THE REFORMATION
IN GERMANY

Volume Two

JOSEPH LORTZ

The Reformation
in Germany

VOLUME TWO

Translated by Ronald Walls

LONDON
DARTON, LONGMAN & TODD
NEW YORK
HERDER AND HERDER

DARTON, LONGMAN & TODD LTD
64 Chiswick High Road, London W4
HERDER AND HERDER, NEW YORK
232 Madison Avenue, New York 10016

Vol 1 of *Die Reformation in Deutschland*
was first published in 1939; Vol 2 in 1940.
This is a translation of the revised edition published
in 1949. The Author's Foreword, the Postscript and
Bibliography are new.

This Translation
© 1968 Darton, Longman & Todd Ltd
First published 1968

Printed in Great Britain by Richard Clay
(The Chaucer Press) Ltd, Bungay, Suffolk

CONTENTS

PART TWO

The New Political and Ecclesio-political Configuration

ONE

Fundamental Forces.
Foreign Politics

I

The observer of the Reformation, whose interest is primarily
in the history of the Church, must take care not to assess the
whole situation at that time purely from the religious or ecclesiastical point of view, or describe the events in purely theological
terms. It is true that in those times religion was the most powerful,
because the deepest rooted, force. For the reasons we have given,
it exercised tremendous weight. Ultimately it is in religion that
we find the motive power behind Reformation history. These were
religious times.

In the events of the period, however, religion was not something
on its own. The many noisy and passionate religious and ecclesiastical discussions were not a complete reflection of all that was
going on in those years. In those days the Germans were not
predominantly concerned with these things. As in every age life
pressed on, impelled by political, social and economic forces,
which shaded off into one another, and interacted in various ways.
Throughout the twenties of the century Germany never came too
dangerously near a religious war, not even in the Peasants' War.
Even the *Reichstags* of Speyer in 1526 and 1529, so revolutionary

in respect of the public and legal reforming of the Church, were not substantially determined by religious factors. Consider the leading political figures: Gattinara, 'high chancellor of all realms and territories of the king', in whose universal schemes the Church and the unity of Christendom did indeed play a part, was able in 1523 to conduct a thorough and all-embracing discussion of the whole domestic and foreign political situation, without ever mentioning the Lutheran affair.

The same can be said of the *Reichstag* at Worms in 1521. Historically, the religious transactions concerning Luther became its chief topic; but in the total agenda of this assembly, at which the princes amused themselves with 'coursing and jousting', it was only one topic amongst many others; and to many of the princes and counsellors the other topics seemed to be much more urgent. How could it be otherwise? The game of power politics: the emperor – the German territorial princes and the emperor – the pope – France – England had reached a new phase and pressed for urgent decisions. This was first and foremost in their minds and seemed to be the stuff of which future visible history would be constructed.

The position of the young emperor, the vessel of supreme dignity, was not a happy one. All had first to be won, put in order and then used in the execution of vast designs.

There had already been unrest in Spain before he ever went there from the Netherlands as Charles I in 1517. In spite of the unique labours of the regent, Cardinal Ximenes de Cisneros, the Spanish kingdom did not escape the consequences of profound unrest. The departure soon afterwards of the emperor elect revealed this in its true light. Revolution broke out. The variety of people of all classes, who took a hand in the devastation and plundering, plainly revealed how deep the disturbance went.

In relation to France, since the rivalry over the imperial office, nothing remained of that superficial fraternisation which Charles had struck up with Francis I in Noyon in 1516. France had supported the revolutionaries in Spain, and attempted to annex Navarre, even the parts lying south of the Pyrenees. The Spanish victory, on the other hand, did nothing to stop the claims of Francis I to Naples. The Italian problem emerged clearly and acutely. Charles would have to settle things with the pope who, before the election, had been his strongest opponent. But the loudest complaints of the German princes were against Rome, and these complaints were now finding specially sharp formulation. We have seen also how strong were their feelings about the imperial government. The electors had done business over the imperial election; they had forced Charles to come to strict terms with them. At Worms and later they thought they could bargain their wishes against those of the emperor, thoroughly exploiting Charles' difficulties. They did this, in fact, throughout the whole period we have been considering. Ruthless self-interest on the part of the German territorial rulers dominated the course of the German Reformation. This became the most important force in shaping the political and ecclesio-political configuration.

In spite of everything the emperor temporarily gained his objective at Worms; but the arrangement was the result of haggling, and in all of the agreements made between him and the estates down to 1544, this same spirit prevailed. Only then, after all sorts of devious and temporary solutions, was he able to reduce overstrained presumptions to a definitive settlement, and introduce it as such.

The whole foreign political situation of the empire depended upon a trial of strength after which there would be not many masters in the empire, held in eternal uneasy equilibrium, but a single ruler. Throughout countless dangerous and crushing ups and downs, Charles had always kept this goal in view. From 1530 until the religious conversations at Regensburg in 1541 he had deliberately allowed it to fall into the background, in order to arrive at an honourable, earnest, highly responsible and peaceful solution. He went after this objective with the amazing and stubborn tenacity, of which he was a master. But the question was never absent, outwardly as in his inner mind: negotiation or force? The final answer was to be force, and it did not achieve his aim.

There is a special charm about the whole of European history in the Reformation period, because we find the same characters in the drama still on the stage at the end as were there at the beginning. Charles V was German emperor from 1519 until 1556, Francis I king of France from 1515 until 1547, Henry VIII king of

England from 1509 until 1547 and Suliman II was grand sultan of Turkey from 1520 until 1566. The only persons to change were the popes. This was of great importance in the intimate mechanics of political life in those years. In all of the varied demands, transactions, contracts, marriage projects, personal encounters and discussions, which were constantly arising, at the end of the day it was the same personalities who were encountering each other.

At the time of the schism the shape of foreign policy in German history was based upon the interweaving of the empire into the Spanish–Habsburg power complex. The destiny of this power was strongly and essentially conditioned by three facts: its extraordinary geographical extention, allied to a disparate and hence highly vulnerable structure; the European tension between this power complex and the nationally more unified France, which pressed towards the east; the energetic advance of Islam from east and south into the heart of Europe. The whole political problem was thus dominated by two mighty foreign political antitheses, which for their part engendered a host of political forces and combinations of forces: Christianity – the Turks; the empire or emperor – France.

The second of these tensions and its effects played by far the more important role, for the very reason that in the thirties and forties the Turks had become direct allies of France against the emperor. In addition French pressure upon Habsburg positions was supported, even from German bases, by the pope himself.

To understand the way things were going we require a brief description of the geographically loose structure of the empire of Charles V. On the one hand this empire, by its vast extent and powerful geographical and political influence, represented a dangerous encirclement of France. On the other hand, the vast extension of its highly unstable frontiers presented France with a constant temptation to break into the empire. In its structure, France was unlike the Habsburg empire, and in every respect had the advantage. True, it had not yet fully attained its natural compactness, but in all essentials this was complete, with the acquisitions of Louis XI in 1477 and 1481. It possessed a royal power, already to some extent domestically concentrated, which extensively controlled the country's economic resources, and which, thanks to an advanced administration, was able to mobilise these resources relatively quickly. In contrast, Charles' power rested not only upon widely scattered and ethnically different lands but upon lands that were still largely undeveloped. Charles' gigantic inherited realm was held together by a personal union, but it possessed no unity. The lack of a sense of unity is much less surprising than the enormous efforts made by Spain, for example, to advance interests that seemed quite foreign to herself, or than the proud sacrifice with which, once again, the Spaniards accepted the role of executors of the plans of their imperial ruler, whom they were unable to keep permanently on their own soil.

The point at which an attack upon the Spanish–Habsburg coalition would have to begin was geographically and historically clearly determined: northern Italy. This was the focal point of the empire of Charles V, and its most vulnerable spot. This, too, was the territory that France would have to control if she wanted to achieve the status of a world power. The function of northern Italy as focal point of the whole Spanish–Habsburg power complex emerged from the necessity of holding the widely scattered lands of the empire in union. Without northern Italy there was nothing to join Spain and Naples with the Austrian and Netherland possessions. An essential link would have been missing in the chain, and the chain itself could easily have been broken. The chain comprised Spain – Naples and Sicily – northern Italy – the Austrian hereditary lands, including possessions in the upper Rhineland – (Germany) – Burgundy – the Netherlands.

In addition the opposition between France and the empire was also an historical struggle for power in southern and northern Italy, deeply rooted in centuries-old efforts aimed at making emergent France the possessor of the universal imperial power. Shortly before the Reformation this opposition had acquired new life, after the campaign of Charles VIII in 1494, when he tried to assert his claims upon the inheritance of Anjou in southern Italy, against Aragon. From a different angle fresh areas of friction had arisen on account of the new state of Burgundy (which embraced imperial fiefs, as well as French royal fiefs), for Maximilian's marriage had brought this country within the Habsburg-imperial sphere of influence. The difficulties naturally precipitated a decisive conflict, because, with the marriage of the Burgundian heir, Spain, too, had become drawn into the Habsburg block, and Charles' gigantic empire was the result; and then this emperor turned out, as we have seen, to be a man who felt and ruled as a Burgundian.

The struggle for northern and southern Italy (Sicily and its link with Spain was vital on account of grain supplies) threw the political and moral power of the papacy directly into the fray, and posed the eternal question: who would the curia support, the emperor or France? The wealthy Netherlands were, along with Spanish money, the strongest economic foundation of Charles' power, and through trade, which was the source of their wealth, they pointed both to England and to the rival German Hanseatic League. This presented a still quite immature structure, with highly vulnerable frontiers. They were exposed to France on the west, to England and Denmark from the sea, to the pro-French duke of Gueldres on the east.

The complexity of the course of this mutual struggle, as it developed from all these different factors, always inextricably bound up with the religious question, is utterly confusing. The alignment of forces was continually changing with almost nonsensical rapidity. The course of events displays a number of isolated developments and processes, which are of prime importance for a close understanding of Reformation history, and we shall recount these in the appropriate place. There are a greater number, however, which are of interest only to the specialist. As Karl Brandi said, in the end 'almost with the precision of the constellations, in the European political sky things were once again running in their accustomed grooves'. We must, however, trace the basic lines of development in all the confused variety, and pick out what is typical from the eternal flux.

The most important facts are these: (a) Every time France set about trying to acquire Italy in order to break through the Spanish–Habsburg ring, and every time it took Milan, it failed, and Charles V was left the victor. After every victory, however, Charles found himself face to face with the same task as he had faced in 1521, and in 1556, as far as concerned Germany, the Netherlands and Italy he had to begin his political work all over again. (b) All the participants naïvely took it for granted that peace treaties were scarcely binding at all, and so peace was always followed – almost at once – by a fresh political dispute.

France's first attempt, during the period we are studying, to escape threatening encirclement by Spain–Habsburg, was Francis I's bid for the German imperial crown. Charles V's victory in this issue was followed almost immediately by the first war between the two rulers over northern Italy (1521–25). This ended in the captivity of Francis I and the acquisition of northern Italy by Charles. Immediately France, assisted by a European coalition – the Holy League of Cognac, with the pope, Milan, Venice and England – started up the war afresh. Again Charles was the victor (the peace of Cambrai, 1529), and for a second time Francis had to give up his claim to Italy. Charles, however, was unable to utilise his victory to consolidate the situation in Germany, for in the east the Turks had pressed forward to the gates of Vienna, retreated and then pressed on anew. This embarrassment was exploited by the French king to precipitate another war. And so, from 1536–44, Spain–Habsburg had to make two attempts to carry on a war on a double front (1536–38 and 1542–44): against the French in the west and the Turks in the east. This conflict, too, ended in the west in a victory for Charles. At the peace of Crépy, 1544, Francis finally renounced claims to Italy.

This confusingly rapid change of alignments, which seemed to invalidate every victory, and caused every declaration of peace to be followed by a new belligerent alliance, had its roots deep in the defects of methods of warfare. The planned conduct of campaigns was frustrated by far too much fantasy and precipitation. Mighty beginnings came to nothing because no thought had been given to reinforcement and supplies, or because a campaign was irresponsibly delayed until rain, cold and sickness brought disaster. Most of all, however, and especially on the emperor's side, there was the constant cry – no money! On the whole they were living from hand to mouth. Charles' vast political designs, which he pursued with such incredible persistence, were not supported in the slightest degree by any comparable technical preparation. Money to prosecute his campaigns was not raised methodically, and so he could never rely upon a sure supply.

And so military contests were doomed, from sheer inner necessity, to failure through the destructive forces of disorganisation. Even the campaign against the only power that had at its

disposal a huge standing army, that is the Turks, were cursed
by this same defect. Were it not so, how could territory right up to
the Danube have been surrendered after the defeat of the Hungar-
ians at Mohacs, and the campaign have been resumed again the
next year?

The French and the emperor both faced the problem of recruit-
ing men. The use of Swiss mercenaries was comical – to say
the least. These served now the French, now the emperor, now
the pope. All they were interested in was their pay. Swiss were
to be found fighting on both sides. Ought fellow-countrymen
thus to kill one another? 'A hundred years of war, but not one
day of battle!' Instead, there was endless opportunity for plunder;
and they could go back to till the land at the appropriate seasons,
too. At times it happened that the mood of battle prevailed, and
they felt a certain conviction in favour of Germany and the
Habsburgs against the French. In general, however, they sold
their services for money. If the pay did not come regularly, they
threatened to change sides, or to go home.

It was with such soldiers as these that Charles had to fight
his battles. Even the German troopers fought only for money;
and as Protestants these were ready to serve the pope – for
money.

It is true that even these soldiers had acquired some kind of
community spirit. The concept of the emperor contributed to
this – powerfully, even. But stronger still was the influence
of the genuine leader of the troopers – Frundsberg, for example.
At times he had kept his troopers together and urged them on,
even without pay. The same was true of the experienced art of
war of some generals like the imperial Pescara and Leywa, who
were more feared than their armies. Such personalities, however,
were rare; and when they had gone, what was left? The grisly
fate of Rome, plundered in 1527, and the voluntary disbanding of
the armies there, are a plain answer to that question.

All we have to do is to list the separate events of but a single
one of these wars to have a clear picture of the utter senselessness
of it all. Take 1527, for example. The sack of Rome smashed the
front that was threatening the emperor; but now the imperial
army spent months hanging about Rome, and once again
northern Italy was lost. The French with the Genoese practically

became masters of Naples. Again the emperor's power had gone; and then Admiral Andria Doria defected to the emperor's side, and once more northern Italy was defeated on 21 June 1529. The fate of Milan was the supreme example: 1494 – French; 1495 – autonomous; 1499 – French; 1512 – Italian once again; 1514 – French; 1521–22 – acquired by the empire; 1524 – French; 1525 – imperial; 1526 – in the League of Cognac; 1528 – imperial; 1534–36 – Francis again laid claim to his 'inheritance'; 1540 – Charles feued it to his son Philip; from 1549, and especially from 1555, France renewed her ancient demands.

It is easy to see what little authority peace treaties possessed, which were the result of such inconclusive battles, of such meaningless power relationships, and how little they were regarded as definitive by the temporarily defeated or exhausted party. There were always reservations. All the concessions in the peace contracts, and all conquests, were perpetually coming up for revision.

They were regarded as provisional arrangements by Francis of France (out of sheer frivolity and love of life); and Charles V, too, regarded them in the same light (from earlier insight and quiet superiority). It is true that the first big successes of 1521 and 1525 – all unexpected – vastly increased his self-assurance. He already felt that he had reached the point from which he could do his work for Christianity, interiorly and externally, as the universal emperor. Soon, however, he was to learn how long the road would be that he still had to travel, before he could establish permanent inner unity and outward security. At all events he refused to give up his clear aim. On the contrary, he learned more and more the art of appearing to yield, in order to achieve ultimate victory for his boundless claims.

What was the reaction of these foreign political developments upon the course of domestic German history? This history was dominated by the advance of the Reformation to the disadvantage of the ancient Catholic position, as defended by the Edict of Worms and thereafter by the Catholic princes, chief of whom was Charles himself. In power politics and in his solicitude for the old Church Charles required the co-operation of the territorial rulers, of the princes, dukes, knights and cities. Failing this, he would have to overcome them. The foreign political situation affected the religious negotiations within Germany because the emperor had to rely upon the support of the territorial rulers whether they were Lutheran or Catholic. These territorial rulers – deeply divided politically, dynastically and, later, confessionally, and liable to change sides – as a result of the foreign political situation became the lever which largely determined the course of the Reformation in Germany. After 1527 they determined it decisively. The foreign situation was constantly forcing Charles to come to terms with the Protestants in Germany, granting them concessions that were in contradiction of his own political and religious convictions. This in turn gave the Catholic estates the opportunity to announce their demands more noisily. The emperor's proposals to the *Reichstag* in those days, and the resolution of the *Reichstag*, clearly evidence this fact. All of these resolutions were closely related to the foreign political situation. If at times they were a direct expression of the emperor's power, then others reflected the foreign political pressure that the estates were able to bring to bear upon the emperor; or settlements, containing severe demands by the emperor, were negated by a succeeding *Reichstag* with its more lenient concessions. The political history of German Protestantism in the Reformation period is a direct reflection of the freedom or obstruction of the Catholic emperor arising from the exigencies of foreign policy.

The political course of Reformation history – and hence, too, in a most significant fashion its religious and ecclesiastical development – depended also upon the fact that there was no central, constantly applicable, executive in Germany. The misfiring of the plans for the reform of the empire under Maximilian set the pace for the whole of the sixteenth century. The constant changing of alliances, the perpetual haggling and compounding of the estates with the emperor, the princes and the cities, the vacillation of every kind of authority, all of these things arose because none of these powers had a standing army. Whenever a competent military power seemed to emerge, as in the Swabian League, or in the person of Sickingen with his soldiers, it at once gained an advantage quite disproportionate to its real resources or to the number, extent and force, of the power that had to be held in check.

A specially interesting complication of the interplay of forces was provided by the person of the emperor's brother. He was at once a help and an embarrassment to the emperor's cause. The emperor's German policy was profoundly influenced by his frequent, necessary absence from the empire. To provide for this situation, an imperial government was formed. Charles knew well how to give this government an imperial stamp from the day of its inception. He made Ferdinand his representative. As early as 1519 the emperor saw great possibilities in the Charles–Ferdinand combination. At that time he told his brother that the undivided unity of their lands was the only thing that could provide the possibility of his achieving his purposes. With this in mind, in 1521 he began to endow his brother with lands and honours in keeping with the role he was to play. In all of this the emperor was still the authoritative power, who liked, with all his gifts to his brother, to add reservations, which stressed the attachment of the archduke to the emperor. As leader of the imperial government, by his share in the elaboration of the pro-positions to the *Reichstags* that were to be summoned, or through his own composition of these propositions, and by the direction of the *Reichstags*, Ferdinand's influence upon German imperial policy became most important. It was only natural that he should have tried to move out of the shadow of the emperor. He made a fair bid to do so by being elected king of Bohemia and Hungary in 1526, and by the victory over his rival Sapolya, and by the repulse of the Turks before Vienna in 1529, and finally by his election as king of the Romans in 1531. Ferdinand's elevation to be a king was admittedly part of the extension of the imperial ascendancy, the end of which Charles saw as an hereditary Spanish–Habsburg empire. And so, as a king, Ferdinand was more of an executive instrument than an autonomous director of the empire. Regular and extraordinary emissaries of the emperor and his detailed written instructions saw to that.

The growing Turkish menace on the eastern flank of the empire – on Ferdinand's own territories – concentrated his attention more and more upon the battle with the infidel. In the end the two brothers parted company. It is conceivable that Ferdinand was opposed to Charles' plans to secure the Spanish succession within the empire. However, his feudal loyalty remained when in 1552 disaster overtook the emperor: Ferdinand voluntarily shared his flight.

The whole development of the Reformation within Germany hung upon the fate of the Edict of Worms. If this had been carried out, as it should have been according to imperial law, it would have put an end to the Reformation on any great scale. But the fate of this edict was the very thing which brightly illuminated the whole confusion of the political and ecclesio-political condition – the almost unimaginable weakness of the empire. Real results in the form of an inquisitorial persecution of the new doctrine, its preachers, adherents and books, were produced only in the Habsburg and Netherland–Burgundian lands, where the ground had been prepared by severe decrees of Charles. The labours of the loyal Catholic duke George of Saxony or the elector Joachim I of Brandenburg or the duke of Brunswick were of very little consequence, taken as a whole. Bavaria was very far from truly implementing the Edict of Worms. In Bavaria the edict was promulgated, and on 5 March 1522 a ducal mandate was issued proscribing Luther's doctrine. However, Leonard of Eck, who managed the affair in that region, had but one end in view: to make the country politically strong and so safe from revolution. Throughout the entire Reformation he achieved this end without any bloodshed. But Bavaria was not, and never became, a real reserve of Catholic ecclesio-political power. The Bavarian prince-bishops displayed the same failure in duty and laziness or cowardly fear as their colleagues in other regions. The attitude of the councillors was in harmony with that of the rulers – indeed, the councillors were often secretly Lutheran.

For the rest, the manner in which this edict arose suggested that weighty political forces would be thrown in against its execution. The struggle had a twofold root, one ecclesiastical and religious, the other political. The ecclesiastical and religious root embraced the emerging new attitudes to canon law, which were connected with the notion of the territorial Church and its extension into the Protestant territorial Church (*cuius regio*, right to reform, secularisation), and which led, after 1525, to the transition from the congregational Reformation to the princes' Reformation. The second, political, root was the emerging

Protestant-confessional principle that sought for itself a corresponding political expression.

The battle over the Edict of Worms, the elaboration of the new Evangelical views of canon law and the development of the confessional principle, were all represented in significant measure in the *Reichstags* of those days. This provides us with the basis for our further exposition.

First of all, however, we must consider the mighty double dispute with France. This disclosed much of the inner rhythm of all future disputes; and it seemed, too, that this would have to provide the platform from which the victorous emperor would set about solving the domestic German question.

II

On 29 April 1521 it became known in Worms that the *Comuneros* in Spain had been defeated. This opened up two vast prospects: Charles was able to take a real grip of his inheritance in Spain, and organise it; and the skirmishing with France on the Netherland frontier could be stepped up to the scale of a regular attack.

The fact that Charles and his advisers put the first task in front of all other, indicates their clear weighing up of what was necessary for the organic construction of a universal policy. It is true that the emperor simply had to accept his seven-year absence from Germany. He did this, perhaps unaware of the ecclesiastical and political import of the Lutheran revolution. Even when he wrote his memoirs, after feeling the full impact of the Thirty Years War, he still placed the Lutheran movement on a par with the revolt of the *Comuneros*. And yet, this long absence of the emperor from Germany – to be repeated in the following decade with a like result – was one of the principal causes of the new doctrine taking root. Moreover, in the end this was the rock on which Charles' whole work foundered.

As we have observed, the dispute with France was inevitable for several reasons. Not only was a Spaniard on the imperial throne a threat to France but the French were very much alive to the fact, and Francis I had frequently adverted to it.

Conversely, France's desire to expand into Germany could

count on support from many quarters. Alliances between a German prince and the king of France were not exactly unknown. In the recent imperial election, the Hildesheim feud had been a threat to the emperor. The victorious army stood ready to support Charles of Gueldres, who was sympathetic to France, and a bitter opponent of the Habsburgs all his life. At that time the idea of a French emperor was far from absurd. Many would not have regarded him as so different from the Spanish–Burgundian Charles V.

Against such a background as this we must understand the rather strange letters of Francis I (and his successors) to the German princes, excusing himself for making war on the emperor. For example, on 11 May 1521 he maintained that he was not waging war on the empire 'whose ally he was, as king of France, and whose vassal, as duke of Milan'.

Basically, for Francis, the issue was Italy; and even this worked to the emperor's advantage. Perhaps as a result of the rising Lutheran danger, and certainly on account of France's designs on Naples, Leo X became more friendly towards the emperor. In fact, he pressed for an offensive alliance with the emperor against France. At the end of May just when the Edict of Worms had been completed against Luther, an agreement was made between these two universal powers, whereby Milan was assured to Sforza, Genoa to the Doge Adorno, Parma and Piacenza to the pope. Similar forces drew Charles towards Henry VIII, and in 1521, at the instigation of Cardinal Wolsey, a secret agreement was made leading to a treaty against France in June 1522. (This treaty contained one of those many marriage projects by which Charles, since his childhood, had so often been betrothed. This was an instrument of diplomacy that he was to use all this life – with virtuosity, we might say, but also to the point of excess, and with every conceivable complication. On this occasion it was Henry's daughter Mary, who was the lady selected.) The following year saw alliances between the emperor and England and Ferdinand and Venice; and between the emperor, England, Ferdinand and the pope, Milan, Florence. For the emperor this was flank protection on a grand scale. From the point of view of power politics it rested upon an inadequate foundation. None the less it was supported by the grand concept of Europe, which Charles learned from his first minister, Gattarina, who was to control his political thought until his death, and raise him far above the petty interests of the territorial rulers.

The lack of real political foundation soon became obvious. Most of the signatories defected to France. The grand sultan Suliman, having taken Belgrade, pressed into Hungary. The treaties with England were only a kind of credit against the future. On 1 December 1521 Leo X died. All depended upon his immediate successor. Things looked bad for the emperor. All the same it was his armies that were successful. In November, even before Leo had died, papal and imperial troops took Milan, and in the following April Spanish troops and German troopers under Frundsberg performed their great feat: they beat the famous Swiss mercenaries and the French at Bicocca. The French vacated northern Italy.

These victories were followed by an attack the next year on France, along a wide front. France meanwhile was beginning to display increasing national strength. Charles of Bourbon, who had gone over to the emperor's side, possessor of important, compact territory in the south of France, was unable to alienate other great lords from the kingdom – as he had hoped to do, and as had been expected. On the contrary, France was strong enough to repulse the imperial thrust as far as Marseilles, and to mount a successful counter-attack, ending in the recovery of Lombardy (autumn 1524) and in a treaty with the new pope, Clement VII.

It is true that France could not take Pavia; and it was at Pavia that the fortunes of war seemed to favour the emperor in a way that was comparable with the vast extent of his realm. This was the great crisis of the century. The emperor's good fortune here was not in accordance with the military prospects, but rather in defiance of them; Frundsberg had indeed succeeded in bringing his troopers over the Alps in the dead of winter, but none the less the imperial prospects were bad. In Spain the emperor expected that the campaign would end in disaster. The news of the resounding victory on 24 February 1525 (his birthday), when the French army was destroyed, and the king taken prisoner, took him completely by surprise. The emperor was ruler of the world. The French king was taken in Spain. A fresh treaty now united (to outward appearance) the emperor, the pope and England (April 1525).

All the earlier battles for north Italy and even for southern France had been no more than a provisional scamper. Pavia was the first decisive battle. As Lannoy said, it had been the one true harvest for the emperor, sent by God – his golden opportunity. Certainly, only a peace that corresponded to the true balance of power could make this permanently decisive. The war against France had been unavoidable and necessary. The time had come for intelligent reorganisation. This was where Charles failed, as he did later when his immoderately long and humiliating imprisonment of Philip of Hesse and Frederick of Saxony jeopardised his victory over the Protestants. The exaggerated peace demands of the emperor, composed after a full year's reflection, indicate a lost opportunity for world history. In a sense we may assert that it was the peace of Madrid, embodying these proposals, that condemned Charles' life work to failure, on the stage of European, as of German, politics. The enormous advantage which the emperor had gained by this victory and the capture of the French king, aroused the opposing might of England (which, despite its alliance with the emperor, had made no peace with France in August) and of Italy. In addition, France once again showed herself to be an extraordinarily resilient nation. We find ourselves constantly comparing this France with the Germany of the merchant princes, and at this point in history, long before the Gallicanism of the seventeenth century, we can discern the colossal national superiority of France. The territorial demands which Charles presented to Louise of Savoy, the king's mother, who conducted the negotiations, were rejected at once with an imposing self-assurance. The terms of the peace of Madrid, however, concluded on 14 January 1526, between Charles and Francis (marriage contract between Francis and Eleanor, Charles' sister, and widow of the king of Portugal; French renunciation of Italy, Flanders and Burgundy; a united crusade) were evaded by Francis simply by breaking his word. He had already announced his intention to do this to his councillors at two secret meetings before signing the treaty. This word-breaking was calmly accepted by the nation, although Charles denounced it as cowardly and dishonest. It was maintained by France that the contract made in Madrid was coerced and hence not binding. Immediately the king broke his defence and non-aggression treaty with the emperor, by joining the Holy League of Cognac, comprising France, the papal states, Venice, Milan, Florence (secretly) and England (a silent partner in the background). This league formed a broad phalanx against Charles. At one blow the whole preponderance of imperial power seemed to change to its opposite, and Charles' very existence to be threatened. In the same year, 1525, electoral Saxony and electoral Hesse made a pact at Gotha-Torgau. On 29 August the power of Hungary collapsed at Mohacs under Turkish attack.

Once again the luck of war saved the emperor in a second clash with France. This was accomplished by a vast detour, carried out against the emperor's will – the sack of Rome in 1527.

Colonna, enemy of the Medicis, had suddenly risen against Clement VII. In September 1526 he broke into Rome. This was a wonderful opportunity for the emperor, but one that he was ready to exploit only in case of extremity. He preferred to come to terms with the pope. In June, however, the pope decisively turned his back on the emperor. Charles reacted by writing a violent letter in which he threatened to appeal from the pope ('wolf' not 'shepherd') to a council. In a second communication he called upon the cardinals, for their part, to call a council. Meanwhile military events were running their course. Frundsberg had brought fresh mercenaries across the Alps. Most important of all, the military command of the army of the League hesitated, while, for their part, the demoralised, hungry, cold soldiers of the emperor no longer held back. They would obey none but Lannoy or Charles of Bourbon; even Frundsberg was unable to hold them in check, and the mutiny brought on a stroke from which he died. The soldiers rushed upon the treasures of Rome and upon their emperor's enemy, the pope. Bourbon fell in the assault upon the city. The soldiers were without a commander. The sack of Rome broke over the unhappy Renaissance city, and the Renaissance was buried beneath a sea of Italian, Spanish and German horror. This lasted for months. Divine punishment, so often and for so long foretold, had at last come terribly upon the sinful city. Through the German Lutheran mercenaries the Reformation had its share in this event. The pope, now besieged in the castle of St Angelo, and left in the lurch by the League, gave himself up. The emperor held a sufficient number of strong-

holds within the papal states; but a fresh, victorious advance of the
French and the English as far as Naples once again called everything in question. Nothing came of the threat, however, because
of the defection of Admiral Doria to the imperial side. Again
battle flared up in north Italy. Doria took Genoa. On the
imperial side, the troops of the duke of Braunschweig-Wolfenbüttel mutined, and the French threw another force against
Lombardy. The imperial forces won the day. For a second time
the battle for Italy came to an end. On 29 June Charles made
peace with the pope (Barcelona). On 3 August 1529, the peace
of the Women was settled in Cambrai (between the emperor's Aunt
Margaret, regent of the Netherlands, and the king's mother):
Francis gave up claim to Italy, Eleanor would now really ascend
the throne of France.

Peace now seemed to be reasonably well guaranteed. Charles
was aware of having accomplished the securing of Christendom
against heretics and infidels, and, as Gattarina had taught him,
this was the precondition of real imperial policy. More than
this: he now fulfilled his long-considered project of travelling
to Italy. On entering Bologna, where he was to be crowned
emperor by the pope, he received the wonderful news that the
Turkish threat, too, had been averted. Vienna had repulsed the
infidel.

Could Charles have received any better omen for the work he
now proposed to carry out in Germany?

All very well – but in Germany the Reformation had taken a
turn which the emperor failed utterly to comprehend. Our first
task now is to examine the situation.

TWO

Reformed Rulers and the Church's Rights

I

The subject matter of this chapter is not derivative theory but the immediate, concrete course of Reformation history. The detailed development is so lacking in uniformity that it is expedient to highlight certain basic features, and discuss them now in their context.

We are dealing with a development arising from a double root: (*a*) from the pre-Reformation territorial Church system which – (*b*) experienced radical elaboration by reason of the new theological views of the Reformers.

The breaking loose of the princely and civic authorities from the former ecclesiastical system took place without any uniformity. This was in keeping with the issue itself, and with the resolution of the *Reichstags*. The objective, however, of declaring for Luther and his Reform, and of exploiting the situation to the advantage of one's own power – in the sense we have already described – became more and more clearly formulated in the states and cities. On the other hand, the necessity had urgently arisen of preserving order in face of revolution, in the midst of a variety of changes in the ecclesiastical system. From 1523 onwards Luther's liturgical writings were directed to this end. Not least effective was the fear of violence by the peasants and the fanatics.

Some sort of intervention by the civil authorities in the regulation of Church affairs became almost taken for granted, because of the situation. Moreover, with the overthrow of the clerical estate, secular authority to some extent was set on a level with that of the former spiritual power. It was in the cities especially that a practical solution had to be found, for here most of all social functions, such as care of the poor and the education of children, once fulfilled by the Church, were now being taken over by the town councils. As yet, however, there was no clear, fundamental concept of the new forms of life, no formulation of their rights and delimitations.

At its core and origin the question posed by the Reformers was religious through and through. Automatically, the first reforms were initiated in the sacral sphere – in public worship. Karlstadt, Zwingli and Müntzer set about in this way, as did Luther. This activity in turn set off questions about canon law; for, as soon as the realisation of the new dogmatic-liturgical views affected the churches with their endowments, to which were attached very real obligations, and demanded the discontinuance of former liturgical life, encumbered as it was with material entanglements, the whole question of Church property had to be raised.

And so, confusedly at first, but urgent in practice, the question arose of who were the legitimate successors to the old Church, more precisely, to the pope, the bishops, the monasteries and the parishes. Who owned the churches and the altars, the endowments of which were explicitly tied to the celebration of mass? Whose duty was it to regulate public worship? As there was no longer any special priesthood, no bishop in the old sacramental sense, who was to nominate the parish priest, and to whom was he answerable? This was the actual situation with which Luther had to deal: no bishop ought to be set over the parish clergy. Later, he occasionally expressed the opinion that he would gladly yield to the rule and consecration of bishops, if only they would acknowledge true doctrine, but that is only a vague and peripheral statement by which he cannot be bound – in spite of the change he underwent after 1525. Such statements in no way alter his complete rejection of the special priesthood, of the sacramental office of bishop.

The question thus emerged: did the new confession of faith provide a way of laying hands upon the existent ecclesiastical system of property? In the nature of the case, the answer varied according to the percentage of persons in any given parish or religious community who subscribed to the new doctrines; often it was affected most of all by the aggressive activity of the Reformers in contrast to the inertia of those upholding the old faith. The problem was specially complicated in places where Reformed victory seemed to be impossible on account of Catholic resistance. This situation was eased in places where the new Evangelical ruler had already controlled both secular and spiritual power in the past. This was notably the case in Prussia, where the duke had been grand master of the German Order, and in that capacity enjoyed ecclesiastical rights. In addition the bishops of Samland and Pomesia abdicated in favour of the new duke, and in the new Church exercised their authority in co-operation with him. It was quite natural in these circumstances for the duke to appoint successors to the bishops as they died.

How were matters to be decided in the many complicated cases where the personal possessors of indisputable titles to Church property – bishops, cathedral chapters, monastic communities – remained loyal to the old faith, while the town council went over to the Reformers? What happened when the titles to Church property were held by absentee bishops and religious in a region which went over to the Reformation? The question here had long since ceased to be solely about the truth or falsity of the new doctrine. It was, rather, the question: what basis in law can be found for introducing the new doctrine into the public order of life?

There can be no doubt that this question was of fundamental importance. The representatives of the old Church dutifully upheld their rights, and legitimately defended themselves against deprivation. But this sank to the level of a secondary question in comparison with the first: where is the truth of God? Where this truth is, there too is divine light; and this concept was at the foundation of all canon law in the old Church. This had been amazingly clearly formulated by Wycliffe in terms of his criticism of the existence of the papacy, and applied against the old Church, as the law of God. The same question with the same answer had been put forward repeatedly by the spiritualist and natural law movements right down to the latest Middle Ages. This way of thinking found its ultimate and sharpest expression in the twisting of the social demands of 'ancient law' into 'divine right' in the peasants' risings.

The new Evangelical Church systems were introduced, backed by the same concepts. In the riotous proceedings at Wittenberg or Allstedt, as in more peaceful transitions into the new ways, the same concept was at work: ancient divine right was violating human rights. In Leisnig, a city in electoral Saxony, which had whole-heartedly accepted Luther's doctrine at an early date, an Evangelical pastor and preacher was installed, on the citizens' own initiative and 'on the trustworthy advice of godly scripture scholars' – of whom Luther was one. It is true that the Cistercian monastery of Buch held the right of patronage over the parish church. 'In contradiction of this, however, they appealed to the much more ancient right, which could oust all earthly and human power, reason, and law for it derived from Christ himself.'

In the foundation period Luther's ideal rested wholly upon the notion of the radical separation of the secular from the spiritual; the worldly, the organisational, appearing as utterly insignificant in contrast to the inward and spiritual. Everything was swept away by the freedom of the Christian man and the priesthood of all believers. For him, the Christian congregation was and remained the great subject of Christianity in its social manifestation. This was the guarantee that Christ was alive and speaking. 'A Christian assembly or congregation have the right and the power to judge every doctrine, to call, install or depose, a teacher, on the basis of scripture' (1523). In his exposition of this thesis, from the first sentence Luther distinguishes between the Christian congregation and one 'wherein men undertake human business'. Christianity exists only 'where the gospel is preached'. 'Bishops, collegiate clergy, monastic communities, and whatever else is of the people, drive out the gospel, for they rely upon human doctrines. Therefore their actions are heathenish and worldly. In respect, therefore, of doctrine, of the installation and deposition of pastors, we must not in any way turn to human laws, rights, traditions, custom and usage.' The fact that a custom has endured for one or for a thousand years does not affect the issue – man's soul is an eternal thing.

Today we are no longer astonished that such universal, spiritual principles did not possess the power to remove the deeply rooted ecclesiastical legal system without friction, and erect in its place a new and lasting order. Luther's principles were a bit obscure. Even the notion of the priesthood of all believers, on the one hand, and of the special rights of the theological preacher and of the pastor, on the other, and also of the Christian secular power, conceal unresolvable and contradictory tensions in doctrine. The designation of the congregation as the vehicle of new Christian life had the important result that the political authorities almost certainly had to take over the direction of the Christian congregation, without any compunction. This was specially true in the cities where direction of the Christian congregation involved at the same time the direction of a highly complicated political common life. In Zwingli's system of Church government – a product of the city – this form was most clearly expressed. Butzer's government of the congregation in Strasburg became in turn a model or stimulus for Calvin.

An accommodation could be reached here only on the basis of the view of the Church as a community of the elect – the view, that is, that the true Christian congregation is and can only be a little flock.

With a rather rough hand, the course of events seems to have pushed this view to the side. The first organised Lutheran visitation of churches was carried out between 1527 and 1529 in electoral Saxony by officials of the elector. Such a proceeding, as we saw, followed the pattern of the uninterrupted practice of Catholic princes. These visitations had either been tolerated or directly requested by the Church. It is obvious, however, that with the emerging Evangelical system the prince could come advancing far greater claims than before, while at the same time having his ecclesiastical power greatly enhanced on account of former Catholic custom.

It was on these visitations that all of these questions first became really evident. A host of uneducated pastors were discovered, whose ignorance had been their best aid of all for the Reformation, for they had no idea at all of what it was all about, nor did they see that by the Reform of worship they would lose something essential, that Christianity was being changed at the deepest level. In 1528 the cautious pedagogic, and moralistic Melanchthon sent his instructions for the visitators to the pastors in the electorate of Saxony. This contained advice on the treatment of these questions and pastors. At the visitations themselves, as at the planning stage, the faculty of theology at Wittenberg assisted. With ever-increasing exclusiveness, the orders of the territorial ruler became the source of legality. The estates fell more and more into the background. In all places there were cases of sheer administration (endowments and benefices; preacher's stipends), of a mixed kind (education and placing of clergy), as well as questions concerning doctrine (regulation of the dispensing of sacraments, of public worship in general, protection against those teaching heresy).

Things took the same course in other states which decided for the Reformation as they did in Saxony. In this process a great variety of Church orders emerged, corresponding to the dissimilar requirements and opinions of the rulers and theologians. This variety was qualified, however, for all the Church orders, with the exception of the Palatinate, which showed Calvinist influences, were Lutheran, and derived primarily from the instruction of Melanchthon (1528) and the visitation regulations of the margrave of Brandenburg (1528). This holds good of Hesse as well, where the Reformation had occurred to begin with through the influence of the ex-Franciscan, Lambert, from Strasburg. One of the most influential collaborators in the ensuing Reformation of Hesse was John Bugenhagen, Luther's closest friend, the witness to his marriage, his lifelong confessor and the eulogist at his funeral.

In the cities the development was less uniform. There were deviations everywhere from the customary party alignments. The religious schisms manifested themselves in the imperial cities of southern Germany. Zwinglian and fanatical sects of various sorts made their mark. In 1530 Strasburg was one of the most important sectarian centres in Germany. And here, too, were to be found Church orders which derived from Saxony.

Luther played his part in this development. His most important contribution was admittedly the rejection of the old order.

Revolution begets revolution – all the more if it allows a fundamentally subjective ideal to take command. Because in addition
the old order had been ecclesio-political, it could be replaced in
the full sense and along the lines of a conservative revolution,
such as Luther envisaged, only by an ecclesio-political power.
This would have been true even in the absence of very strong
egoism in the secular rulers. On this score Luther suffered deep
disillusionment. From 1517 onwards, and with increased intensity
from 1520 and 1521, his battle boldly relied upon trust in the
immanent power of truth. He gave clear proof of this in Worms, by
his ride to Wittenberg in 1523, and, in a different fashion, by his
clash with Müntzer, when he rejected the use of force to suppress
what he regarded as heretical preaching. But now, under pressure
from outward events and the complexity of circumstances, these
simple basic lines were abandoned. Once again things developed
unevenly. For this reason, too, Luther's attitude towards the
authorities, especially to the state, is hard to describe. Moreover,
vital as these questions were for the growth and elaboration of
Luther's work, they were not central interests to him personally.
He concentrated much more on an exclusively religious theme:
the justification of the individual soul. Thus it came about that
these questions were dealt with from case to case – dealt with,
not solved.

Christian doctrine implied a clear, unambiguous, immovable
principle: under all circumstances – sin apart – one must obey
legitimate authority. In 1525 Luther applied this principle with
special rigidity in respect of aspirations of the peasants. He accepted
these, but insisted that a Christian must rather suffer injustice
from his superiors than take the law into his own hands. His
second treatise written in that period and opposing the peasants,
drew its conclusions mercilessly. None the less, in these basic
problems, Luther does not fall under any suspicion of flattering
those in power. A certain preference for the state before the hated
curia had not prevented the young professor from ingenuously
attacking the great lords in 1515–16 in the coarsest democratic
manner. They 'rob and steal on such a scale that there is scarcely
one who is not at the game'. These are the 'mighty oafs' whom he
later (1525, 1529) reproached for their raging against their
subjects, and from whom Luther showed such independence in

B

1517 and 1522 (letter to his elector on returning from the Wartburg).

The violent spread of the Anabaptist movement and of the Peasants' War on the one hand, and, on the other, the rather disappointing fruits yielded by the free gospel, reduced Luther's boldness. He lost his belief in the free, self-governing congregation of true Christians.[1] Gradually he began to see clearly, that there could only be very few who were wholly Christian. 'A rare bird the true Christian. Would to God that most of us were good, devout heathen, living by the natural law – never mind being Christians' (*Admonition on Peace*, 1525). Even more insistently, he recognised that the Christian, even more the whole congregation, must be held in check by discipline. He returned to the view that truth and grace require help, that government and doctrinal precepts are necessary if disorder is to be avoided.

After 1526 at the latest Luther was no longer master of the ecclesiastical situation, much less of the ecclesio-political situation. Quite apart from the rising influence of other theologians (Melanchthon included), a sense of ecclesiastical power was growing amongst the princes, who more and more took over the direction of religious affairs from the political and economic angle. The outcome of the Peasants' War provided special encouragement for this kind of territorial Church order. The territorial princes were the victors – not merely over the peasants but also to some extent over the emperor and the imperial government, which had done, or been able to do, nothing in this dangerous business.

As early as 1524 Luther had agreed to a free secularisation by the princes of the 'defunct' churches and monasteries. In so doing, somewhat tastelessly he had joined together as fruits of the new doctrine, the eternal salvation of the elector and the daily increase of considerable material wealth. Following certain beginnings in 1525 and after the *Reichstag* at Speyer in 1526 he ordered those visitations of churches, recognising the primary right of the elector in these things. In 1527–28 he explained that

---

[1] The modern reader is in danger of interpreting the terms 'free' and 'free congregation' in the light of his own concept of autonomy. From the start, however, Luther did not have in mind an amorphous, communistic kind of community, but a natural organism under a guiding authority.

'without bold regulation' by the elector nothing could be done properly. On the regulation of schools serving the new doctrine (to town councillors, 1524) Luther gave personal assistance by the definitive composition of his larger catechism (1529). Set rules were provided there for preaching, dispensing the sacraments, and for reception of the sacraments, and these were binding on the clergy and faithful respectively. These things no longer concerned merely the sphere of private conscience but also public, civic, Christian life. Then there emerged a graduation of offices from pastor, to superintendent, to territorial ruler. Towards the end of the *Reichstag* at Augsburg in 1530 the theologians from electoral Saxony along with Melanchthon explained clearly enough that teachers and preachers would make no attacks upon the mass if the princes did not wish to forbid it.

This abandonment by Luther of the notion of the congregation in favour of Reformation by the Christian authorities, especially by the princes, represented a serious dimming of his early, genuine Reformation ideals. The fact is by no means illogical, however, in view of the actual disposition of forces, of that living development, which had begun in the territorial Church system of pre-Reformation times. Nor may we overlook the fact that Luther's assent to the princes' right to initiate reform was accompanied by weighty reservations. In his preface to the instruction to visitators in 1528 he protested against the interference of the secular power in Church affairs. He refused to tolerate them in the Church or in the realm of conscience. In 1534, in his preface to the exposition of Psalm 101, he denied the right of the political power to interfere in spiritual things: 'I must constantly harp on this distinction between the two kingdoms, no matter how often it has been stated; for the old devil never ceases trying to mix up and confuse the two. The secular rulers are always wanting to teach and control Christ's heritage in the devil's name. ... Likewise false priests and rabble rousers always like to teach and ordain how the world ought to be governed ...'

A considerable part of the Church property acquired was applied to the erection of schools, the making of fresh endowments or the reorganisation of existing ones. In this field the Reformed territorial rulers accomplished a great deal. A new Protestant form of education emerged from these schools. In them Protestant piety and life had their roots. Very often, indeed, it happened that these and other purposes, notably charitable endowments, remained mere projects, and were never carried out. In the Mecklenburg Church order of 1552 we read: '. . . for it is Christian and in accord with written law, that these donations, designed from time immemorial to support Christian offices, be still applied to the maintenance of Christian doctrine, churches, schools and hospitals.' The proceedings of the state parliaments in the same year and the proposals of the dukes to these assemblies in 1555 express the same sentiments. Things worked out differently in practice. Blatant egoism directed the development, whether it was that of the dukes, or of the estates, each using their own appropriate tactics. The application in 1552 of Church property to the use of the universities, of students, and of the poor in Mecklenburg became a type of secularisation, which caused the Lutheran professor, David Chytraeus to speak of 'birds of prey at court'.

Amongst the princes it was the same man, for the most part, who set the pace in the matter of secularisation, as took the chief initiative politically: the landgrave Philip of Hesse. He was remarkably clever, but equivocal, too, so that the Catholics within his territories were able at first to put their minds at rest: who could not acquiesce when abuses were being corrected? Very few of them could see through the deception, as did the guardian of Marburg at the Synod of Hesse in 1526.

Indeed, it was no accident that the great ecclesio-political advance of the Reformation in Germany was a mark of the second generation of princes, in whose time political and economic impulses far outweighed religious and evangelical motives. In this generation, too, Hesse was one of the younger members.

THREE

The Birth of the Confessional and Politico-confessional Principle (1521–29)

I

The duty of obedience to the authorities – unconditionally demanded by Luther – led in Germany to special difficulties on account of the class structure of the empire. What the various secular powers were allowed and obliged to do in religious matters within their own territories, gradually became more or less defined. In Worms in 1521, however, legitimate imperial authority had opposed the doctrine which Luther claimed to be the only true Christian doctrine. The new gospel faced the threat of outlawry and perhaps the use of military force. In this case what were the rights and duties of subjects? What was meant by the term 'subject'? At first Luther had no doubt at all that a Christian is still bound to show obedience to the authorities, even when they persecute him on account of faith. True, one is not bound to follow the emperor into battle against one's co-religionists, but one must patiently tolerate the injustice of the authorities oneself; for legitimate authority is ordained by God. All the same, a person attacked on account of his faith may claim the right of self-defence.

At the Lutheran court of electoral Saxony this was the accepted view; and that explains why for so long the political development of the Protestant confessional principle, in so far as it called in question the relationship to the emperor, lacked action and any aggressive spirit.

Philip of Hesse saw things in a totally different light. He had Zwinglian leanings; and for Zwingli the preaching of the word and its expansion by means of politics and the sword went hand in hand. He felt obligated to no man. Long before any of the other princes he saw the emperor, not as a superior authority but as an opponent, to be fought with every available means. Zwingli was the driving force in the development of the political Protestant confessional principle. Afterwards, he dragged Saxony along with him – but slowly, for the innate defensive spirit of Saxony was finally overcome and replaced by positive adherence to the political Protestant principle (opposing the emperor) only in the rebel Maurice of Saxony.

As late as 1530 Luther himself still represented the passive view (admonition to his beloved Germans, a *Memorandum to the Electors*), Osiander in Augsburg having already asserted the right to oppose the emperor. His colleagues at Wittenberg held the same view. The more liberal jurists, however, attached the concept of authority, applicable in this case, to the hereditary territorial princes and to the civic powers, but not to the emperor. In general, however, Luther's attitude was not quite consistent. In the same *Admonition* of 1530 he had the possibility of a real conflict in mind: 'Let us carry on cheerfully, then, come what may – war or insurrection.' By 1532–34, however, his picture of Charles as the enemy of the Turks was becoming really blurred, and he fell into line with his theological colleagues on the question of whether obedience implied patience or revolt. Following the dynamic of outward as well as interior revolt against the old order, he affirmed his belief in the permissibility of resistance to imperial authority, which was persecuting the gospel. The princes were not simply subjects of the emperor; moreover, the imperial promises at the religious peace of Nuremberg had created a new situation, in which the emperor was restricted, having renounced the right to use coercion in matters of faith.

II

The Edict of Worms was the expression of the prevailing state of affairs according to ancient legal tradition in the empire. The attempt to overthrow this represented a battle for the legality of a new private opinion in basic questions concerning Church and State, in opposition to former authority. The Edict of Worms expressed the binding authority of Church and empire. The battle against the edict expressed the right of self-determination. From the Church's angle, this meant the revolutionary freedom of the individual conscience. This was not quite the same as private individual conscience – the understanding of events did not go so deep – but it meant freedom for the separate historical, political and civic, powers, who were soon to declare their right of intervention in the sphere of conscience.

The victory for this view was the victory of the Lutheran Reformation. The gradual elaboration of this view, its outward manifestation, its results and repercussions, are a description of the path followed by the German Reformation, which we have already studied in respect of its more spiritual aspects during the twenties of the century. Now we must examine the political aspect of this development.

The Edict of Worms provoked quite violent reactions; but these were confused in intention and insufficiently recognised in their import, expressing as they did a mere passive resistance. The resolution of the *Reichstag* at Speyer in 1526, however, produced the first fundamental formulation of the new Protestant confessional principle. Ranke was perfectly correct in dating a new epoch in German history from this point. This is not contradicted by the fact that the new principle was not yet incorporated in the constitution. The claim had been made; and it won the day.

From 1526 onwards it was the battle over this principle that characterised the history of the Reformation. The battle was waged with varying degrees of ruthlessness. At bottom this principle was nothing other than the transfer of the central slogan of the Reformation: 'Nothing of man!' to the problem of political Power. No majority decision may bind or loose the conscience.

What bitter tragedy! This same principle led to its direct opposite in the *cuius regio, illius religio*.

The Edict of Worms threatened outlawry. Its execution was a question of power. Resistance against this was a question of power also. The elaboration of the Protestant principle in the political sphere was thus necessarily a question of power and a trial of strength. Who were to be the vehicles of this elaboration depended upon which political power would most strongly and most quickly attach itself to Luther's gospel, and upon the political, economic and military force which it had at its command.

The first putting into practice and public legal presentation of the Protestant principle was effected outside the empire by Zwingli in and through the Confederacy (1519 onwards in Zürich). None of the political forces which accepted Reformation doctrine in Germany effected such an intense integration of religious belief and political action as the Swiss had done. In Germany we have seen that the development was carried out essentially by two historical rulers, one of whom stressed the religious aspect, the other the political aspect. These were electoral Saxony, and Hesse, represented by Frederick the Wise, his brother, John the Steadfast, John's son, John Frederick, and the landgrave Philip. That is not to say that Frederick cared nothing for political advantage and that Philip had no interest in profession of faith; but it is a true statement of their characteristic difference in approach.

The correctness of this thesis is easily confirmed. Quite apart from the Lutheran business we know that Frederick the Wise was a man of fairly explicit religious interests. His zeal over his collection of relics and of indulgences are not so important on this score as the fact that he used to spend Holy Week listening to pious discourses in a monastery. This was perfectly in keeping with his manner of approaching Luther, from whom in 1518 he sought instruction on the question of indulgences and justification. At an early stage he became a convinced Lutheran. Aleander's description of the *Reichstag* at Worms in 1521 states this fact, although with some hesitation. The Lutherans, he said, had turned his head, to this extent, that he seemed to believe that Lutheran doctrine was the true Catholic faith. Throughout his whole life Frederich may have been cautious and hesitant in choosing his exact position, but his attitude is most easily explained if we assume that he was personally convinced of the truth of Luther's doctrine. His hesitation in spreading the new doctrine was perfectly in line with Luther's views. There should be no suppression by princely power of freedom of preaching, no resistance, either, to unjust superior authority. His successors adopted the same attitude. Increased action merely modified the picture but did not change the essence. The history of the *Schmalkald League* provides proof of this.

Philip of Hesse, the politically active partner, was by no means primarily animated by religious concern. He lived for politics and sensuality. It has been said that in return for Ferdinand's renunciation of Nuremberg he would have been prepared to accept peace and religious compromise. The much later threat that he would go over to the emperor if the Reformers failed to allow his marriage has the ring of probability about it. Philip was all for an unfettered, bold conscience, especially if it were to his own private or public advantage. An affair so eminently religious as the Marburg conversations was inaugurated by him only from far-sighted political considerations. It was thoroughly characteristic that the first aggressive expansion of the gospel through military force was carried out by him.

In Charles V the Catholic opposition possessed a combination of religious loyalty and political initiative. His manifesto at Worms on the day after Luther's great declaration provides fully adequate proof of this. All his life he was ruled by these qualities, in spite of tactical vacillations. He was in deadly earnest about restoring peace and unity to the whole of Christendom, and ready to apply force of arms to that end. He was a product of the classical Spanish concept of the unity of the politico-religious and the religio-political, in which each element served the other, neither, however, being affirmed as less original than the other, and in which above all the religious element lost nothing of its sublimity and integrity because it seemed to serve politics. This question must be examined again later.

This unity gave Charles an unconditional superiority over his opponents. On the other hand, he was crippled by the vacillating and weak crowd of German territorial rulers, who, as Catholics, ought to have been the supports of his work.

(a) Charles must have been more than content with the choice
of the new pope on 9 January 1522. He was Adrian of Utrecht,
his former tutor, then his regent in Spain. This man was an
epoch-making personality in the history of reform within Catholicism. We will discuss this in Part Three. Politically he was not one
of those popes who wanted to build a personal dynasty upon the
papal states. There was no trace of the Machiavelli in him.
He felt responsible to every member of the universal Church.
Thus it came about that this German, so closely attached to
Charles, was far from being disposed to become a tool of imperial
policy or of the wishes of the emperor.

The first *Reichstag* since Worms in 1521,[1] the first, also, in the
new pontificate (Nuremberg, November 1522 – February 1523),
clearly displayed the strength of those forces opposing the emperor
and the execution of the Edict of Worms. For the execution of the
Edict of Worms the papal nuncio, Chieregati, offered an unheard
of price: a confession of sins by the curia and reform proposal
that arose from a truly great-hearted Christianity. The response
was discouraging in the extreme. The execution of the edict was
refused, allegedly because it would lead to disturbances. For a
settlement of the religious dispute, the antecedent correction of the
Gravamina was demanded. In addition, a totally fresh basis of
negotiation was proposed: a general council on German soil.
Until then, however, nothing was to be preached except 'the true,
pure, clear and holy gospel and the approved scriptures'. The
meaning of this formula was absolutely plain. In face of this the
Reichstag's demand that Frederick the Wise for the time being
prevent his professor and his adherents from making public
utterances, carried little weight.

And so, after the bull of excommunication and after the
imperial ban there was to be a council. This implied complete
disregard of the supreme sentences passed by Church and empire.
The conciliar idea, which we are to meet over and over again, at
once took on a revolutionary colour, which went far beyond
anything hitherto known in Catholic conciliarism. This tendency
persisted in all of the future related propositions of the Reformers.
That was fundamental. If we lose sight of the fact, we will

[1] The *Reichstag* at Nuremberg in March 1522 was so poorly attended that
a second was called in November.

completely misunderstand the possibilities of union and the negotiations that were aimed at that end. The tragedy was that most
of the Catholic powers for so long were deceived by this
misunderstanding, and even helped to create it.

In a very real sense the resolutions of this *Reichstag* were quite
incredible. How had it become possible to reach such conclusions?
Luther's followers were a powerless minority in the estates of the
realm; and yet a committee proposal, clearly sympathetic to
Luther and antagonistic to the Church, was put forward, and the
final resolution of the diet included the demand that at the
coming council the secular powers, too, must have a voice.
People were speaking openly of the Lutheran affair as 'the
evangelical truth, which ought not to be suppressed by the
tyranny of the Edict of Worms, and in place of which abuses ought
not to be tolerated'.

These few supporters of Luther in the *Reichstag* exploited the
situation more zealously and purposefully than those who were
loyal to the Church: they had control of the key positions – were
on the committees of the *Reichstag*. The Reformers dominated the
new class of learned advisers, who played such a big part in the
formation of modern times. These men directed their princes,
sometimes against their own wills, sometimes took their places;
they thought and acted for them. The activities, for example, of
John of Schwarzenberg, or of Planitz, were decisive. These men
were opposed by that enormous uncertainty, lukewarmness and
confusion of mind of Catholics, which Cochlaeus had reprimanded
so vigorously, and by the culpable selfishness of the rulers, who
saw a means of advantage for themselves in Luther's attack upon
Rome. The prince-bishops were characterised by criminal carelessness and thus encouraged the devastating confusion of anti-
Roman *Gravamina* with anti-Roman Lutheran doctrine. The
representatives of cities already displayed the spirit of compromise
which, lacking clear principles of belief, desired merely to follow
the line of least resistance. Severe persecution, they thought,
would only make matters worse. The extent to which the whole
question of blame had become utterly confused in the minds of
large sections of the public is shown by the admonition to the
nation, issued at the same time by the estates of the realm, and
supposed to be announced every Sunday from the pulpit, which

quite openly spoke in one breath of 'errors' amongst clergy, secular rulers and other Christians, without indicating that by 'errors' it meant only 'abuses'.

In this way the Lutherans gained what they most required: time. With every month that passed undisturbed by the execution of the edict, Luther and his followers were able to preach and print as they pleased. Thus the edict lost its weight, and, conversely, Luther's cause gained in power and in apparent legality.

On the other hand the fate of this *Reichstag* presupposes a serious impotence on the part of the emperor and the empire *vis-à-vis* the territorial rulers, and a corresponding sense of independence amongst these princes *vis-à-vis* the empire and the sanctions it might try to bring to bear. This fact had been highlighted in that very year – 1522, when, at the beginning of March, Luther had gone to Wittenberg against the wishes of the elector, had preached on his journey, then in Wittenberg, and in the course of subsequent lesser journeys, and had been publicly acclaimed. No one seemed to have regarded him as a notorious outlaw. Now, after the Nuremberg resolution of 1523, he could even dare to threaten 'the drunken and besotted princes' at whose door stood the wrath of God.

We can see that everything was topsy turvy. The Lutheran movement had already seriously shaken the foundations of life according to the ways of the old Church; or it had uncoverd the fact that these foundations were already gone.

(*b*) In the very next year things moved on with uncanny speed to a catastrophe. What had provoked amazement in 1523 was far exceeded in the Nuremburg *Reichstag* by the same forces, in spite of seemingly greater opposition. It is in the resolutions of this *Reichstag* that we see for the first time that 'so far as possible' which was so much in harmony with subjective autonomy, with the Protestant principle. The estates promised to carry out the Edict of Worms 'as far as they were able'.

Once again the main work was done by the juridically educated advisers, most of whom represented the cities. Once again they averted to the danger of revolution by the common man, who was thirsting for the gospel – as they had expressed it in their message to the emperor in Spain. Quite openly they proposed to judge religion from the standpoint of the empire, and to judge preaching, not by the Edict of Worms but by scripture as the sole norm. One thing was clearer now than in the previous year: the authoritative decisions of pope and emperor were no longer regarded as final. The separate estates, those, that is, who 'have universities', were to make extracts of 'the disputed material' from all new doctrines and books.

It was the cities, too, who kept up the frequent demand for a general council, so that 'it could at last be discussed, how each ought to behave in this matter for the time being'. Meantime there should be a 'general assembly of the German nation' (in November) to review the former attitude. The really astonishing thing was that Bavaria too, subscribed to these demands, and that an assembly of princes and an assembly of electors agreed to them. At first, even Ferdinand agreed to the scheme.

Luther did not let slip this opportunity of exploiting the obvious contradictions in the resolution of the *Reichstag*. In violent terms he denounced the princes, and severely prejudiced every form of authority, 'for I am at once damned and spared future judgment . . . these princes must be fools and drunkards. All right then – we Germans will have to remain Germans, asses and martyrs of the pope, as though ground in a mortar. . . . What do you want dear Lords? God is too clever for you . . . he has soon fixed you. Do not march against the Turks, for the Turks are ten times cleverer and more devout than our princes . . . the crazy, foolish, raving, lunatics . . . God deliver us from them and send us, by his grace, other rulers. Amen.'

This *Reichstag* was significant in another respect for the alignment of forces. The imperial government required funds; but the estates were unwilling to pay. And so the Habsburgs paid, and because they paid, they used the imperial organisation more for their own dynastic interests than for the common good. This was specially important in the development of secularisation during the thirties.

(c) The *Reichstag* of Speyer in 1526 had already defined the issue. It realised the possibilities opened up for Lutheranism in Nuremberg in 1523–24.

That things should have progressed in that direction at that particular time once again revealed the extraordinary alignment of forces in the empire. A reaction is what we should have expected; for meanwhile, Charles' troops had won the secular victory of Pavia; the suppression of the peasants' revolts had consolidated conservative forces, increased the fear of change and thus damaged the cause of the Reformation. It was the mighty victor of 1525 who had put the proposal to the *Reichstag:* 'having put down the peasants' revolt, now the Edict of Worms will be carried out ... '

In reality, few representatives of the estates had the courage to present themselves in person. The most active appeared: the electors of Saxony and of Hesse. The slogan which their specially numerous followers bore upon their doublets: 'God's Word Endures For Ever', proclaimed their self-assurance and sense of purpose, as did the ingenuousness with which Philip of Hesse publicly appeared as a Lutheran. These became the victors, in spite of the fact that now their representatives on the committees were in a minority.

A protest had already been made that profession of faith and collection of Church endowments be freed from all control. When this was countered by the demand that the Edict of Worms be carried out, there was a move in the cities to deprive the clergy of their privileges, and make them subject to the one law of the land. This move was not more violent than with the territorial princes, but it was more sharply expressed. It became apparent that secularisation and hence Reform of Church policy was going ahead most consciously and most boldy in the cities. Once again we encounter the vague idea of a general council. On the other hand, on account of the Turkish threat, Ferdinand was thrown upon the estates for support. And so the *Reichstag* ended in a compromise which opened up the way to victory for the Protestant principle: until a council could be called, concerning the Edict of Worms, each estate should act as it dared to answer God, the imperial majesty, and the realm. This was the very principle to which Hesse and electoral Saxony found themselves subscribing in October 1525: in matters of faith one is responsible to God alone.

In these transactions the notion of 'ecclesiastical abuses' and 'ordinances of men' had once again (as in 1524) been expounded with a vagueness that was very dangerous. The estates of the realm were beginning to interfere in the Church's own doctrinal sphere. The resolution itself was the most significant and most fateful thing of all, principally because it did not present a common front to the principle behind the protest we have mentioned. As a result it became one of these fatal, ambiguous half efforts which, in times of revolution, always play into the hands of the innovators. On this occasion in Germany it assured the victory of the Reformation by providing it with means of growth.

In fact, the Speyer formula had been thoroughly exploited in the elaboration of a new form of Church government. Obviously the renewed shift in foreign political alignment was an important contributory cause: the very comprehensive League of Cognac now faced the recently omnipotent emperor. It was during the Speyer *Reichstag* (23 June 1526) that the emperor in Spain was rebuffed by the pope.

(*d*) If we would judge the pope by the truly binding law of Christ's Church, we must see this rebuff of Charles on 23 June 1526 chiefly in the context of the ecclesiastical situation in Germany. For years the spread of the religious revolution had been greatly increasing. In particular the attempts of the juridical advisers to place intra-ecclesiastical reform in the hands of the secular authorities had been obviously successful. By demanding an independent council in Germany the danger had become felt in Rome in its most feared and most detested form. In various ways the curia had emphatically protested against the development. On the other hand, Charles remained loyal to the Church. He forbade a national council, and demanded the execution of the Edict of Worms. He was able to do this because he had political power. At this juncture the pope parted company with him – appeared as his emeny. He weakened Charles' political position, thus strengthening the political power of the Lutheranisers and of the Reformation, and, in addition, favoured, of necessity, deep-rooted, state–Church and Erasmian–relativist tendencies that existed quite close to the emperor. From political considerations the pope damaged the ecclesiastical and religious situation, as his predecessor Leo X had done. His change of position aided heresy. Nor was this burdensome fact cancelled out by Charles' undoubtedly improper political conduct towards the pope – his part in the piracy of Colonna, for example.

This pope, Clement VII (1523–34), a Medici, was in general a great disillusionment for the emperor. A model emperor's man when a cardinal, hence Charles' first choice as pope, this man became a broken reed once in that office. There was his inglorious defection to Francis I, conqueror of Milan, his return to the imperial party after the fall of Pavia, then his joining in the League of Cognac. The sack of Rome brought him to his senses, but he never became strong enough to adopt a consistent attitude. How tragic, that in the midst of the Church's battle for its very life, this pope never saw further than petty worries of domestic policy!

Charles was never so enraged as in 1526 when, for the first time, he experienced how the sacerdotal head of Christendom could leave him in the lurch, to face his problem of political power, at the same time shelving the religious problem in Germany, and for such petty reasons. In language which expressed the general bitterness felt in Germany, he denounced the pope's faithlessness. The statement is a famous state document – perhaps a little one-sided. He held the threat of a council over Clement's too frightened head; and as later statements show, he shared the conciliar view-point. This statement, however, stressed also – now allusively, now plainly – a circumstance that is decisive in a verdict upon the ecclesiastical and religious situation. When it was stated – although with hesitation – that the pope had provoked nothing but scandal and destruction of Christian common life, this must be taken as the exaggeration typical of Lutheran polemics as of the spirit of the author – Alfonso Valdes, brother of the later Reformed Juan Valdes, and an enthusiastic admirer of Erasmus. The question was asked: was it permissible for the pope to weaken Christian powers and strengthen the heretics? The answer was that if the pope had not taken arms against the emperor it would have been easy to destroy the errors of the Lutherans and the Reformers.

Basically, Clement was merely carrying on an ancient tradition of the Renaissance curia, who thought primarily in terms of Italian politics, even in terms of dynastic self-interest. We have already noted how fatal was Leo X's intervention from political motives in the process against Luther. Even his first alliance with the emperor at the end of May 1521, revealed him as nothing but a politician, and one deeply involved in nepotism. If we want to see how the confusion of religion and politics in these days went down to the merest trifling details, we need only look at the despatches of Aleander from Worms. In turning to Francis I Clement was only displaying this confusion on its highest level. Ranke and Pastor have described his pontificate as the most fateful in the whole history of the papacy; and it was this change of allegiance, chiefly, which led them to this assessment. 'By making himself the fulcrum of opposition to Charles V, the politico-ecclesiastical revolution in Germany was allowed to have free play' (Pastor).

In fairness to truth we must point out that the vacillating Clement was more than cleverly outplayed by Francis I. We ought to remember, too, that no contemporary could be expected to see the full import of that mistake as we can see it today. It remains true, however, that the fatal dullness of vision we see at work in these events was chiefly caused by the colossal, and accepted, mixing up of political, economic and family, interests with those of religion.

Clement VII contributed to the strengthening of Protestantism not least by his stubborn resistance to the calling of a council. People were looking to a council as a means of reuniting Christendom, and had this been called in good time, the object might well have been achieved. 'Thanks,' however, 'to the constant putting off and upsetting of a council by papal policy, Protestantism gained more and more time in which to take root and spread' (Merkle). By comparison delay over the English divorce affair was of lesser importance, although that, too, formed part of the general picture.

These things became no less true and no less urgent by being seldom expressed. To disguise these facts is unchristian, for it is an offence against a basic requirement of Christianity: the necessity of admitting one's own faults. The blame on that occasion was ours, and we admit it with sorrow.

In fact, in this harm which politically- and dynastically-minded popes were doing to the cause of religion we see beyond the so-called secularisation of the leaders of the Church to such a shifting of emphasis in ecclesiastical interest that an inversion of essence seems to threaten. At this point we begin to see what might almost be called the 'legitimation' of the Reformation. We do not mean that schism and heresy are justified; but, accepting man as he is, and assuming that even within the life of faith his natural energies still operate, then the experience of history tells us that – the question of culpable apostasy aside – a radical attack upon the Church such as many most loyal Catholics of that time expected, was inevitable.

No true Christian can rest content merely with reading this statement; he must weigh up and help to bear the colossal weight of guilt, if something is to be gained for the sake of the still unresolved problem of the Reformation – for the rent is still unmended.

Nowhere is this inversion of values such a crying scandal as in the representative of Christ. Equally plainly, however, must it be said of those who initiated the Reformation under the slogan of 'God's Word Alone!' that the same inversion was very often to be found in their ranks.

At this point we are more interested in the question of the testing of the Catholic powers, France in particular. The contradiction between her domestic policy and her foreign policy in the Lutheran affair is so obvious that no extensive proof is required. France burned Protestants at home and supported them in Germany. She gave them substantial help, what is more, reinforced by her alliance with the Turks. Quite openly Pope Clement took this into his reckoning in order to force the emperor to abandon his demand for a council. We can sense how the loyal Catholic Charles V was unable to understand why he should be treated in the very same manner as Francis I, who betrayed the Church's cause.

The policy pursued by the Bavarians who remained Catholic displayed suspiciously similar features. In 1524 Bavaria supported the idea of a national assembly. It opposed any vigorous suppression of the Reformation, at the *Reichstag* of 1530 in Augsburg, for it did not want Ferdinand to be made king of the Romans. From 1534 it was in alliance with the Schmalkald League and with France – a shamelessly two-faced policy. In 1548 it made alliance with Protestant powers to prevent any increase in imperial power. These things were done by the same Bavarians who were loudest in their demand that the 'weak emperor' should use force to suppress Protestantism.

These things are not secondary matters in Reformation history – least of all from the Christian point of view. They aggravated the essential weakness of Catholic resistance in Germany, and partly explain how the Reformation was able to make such unimaginably deep inroads into the Church's domain.

(e) Had the Catholic powers in Germany, with the emperor as their strongest representative, been at all in earnest about fighting to maintain their position they would have been obliged to oppose the resolution of 1526. The emperor's proposals to the *Reichstag* of Speyer in 1529 were in line with the realisation of this fact. In virtue of imperial authority it rejected the resolution 'which had been instrumental in producing so much nonsense and misunderstanding against the faith' and had 'been used to excuse all manner of frightful new doctrines and sects'. This move was designed to prevent the actual growth of the Reformation and its legalisation.

This *Reichstag* was unusually well attended. All seven electors were present. Once again Catholics had a clear majority, and even the lords spiritual displayed a more resolute attitude. By this time the catastrophic development, that now really threatened their power, had shaken them up to some extent. Now they were fighting vigorously for their own personal power at least. The expression of this power, however, within and without the territories of their princes, was their episcopal jurisdiction and the holy mass. As a result the resolution of the committee was strongly Catholic in tone. The old religion was to claim unrestricted acceptance everywhere. Any Reforms that had been introduced were to be permitted only until the council. This tolerance did not apply to Zwinglians and Anabaptists, however.

The final resolution of the *Reichstag* (designed by Ferdinand) was in line with this proposal. The matter was more definitely settled than the emperor's advisers would have wished. All the same there was still that fatal vagueness of statement: where the Reformation had gained entrance any further change in the meantime was to be 'prevented as far as humanly possible'. In addition, stress was laid on the fact that no power was permitted to assist alien subjects against their own ruler.

This final resolution of the *Reichstag* was followed by the famous protest from which the followers of the Reformation got the name of *Protestants*. This protest set an autonomous minority in opposition to the decree of the realm, and split up the political unity of the estates of the empire. This protest was the first formulation of the subjectivist standpoint of the Reformation, in the form of a claim for imperial legality. The resolution of the *Reichstag* was rejected 'because in matters touching the glory of God and the salvation of our souls each man stands alone before God to whom he must account, and none in any place can excuse himself on the grounds of what others do and decide – be they few or many'.[2] They demanded a return to the resolution of 1526, which, having been unanimously accepted, could be abrogated only by a unanimous vote. This was a reiteration of the principle enunciated by the Hussites who had been invited to the Council of Basel: matters of faith cannot be settled by majority vote. Now this was being put forward by the estates against the resolution of the *Reichstag*, and so from then onwards 'every possibility of restoring unity by imperial constitutional means was thrown overboard' (Mentz). Should the opposition remain firm, force alone remained as a means of healing the division.

For a long time, through the preparation of confessional alliances between states, things had been moving towards this *ultima ratio*.

III

The intervention of armed force in settling the religious question of the Reformation was perfectly acceptable in terms of all medieval tradition and constitution. All religious affairs were the concerns of the Church and of the secular state. Charles' announcement in Worms that he would devote his life and his crown to the suppression of the Lutheran system was a clear expression of this mentality, which then found concrete expression in the outlawing of Luther. Even before this happened the view had been expressed

[2] Again it was Philip of Hesse who was first to make this objection to the proposal of the committee. Electoral Saxony joined him in this. These two became the leaders of the opposition party. Besides them the party included the margrave of Brandenburg, the prince of Anhalt, the prince of Lüneburg, the cities of Strasburg, Nuremberg, Ulm, Constance, Lindau, Memmingen, Kempten, Nördlingen, Heilbronn, Reutlingen, Isny, St Gallen, Weissenburg a/S, Windsheim,

on the Reformed side that the Reformation should be accomplished by force of arms, in general, through the intervention of the secular power; and this had in fact been carried out by Zwingli in Zürich.

Both of these statements – alike in principle – were taken up by the estates of the empire. The result had to be that the religious and ecclesiastical schism found political expression; and it was obvious that the adherents of each viewpoint would close their ranks in confessional alliance.

This development naturally went parallel to those we have already examined. The obscurity of the situation and the uncertainty of the aims, from which definite features gradually developed, although with considerable instability, were more than ever obvious now. The reason for this was territorial self-interest, which had no regard at all for the primacy of religion – at least not on the average and not when it came to action. Even in later years when politico-confessional grouping was much further advanced, this political self-interest was often much more evident than confessional ties. In 1538 the Archbishop of Trier, for example, successor of Richard of Greiffenklau, approached Hesse with the proposal that they stick together, 'as though we professed the same faith'. In other words, all of the powers were by no means convinced that in all circumstances they should align their political and military power with their religious convictions. The contradictory attitude towards the curia of Philip of Hesse, the Bavarian dukes and France, are all too sad an illustration of this fact. In addition there was the lukewarmness of Catholics, not least of their spiritual leaders. It is true that the situation was always made worse than the facts need have demanded, through the sheer confusion that was rampant. It is certainly not true that anyone really grasped the full import of a schism in the Church, so often rumoured in political and governing circles in the thirties. For countless numbers of people as late as 1555 it was still no more than an episode that would soon be at an end.

The year 1524, when the fate of the Edict of Worms was sealed at the Nuremberg *Reichstag* by the dangerous formula 'as far as they are able', saw the first attempt at mutual help amongst the Catholic estates. The assembly in July of that year at Regensburg, under the leadership of Ferdinand and the Nuncio Campeggi, united the dukes of Bavaria and the bishops of southern Germany, and had a primarily religious and ecclesiastical orientation. Existent alliances were in fact explicitly excepted. Mutual help was promised in case of possible unrest. Opposition to the Edict of Worms was to be treated as heresy, the spreading of Lutheran doctrine banned, and attendance at the university of Wittenberg prohibited.

Even these modest treaties were exposed to serious interior difficulties. Was there any more violent inter-German antithesis than that between Austria and Bavaria? This animosity sapped the strength of any alliance. In the following centuries Bavaria was repeatedly to be the great hindrance to the forming of a solid Catholic political front.

The same month of July saw the first beginnings of a political Reformed front in Speyer. In December the same thing happened in Ulm. The prime movers were cities that had been the first and the most energetic in allowing the new doctrines to mould public life. Now they openly professed Lutheranism and promised each other mutual assistance in resisting the execution of the Edict of Worms.

From the very start of literary polemic it had been a commonplace for Catholics to point to the revolutionary character of the religious Reformation. Rejection of the Church's authority would not stop short at that of the secular power. Luther's doctrine of the freedom of the Christian man would lead to anarchy. The curia in particular had relied greatly upon this argument. The peasants' risings in southern Germany, and the radical insurrections in central Germany in 1525 had demonstrated the truth of this argument to the princes. Having first sunk religious differences in a common effort to put down the risings (as with Sickingen in 1522 and the Münster Anabaptists in 1535), it then became obvious that the Catholic princes should form an alliance for their common defence, for religious Reform was blamed for the insurrections. In the same year – 1525 – they assembled in Dessau in order to root out 'the damned Lutheran sect which was the cause of the insurrection'. Duke George of Saxony, Elector Joachim of Brandenburg, Elector Albrecht of Mainz, Duke Henry of Braunschweig-Wolfenbüttel and Duke Eric of Calenberg were all there.

CONFESSIONAL AND POLITICO-CONFESSIONAL   49

This was the year of the emperor's victory at Pavia. The situation looked dangerous for the Reformers. The Catholic alliance of Dessau provoked a similar Reformed alliance, and this time the sapling was really vigorous.

Again the religious basis was to be given pride of place. The Reformation demand: 'no ordinances of men, nothing but the eternal word of God!' with its marvellous one-sided appeal to countless people, now dominated the ecclesio-political course of the Reformation. It was not simply the most powerful factor; it was the all-controlling root. As in Worms Luther had appealed to his conscience as the final, inviolable authority, so now the proposition was enunciated, in defiance of the Edict of Worms, that in matters of conscience and religion each must stand on his own, that God alone has power of entry into a man's conscience. Because the opposite view relied upon the power of the empire, therefore it could be resisted ultimately only by similar power. To help in the assertion of this view a conference took place in October 1525 between the young Hesse and the new elector of Saxony in the hunting lodge at Friedewald. All that was agreed upon there was mutual assistance at the coming *Reichstag*. This alliance was first brought into operation at Speyer in 1526, after it had been strengthened internally and received additional support from northern Germany. Here the Reformed cause was represented by a proper alliance, the first Protestant alliance, based upon the Torgau agreements of February 1526; and it was this coalition which very largely provided the basis for the famous resolution of the *Reichstag*, which, for practical purposes, formulated the Protestant principle, and ensured the tremendous growth of the Reformation in the following years. These years saw a decisive remoulding of Church life in Saxony and Hesse and in several smaller states and in a number of cities, which we have mentioned.

In order to assess the importance of this first Protestant alliance we must remember that meanwhile the Catholic union of Regensburg was already bereft of power. We must take into account also the foreign political situation, especially Turkish pressure upon the territories belonging to the Catholic Ferdinand.

Fundamentally, those agreements of 1525–26 were relatively

unimportant because military conflict was not envisaged. The explosive state of affairs, however, was proved in 1527 – despite the harmless appearance of the as yet inarticulate views of the landgrave – by the unique incident now known as the Packschen affair.

Producing a forged document, one of the advisers of Duke George of Saxony, Otto von Pack, told Philip of Hesse of consultations between George and Frederick, the object of which was to make a pact of aggression, to which the electors of Mainz and of Brandenburg, the archbishop of Salzburg, the dukes of Bavaria, and the bishops of Würzburg and Bamberg, were parties. If necessary they would go so far as to drive out the rulers of electoral Saxony and of Hesse. Philip was taken in by the forgery. He was not too unhappy about this, because it was in line with his constant theory that one must always anticipate the threatening danger from the opposition. At once he displayed enormous activity. He prepared for war, gathered the elector of Saxony to his side, made alliance with France, with Frederick's rival Zapolya, and with Denmark. For the first time the Reformation movement in Germany, in its political aspect, appeared in all its harshness. The first rumblings of a religious war were heard. Luther must be given credit for averting war on that occasion, for he had a moderating influence upon the elector.

The *Reichstag* resolution of 1526 and the speeding up of Reform within the states of Hesse and Saxony (including the visitations after 1527 and the founding of Marburg university in 1527) along with this resolute taking up of arms, made the mighty advance of the Reformation visible, just as on the other side it made the rising fear of the Catholic princes apparent. Philip succeeded in making the prince-bishops of Würzburg and Bamberg renounce their episcopal jurisdiction in Hessian territory. In addition he was able to exact monetary compensation for his completely unjustified armament. On the Catholic side this false alarm created greater alertness and readiness for defence.

In 1529 the confessional powers stood so sharply oppposed, and the *Reichstag* resolution signified such a confirmed 'No' to the mighty reinforcement of the Reformation, that the resulting protest cried out for an immediate alliance. Hitherto the progress of the Reformation in the formation of public life in Saxony,

Hesse, Lüneberg and the imperial cities of southern Germany had developed on the basis of a deliberately vague ecclesio-political situation. Clear formulation had been avoided, and vagueness exploited. More than this, after the official protest of a group of imperial estates, a clearly discernible secession was at hand. The question was whether the imperial government would recognise this secession. If it did not, had it the power to lead back the seceders to the idea of the empire as the political form of the universal Church, whose one faith all princes and their subjects must accept? At all events there was an obvious danger of conflict, and hence the desire for confessional alliance amongst those who felt isolated or threatened was understandable. On the day the resolution of the *Reichstag* was signed, 22 April 1529, a defensive pact was made – 'a special understanding' – between Saxony, Hesse, Nuremberg, Strasburg and Ulm.

This alliance, too, had internal problems, this time dogmatic, for Luther would have nothing to do with the Zwinglians of south Germany. The religious and ecclesiastical schism within Protestantism, that had been developing for a long time, was now being followed by a threatened political division, and thus by apparent decline.

As might have been expected, the politician, Philip of Hesse, was the man who recognised the danger most clearly. At that time a durable political alliance of the whole Protestant interest would be possible only on a basis of religious, dogmatic unity. Again it is understandable that this goal would appear more easily attainable to a humanist, relativist Zwinglian like Philip of Hesse, than to an uncompromising, genuine Lutheran. On that same day, 22 April, the first letter was sent from the landgrave to Zwingli inviting him to meet Luther and Melanchthon. Zwingli saw at once the danger threatening Protestantism. He strove passionately for a union between north and south. The problem was Luther, who would only agree to a meeting after severe pressure was put on him by Philip.

The outcome of these efforts was the celebrated Marburg conversations from 1–3 October 1529. We know what the result of these was. The essential difference between the two Protestant parties became sharply focused in the article of belief concerning the Lord's Supper. Here was the clash between rationalist, humanist, relativist Zwinglianism and the robust, intolerant dogmatism of Lutheranism which was tied to the unaltered word of God. This difference remained, although Luther did not completely shut the door on agreement, but modified the Schwabacher Articles produced by the Wittenbergers, and produced the Marburg Articles, in which the antithesis was softened. The validity of these articles did not, it is true, outlast the Marburg conversations. Before the start of the disputation Luther had written down the words of institution in chalk on the table: 'This is my body.' In the course of the dispute he lifted the cover and pointed to the words. The 'is' in contrast to Zwingli's 'signifies' – taken over from Honius – illustrates the antithesis. A series of articles was produced in which an understanding was reached, or in which it was imagined that understanding had been reached; but the true state of affairs and the dominant mood are shown in Luther's statement: 'They possess a different spirit from us.' This statement gives a truer picture of things than Luther's words to his wife on the day after the last session: 'Our friendly conversations in Marburg are at an end, and we are agreed on almost every point.' Obviously this does not ring true. We ought to remember that Luther's verdict on Zwingli in general was very far from suggesting any unity between the two men. Any development towards unity can be found only by means of a very forced interpretation of the facts. Taking a broad view, we would have to admit that it would have been contrary to Luther's nature for him not to have condemned this 'wild Swiss' with his human self-assurance. The man 'who is deceived into seeking his own honour and deeds instead of displaying a contrite spirit, is our own creation'. His return to the Schwabacher Articles in the same month, and the attempt to continue the alliance without Hesse; the embassy from electoral Saxony which approached the emperor with the plan eventually to part company with the rest of the Protestants; the angry scenes during the Schmalkald negotiations in December, when the Upper Germans were denounced as sacramentarians; all of these facts speak for themselves. Luther the dogmatist had no time for politics. Zwingli, on the other hand, was unable to relinquish his pre-religious, pre-biblical rationalism precisely on account of his political views.

Thus the political alliance between the north and south, between the country and the towns, never took place. Even in their own southern region the Swiss were unable to effect a league. Soon after, with the defeat of Zürich at Kappel on 11 October 1531, they disappeared from the scene. Zwingli having fallen in battle, the personal, ecclesio-political pivot of the Upper German cities was gone, and thereafter it became easier to unite them with the whole of German Protestantism.

For a time, however, the rift had been a reality. Electoral Saxony laid down the dogmatic conditions for a political pact, and these conditions were conceived in true medieval style as making a total claim upon people. So little did they see the full import of the Reformation.

By the end of 1529 the confessional, Protestant alliances or attempts at alliance had once again come to nothing. Contradictions within Protestantism were growing. This itself gives us a new insight into the power of the Reformed revolt; for the Reformed faith grew in spite of these diversions. This can be proved even of Melanchthon's watered-down version of Lutheranism in the Augsburg Confession. The enduring effect of the division between Luther and Zwingli was not the ensuing split up of the political alliance. The idea and sense of solidarity amongst all Reformed Christians – even including the fanatics – was greater than their divisions, even although unification had in the end to be effected without the Swiss. The power of this idea was seen in that, despite the narrow Lutheran intolerance which refused to make an alliance with the Zwinglians, the Protestant principle won the day, and was able to overcome the dangers into which the movement had fallen.

More than this: in a sense the disruption of those days, on account of Lutheran intolerance, was the saving of Protestantism as a religion. An alliance at that time could only have been reached at the expense of dogmatic rigidity on a central point. That would have meant a watering down of German Protestantism at a very early stage, and the result could only have been a further weakening of Christian forces in Germany.

FOUR

The Progress of the Reformation
and the Victory of the Confessional–
Political Principle (1530–39)

The years from 1530 until the start of the Schmalkald War, that
is until the final repulse of Francis I by the emperor in 1544,
display a series of unique, new features, over and above the
continuation and further elaboration of the religious, ecclesiastical
and political forces we have already examined. On the other hand
those years reveal, as well as a clear sharpening of antitheses, a
certain relaxation after a temporarily achieved victory.

If we ask what it was that really animated the man of the
Reformation period, it is not in those years that we will find an
answer. At the beginning of this decade Riemenschneider,
Burkmair (1531) and Veit Stoss (1533) died, the last representatives of a great artistic epoch; and none was there to succeed them.
But, we see on the other side a greater number of non-religious
questions appearing in literature. In Luther's own writings do we
not detect a certain relaxation in respect of the exclusive *sola fide*?
Melanchthon is found pursuing the moral and pedagogic line
which he had begun in his practical, public work after 1527.
Once again natural faculties and something of humanist relativism
came strongly to the fore in Protestantism. The Augsburg Confession (*Confessio Augustana*) of 1530 and the highly important

variations in Melanchthon's *Dogmatics* (*Loci communes*, edition of 1534) provide important evidence of this. In 1535 in his *Ecclesiastes* Erasmus once again gave what Huizing described as an 'ingenuously moralistic interpretation of the faith' – even of its very core. In the same period the Stock Exchange was built in Antwerp – a significant symbol.

The emperor's attitude to the German question changed also. He began to treat the religious issue in a more compromising, tactically more pliable, manner, which led in logical sequence from religious conversations to the new idea of religious equality (1539), to the Schmalkald War and, even further, to the interim following the imperial victory. This was supplemented by striking hopes of union.

In the end an element appeared that was not entirely new, but it appeared with renewed energy – positive Catholic reform in many forms. This will be discussed in Part Three. The great symbol of this reform was to be the Catholic council.

I

On 29 June 1529 peace had been signed in Barcelona between the emperor and the pope. The pope was easily won over, for what lay nearest this heart – the reinstatement of the Medicis in Florence – Charles was willing to grant. The next year, 1530, on 24 February, which was Charles' birthday and the anniversary of the battle of Pavia, the coronation of the emperor took place in Bologna. This was the last crowning of a German emperor by the pope. Even then it meant very little in the life of the German nation. Charles' empire was no longer German and Roman; it was a universal state, much wider geographically, and much narrower ideologically, than the original medieval empire had been.

Charles had set out for his coronation in Bologna not from Germany but from Spain. In his retinue the German princes were conspicious by their almost entire absence, although this was quite contrary to Charles' wishes. He came accompanied by the Italian and Spanish aristocracy. Duke Philip of the Palatinate, however, was there to carry the orb of the empire. The absence of Germans was due to the short notice they had received; none the less their absence was a highly significant symbol.

Germany in those days was not the support of the empire but its opponent. Charles, on the other hand, could completely rely upon his sovereignty over Spain and Italy. The years spent away from Germany – 1522–29 – preoccupied with war in Italy and with Burgundian aspirations, he had profitably employed in Spain where he had consolidated his royal absolutism. The nobility at home as in the rapidly growing vast colonies abroad proved themselves in the service of this absolutism; and the country's economic power, too, stood at its disposal in an extraordinary degree. This new power – a reality as well as a notion in the European mind – and the possessions won in Italy through the double victory over Francis I, were the foundation upon which he now built up his German enterprise.

With the emperor's announcement of his imminent return to Germany, included in the proposition to the *Protest-Reichstag* of Speyer in 1529, Germany was once again brought into the forefront of his political calculations. The historical and human resolution with which he alone on 19 April 1521 had briskly and boldly declared himself the opponent of the religious Reformation had not weakened. He had let the empire fall into the background of political interest during his seven-year absence in Spain, and thus had contributed to saving the Reformation. In so doing he had, however, obeyed the law of his universal empire, which was a political empire; the pope, on the other hand, had contravened the law of his universal empire, which was a religious and ecclesiastical empire.

On his journey to Germany for the *Reichstag* at Augsburg in 1530, Gattinara died. He had been the real educator of the emperor as a statesman with a universal and imperial outlook. Half a year later Charles' Aunt Margaret died. She had governed the Netherlands, the highly important residue of the Burgundian ancestral territory, for him in a masterly way. It is true that a worthy successor was found to Margaret in the twenty-six-year-old queen widow, Maria, Charles' sister; but the relationship could never be quite the same. Charles entered the decisive period of his life's work alone.

The *Reichstag* at Augsburg in 1530 displayed many strikingly conflicting features. Both sides displayed inflexibility supported by threats, and also an astonishing readiness to compromise. Following the open breach between the old and the new faith at Speyer in 1529, Augsburg was meant to be an all-out attempt to restore complete unity. Both sides approached the diet in this spirit, and both applied harshness and meekness to attain that end.

The announcement of this diet was made by the doubly victorious emperor from Bologna. Even England had offered its services, if the emperor would but help on the divorce case, and the previous year the king of Denmark had declared complete subservience. Most of the document dealt primarily with political questions (the Turks, Italy, Spain), and certainly these themes were of central interest to Charles. In particular, the Turkish question, or the problem of defending Ferdinand's territories in conjunction with the plan to make him king of Rome, was tied up with the Habsburg hereditary succession in the empire. The chief objective, however, was to take action against 'error and schism in the holy faith; to submit all past error to our Saviour, to hear with all possible discretion and in love and kindness the diverse opinions that exist amongst us, to understand and to weigh them, and to bring them together in a single Christian truth ... and as we all fight under the one Christ, so shall we all live in unity in a common Church'.

The tone of this document was more than 'peaceable beyond all expectations'. In respect of the religious question itself it was not simply dictated by solicitude for religion. Once again we see that unhappy dogmatic and theological vagueness, allied to a readiness to compromise, which was to become one of the most important preconditions for the spread of Reformation doctrine. This interpretation is not overthrown even if we see the formulation of this document as largely tactical, having the aim of at first appeasing the followers of the Reformation by an expression of accommodation.

The great conflict, expressed by the protest of 1529, rested ultimately upon the demand that in matters of religion one was bound only by one's decision, and not by majority vote. The document tried to by-pass this controversial material by making attendance obligatory. The emperor would, in any case, 'deal and consult with the estates present in every way' as though those invited were there.

Attendance came up to expectations. The emperor was there with Campeggi, the papal legate. The electors and the other estates were well represented. The rulers of electoral Saxony and of Hesse were there in person. Luther looked on from the relatively close Coburg – an observer and an adviser. Melanchthon now a Reformer, appeared in person in Augsburg as theological spokesman. Every Catholic theologian of repute was there; Eck, Cochleaus, Fabri were the leaders.

The emperor's last personal encounter with the German Lutheran movement had been in Worms in 1521. On that occasion Luther had made little impression on him, and the emperor's own firm and threatening declaration had met with no active resistance. Since that time he had formed no higher estimate of the German princes, and at the coming *Reichstag* he was again to show his contempt of the estates. And so we can understand how the emperor was tempted to think that he would meet the same sort of situation in Augsburg in 1530 as he had met in Worms – a situation that could fairly easily be mastered by a combination of firmness and prudent temporising. But the thoroughly self-assured and most abrupt attitude of the Protestant princes at Augsburg very quickly and plainly showed the emperor how radically things had changed since Worms. The elector of Saxony, for example, had coins minted in Augsburg during the diet, bearing his own image, and describing him as defender of the gospel. Admittedly, this was illogical, for, as we have seen, after the failure of Marburg, and Philip's alliance with Zürich, he felt inclined to come to terms with the emperor. Melanchthon's mediatorial activity perfectly expressed the attitude of Saxony at that time. He would gladly have seen an understanding arrived at between Catholics and Lutherans in opposition to the Zwinglians.

However that might be, to begin with the emperor reacted in terms of the proposition by a conciliatory treatment of the princes. In the peace of Barcelona he had promised the pope to lead back the Protestants either by kindness or by force. He kept both of these methods in mind.

To be ready for the intimated theological comparison, the elector of Saxony had asked his theologians for a short collection of all the chief points of the Christian religion. In March a common scheme was prepared by Luther, Jonas, Bugenhagen and Melanchthon. Taking this as his basis and with the aid of the Schmalkald and the Marburg articles Melanchthon composed a 'justification of the Church Reforms inaugurated in Saxon territories'. On the other side the dukes of Bavaria had asked Dr Eck to collect Luther's errors. He did this in his *Four Hundred and Four Articles* which, in tune with his own mood and that of those who commissioned him, once again set about encouraging the emperor to proceed sternly against the revolution. Influenced by this belligerent document, Melanchthon modified his justification (Gusmann). He wrote the first historic Protestant confessional document – the Augsburg Confession. This was directed explicitly at the emperor and was read out in German on 25 June 1530 'before the whole realm, the princes and the estates' as the profession of the Reformed signatories. This was a momentous hour, and Luther rightly regarded it thus. Moreover, as he said himself, it was an hour of consolation.

This Protestant–Lutheran confession was refuted by the Catholic *Confutatio* (John Faber, Eck, Cochlaeus, Wimpina). After much chopping and changing, the emperor himself took a hand in its formulation, trying to avoid harshness wherever possible. In turn Melanchthon defended the confession against the *Confutatio* in his *Apologia*, in which unfortunately he represented as the Church's teaching much that had already been rejected as uncatholic by the Catholics. The emperor rejected Melanchthon's *Apologia* and decided that the *Confutatio* had refuted the confession from holy scripture and by sound rational arguments.

The Augsburg Confession was signed by the elector of Saxony, the margrave of Brandenburg, the dukes of Lüneburg and the prince of Anhalt, by Nuremberg and Reutlingen. The landgrave of Hesse eventually joined in. Four Zwinglian cities in the south (Strasburg, Constance, Memmingen, Lindau) which had not been allowed to sign the confession, made their own official confession in the *Tetrapolitana*. This was not read out in public, but only before the Catholics in committee.

There was a host of cities besides who did not know what they wanted or what they ought to do, and who did not grasp the

c

significance of all the fuss over the confession. They would rather have kept right out of it.

In the end Zwingli, too, sent his own confession (*Ratio fidei*), wherein he allusively reproached the Protestants with nostalgia for the fleshpots of Egypt. Melanchthon dismissed the *Ratio fidei* with the remark that Zwingli had gone mad.

As well as the literary duel between the Lutherans and the Catholics there was a long-drawn-out verbal debate between Melanchthon, Brenz, Schnepf, and Eck, Wimpina, Cochlaeus. Even the princes and their lawyers joined in. Here, too, it became obvious that even a soft-pedalling document like the Augsburg Confession could achieve nothing. Even if Eck had not made unnecessary difficulties over the question of veneration of the saints, there could still have been no agreement on article twelve concerning satisfaction and the sacrificial character of the mass. The contradictions cannot be explained away.

The Augsburg Confession became and has remained the most important of all Protestant confessions. This is a fact of immeasurable significance; for it was not Luther, creator and life-giver of Reformed doctrine, who fashioned the greater part of Protestantism, but Melanchthon, a genius no doubt, but essentially a scholar, a schoolmaster and a humanist. It will be necessary to examine this document more thoroughly. It has to be viewed from many angles if we are to see beyond the content of its articles and grasp its real significance.

This confession was the supreme bid of humanism to penetrate Lutheranism without cancelling it out. It was of little moment for the larger historical development that towards the close of the *Reichstag* Melanchthon grew more obstinate, under Luther's influence. The basic attitude of the confession remained unchanged and its influence endured for centuries. This was fatal for Protestantism, for the unfathomable, overwhelming, paradoxical power of Luther's doctrine was thus turned into a much thinner, more formal Lutheranism of mediocrity, which often took refuge in all too smooth formulae. The roughness and internal contradiction of Luther's sayings had been ironed out; and in the process the indestructible quality, the infinite growing potential, that which could not be taught in the classroom; in short, the primeval quality had been destroyed also. Luther's friend Baumgärtner said that at Augsburg nobody did so much damage to the gospel as Melanchthon.

Strange as it may seem this change of attitude damaged the Catholic Church too. The colossal weakening of Christianity in the post-Reformation period is clearly characterised by the rise of the relativist spirit of the Enlightenment. A reunion of the two confessional groups, the Catholic and the Evangelical, became all the less likely the more the new religion became robbed of its deeper values, the more dogma was underrated, Christianity made a relative value, and revelation destroyed.

The inroad of this relativism into Lutheran Christianity coincided with the Augsburg Confession of Melanchthon the humanist. There is no disputing this fact, even if Melanchthon did describe his own work as most vehement. The most important distinctions and essential deviations of the new doctrine from the old were not dealt with at all. The absence of free will was ignored, as was the fundamental refutation of the primacy of the pope. The 'power' of the bishops was to be retained, so long as they had the gospel truly preached. But what was the point of all this if the issue was represented as if the antithesis were limited to those 'abuses', which had long since become the outward symbol of the programme, but did not belong to the sphere of dogma: communion under both kinds; marriage of the clergy; abolition of saying masses, of obligatory confession, of fasting laws and religious vows? The antithesis had been falsified, and Catholic polemic was quick to fasten upon this and reproach the Augsburg Confessions with having presented the Protestant viewpoint incompletely and dishonestly.

Melanchthon approached his work with a holy zeal. He was concerned about unity, for which he anxiously laboured for many long weeks. He was filled, too, with a great missionary zeal such as he saw in St Paul, who had become a Jew to the Jews. Thus, free Christians ought to adopt much of former papist practice. He saw, too, how all around him Christian discipline was on the wane. Thus he conceded episopal jurisdiction not merely to accommodate Catholics; he sought afresh for a fixed order with which to counter the abuse of evangelical freedom around him. But it was a matter of the formulation of the faith, not just of moral earnestness or of fervent personal faith itself. Here Melanchthon had taken on an impossible task. His veering course at the *Reichstag* was marred by dark blemishes, which his contemporaries saw as dishonesty, damaging to the gospel. The timid, petty, sly dishonesty of Erasmus cast its shadow upon Melanchthon's image. It is true that when Campeggi reproached the Protestant spokesmen with acting like the heretics, who answer with furtive, equivocal words, he was parodying the facts quite unjustifiably. For when Melanchthon expressed the opinion that articles of faith must be accommodated to the situation of the moment, we cannot say that he was indulging in deliberate deception. This opinion, too, was an expression of the fundamental mediatorial attitude of the humanists.

Once again we have to refer to the theological confusion and the obscurity that necessarily attaches to the mighty procreative force of every revolution. We must note, too, how long it was before many Catholics recognised the incompatibility of the two doctrines – of the two modes of life. For a long time people had imagined that if the separate propositions of Lutheran doctrine could only be refuted, all would be well. Few people realised that the real division lay between two opposed ways of thinking: on the one side were the tradition and the organism of the Church, on the other, subjectivism – an essentially unfettered attitude of mind. This second attitude was fundamentally uncatholic. The still unresolved controversy over basic questions about Lutheran ideas ought to be a warning to us to be cautious in our verdict upon Melanchthon. He still hoped for a move towards reunion from both sides. It seemed quite possible to him, that the 'abuses' mentioned would be abolished, and also that the Evangelicals would once again lay more stress on certain Catholic conceptions. In such a highly charged political situation as existed in 1530, and considering the world-historical repercussions of an official formulation of the new doctrine, it was hardly possible for a peaceable nature like Melanchthon's to escape the temptation to ease his official party position by a few distinct concessions to the pope. It was a bit too much when he addressed Cardinal Campeggi, speaking of 'reverence for the authority of the pope and the whole government of the Church'. The main point remains: for him the definitive thing lay in the non-dogmatic sphere. Such distinctions might well have seemed unimportant to him. He was truly convinced that the chalice for the laity and the marriage of the clergy were the only things that divided the two parties. (Luther dispelled this misunderstanding by his coarse invitation to the cardinal and the pope to '*Götz von Berlichingen*'.) Nor may we forget the theological, political, legal and psychological, importance for the Reformation, of maintaining legal connection with the institutions of the old Church. This, too, throws light on Melanchthon's mediatorial activities in Augsburg, as, for example, when he stressed to Brenz the authority of the bishops. There was no question of their divine right. How important it was for the Reformation, however, that the external, secular–legal image should not be changed, that the bishops be taken over into the new Church. It is true that Melanchthon did not state the fact that their whole nature had, of necessity, to be altered. Brenz was more frank: 'The main thing is that we (by appearing to yield) should gain the toleration of our doctrine.'

We are not yet in a position to judge the Confession of Augsburg in terms of the political purpose it was designed to serve in the dispute with the emperor over the Edict of Worms and the Reformation as a whole. This was its primary purpose for the princes at least. Each according to his opinion and needs thoroughly exploited the vagueness of the confession for his own political advantage.

On the other hand, the behaviour of the emperor, too, was strongly influenced by political calculation. His oscillation, however, from the energetic speech of his first conversations with the Protesters to the dogged efforts to reach union through proof and counter-proof, was a clear expression of the theological confusion of the situation, and of the hope against hope which it nourished. We might be tempted to regard the action of the emperor in 1530 at Augsburg as mere tactics, but the imperial religious conversations of the forties show that such a view is inadequate. Against that wider background even Melanchthon's vacillation loses some of its enigmatic quality.

Luther's inability to see beyond the real abuses in the Church to the true features of the Church has frequently been discussed.

How successfully he and his followers had built up the incredible theory of Catholic *work-righteousness*, and how little effort had been made to understand the clearly stated doctrine of the old Church, was once again revealed in the Confession of Augsburg and even more in the *Apologia*, written in reply to the Catholic *Refutatio*, and which later found its way into the official credal statements of the Lutheran Church. It was said, for example, that in the Church until Luther's day, forgiveness of sins could be obtained only by the performance of human works; that therefore the necessity of grace had virtually to be rediscovered. This was the heart of the controversy and it rested upon a colossal misinterpretation, which must frequently be called a calumny. Why is this fact scarcely ever stated in Evangelical studies? The reason is that Luther's vast reorientation entered into the substance of history, and his followers became bound to this reorientation, oblivious of the manner of its origin.

Of all the private and official documents, the Augsburg Confession is the one which reveals most clearly what the Reformation was all about. In view of all that has been said it is an astonishing thing to have to assert this of a document which took so much trouble to conceal the rough edges of Lutheranism, and prove that its authors still stood within the ancient Christian community.

This is the most revealing thing, however. The essence of the novelty did not lie in dogmatic deviation in one, two or even twenty articles. It lay in a new style of faith. If this were maintained, the Reformation would persist; and it mattered nothing whether one appeared to return in many things to the old Church, or broke more radically away from it. Here, too, was the mystery of the unity of an essentially divided Protestantism. We will see in more detail later how much Catholics, from the very start reproached Protestantism with this division. Violent contradictions and sharp variations were exposed – and rightly. Leaving out of account the oscillations and tensions in Luther himself, in Melanchthon and amongst Luther's followers, there was an abundance of contradictions of all grades of intensity in the Augsburg *Reichstag* itself. Not only did it produce the official *Confessio Augustana* but there was the *Tetrapolitana* as well, and then Zwingli's confession. Already the devastating effect of subjectivism was at work, as was that of mutual hatred, not only between Lutherans and Anabaptists but – in a violent form – between Lutherans and Zwinglians. Sturm, Butzer and Melanchthon provide plenty of evidence of this. The conclusions drawn by Catholic polemicists, however, were not expressed with sufficient precision. They proceeded on the assumption that there was a fixed body of dogma, and that every deviation from it was a contradiction of the whole thing. In this they wrongly transferred a Catholic concept to an essentially non-dogmatic view of faith. Catholic controversial theology was confirmed in this view by Luther's and his followers' radical intolerance of Zwingli and the Anabaptists. This intolerance clearly betrayed fatal illogicality on the part of Luther, who did not see how his basic position demanded complete independence from any particular article of dogma.

Luther's attitude to the events of these weeks was curious. Like Melanchthon in Augsburg, he, at the Coburg, was in a state of great spiritual excitement. In harmony with his vehement nature he presented a forcibly controlled exterior, but underneath was full of violent defiance. At first he had so hedged about the soft-pedalling *Confessio Augustana*, which he did not want to send, but would not obstruct either, by his general reservation, 'so long as the gospel remains free', that all seemed safe enough. He read the text carefully over and over again, and agreed to it. All the same, like many of the Reformers, he thought that Melanchthon was playing a dangerous game. He began to call a halt. There would be no retreat. He would get out of this dangerous atmosphere and back to the security of the home-ground in Wittenberg. His complete confidence in the cause of 'his' gospel found drastic, but too revealing, an expression: 'If we fall, Christ falls. Then let him fall, for I would rather fall with Christ than stand with the emperor.' No compromise there! Admittedly, in the context he stresses specially that he has no wish to be daring; the Spirit itself testified within him, showing him how far he could go in overreaching himself.

All the same we do Melanchthon an injustice by seeing him at this period only in contrast to Luther's intolerance. In those weeks Luther himself was far from preserving the image of constant rigidity. In numerous letters to his assistants in Augsburg and in a public *Admonition to the Clergy Assembled at the Reichstag in Augsburg* he himself had taken part in this work. And then, in repeated, urgent formulae, he added his fervent prayers (not without a measure of presumption) and wrote at the dictates of conscience.

He began gently and with much humility. Then, what he had spoken of to Melanchthon six days after the start of the work, began to show itself. Fury began to boil up within him; he had to guard against the coarseness which erupted all uninvited. Unfortunately he was unsuccessful in restraining coarseness and a quite incredible, as well as incomprehensible, portrayal of Catholic doctrine. He gave vent to coarse outbursts about 'abominations and blasphemy in the manner of the Turks' who dwelt in 'the devil's Church', about whores filled with inexorable lust, in whose company, for centuries no bishop had ever heard of the creed – instead they had enjoyed living in luxury. These followed more or less open threats to the bishops – who were 'far from safe in their seats'.

By these Luther hopelessly destroyed his case in the eyes of those he was addressing. And yet the amazing thing is that the ultimate object of this communication was to win over the bishops. It meant to achieve this end even by threats. The whole thing was a remarkable oscillation between wild caricature and cordial entreaty. It was an agitated, a distorted mind that spoke here. At times the language threatened to overturn. But the object remained. 'We will leave you alone as you are, to teach what you like, will leave you your princes and rulers and property for the sake of peace – a thing that the Hussites and Wycliffites never did. Only keep the peace and do not persecute us. . . . We can help each other to live in peace. . . . Let us teach the gospel freely.' The earnestness of Luther's intention to win over the bishops is demonstrated by that document – to his dear Germans – in which he expressed his deep disappointment over the outcome of the *Reichstag*.

In harmony with this objective, Luther now presented his own doctrine entirely in a form which expressed the difference to Catholic dogma – not to the hated pope himself – purely in terms of the powerful penetration of what was human into the elaboration of Catholic doctrine. The mass, even, became 'our one supreme treasure' – and this was not meant ironically.

This ironing out of authentic Lutheran paradoxes did not come about unprepared. We know of the reaction after the terrible display of the rising of the peasants, who were screaming for evangelical freedom. This reaction led to the inauguration of the visitations, and these quickly forced the production of defined doctrine. In 1525 the *Instruction for Visitators* appeared, and Luther wrote the foreword. Cochlaeus seized on this eagerly. Was Luther now returning to a dogmatically fixed and ecclesiastically ordered earlier system? Was Luther turning about; was he returning to the Church? Cochlaeus saw Luther's development change several times, and wrote his *Luther septiceps*, documenting the seven stages in development with specific contradictory texts from Luther. Luther's *Admonition* must be seen in the context of this development.[1] It is true that this attitude rapidly and radically changed under the influence of the various complaints about Melanchthon's compromising. It was not until the firm resolution of the *Reichstag* had been passed that the infuriated opponent began to talk. He saw battle coming, his self-confidence rose mightily, and he called upon the Germans to make their choice between the emperor and God. He also found opportunity to defend himself against the suspicion of fomenting insurrection. 'They will neither terrify me nor make me faint-hearted. It is I who will terrify them. I will remain – they will disappear. They have made too big a mistake. My life will be their hangman; my death their devil.'

When he rejected the emperor's draft of 22 September, Luther, whose opinion had been asked, expressed himself with that exaggeration which was for ever weakening his opposition: the Augsburg Confession must remain as the true word of God until the Day of Judgment. No angel in heaven may alter a word of it,

---

[1] In 1530 and the years following the atmosphere was full of the spirit of accommodation and fraternisation in another curious way. The curia placed great hopes upon Melanchthon. Their representatives tried to entice him away from Luther. On 6 June 1530 had he not written a submissive letter in which he recognised the Roman Church, and even commended the mass and objected to the chalice for the laity and marriage of the clergy? In November 1531 Clement VII thought he could assume that the elector of Saxony had been converted. In 1532 Cochlaeus, Campeggi and Aleander had to combine to dispel the good impression Melanchthon had made upon the curia by his muddled gentleness.

without incurring damnation and eternal fire. The mass is the
greatest abomination on earth – and so on. . . . One dare not
budge a hair's-breadth on any of these articles if Germany is not
to fall to pieces. True, the calmness with which Luther refused to
allow the least deviation from the truth, even although 'the whole
world should fall in ruins as a result' is amazing. But what are we
to think when we compare the Augsburg Confession with the
Apologia or with Luther's verdict on their soft-pedalling, or when
we include the confession of faith placed by Butzer before Luther
and Zwingli for approval? What are we to think when we compare
Luther's common verdict on the mass as the worst abomination
on earth with his affirmation about 'our one supreme treasure',
and with the protestations of the Augsburg Confession? We
would do an injustice to his followers if we said that they had
abolished the mass.

The princes and the cities of the opposition rejected the settlement proposed by the emperor, 'for the sake of God and their
consciences'. The diversity and uncertainty of the cities with
regard to doctrine was, however, rather grotesque. The emperor
was right when he informed them that he did not know what
faith any of them professed, and would like them to enlighten him
on that point. Not only was there the split between Zwinglians and
Lutherans, but the Zwinglians were divided amongst themselves.
The more cautious held aloof from the radical haters of the mass,
and the neutrals from the Swiss. Biberach's instructions to its
emissaries was almost incredible: 'For the sake of faith and the
sects, follow the line taken by Mayor Besserer of Ulm. If Ulm
wants to become Catholic once again, let Biberach follow; if
Ulm wants to become Zwinglian, let Biberach become Zwinglian
too.' Besserer himself was equivocal in the extreme. He insulted
the pope, but assured Campeggi's secretary that he hated none so
much as the Lutherans, unless it were the sacramentarians. 'The
representatives of Reutlingen signed the Augsburg Confession
although they had brought a basically different one of their own.'
Amongst these people the confession had become a political
bargaining counter in a frightful degree. We can understand how
the poor opinion the emperor had of the cities was not elevated
by such muddle. He concluded the rejection of the *Tetrapolitana*

with the threat: 'If the cities do not change their tune, the emperor will do all that his office demands.'

But it never went as far as that, for various reasons: he had no army; there was a possibility of a civil war – as Charles told Campeggi; the irresolution of the Catholic princes was surpassed only by their obvious disunity; their vigorous protestations of support of the emperor were vitiated by vague reservations. Only two of the Catholic princes – Duke George of Saxony, and Elector Joachim of Brandenburg – were for the use of force. The dukes of Bavaria were strongly opposed to its use, and at the same time tried to circumvent union between the emperor and the Protestants, for they did not want to see any increase of Habsburg power. Of the lords spiritual, Cologne and Augsburg (Bishop Christopher v. Stadion) were sympathetic rather than antagonistic to the Reformation. The leader of the German Church, the archbishop of Mainz, did not know what he wanted. He was a broken reed, taking now this line, now that. In 1532 he accepted and rewarded the dedication of Melanchthon's commentary on Romans. He even sent money to Catherine von Bora, but Luther refused to accept it. (His friend Doctor Rübel kept it, however.) The emperor's own confessor advised compromise. Why should not Ferdinand eventually have Protestants for subjects, like the Bohemians? To suppress them, was a war really necessary, especially when the outcome was so uncertain?

We can see how on both sides the theological situation was frightfully muddled and the political situation utterly obscure. In the end the emperor tried energetically to clarify both. He refused to admit that the Protestants could claim – against the whole world and against himself – that they had a monopoly of the gospel. His threats and his approval of the *Confutatio* had convinced Philip of Hesse that further consultations were a waste of time. Philip left the *Reichstag* and wanted to make serious preparations for war. When the emperor's proposal was proclaimed as the final resolution of the *Reichstag*, the elector of Saxony departed also. Thus the resolution in its definitive form of 19 November was the work of the emperor and the Catholics. The Reformed party stuck by the protest of 1529. However, 'the political group of Protestants were now joined by those who had been dogmatically united by the Augsburg Confession' (Brandi).

In substance this resolution was a firm renewal of the Edict of Worms, without any of the later mitigations. It was much more detailed, too. Special mention was made of the vast spread of the Reformation through coercion of laity and religious, and of the resulting spoliation of the monasteries and the expulsion of the occupants. Finally a plain protest was made against the deadly calumny that Catholics wanted to suppress the word of God. The unhealthy subjectivism of the preachers, who preached according to their own judgment, was laid bare. It was no accident that the coarseness of the preachers was seen as specially dangerous. Full material and legal restitution was to be made for the forcible suppression of bishoprics, monasteries and churches. Resistance was to be treated as a breach of the Land Peace and punished with outlawry. Luther's doctrine must no longer be preached. All apostates were to return to the Church. Binding articles of faith were laid down. Only approved and celibate clergy were to be allowed to officiate. Everything Catholic was to be protected, and the alliance between the emperor and the Catholics was designed particularly to ensure this protection. Submission had to be made by 15 April 1531.

No one had imagined that this resolution would automatically restore the old order; but at least the subjects of Reformed princes were assured the right of escape.

How seriously was this enactment taken by those who were chiefly responsible for it? There can be no doubt that the resolution reflected Charles' deep conviction about what really ought to be done; but the memory of his curious oscillation at the start of his reign, from unusual abruptness to protracted and accommodating negotiations, aroused suspicions. Above all, on the Catholic side the mighty threats were followed by nothing. The continuation of the affair, on the emperor's side, was in line with the genial negotiations that went on during the *Reichstag*, and not with the abrupt demands with which it opened and closed.

In all of their negotiations during the Reformation period, the chief thing the Protestants demanded – besides the marriage of the clergy – was the chalice for the laity. It often seemed as though their practical demands were exhausted by these two items. We have just heard Melanchthon's views. In the interim of 1547 Charles V tried to heal the division by proposing to concede these points. As late as the reform manifesto of Ferdinand II, during the final phase of the Council of Trent, it was believed that a way to heal the schism could be found by the granting of this request by the pope. The negative result quickly proved this belief false. This does not mean, however, that the scheme would have been bound to fail thirty or forty years earlier. It is not idle to ask whether perhaps in denying the cup to the laity, the old Church was not demanding too high a price for loyalty, especially as granting the cup would have made no inroads upon her inviolable inheritance. It is no idle question, indeed, because the answer illumines further the inner problems concerning Reformation growth and its 'causation' from the Catholic side.

We cannot, it is true, fairly judge Catholic opposition to the chalice for the laity without taking into account the earlier history of the Hussites. With them this same demand had been bound up with revolution; and on the Protestant side mention of the chalice often seems to have implied a rejection of the consecration (Eder). None the less, a satisfactory clarification of this point could have been achieved, because at the start of the Reformation the Hussites were universally abhorred in Germany, in spite of violent hatred of Rome, and rejection of the consecration had not yet become a reality. Misunderstanding of the chalice for the laity could, therefore, have been avoided.

Let us now place this question alongside our definition of the Reformation as a revolutionary declaration of maturity of the people of the Church. What would have happened had the Church not been so predominantly clerical, and the idea had been alive amongst theologians and prelates of a co-responsible laity? In respect, even, of the above-mentioned Hussite embarrassment, Catholic resistance to the cup for the laity might have been more positive and intelligent. Within society there were deep religious energies which could have been integrated into the old Church, as St Francis once had done through his third order. The rejection of the demand itself need not have put ecclesiastical, clerical prescription so exclusively in the forefront, nor sought the good of the Church merely in the negative correctness of an almost nominalist theology. In the whole affair we see far too much short-sighted fear, and a lack of inner freedom at work.

By her labours, including this very refusal, the Church fulfilled her essential task: she had preserved the substance of truth and power undiminished, and passed these on down to our own day. That is not to say that she performed her task perfectly, by any means. She would indeed have acted perfectly had she healed the schism, by dogmatically purifying and integrating within her own life the mighty surge of religious Reform. That, however, was not entirely within her power. Even so, she could have come closer to perfection had she done everything possible to attain that end.

We study the past, because it still lives, still affects us, and we hope to learn from it. Catholic daring, as an expression of the inviolable objective truth and holiness of the Church, and of the strong inner freedom of the Christian man in face of threatening danger, that is the overcoming of a too one-sided denial or a too negative correctness, is useful to the Church in every age.

II

In his *Admonition* of 1530 Luther had given a very one-sided portrayal of the situation, it is true. All he saw was the victory of his own cause. He would not have been Luther had it been otherwise. None the less he was right in thinking that things had slowly been maturing and that the moment had come for the tension to be resolved. 'Things cannot rest at this stage any longer.' Luther smelled the morning air. The outlawed heretic dared not appear at the *Reichstag*, but he sat there in the Coburg, like a superior judge, and, all uninvited, on his own authority, publicly admonished the *Reichstag*, saying that they would have to acknowledge him in the end. He was fully aware of this autocratic spirit. In the introduction to his letter he had overcome it with Christian humility, and had maintained a superior composure. Then he allowed it to emerge in his colossal self-assurance in God and in Jesus Christ. It is true that Luther saw loyalty to the old Church as reprehensible faithlessness. But he was right in complaining that in all these decades of striving, one thing had been sadly lacking – humble prayer. 'Who is there among you who has once done penance for such terrible abominations, who has uttered one sigh or shed one tear?' The substance of Christianity was at stake. Would not the whole struggle have ended very differently had there been an atmosphere all the time of devout prayer? 'In truth, the matter is too great. Human wisdom and strength are too small. God must help . . . and you must make sure of his help and grace by earnest prayer.'

At the end of his *Admonition* as at the end of the *Warning* Luther spoke of a future shedding of blood. This is a further revelation of the mood of this year, which was somewhat obscured by the protracted theological discussions at the *Reichstag* and with Rome (Melanchthon).

The *Reichstag* of Augsburg was supposed to have effected a settlement between the two confessional groups. In reality it widened the schism. It made clear to the Reformers the great danger in which they stood. This caused the division, that so recently threatened to weaken the Evangelical movement, to fall into the background. On the other hand, their self-assurance and initiative increased. Moreover, as we saw, the emperor's threats were followed by no action. Butzer and Sturm tried to draw the Lutherans away from their notion of patient obedience. Wittenberg jurists, as we learned, arrived at conclusions very like those expressed by Luther himself. Finally it was most opportune for the Reformers when on 15 January 1531 Ferdinand was elected king of the Romans (in Cologne instead of Frankfurt), under protest from the elector of Saxony, for this aggravated Bavaria's ancient hatred of Austria, thus weakening the Catholic front.

Thus Augsburg 1530 gave impetus to the politico-Evangelical alliance which gradually grew into the official political vehicle for the whole of German Protestantism – the Schmalkald League.

This alliance, with its unimpressive, halting progress, was unhappily a reflection of the divided, particularistic, egoistic designs of its members. It was no parallel at all to the intellectual and religious revolt which gave such power to the beginnings of the Reformation. It is true that they sought protection against the threat from the emperor, but no one was clear how this was to be done. This remained so even after the constitution was fixed. The chief lack, however, was any clear realisation that a mighty effort would have to be made. No one possessed the required resolution or spirit of sacrifice. Once again we encounter the lamentable pettiness of the German territorial rulers.

Again, the most energetic was Philip of Hesse. In November 1530, in consultation with Basel and Strasburg, he had joined in a common defence bond with Zwingli. Indeed, Zwingli and Philip were the only Protestant leaders capable of thinking about the larger political context, and with any experience in the matter. It had already occurred to them to make an alliance with France and Zapolya against the emperor. In this Philip's chief end was egoistic and political. He wanted to take Würtemberg away from the Austrians. He was not interested in opening up the way for the Reformation in south Germany. He was set on the substantial increase of his own political power and the repulse of his dangerous rival, Austria.

In any case, by December 1530 the negotiations between the supporters of the Augsburg Confession had led to a kind of defence pact against the emperor. Members were: electoral Saxony, Hesse, the two Brunswicks, the prince of Anhalt, the two counts of Mansfeld, Magdeburg and Bremen. In spite of all weaknesses, this was an important event, for it provided a 'core of resistance' as Ranke described it. The settlements, so much disputed in 1529, were found once again in the Schmalkald Articles. The place too, was symbolic: between electoral Saxony and Hesse, the two upon which the League was chiefly to rest, just as it took its origin in that first agreement between Saxony and Hesse at Torgau in 1526.

In February 1531 Strassburg and various south German cities joined in. An 'understanding' was born. Confessional interests now began to give way to political interests. The Zwinglians were excluded, strictly speaking, but a political alliance was created for religious Zwinglianism. Through Hesse, Strasburg and Constance, who belonged to the Zürich–Basel defence pact, this grew into an alliance with political Zwinglianism as well. When Zwingli died on 11 October 1531, this most important tendency was complete: the south German cities orientated themselves of necessity towards the north. The political unity of a doctrinally split German Protestantism received considerable reinforcement.

In that same October the Schmalkald League gained the highly important rear cover, of which we spoke, as a result of the support of Catholic Bavaria.

The decisive rise of Protestantism coincided with the emergence of the Schmalkald League. This happened in the fourth decade of the century. The decisive year was 1532. On 27 February 1532, a draft of the Schmalkald League was signed. In December the final redaction (*A Scheme for Defence*) was ready, and this was accepted as definitive in Schweinfurt. Common resistance to assault upon Evangelical doctrine had been resolved – involving defiance of the emperor. The right of resistance had been explicitly affirmed. There was a council of war and even a war budget. It is true that no one yet knew how the burdens and duties would be apportioned. The burdens were the first to be settled: following an old recipe, these were laid chiefly upon the cities. The great question remained: who was to be the leader – Hesse or Saxony? In the end both were. It is easy to see how unpropitious that was for the internal unity of the League, and hence for its power of action, and also, therefore, for the prospects of the Reformation. None the less the centre of resistance, thus created, stood firm, to become the greatest threat of all to the unity of the empire.

There was, however, an even broader foundation for the significance of the year 1532, which we have described as the turning-point. Once again one of these notoriously quick redistributions of power-groups had taken place. In addition to the growing power of the Schmalkalders themselves, once more it was the foreign political situation that determined the issue. This led to a completely new state of affairs – to the religious peace of Nuremberg of 1532, the interpretation of which was to be a bone of contention for years.

This time the Turkish threat was the dominant factor. Suliman II had again pressed forward to the Danube, and Ferdinand and the emperor simply had to seek Protestant support. Moreover, since 1531 the unpredictable Pope Clement VII had been veering towards France. His nepotism overshadowed the Church's universal interests. He was then involved in the betrothal and later – in 1533 after frequent return to, and re-enstrangement from, the emperor – in the marriage of his niece, Catherine of

Medici, to the son of Francis I, later to be Henry II. At the same time, in 1531, the Church of England broke with Rome, making their king the head of the Church in England – yet another important reinforcement of Protestant self-assurance.

In short, by 1531–32 the political situation was quite different from what it was in 1530. This is proved by the *Reichstag* at Regensburg in 1532; for this *Reichstag* was completely overshadowed by the special negotiations with the Schmalkald League in Schweinfurt and Nuremberg. These *special* negotiations in fact presupposed an essentially different relationship between the parties. This was no *Reichstag* called by the emperor and conducted under imperial law. Two parties met, on equal terms, in an agreed place, to negotiate. Already the League was interested in much more than mere recognition of what it had already accomplished or in the abolition of supreme court processes, or in the reversal of Ferdinand's election as king of the Romans. It pressed now for a universal, fundamental regulation, for confessional freedom, not just for themselves, but also for those who might want to join their ranks today or tomorrow. It is true that a legal device was found by which the desired formal agreement could be circumvented. The resolution of the *Reichstag*, which refused any change in imperial law, was supplemented by other decrees that provided purely provisional and political regulation for the present members of the League until the next *Reichstag*: the greater part of the supreme court process against the Reformers was to be held in abeyance meantime; the estates were to refrain from 'war or pillage amongst one another on the grounds of religion or belief, . . . until the next universal, free, Christian council, as was agreed at the *Reichstag* at Nuremberg'. The estates voted a huge army 80,000 strong. The result demonstrated the strength of a united German effort. August–September saw the decisive defeat of the Turks, a precondition of which, however, had been the victorious resistance put up by the Hungarian fortress of Güns. Charles was able to celebrate this victory in person in Vienna.

Regensburg 1532, the religious peace of Nuremberg, and the victory over the Turks represented a success for the Schmalkald League, which mightily advanced its cause. The diet of the League in Schmalkalden in December 1535 extended the League for another ten years or so, until February 1547. New members joined: Würtemberg, Pommerania, Anhalt, Dessau, Augsburg, Kempten, Frankfurt, Hanover, Hamburg. Gradually German activism became centred in the League – a result of the Reformation and secularisation of whole states, which had characterised the triumphant progress of Protestantism in the thirties. Meanwhile the Catholic camp, minus the emperor, adopted a typical attitude of conservation and defence.

Most important, however, was the fact, that the anti-Habsburg policies of the Catholic Bavarians in alliance with the Schmalkalders, Hesse and France, led to the return of Duke Ulrich to Würtemberg in 1534.[2] He and the landgrave, supplied by Francis I with money to equip the army, took the state by means of a devastating defeat of the Austrians. It was not the power of the Habsburgs – who at that time kept noticeably well out of things – but the Catholic cause, that suffered a severe blow in the loss of the important alliance between Austria and the Rhineland and Burgundy. In the same year Würtemberg went over to the new doctrine. Protestantism now had a focal point in south Germany, and thus a new potential for expansion. It was at this point that Lutheranism fused with Zwinglianism to form a single consolidated block.

In 1536 the religious unity of the League was assured for a time by the Wittenberg Concordat. This document was in harmony with the spirit of the man behind it – Butzer. But the Lutheran formula on the Lord's Supper, framed by Melanchthon and watered down by Butzer, achieved its purpose only temporarily. That purpose was to secure the Schmalkald League.

Today no one doubts that in his fight against the Reformation, the emperor should have been able to count on the whole-hearted backing of the pope. He was the *sacra Caesarea maiestas*, the steward and protector of the Church, leader of Christianity in the battle with heretics and infidels. Moreover, he was very conscious of this status and office, and thus saw very clearly the importance of standing side by side with the pope. In the thirties, therefore, he

[2] It is interesting that it was immediately after the loss of Würtemberg for the first time that the idea of a Bavarian–Austrian marriage emerged. In 1546 this led to an enormous change in Bavarian policy.

staked everything on enlisting the pope in his cause. In 1532–33 once again he visited Clement in Bologna. The result of this, on the broad view, was absolutely nothing. Certainly the measures taken by the pope of that time must be seen in the light of the political necessities of the papal states. Even so, they are embarrassing in many respects – especially in respect of the Turkish threat.

People had long since ceased to imagine that the popes and emperors were unaware of the Turkish threat or were disinclined to wage war on the Turks; none the less, the idea that making war on the Turks as a Christian duty was still a powerful force in people's minds. The candidature of Francis I for the imperial throne was supported mainly by the fact that he had the power, the money, and the bravery to fight against the Turks.

Francis I, however, had in fact shown very little interest in this task. He followed the bad example of the Venetians, who had performed espionage for Suliman in 1529, and to some extent of Bavaria, which had been in alliance with Zapolya, an ally of the Turks, since 1529.

It is worth noting that the question was not whether peace should be made with the Turks, as Ferdinand had suggested to the emperor, and as was done in 1533; it was rather the question of the exploitation of infidel military power against Christians. Since the end of the twenties at least, France had used its ties with Turkey in this fashion. In 1535 the first French legation was sent to the sultan's court and concluded a treaty in 1536. Even the Moslem pirates in the Mediterranean who, with the sultan's express approval, made war on Charles, were supported by France. In 1537 a Turkish–French fleet defeated the emperor's fleet in the Mediterranean. The emperor was full of the notion – almost intoxicated by it – that a crusade was the essential expression of a European empire. At the same time Francis I had strong sympathy with the Protestants.

From serious considerations of power politics this Catholic king put political interests before religious and ecclesiastical interests. The Schmalkalders were more timid than he when, in December 1535 they made an alliance with his most Christian majesty only on condition that their obligations to the emperor and the empire would not be affected.

The curia, too, once again displayed similar perversions of the order of duty. The mighty anti-Habsburg front of 1533–34 included France, the Turks, the German Protestants and the pope. In 1535–36 things were even worse. At that time the emperor once again was at the peak of his power as a result of his world-shattering victory over the Moslem pirate, Chaireddin Barbarossa. Even amongst Protestants he received some acclaim as protector of Christendom. Italy had been pacified since 1533 as a result of the alliance between the emperor and the pope, and as a result of the alliance based upon the universal Italian-imperial League. France respected the peace of Cambrai, the fruit of the peace of Madrid; under pressure from the emperor the curia had set about reform by calling the epoch-making commission of cardinals. This was the state of affairs for which the emperor had been working for fifteen years. And it was at this very juncture in 1536 that Francis I made war. He marched on Italy in order to win Milan – in straits through the death of Francesco II – for his son. He made a pact with the Turks, supported the excommunicate king of England, and fostered links with the German Protestants.

It is true that even in the midst of effusive scenes of fraternisation with Francis I, and while enjoying to the full his sense of victory, Charles had written to Ferdinand in 1529 and said: 'It is always uncertain whether France will keep the peace.' Certainly the machinations of the French in the Würtemberg affair were no secret. On 1 February 1535 the French king had finally issued his manifesto to the Germans. This was a most unheard of breach of the peace.

Early on Easter Monday, before the high mass, under pressure of this mountain of perfidy, Charles made his unexpected, passionate complaint to the pope and cardinals. He denounced Francis' unchristian behaviour and tried to force the lord of the Vatican to do his Christian duty, and make a definite decision for the imperial-Catholic cause. In the war that was becoming unavoidable with France he saw the utter ruin of Christendom on account of the Lutherans and the Turks. He offered to fight a duel with the French king, as a sort of divine judgment, in order to avoid a battle between brother Christians. What was the result? The pope preferred to remain neutral.

Charles had asked the question in the proper quarter and in the correct form: he had put it to the pope and hence to the

whole Christian world, and had done so in his capacity as the
Christian emperor, who was aware of his duty to save Christendom
from the heresy and infidelity which threatened it. The king of
France, self-styled 'his most Christian majesty', stood in his way.

For the emperor the start of the military dispute did not look
very promising. He let himself be sidetracked into an unsuccessful
attack upon Savoy. The following year his fleet was defeated in the
Mediterranean by the Turko-French fleet. Early the same year
a French army had made a vigorous assault into the Netherlands.
Here was where the equilibrium might have been restored in this
developing bloody conflict.

Even in the midst of all this confusion Charles did not neglect
to strive for peace with France, as the one sensible objective. This
time, however, no peace ensued from the cessation of hostilities on
the southern and northern scene of battle. All that was achieved
in Nice, where the pope, the emperor and the king simultaneously
halted, was a ten-year truce. This was a makeshift arrangement;
and Charles was no longer able to set about his task within Germany with a free mind, for, until the end, he had to fight a battle
on two fronts with two armies.

At this time the Protestant forces had to overcome manifestations of interior disintegration. Paul III had, in fact, scheduled
a council and invited the Protestants to take part. The elector of
Saxony asked Luther to produce a comprehensive statement of his
position. The Reformers provided this in the Schmalkald Articles
of 1537. In their general trend these were the antithesis to the
Augsburg Confession of Melanchthon. The irreconcilability of the
Reformation with the old Church now became a glaring fact.
During the Schmalkald assembly Luther was mortally ill.
In severe pain, praying and longing to be released, he preached –
as he had done in the Coburg and at Altenburg in 1530 – his
testament of hatred of the papacy: *Pestis eram vivens, moriens ero mors
tua, papa!* If only he might live until Pentecost and give the pope
one last dressing down!

As we shall see, the inter-Protestant schism that was begin-
ning to show at that time became worse through the action of
Philip of Hesse, but did not prevent the growth of German
Protestantism as an ecclesiastical and political force. One state

after another joined forces with him; and since 1537, Duke Henry
of Saxony, too, had been a member of the Schmalkald League.
He was not an important man himself, but was brother and –
owing to the death of the heir – himself now heir to Duke George,
the greatest support of Catholicism amongst the German princes.
When George died on 17 April 1539, the duchy became Reformed
– with the assistance of electoral Saxony. Immediately after the
death of Elector Joachim I, in 1535, the margravedom of Küstrin
in Brandenburg was ready to go over to the Reformation. In 1539
the electorate went the same way. In that place the Reformation
was a markedly external affair. The mood prevailing in the state,
supposedly desirous of a new Church order, was far from predominantly religious. The new ruler, Joachim II, was an open compromiser, little interested in the religious problem, and hence
unsympathetic to the rigid Lutheran theology of Wittenberg. He
could easily have been kept within the old Church, had the general
situation seemed to offer better prospects for the old faith.

In addition, the growing Turkish threat made any large-scale
Catholic action against Protestantism impossible. It led, rather,
in the Frankfurt postponement of 15 April 1539, to a truce
between the emperor and the Reformation party, involving
nothing less than the recognition of the positions gained by the
Reformers. This was scarcely altered in practice by the fifteen-
month time-limit; for after it had expired, the peace of Nuremberg
of 1532 once again came into force, and the advantage which this
gave to the Reformers had already been sufficiently demonstrated:
once more Protestantism was gaining time in which to take root.

In truth there was a victorious advance of Lutheranism which
took the Evangelicals themselves by surprise. At the end of 1539
Cochlaeus thought that the Church's situation was hopeless.

At this very moment Protestantism was presented with a fresh
and, it might have seemed, decisive, opportunity of gaining all
that remained (apart from Bavaria) of free Germany. This
opportunity was provided by the union of Jülich-Cleve and
Gueldres, in the person of Duke William, elected in 1538 by the
estates of Gueldres, and who had now become supreme ruler on
his father's death in 1539. He was related to electoral Saxony
through his sister, Sybil, wife of John Frederick, and to England
through his second sister, the fourth wife of Henry VIII. The

Reformation of those territories on both sides of the Rhine, close to the imperial Netherlands, by a young ruler with such wide family connections, could have proved an unusually great political and religious threat to the Catholic-imperial cause. An expansion of the Reformation into the regions around Münster and Cologne was probable; for in Minden–Münster–Osnabrück there ruled the prince-bishop, Francis von Waldeck, who, after the Anabaptist troubles, had shown such sympathy for the new faith, or, rather, for the possibilities contained in secularisation. Cologne still had its archbishop, Hermann von Wied, who was a radical Reformer. Moreover, a Protestant Jülich–Cleve–Berg–Gueldres block threatened the links between the imperial Netherlands and the south, which formed a vital interior front within the Habsburg–Spanish system. Not least – a Reformed area comprising Osnabrück–Münster–Cologne was a Protestant threat to all the ecclesiastical territories of the west. Success here would mean the end of Catholicism in Germany.

The situation had become a threat to the very survival of the emperor's cause.

What of the Catholic estates in Germany? Were they utterly powerless? Could they form no kind of alliance?

It is well to note carefully the following: it is wrong to set Catholic alliances or attempts at alliance alongside Protestant leagues. To arise, the latter required greater energy, and so, because they did arise, are an expression of such energy. We know, indeed, that there were countless tensions and petty jealousies within Protestant political leagues. The suspicion with which the rulers regarded each other, and that with which the cities regarded all of the rulers, was great. Seen as a whole, however, the relative unity of the Protestant league was incomparably stronger than that of the Catholics, so many of whom remained aloof, disinterested or afraid, while important states like Cologne and Westphalia were a heavy burden upon the Catholic cause, and Bavaria, the greatest power of all, made common cause with the Schmalkalders and their allies, the French, playing a double political game with a vengeance. The verdict passed by the emperor at the bitter end of the whole period was true: 'the obedient estates were utterly faint-hearted and no comfort at all', . . . 'the Catholic princes think only of themselves'. As we saw, various Catholic alliances were in fact accomplished. What we have said of the political agreements of the period in general applies to them also: in themselves they were worthless, except when, from time to time, they were put into action. They possessed only that power which was injected into them year by year through activity. Even this did not happen. There was no Catholic counterpart to the regular and highly active Schmalkalden assemblies.

The Packschen affair had somewhat scared the Catholic estates. In Augsburg in 1530 there was much serious talk about an alliance with the emperor, but no one was prepared to accept the corresponding financial burdens. And so this plan, too, came too nothing. Taken all in all, the rulers did not want to give too much power to the Habsburgs.

In 1531, after having been elected king of the Romans, Ferdinand disavowed before the electors the capitulation which bound him to carry out the resolution of the *Reichstag* of 1530. This resulted in his making a ten-year defensive pact with them; but history shows no effects produced by this pact.

In November 1533 Duke George of Saxony entered into alliance with the princes of north Germany. This was known as the league of Halle. It never acquired any importance, however, because, with the death of the elector of Brandenburg, the whole state of affairs changed in favour of the Protestants.

The emperor's vice-chancellor, Held, a Luxemburger from Arlon, who dealt so unnecessarily abruptly with the Schmalkalders in 1536, saw clearly what the decisive thing was: future *Reichstags* would make no sense unless the religious issue was settled first. Unfortunately his efforts to bring about a Catholic league at that time were in vain. He, however, was the moving spirit who, on 10 June 1538, ultimately brought into existence the Nuremberg Christian Union. An essential defect was all too obvious: this union included none of the electors. Only two bishops, Salzburg and Magdeburg, joined in. Even the pope was not a party to the league. The emperor, whose whole mind was set on making peace with the opposition, was well aware of the weakness of the arrangement. He joined in only later on; and the whole project remained a miserable affair. Not only did it lack power but it lacked purpose also. The fact that the alliance (Duke George, Brunswick, Bavaria were the most powerful parties) made such an impression upon the enemy may be its objective justification; but the impression depended solely upon the enemy's fear and ignorance.

III

At this point we must go back a few years. In the episcopal states of the Rhineland, since the fifteenth century, the enmity between the citizens and their bishop had expressed itself most violently in the interplay of economic and social interests. Enmity was also seen in the citizen's attitude to the business activities of the clergy. This was what set off the minor revolutions in these cities, which in the sixteenth century were accompanied by the peasants' risings. As yet, however, no real explosion had occurred – certainly not in the lower Rhine, in the Habsburg Netherlands.

All the same, it was this region that became the breeding ground of a final spiritualistic–communistic movement of fanaticism. This reached its peak in the rule of the Anabaptists in Münster. Here the restless, unstable, missionary wanderlust of 'inspired' individuals found the right material and favourable circumstances for setting up the kingdom of God, according to their own highly egoistic fanatical recipe. This movement drew strength chiefly from the artisan class. This region became a focus of fantastic distortion, of acute social sickness, a witches' Sabbath, which a handful of curiously gifted and ruthless fellows knew how to manipulate. This was an explosion, which clearly indicated the degree to which the old accustomed order of life was being shattered to the foundations, and turned upside down.

The empire had already known important Evangelical–fanatical groups; for the threatening Protestant tendency to schism had continued after the collapse of the Müntzer fanatics and produced a host of queer and significant fanatical sects and personalities, who gradually became the dreaded common enemy of Reformed and Catholic alike. In 1535 both parties were to make common cause against these fanatics in Münster. This was not the beginning, however: sword and stake had already been used against them, especially in Switzerland and south Germany; in 1528 the

Swabian League had taken strong measures against the Anabaptists in south Germany; and then in 1529 and 1530 the *Reichstag* gave orders for their bloody suppression.

These Anabaptists were characterised by an explicit lay Christianity, by opposition to fixed dogma and hence also to the official Reformed Churches, which were now becoming more and more committed to a constitution. Under the force of inner logic, this enmity became much more violent after 1527–28, when there was no longer any doubt that Lutheranism was changing from the Reformation of the congregation to the establishment of a Church government. It was in 1527 that Michael Sattler – an ex-monk born about 1500 – had welded the gentle Anabaptists, who renounced all force, but demanded separation from the world, into some sort of a unity at the great Anabaptist assembly at Schlatt. These were the 'fraternal children of God'. The ensuing general persecution of Anabaptists had two results. Both of the basic types of fanatic stressed their characteristics even more strongly: the agitation which produced fantastic apocalypsism and expressed itself in rousing sermons, revolutionary speeches and threats, even in the hour of execution, increased; but so did humble spirituality, the pure and gentle mark of sonship of God, involving renunciation of the world, its ordinances, the sword and oaths, and encouraging a corresponding expectation of the Parousia.

Caspar von Schwenkfeld (1489–1561) belonged to the first type. He saw the fatal decline of Lutheranism into a banal 'fleshly freedom' (1524). Compelled by his persecutors to become a restless wanderer, he became a pious model for his congregation of saints, the predestined, who form part of the totally invisible Church, to whom God has given his Spirit, without any form of mediation. Even the Bible is only a control. This man was able to set the whole south and east of the empire in a ferment.

Sebastian Frank (d. 1542/3 in Basel) criticised everything without restraint, not excluding the secular powers and the Anabaptists. Luther called him 'the devil's favourite blasphemer'. In 1528 this man had begun his career as a Lutheran preacher in Nuremberg. By 1531 he was preaching a pantheistic and spiritualistic doctrine in Strasburg, where Sattler had published his twenty articles, which were to become so important in the spread of the movement to the Netherlands. From 1534 onwards he worked in Ulm (where Schwenkfeld died later) as a soap-boiler.

In Moravia, Hungary and Siebenbürgen, the Anabaptists of the gentler variety had great success, and were even able to achieve a significant measure of actualisation of their unrealistic ideals in a hard-working community with no property. The Moravian Brethren practised a communism of love allied to explicit Quietism, which was in marked contrast to the orgiastic radicalism of Münster.

In a remarkable degree, these spiritualistic–apocalyptic–Anabaptist forces kept far away from all contact with the stage of secular history. They were but a surge, a movement, having no formal expression. Moreover, this movement was full of variety and contradiction. On the other hand, it would be a mistake to think of it as a mere side-issue amongst the whole pattern of forces at work. It was amazingly powerful and the ever-present cause of development of moral and religious energies below the surface of conceptual life. It provided a large part of the universal activity of the fundamental forces of the epoch, and could be likened to the formation of the humus which nourishes a whole forest. The sheer lack of form in this movement bred destruction and the rapid spending of momentum; but fantasy and whimsicality were far from the chief characteristics of this movement. We do not sufficiently recognise the revolutionary element of this seething, chaotic period, or the mysterious forces pressing for a change within Christendom if we do not include in our picture the Anabaptist movement, and see it as a very distinct phenomenon. The mighty revolutionary metamorphoses of the fifteenth and sixteenth centuries were ultimately based upon those dull stirrings which manifested themselves in those whom Luther classed together and denounced as 'rabble-rousers and fanatics'. They were not just occasional deviations from the large, official patterns.

A first hint about the nature of the Münster Anabaptists is provided by the time of their appearance. Münster had been a product of the period when Lutheranism was still enjoying vigorous interior development; the revolution was still conceived in ecclesiastical terms; the secular power had not yet interfered to transform development along political lines. After the *Reichstag* of 1530, however, after various preliminary steps had been accomplished, the conflict became very largely a political affair.

The emperor's opponents at Augsburg were no longer the Reformers, but the protesting estates, soon to become the Schmalkald League. The Münster Anabaptists were an exact counterpart of this development. Their central stress was on 'the spirit' but they still demanded the setting up of the kingdom of God and his law, conceived as the establishment of a visible communistic 'city of God'.

The expansion of the fanatical ferment in the region of the lower Rhine drew strength as much from insidious infection as from the impressive oratory of 'inspired' agitators. The propaganda was spread by preaching the spirit, by giving testimony to the worship of God of the pure, by uttering apocalyptic threats concerning the coming of the Lord, in the tiniest back rooms, as well as by fanatical and rousing declamations of faith on the scaffold and during the trial, or by haranguing and moulding the people at mass meetings.

We may not say that the Reformation period was one of general agitation amongst the entire populace; it was, however, a time when the world was out of joint—on the verge of disintegration. We can feel this. Luther's thunderings had sounded. Germany had witnessed the tremendous scene at Worms, and had known what it meant. The land had felt the terrifying threat of the Peasants' War; the imagination of Europe had been fired by the mighty battle of Pavia; the sack of Rome had created a universal sense that the world must quickly change its course if utter disaster was to be avoided, not only in the world, but in the Church also; the Turks had been at the gates of Vienna. Germany was primed for a vast explosion. The most obvious scene for the radical explosion of all this dangerous material would be populous places where there was most industry and the biggest proletariat, in places, moreover, where the repressive policy of the Habsburgs most severely obstructed outward expression: that is the Netherlands.

And so, at the very start of the movement there were to be found in the Netherlands representatives of both of the extremes we have mentioned. Melchior Hofmann, the furrier from Swabia, was devoted to the cause of patient Christian expectation of the Parousia. Later on he worked at various times in Strasburg, where he died. More extreme, however, was the 'prophet' Matthys-

zoon, a baker from Harlem who appeared on the scene after
1530. The kingdom of God, with the enlightened for its vehicle,
must be spread by force, and its enemies must be destroyed.
He himself was prepared to shed the blood of both Catholics and
Protestants in Münster. The chief agent in introducing and
establishing Reformed doctrine in the churches of Münster had
been the eloquent chaplain, Bernd Rothmann. Victory was
assured by summer 1532. For years the country-folk and towns-
people in Westphalia had been in a ferment as a result of social and
economic distress. In association with the utterly selfish cloth
merchant, Bernd Knipperdolling and his work of agitation in the
guilds, influenced also, and finally dominated, by the Anabaptist
preachers from the Netherlands, Rothmann now fell in with the
social and religious revolutionary demands. The town council
was ousted and the ancient objective of the corporation – to be
free from the bishop – was accomplished. The bishop had to give
way and peaceably allow a radical Reformation to take over. The
line of development fostered violence. Outsiders took over the
leadership: the baker, Jan Matthys and, after his death, the
tailor, Jan Bockelson from Leyden. Being strangers, it was
easier for them to establish their régime with increasing despotism.
Knipperdolling, the former mayor aided and abetted the alliance,
especially in his judicial capacity, for he soon began to condemn
and then try afterwards.

The original Reformation programme of 'no works of men' was
now put into effect in its most extreme and most distorted form.
They wanted to get back to the utter simplicity of primeval
humanity, but saw this original human state through the eyes of
the Old Testament. All institutions which men had evolved in the
course of history were to be overturned. This was the Reformation
concept of a totally non-historical Christian mentality carried to
its extreme of abstruseness, and yet applied to concrete daily life.
At the same time we must not allow the fanatical absurdities and
utter madness of a primarily pathological upheaval to blind us to
the reason and sanity in the second prophet of this movement,
Jan of Leyden – a sanity which existed alongside his criminal
irrationality. The fortification of the city, the military and economic mobilisation of all available forces and potentialities were
evidence of perspicacity and purposeful energy. Only because of

this was the city able to stand such a long siege, and repulse two bloody general assaults.

It is also very easy to understand how such violent pseudo-natural impulse would turn into the antithesis of nature and into the crudest naturalism. The young Bockelson, in particular, with his unrestrained passion for horror, combined with the exigencies of the siege – terrible starvation – urged on his fanatical supporters in every class to the bitter extreme of irrationality; for they refused to give in. In that year and a half when this city of the lower Rhine was sealed off, the epidemic psychological material, that we know from the late Middle Ages, worked away until it became virulent poison. By an amazing, hair-raising and blood-curdling inversion, an alleged kingdom of God arose – God's most Christian city', 'the whole congregation and brotherhood of Christ', where the annihilation of all freedom became the norm, where Jan Bockelson ruled upon the 'throne of David', not over this 'supreme city of God' alone, but over the whole world, the superior of all princes and the emperor.

After 23 July 1534, complete communism was in force. This involved community of food and of wives, the latter being regulated by a frightful marriage code which led to the dissolution of all bonds. The sensual court of the king of Sion with his sixteen wives provided a foil to large-scale mass hysteria, which made a treason out of every sin, and punished it accordingly, put down revolt bloodily, and held everything in sullen subjection, not least by the employment of a poisonous system of spying.

All the while there was the most improbable nonsense of alleged prophecies, resulting, in spite of all that has been said, in the unshakeable and magnanimous fanatical faith of many robust men and hysterical women, filled with the 'spirit' of illumination. There was an uncanny coupling together of leaders and the misled. Apart from a few hours of intense excitement, when responsibility may well have been diminished, it is hard to impute even a measure of good faith to the few leading personalities, especially Bockelson. They were men of a different stamp from the mighty early prophet, Matthys and the enthusiastic wandering preachers, who went out from the besieged city of Münster to preach their Anabaptist faith and to die for it. Whatever confused belief Bockelson may have had to begin with in his own prophetic office, had long since been overwhelmed by his unrestrained sensuality, violence, desire for position and power, and, in the end, the sheer urge to keep alive. While his subjects died from hunger, this prophet of God was living in luxury.

Then there were the very necessary propaganda tractates. These were smuggled out of the city in thousands, in order to break the resistance outside, and enlist the help of the Anabaptist movement all around. These tractates spoke in all seriousness of the order and sinlessness and communism of love that prevailed, and affirmed that they would gladly be taught out of scripture by their betters – only that was unfortunately impossible. With the naïvety of children, fools and criminals, the horrible reality was turned into its exact opposite. The self-assured threat was thrown at the obstinate outside: 'Our redemption does not wait, and the fire that is kindled cannot be quenched – not by all the water in the world.'

Münster communism once again became the great common enemy of the Germans, now divided into Catholics and Evangelicals. The defensive action of the bishop and his immediate circle proving ineffective, and there being considerable danger that the trouble would spread, a general district council at Worms voted the necessary means to continue the siege. Cologne, Cleve, Saxony and Hesse gave their support to Bishop Francis von Waldeck. The toughness of the fanatical defenders increased. After several months more, it was treachery alone that broke down the resistance. On the night of the eve of St John the Baptist, 23/4 June 1535, the city, devastated by the militant Anabaptists, and containing few survivors, fell to the besiegers, who drenched it in a sea of blood. The Anabaptists within the city were simply annihilated. At the end the leaders had shown little heroism, and had avoided the hopeless final battle against the besiegers who suddenly appeared within the city. On 22 January 1536 Jan of Leyden, Knipperdolling and Krechting were killed with daggers and glowing tongs in front of the town hall, the very place where the 'king' had sat in splendour in view of his wives, dispensing justice, with Bible and sword. Their bodies were hung up in the notorious iron cage on the tower of the Lambert church, as a terrifying example.

The grisly aberration and deception of a deep-seated restless search for the solution of all riddles through immediate contact with the divine was at an end. Indiscipline had led to self-annihilation, and, once again, through an ocean of suffering, the absolute necessity of a fixed form to ensure the continuance of religious life was proved.

In its ultimate effects, the overthrow of the revolutionaries in Münster represented the end of the promising expansion of the Reformation in that place, despite the increasing trend to the bishop in that direction. The whole pitiable state of Catholicism was represented by this miserable Francis von Waldeck. In the battle with the Reformers his predecessors had capitulated by abdication. Francis would gladly have turned his see into an hereditary principality. Even after 1535 he cheerfully proposed Reformation for Osnabrück on the lines of the Augsburg Confession. Only in 1548 under severe political pressure did he solemnly reject Reformation views, without binding himself to honour these affirmations any longer than the emperor's power lasted.

In the end the Anabaptist régime in Münster had become a reign of terror; but this fact did not alter its basic structure, which was democratic, supported by the masses, and an enemy of domination by princes. Thus the victory of the princes at Münster destroyed the Reformation as a popular movement, and once again the adult responsibility and autonomy of the people was further suppressed. Even Münster became a stage on the road to the territorial Church system and to absolutism.

A similar crisis occurred amongst the Hanseatic towns of north Germany in 1535–36. In Lübeck, Jürgen Wullenweber tried to overthrow the old council and establish an ecclesio-political democracy. His first aim was to spread this democracy further afield than the North Sea coasts. To the suspicious guardians of the old order, in those days such tendencies must have appeared as an offshoot from the dangerous rabble-rousing spirit of Münster. A war with Denmark turned out badly. The nobility of Holstein and Gustav Wasa defeated the democrats. The old town council were reinstated and Wullenweber executed.

In the north as well the Reformation now depended upon the will of the princes.

D

PART THREE

Catholic Life.
Decline and Renewal

ONE

The Continuance of Catholic Life in Germany

I

At the beginning of this third section it is necessary to be reminded of our purpose, which is to arrive at an understanding of the Reformation in Germany. In the period we are studying, the great intra-Catholic reform which, along with the Reformation and the Counter-Reformation, bulked so large in the general history of the sixteenth century – although its importance has not always been fully appreciated – affected Germany but slightly. We ought therefore to give it relatively small space.

I have, however, decided to give this material more space than it would seem on the surface to merit. I do this in deliberate reaction to the neglect that has hitherto been accorded to Catholic life in Germany in the sixteenth century. The descriptions hitherto given of this period have failed to provide an accurate reflection of the actual state of affairs, and have also lacked the special aim which ought to inspire every present-day German study of this epoch. Only when the whole content of the energies then at work is grasped by the popular mind today, will we be able to understand the problems of the confessional schism, which still divides Germany, so that some headway can be made towards healing that schism, spiritually at least, and perhaps visibly, too. Explanations must be rooted in reality. To this day Catholics must feel some distress on reading many eminent Protestant Reformation histories; for these make it seem as though, apart from the politically motivated emperor and the puny attempts of the still Catholic princes – likewise politically minded – scarcely any real Catholicism was left. Individual Catholics and the expression of Catholic life in Germany are given only the briefest mention. The story of Catholic life in those days can be written – so it would seem – on a couple of pages.

In all truth, the disintegration of Catholic life was far advanced. Our description of the causes of the Reformation and of the state of Catholic life at the beginning of the Reformation has made that fact very plain indeed; and even in the years of incipient Catholic reform we will have to refer back emphatically to these things. So much so, indeed, that it might seem that I am destroying my own thesis. Even the positive religious values we shall find may appear weak and meagre enough when compared with the ardent striving of Luther, and with the massive event of the Reformation. It is to be hoped, therefore, that the reader will continue reading right to the end of this chapter, for in spite of everything, the commonly accepted picture is false, for it lacks the necessary supplement which alone makes intelligible the further development that went beyond the merely political sphere.

There is much more to history than genius, obvious activity and novelty. There is a permanent undercurrent of mediocrity, of almost miserable growth; and this is an essential part of history. And there is, too, an interior history upon which massive outward events depend for their very reality. This third part turns to this all too often forgotten interior history, in so far as Catholic life contributed towards it.

It is true that one cannot paint this picture in its whole extension. That would be too monotonous.[1] If we traversed the length and breadth of Germany we would find the same thing repeated over and over again. A mass in Königsberg would be essentially the same as a mass in Trier or at a thousand altars in between. In contrast, the Protestantism of that period was something new,

---

[1] We must distinguish, however. Hitherto we have been very badly informed about the continuation and progress of Catholic life in Germany. A work like that of Greven on the Carthusians of Cologne leads us to expect pleasant surprises from further research.

something on the move and hence varied. Thus it can be described detail by detail without monotonous repetition. Catholicism, on the other hand – with certain reservations – was a homogeneous unity. It must be said with emphasis, however, that as well as monks who left their monasteries, there were a great many who remained loyal, and who had to be driven out of house and home; that as well as degenerate clergy there were a remarkable number of parish priests and a host of bishops who went on faithfully tending their flocks, celebrating the liturgy, preaching sermons and dispensing charity; that beside Luther's writings there emerged a Catholic anti-Protestant literature, the dogmatic, exegetic and literary soundness of which is still significant, for it was a literary effort which – despite its bitter polemic and calumny, in which it did not fall short of its Protestant counterpart – was the product of genuine Christian missionary zeal.

II

Was this essential Catholic life in Germany strong enough at that time?

It certainly did exist strongly in the ever new creative forms of common life – in parishes and in monasteries; and there was a considerable number of leading individuals.

Fortunately we are able to observe the day to day life of a well-run Catholic parish, at least in external details. Not only do we see that the old forms perished but also that believing ecclesiastical life and activity were vigorous, as a result of co-operation between clergy and people. This was not expressed in a cramped struggle for survival. The reality of Catholic life was, rather, taken for granted in the Catholic regions – just as it always had been. This held true also of a great number of monasteries.

To understand both we must recall a few of the basic facts that characterised life in those days: in spite of commercial links – which, for example, enabled Luther's writings to spread so quickly – most regions enjoyed but the very poorest intercommunication, and hence influenced each other very slightly. The several regions of Germany were still very far apart.

The continuance of Catholic life can be demonstrated, for example, by the parish of Father May of Hildpoltstein, of Father

Diel in Mainz and of Dr John Eck in Ingolstadt. These parishes provide us with records from which we can extract a great deal of information. The chief matters dealt with are the provision of Sunday preaching as required by traditional usage in the parish, and the regulation of external religious observance in the course of the Liturgical Year. In harmony with these prescriptions, the records treat least of all of that which would interest us most: the interior prayer-life of the congregation.

We are at first disappointed when we piece together the material supplied by Diel. He speaks of merits, of increasing the store of grace, of veneration of our Lady, of the indulgences peculiar to their own parish, of the blessing of the ashes, of confession before Christmas, of the fast-days and ember days, of mass endowments, and of stations of St Anthony and St Martin, and of the relics and fraternities belonging to the parish. It is obvious that those who wished to belong to the parish family had to go to confession in the parish church; and one was not permitted to go seeking an ignorant confessor. It speaks of fraternity taxes, and comments that offerings not belonging to the parish priest should be paid in the presence of witnesses. There is, too, the rather unattractive reckoning up of days of indulgence.

There are more heart-warming sections. The pastor was to instruct the people concerning devout reception of Holy Communion; and the collection was to be taken up earlier so as not to disturb people at the reception of Holy Communion. The faithful were to yield themselves up 'in interior contemplation, devotion and love, to him whom they believed to receive in a hidden manner in Holy Communion, and whom one day they hoped to see with unspeakable joy in his heavenly kingdom'.[2] If a sick person was unable to receive viaticum, he should have the Body of the Lord brought to him to venerate, while being consoled in these words: 'Believe and you have received!' There are also passages which make clear how well based upon scripture the precepts were, and how seriously they took true contrition, which could be replaced by no other penance, whether that be prayer, fasting, almsgiving or pilgrimages.

---

[2] Because after Holy Communion a chalice of unconsecrated wine was given to the faithful, the difference between this and the priest's chalice was to be explained.

For the rest, even the silence over the more intimate devotional life of the parish is eloquent. We have only to be acquainted with the atmosphere that prevails in a Catholic country parish to appreciate that. As in a thousand chance remarks in the German chronicles of the period, so here, too, the fact of the continuance of Catholic life is taken for granted; for it was that particular form of life which alone could fill out the whole cycle of the changing year. A very ancient custom was being enacted, but still in organically living forms, constantly nourished from the mystery of redemption in the mass. These forms appeared to be utterly conventional, and very often they were just that – as we have read. None the less this faithfulness in small things reveals genuine strength, and we can perceive that behind these externals the life of real faith still pulsated, uninterrupted.

The work and personality of Eck, parish priest at the church of our Lady in Ingolstadt, is clearer and more tangible. His urgent request for the prayers of his fellow-workers in the Lord's vineyard may sound a little stilted, but his parish record does contain abundant indication that its author was a sound and faithful pastor. He laboured to establish what was essential: that the daily and weekly cycle of liturgical life be assured in an orderly way. In all circumstances the timely administration of the sacraments to the sick and dying must be guaranteed. A priest was made responsible for these things each week, and if need be he had to provide a substitute. Every priest in the parish, however, had to be ready unconditionally to step in in case of necessity. But the routine of parish life never dulled Eck's sensitivity to Christian suffering, for example that of a mother who lost her child. He did not allow prayer to become mechanical but repeatedly stressed the need for unhurried prayer. Quantity must not damage quality. His sermon notes for the beginning of the Easter cycle in 1526 contain these words: 'O that people would not be in such a hurry to get Communion over! Once a year you perform this sublime action, and you rush away as soon as you can. Not so my children, not so!' On Palm Sunday and Holy Thursday that year Eck arranged for confessions to be heard from 3 a.m. onwards.

Eck regarded preaching as the chief duty of the parish priest.

In contrast to the lamentable custom of the times he scarcely ever delegated this function to curates. Study and the recitation of the Breviary, which he loved, and the neglect of which he so strongly condemned, provided the solid theological and devotional basis for his preaching. The average number of his sermons while in charge of the church of our Lady (1525–32) was amazing. There were months when he preached ten, eleven, twelve and fifteen sermons. Considering the enormous burden of work he had at that time, this preaching represents a most unusual effort. He pointed out to his flock: 'He who listens devoutly to a sermon should know that he performs as good a work as though he were at home scourging himself like a Carthusian.' It is pleasing and touching to observe that Eck was not one of those preachers who spoke merely of 'your' sins. He included himself explicitly, named himself first, indeed. The earnestness with which he portrayed at once the dignity, the burden and the responsibility, of the pastoral office, as well as many detailed features of his pastoral work, provide sure evidence that Eck's reform proposals and the pious ideas in his sermons were no merely theoretical concern. He meant all that he said in a simple, sober, practical way. With sure instinct he steered a proper middle course between rigorism and laxity. His dogmatic rigidity found no parallel in the conduct of his pastoral duties. He understood the freedom of man's conscience, assuming that a person did not try to evade the seriousness of the Christian law.

His private life seems to have corresponded to the tone of his parochial sermons. He had put the sins of youth behind him. After about 1528 he no longer drank wine at table, even when the curates offered it to him; he was content with simple food, and he fasted more than the Church's precepts demanded, until shortly before his death.

Eck's enemies have tried to discredit the value of his pastoral work, saying that he was avaricious over benefices. Eck was in fact not badly off. When defending himself against a reproach by Butzer he did not mention all of his benefices. He was incumbent of two parishes (the second in Günzburg), and had to put a vicar into one of them.

But if Eck's letters to Rome were full of requests concerning his own financial affairs, this was because he got no replies. What was due to him was not so very much. When he exchanged his former parish of St Moritz (May 1525) for the parish in Ingolstadt, with his colleague, George Hauer, he made a bad deal financially. Eck certainly cannot be upbraided with the worship of Mammon. He meant what he said: 'Do not rob me of what is lawfully mine. I want no more. You are looking at a theologian who says: enough, I ask for no more' (1538).

Earlier, at the time of the Leipzig disputation, for example, we saw no evidence of these pleasing traits in Eck's character. He seems to have changed about 1525. He became increasingly interested in positive pastoral work, both in practice and in his literary output. He threw in his lot with the work for Catholic renewal. Eck never became one of the outstanding figures in this movement of renewal, but by his work of strengthening and conservation, and then by the guiding principles he worked out, he made a most important contribution to that work.

It is not easy to assess the degree in which Eck advanced the Catholic cause, nor to measure its exact religious value. With renewal, however, almost everything depends upon quality.

We must note first of all, that in those days religious vigour had to express itself as antithetical to the Reformation. If we compare, let us say, Luther's letters with those of Eck and Cochlaeus, at once the vast gulf becomes apparent. In the early Luther there is a total absence of any desire for worldly possessions. Soon, however, gifts were to come, and later a proper financial arrangement was established. All his life, however, he was scarcely interested in his own private financial affairs. There is no blemish of this sort to mar the religious concern in his letters.

We cannot make a comparison of the complete works on both sides.

To arrive at a more precise judgment we first have to distinguish clearly between the correctness of doctrine on the one hand, and the full richness of truth, on the other. Eck himself had little appreciation of this distinction. He lived utterly by correctness of doctrine. This, plus a definite sense of the Church, was the very thing that made his doctrine so important as a means of saving the situation, for the alternative seemed to be corrosive confusion. None the less, divorced from fullness and depth it was somewhat superficial, tending towards a type of nominalism and theological rationalism, instead of apostolic, religious preaching in the power of the Spirit.

Once in his later years (1540), in a remarkable criticism of Witzel, he was to reveal what he considered was required in a Catholic champion of those days. Hatred of, or desire for vengeance upon, the Reformers was not enough. There must also be heart-felt fervour of faith, and utter devotion to religion, and these virtues must possess the power to edify others. His parish records prove that Eck himself fulfilled these requirements.

If, however, we estimate the value of Eck's work solely in terms of its immediate religious power, we do not gain a true picture of its importance for the coming Catholic renewal. The Reformation was a total conflict. Any power, any vitality, was bound to be an asset to those who possessed it. In spite of his unpopularity even on the Catholic side, Eck's moral and spiritual influence was considerable. This Swabian peasant's son had an extraordinary power of perseverance; but he was far from obstinate. His traditionalism was alive. In spite of his intellectualist pedagogism, which knew little of interior anguish, Eck was well aware of the failure of pre-Reformation theology – especially that of the 'justly ridiculed monks'. He saw how the living originality of theology had been lost, as a result of the laziness of theologians, and had gone astray down the blind alleys of endless logic-chopping. More than this: he discovered the positive role of the Reformation in the rebirth of the Church. As always in history, here God was using heresy to direct interest once again to the core of divine doctrine.

Besides this, Eck was amazingly versatile. There were few things in which he was not interested: biblical textual criticism and reference to the original texts, paleography, geography, customs of remote peoples, revision of the calender, jurisprudence, mysticism. In particular he was interested in the whole of theology of every period, including the most modern, and, as a support in the battle now raging, everything that was going on in the literary, political and ecclesio-political field. With great ease he could find his way around in the past as in the present.

Certainly his focal interest was always the refutation of heresy; and that attitude, of course, brought with it the usual defects.

'While I live I will oppose all heretics, apostates, schismatics – firm in our holy faith; and I will fight against them with all my power.' If we admire Luther's power of attack we must also learn to appreciate Eck's stubborn intolerance and indefatigability. Eck's extraordinary energy in the service of the Church is shown both by the impetuous zeal with which, from 1517 onwards, he threw himself into the work of polemics, and by the single-mindedness with which he maintained this zeal all his life. He was one of the few who was able to keep pace with Luther in this game of polemics. At least he kept the pace externally: for the reasons we have shown, he never attained intellectual flexibility, superior elegance or overwhelming cogency. Too often he confined himself to details. At the same time he did not concentrate on mere accidentals. At the very start of the conflict, on the occasion of the indulgence theses, he had recognised Luther's attack for what it was: the expression of a new concept of the Church. And so, with remarkable logic, his first systematic work concerned the primacy of the pope. The book was sparked off by the needs of polemics, and conceived along specifically anti-Lutheran lines. None the less, on account of its comprehensive analysis, it is one of the more fundamental expositions of genuine Catholic doctrine.

A notable feature is the method of proof, which thereafter gradually became standard for Luther's literary adversaries: the scholastic positions, formerly presupposed, were abandoned, and they returned to the sources which Luther himself acknowledged – holy scripture principally, and to some extent, the councils, the decrees and the Fathers.

The decisive thing was this: Eck clearly felt that Luther was challenging something fundamental.

Concerning the evidential value of Eck's citation from Church history, we must not confuse his amazing knowledge with the critical soundness of his position. In the former he was vastly superior to Luther, but in terms of the fixity of his dogmatic position, and considering the embryonic condition of Catholic history of dogma, he could not possess the freedom of mind which Luther had gained from his revolutionary independence. None the less, on account of his vast learning, Eck was the most important amongst the early architects of a positive Catholic theology.

There was a serious lack in Eck's contribution, in respect of its function within the Reformation. Eck was on a battlefield, not in a classroom. At all events his scholastic work had to be a warfare also – in the broad sense. In reality, however, his systematic works were too literary. At that time it seemed as though men were arguing about who had most right on his side; but the real issue was: who would succeed in acquiring power over men's minds and souls? The whole thing began in a time of revolution, and this affected the form, the cogency and the effectiveness of all that was said. Eck's fat volumes reached only the educated. He himself was aware of this defect; and he tried to reach a wider public. He sought a wider public, but not the widest, for his important book in this respect was the *Enchiridion* – written in Latin. Its importance cannot be overrated; it was a mine of material for polemicists, preachers, educated Catholic laity, and to that extent it provided a weapon for the battle with the Reformation. But it simply did not reach the masses and moulded public opinion only in the smallest degree. Even this book remained too strictly enclosed within the sphere of the schools and of scholastic theology.

No one refuted Eck's writings; Eck complained about this – to Butzer, for example; but he never saw the deeper reason for this silence amongst his opponents. The enemy were employing their time influencing the populace and the town councils. Their replies were not addressed to particular arguments, and not given primarily in the form of refutations. Instinctively their attitude remained aggressive. Reply took the form of ruthless, biting mockery, that scarcely stopped short of calumy. They were also contained in the many smears and evil reports which have distorted the picture that has come down to us of the man himself. The very intensity of hatred which he provoked in his enemies proves how much he must have impressed them.

Where do we find the key to Eck's work – its excellence as well as its defects?

Eck himself gives us the formula for analysing his personality. 'I want to be a schoolmaster all my life.' We must take this statement at its face value.

Eck was an early matured schoolmaster, who knew everything,

but had not had to struggle to acquire his knowledge. He had never had to travel the road to Damascus, never experienced purifying interior catastrophe. He possessed no creative temperament. He knew all the old answers, but never made them new. He kept moving along the even course of his early youth, and never knew what it was to *realise* what was simply known. Truth never changes, but its power over people depends upon the impressiveness of the form in which it is cast. Eck's intellect was far superior to that of any of his Catholic colleagues. For this very reason he is specially impressive proof of the impotence of truth when dressed up in worn garments.

Eck's glory was his dogmatic soundness and clarity. He kept himself untainted by the inner structure of nominalism, and followed the old road of realism. He was, however, too little interested in bridging the gulf between the newly emerging antitheses. On his death-bed, Eck is supposed to have affirmed that the schism in the Church could never be healed by this sort of understanding resolution, but only by sheer rigidity. 'Behold Eck, always the same Eck, never afraid, ever unvanquished' (funeral eulogy). He was a man of unshakeable level-headedness, representative of a lucid, resolute, dialectically victorious, but cold, intellectualism.

The rigidity of Eck's theses was genuine. Without attempting to disguise the many weak and scientifically untenable parts of his many-sided works, we may say: neither in Leipzig in 1519, nor later, did he ever unscrupulously and cunningly allow his opinion to approximate to that of his opponent, so that he could say he never had thought otherwise. To say such a thing is to fail to see his power, and to deny the plain facts. At the Leipzig disputation Eck was quite enough of a Catholic to know that the freedom and co-operation of the will in the process of redemption, in no way implied any kind of reservation concerning the statement that nothing can earn redemption without grace. The formal error of the Reformers and hence the reason for their opposition to the Catholic Church in general lay in their one-sidedness, in their selection of doctrines, which they affirmed as the whole truth. The chief aim of the Catholic defence was, therefore, to rectify this one-sided picture by completing it; and this was precisely what Eck did. God and man, grace and free will, had to be united in harmonious co-operation. It was this synthesis which enabled Eck to produce this thesis in Bologna in 1515: 'All that is not of faith is sin.' This thesis, affirmed also by Luther, was not in itself false or uncatholic; the one-sided application given it by Luther was.

Eck's own contemporaries not only complained of Eck's intolerance but considered it to be directly responsible for the permanent schism of Christendom. Had it not been for Eck – so it was whispered – religious peace would long since have been restored. Eck, however, like Luther, lived entirely by the conviction, that in questions of faith, war alone cannot determine peace.

It would be difficult to prove that Eck's intransigence during the forties was essentially mistaken. The question is more to the point when applied to the earlier years of the Reformation. One could ask whether the schismatic movement might not have been arrested, had the representatives of the Church tried to understand Luther's and his colleagues' religious and pastoral distress. Courteous reserve and wise tactics ought at least to have directed the campaign. External and irrevocable, although technically legitimated, heresy trials often produced disastrous results. May we not ask what the outcome might have been, had a Contarini, spiritually free and open-minded and pastorally concerned about his opponent's soul, met with Luther in 1518? At all events the mediatorial theology of the forties came too late. In 1519 Eck was not only a clarifier but a dangerous man also. In no respect at all was his conscience disturbed by the responsibilities of the hour. In Leipzig, on 5 July, he calmly and triumphantly pressed Luther towards his explosive conclusions. This certainly convinced the emerging Reformer – as did the course of events in general from 1517 until 1521–25 – that he was on the right track, and that his deep distress and all his efforts were being met with very little religious understanding – often none at all.

The city chronicles and the monastery records both show that Diel's and Eck's parishes were no isolated examples. On the other hand, we can assess persisting Catholic energies correctly only if we consider the pressures which they resisted. One monastery which held out against all corrosive oppression – intellectual, moral, political and economic – in spite of all the allurements, the crippling decline or the discouraging apostasy in the world around, says more about the strength of the Church, than the collapse of a dozen says about its weakness. It is significant, however, that as the years went by, even in Catholic districts the dissolution of the Church began to move faster. The impotence of the clergy, added to the general contempt into which they had fallen, gave rise to a terrible shortage of priests. Many parishes no longer had an incumbent; mass was no longer offered in them, and the sacraments were not dispensed; very often, because there were no Catholic books, Catholics read Protestant sermons and expositions of Christian doctrine. We must set this picture alongside the positive forces of Catholic renewal, or, rather, alongside the Catholic defence. Eck once again provides material in his reform proposals of 1523 and later.

These proposals were by no means entirely religious. They had a clear political slant, that favoured the Bavarian state Church system. Eck's design in this way was by no means dishonourable; but once again it shows us very clearly how much the Church had become entangled in political life, and thus unable to direct itself entirely according to its own spiritual law.

The details – which could be multiplied at will from the memoranda of Cochlaeus and Aleander during the same period – are much less interesting, for they contain only what is well known. They keep going over the old *Gravamina:* the abuses of the curial benefice and tax systems, the overstepping of the limits of clerical-Roman jurisdiction, the exemption of the mendicant orders from the jurisdiction of the bishops. 'If the pope does not forthwith initiate a reform of the curia by a bull against various public abuses, many will look for a remedy from the Turks or from Antichrist. For then it will be plain to all that God is going to chastise the Church on account of our sins.'

We cannot fail to notice that this warning, uttered frequently by Eck, has rather a formal sound. He was perfectly correct, however, to see that the chief trouble lay in an exaggerated and self-seeking clericalism. Burdens ought to be shared out equitably between laity and clergy.

As with spiritual punishments, so the curia had destroyed the meaning of spiritual benefits by indiscriminate dispensation. Just as people no longer believed the pious mendicant, in spite of all his assurances, so too the Church's treasury of merit had become utterly devalued by the indulgence traffic. Many people had used indulgence certificates to pay hotel bills, and even to pay prostitutes. Rome had to share the blame for this. There were far too many indulgences. Scarcely had one been preached when a new one followed. Like experienced money-makers, pope, emperor, cardinals, bishops and their representatives bargained for their share in the spoils. There could be only one result: indulgences were bound to fall into disrepute. Instead of being a stimulus to piety they became the means of its destruction. The best course, Eck thought, would be to revoke all indulgences and then issue new ones prudently.

Eck recognised a root of this abuse in the commutation of spiritual works of penance into cash payments. This went far back into the past – to the time of Gregory III. The saints and the early Church knew nothing of this 'human invention'. On this point Eck was rightly a radical: 'And so all that we can now find in the papal penitentiary, which is supposed to provide the soul with the means of salvation alone, is silver and gold. And how is it that we are not being asked to perform the one act of satisfaction which the Bible commends?' . . . 'Because Rome is only interested in money. Pay and you will be rewarded.' . . . 'Because the penitential offices are for sale, and so the officials know less about theology, about holy scripture and canon law, than an ass knows about singing. How is it that no one excommunicates big sinners – usurers, sodomites and simoniacs – but only the drunkard who is unable to pay his tax of some eight or ten ducats?' 'The confessors in Rome are looking for their offering, and are unconcerned about sin; for this reason confession must be got over quickly, so that there can be plenty of customers in quick succession.' . . . 'How are officials in the penitentiary able so easily to dispense monks from their vows and habit?'

We must take note that this is Eck the loyal churchman speaking, and that he is attacking the pope. He may have been as little able as his opponents were to avoid exaggeration and generalisation, but what he says sounds uncomfortably like what Luther had to say in condemnation of indulgences.

Eck went thoroughly into the incredible benefice rat-race of Rome. Benefices were snatched and sold with amazing irresponsibility, and to the accompaniment of the most barefaced lies. Deserving men were ousted in favour of mere boys. There were stipulations, reservations and other juridical devices; dishonest legal actions, division or resale of the proceeds of a benefice, without the incumbent's knowledge; protracted, arbitrary citations to Rome, on quite general pretexts, which allowed victory to go to the most shameless or indefatigable; there was the transference of benefices to foreigners. All of these things had become scandals that cried to heaven. 'No wonder if the earth should open and swallow up all who were making merchandise of Christ's patrimony.'

It is pleasing to note how Eck inveighed strongly against the accumulation of benefices, in which malignant practice he saw one of the deepest causes of religious decline.

It is obvious that Eck did not deceive himself about the real state of affairs. His championship of the Church was carried out in the full knowledge of Catholic guilt and of the colossal burden of the labour involved. This enhanced his spiritual stature.

He published his ideas on reform at various times. It is important to see that his sense of the magnitude of the task rapidly increased. It is true that he never gave up hope of rooting out heresy; but if at first it seemed an easy matter to define the danger, later he saw that the whole nation was embracing the Reformation, and that the very survival of the faith was at stake. Something had to be done quickly. In 1524 Eck once again had to make it plain to the Romans, that every delay by the curia was disastrous. He had said these things to Leo X, but to no purpose. So far it had made no impression on Rome that thousands of souls were being lost through heresy. The devil himself was tempting them merely to look with contempt upon the Reformation. Scripture itself teaches us to catch the foxes while they are still young.

One of the demands that was constantly being made by all the loyal supporters of the Church was that all heretical literature be destroyed. Eck demanded that this be done uniformly everywhere. He was unaware that his plan was impossible. He knew, it is true, that he would meet considerable opposition; but the manner in which he spoke (1524) about inquisitorial methods proves how hopeful he still was that strict measures would relatively easily calm the storm; and he still believed that the centres into which heresy had penetrated could be neatly geographically defined.

In particular, strict inflexibility was to be shown to all clergy suspected of heresy; for 'this devil cannot be expelled except by rack and torture'. The clergy, too, were to keep a close watch upon the stubborn mendicant friars, who had been doing so much harm in spreading the Lutheran heresy.

In addition, it was necessary to attack the power centre of the Reformation: the university of Wittenberg must be crushed. Wittenberg, where one could now graduate *auctoritate apostolica*, must be deprived of the rights of a universal centre of study, so that none coming out of that university might claim the doctor's degree.

The special disposition of forces in Germany must be known. Germany was large and far from united. There were so many dukes and counts and the rest. On the other hand, the heresy was already widely disseminated and had reached the whole nation. The problem was to find a method of preventing the whole nation going to pieces as a result of this heresy, while there was still some hope of saving those not yet contaminated. Uniformity of action was more important than anything, and therefore the pope must take charge of the whole campaign. The battle must be fought according to a single plan. Most of all, the bishops must present a common front. It would be fatal if one were to smile upon Luther while another trembled at the sound of his name. Aristocratic connection must not blind people to the blemish of false doctrine. At all events, the task must not be left to the negligence of the bishops. They, indeed, were more to blame for the apostasy than were their secular counterparts.

Eck saw it as a precondition of success that the energies of Germany be thrown in, both to overthrow the new doctrine and to reform the morals of the clergy. And so it was necessary, for example, that the nuncios should have the services of a man who knew exactly what was going on in Germany. Eck may have had himself in mind. In any case, his suggestion was perfectly right.

On the other hand, the means would have to be permanently effective, even if there were no papal nuncio present. History proved the strict necessity for Germany of regular provincial and diocesan synods. These must be re-established.[3] Freedom of speech should be granted to all who wanted to speak for the faith at these synods. Eck frequently and stubbornly returned to his thesis: without a reintroduction of these councils there simply could not be a lasting reform. Had there been wide-awake bishops at the synods, neither Wycliffism in Bohemia, nor Lutheranism in Germany could have taken root. It is worth noting how strongly Eck underlined the efficacy of such synods in preference to a general council. Germany and the whole of Christendom might be shouting for a general council, but the people ought not to be deceived: would there ever be a council? And if one was convened, people would be sure to object that it was not free.

Obviously the bishops, too, would have to be reformed. Eck began right at the critical point. He set out as his first requirement, that the bishops expel all Lutherans from their presence, whether employed as advisers, secretaries, chaplains or servants, at their courts or outside. The second demand was, that they must be in a position to know the state of faith about them, and to refute the subtlety of the Lutherans, and in general be able to fight false doctrine. There were, in fact, scarcely any bishops fit to do these things. Hence it was necessary for them to employ at least one competent theologian at their curias – and such men were rare also. Third: the bishops must curtail their luxury. The picture painted by Eck was excessively dismal. There were bishops who, in return for monetary payments, condoned concubinage amongst their clergy, who robbed poor churches in which they did not even perform their episcopal duties, who installed ignorant representatives, who carried on shady deals with their sacred functions, blessings and consecrations. It was incredible how people were fleeced if a bell had to be blessed or an interdict lifted from a cemetery. 'In one German diocese the bishop ordered his clergy to absolve certain sins only on payment of a specified tax – for example adultery, four gold pieces, adultery by married people, six and unchastity with a nun, ten gold pieces.'

Certain things would have to be given up altogether. It was

[3] So that the functioning of the synods might be in harmony with their overwhelming importance, Eck proposed that the pope have a collection of the councils printed.

a question of directing the course of development by constructive initiative. The closer one could keep to the ancient law, the better. The new rules laid down by the curial chancelleries counted for nothing, and these only damaged common law. It were better for Rome to yield now on certain issues than to be forced to yield later on.

This picture of the life of the lower clergy is likewise very black. There were priests in possession of mass endowments who did not even celebrate mass. When dispensing the sacraments they did not bother about the worthiness of the recipients. Above all – everything had its price. Their private lives were full of cursing, quarrelling, drinking, brawling, hunting and gambling. They had become merchants, money-changers and innkeepers.

All of these things created nothing but endless annoyance amongst the people. Practical life was devoid of any Catholic influence. Eck took this particularly seriously. The abuses must be got rid of for the sake of the people. There must be a renewal of real pastoral care. For this reason special attention must be paid to the coming generation of priests, and to the quality of parish priests and of preachers.

It is plain that all of Eck's proposals for reform were pressing for a purified Christianity. In this respect he adopted the programme both of the humanists and of the Reformers. Obviously he did this in a Catholic manner. Once again, however, the chief question arises: which religious force was at work in Eck? There is not much to the answer. The sacrament of penance was described as 'the nerve of virtuous Christian life'; synods were to be inaugurated with three-day processions to intercede for the peace of the Church; in all papal briefs there should be 'something godly', and they should savour of holy scripture and of the Spirit of God – 'as far as could be done'.

It is all quite astonishing, and we leave the relevant proposals with little hope.

TWO

The Beginnings of Catholic Reform in Germany

I

We shall take the concept of Catholic reform in a wide sense. To allow it merely to denote the continuance of complaint against the morass of abuse, would be to undervalue it; for then one would be falling into the error of the Catholic who sees in Luther's Reformation no more than a battle against abuses in the curia. Just as Luther's work, to this day, consisted in his preaching, so conversely the chief work of Catholic reform consisted in the emergence of a more intensive Catholic life, which found a closer link with the objective authority and sacramental holiness of the Church. The fruitfulness of this process is demonstrated by phenomena that were normative in the Catholic reform of Italy and Spain: the Oratory of Divine Love, the Order of Theatines, the great cardinals of the thirties and forties, the abundance of saints after the middle of the century, and the founding of vital religious orders.

For the most part these foreign centres of Catholic life exerted an influence within German history. This resulted from the very Catholicity of the Church. Fundamental Catholic movements always bear a supranational stamp and have a correspondingly wide effect. The fundamental movements within the Church in the sixteenth century arose and were developed in a specially high degree in Rome. On the other hand, German history in the sixteenth century was basically a conflict with Catholicism. It follows that German history of this period cannot be written without to some extent including in the picture the new radiance of Latin Catholicism. It would be short-sighted, however, were we to look only at the symptoms; that is, at the effects of these new Catholic energies within Germany.

The question we have to ask about this period of real revival of the Church in Germany – through the activity of predominantly Latin Jesuits, the 'Spanish priests' – or about the effect of the reforming of the Council of Trent – chiefly attended by Latins – is this: how far was this work turned to a specifically German use? We are not interested at the moment in discussing the many and delicate details of Latin forms of piety, but turn directly to things of fundamental importance. Scientific discussion today no longer lays much store by the stubborn attitude which regarded any power directed from Rome as un-German. Sebastian Merkle, who is a specially competent judge in these matters, has answered our question in respect of Trent. He affirms that the most effective work gained its value from the very fact that it was done by people who were remote from the immediate scene of religious strife, and who were thus less likely to overestimate the strength of the enemy, or to see the problem too much in terms of accidental or peripheral polemics. They could survey the whole scene calmly. An objective judgment can be based only upon an assessment of the quality of the actual work done. It is pleasant, indeed, to observe how appreciation of the work of Trent in Germany lasted well into the period of liberal Protestant theology. Merkle recalls Harnack, who admitted that Protestant scholars had long realised that scripture cannot be separated from tradition, and he himself affirms: 'The decree on justification is excellently expressed in many respects; indeed one may doubt whether the Reformation would have developed had this decree been issued by the Lateran Council and had become really embodied in the flesh and blood of the Church.' Today we can scarcely fail to be aware of the understanding which Latin theo-

logians like Contarini and Seripando had of important ideas of the
Reformers.

Very often Catholic power was manifested most of all in those
places where the old Church had reached its lowest ebb. In
England apostasy from the Church was effected almost entirely
through the sensual passion of one man – the king; and thanks to
the assistance of the shameless and complaisant clergy, it came
about almost without a fight. Thomas More and Bishop Fisher of
Rochester, however, two men who stood at the peak of the culture
of that period, two of the greatest intellects in England, became
Christian heroes, who died for the old faith.

In Renaissance Italy, when the Church's self-poisoning had
brought her within an inch of her life, the mighty prophetic voice
of Savonarola thundered out. The results of his failure became
apparent much later, once again in one of the intellectual heroes
of the age – Michaelangelo of the Last Judgment.

In both of these cases, however, we are dealing with specially
prominent individuals. They indicate that Catholic life, universally weakened by the same wounds, was still capable of heroic
effort, although in themselves they do not prove that life was
capable of stirring the broad masses of the whole people at that
time. Such a stirring could be accomplished only through widespread popular movements. These, too, were in operation, and
were surprisingly deep.

In great measure the Reformation indictment had been directed
against the papacy. These movements would now have to prevail
with the papacy, and in part have to overcome the resistance of
that papacy. They succeeded.

We know that the attacks of Luther and the other religious
Reformers and of liberal humanism played a large part in the
religious deepening of Catholic life in Germany. Many Catholics
fell by the wayside, but many aspects of Catholic life did go
through the winepress, becoming greatly purified in the process.
Even Eck demonstrates this. The internecine war changed this
supreme self-assurance into a much deeper and more Christian
self-knowledge. Similarly, the emergence of Catholic reform
everywhere went hand in hand with the increasing sense of one's
own guilt and the threatening danger from the enemy. We will

hear more about this later on. With growing religious urgency, indignation against abuses became stronger, even amongst loyal Catholic princes; and after 1530 the clerical estates, too, took part in these protests to Rome. Although often there was little enough true religion and altruism in all this, it formed part of the process of purification. The appeals from papal embassies in Germany to Rome for the correction of blatant faults became more urgent. Little as were the results, all the same, these things contributed to the growth of the seed of purification even in the curia, and they nourished hope in Germany that things would improve even more.

For the Church, the Reformation became a *felix culpa*. It was no accident that this effect was known and expressed at the time: 'The Evangelicals are making the Catholics devout.' This affirmation of Willibald Pirkheimer was in harmony with the attitude of Clement Maria Hofbauer (canonised at the beginning of the nineteenth century): 'Schism came because the Germans were in need and are in need of becoming devout.'

The Augustinian monk John Hoffmeister was specially moved by these things. Like Cochlaeus he saw and complained about Catholic indolence, about the lack of zest and courage there was in contrast to the zeal of the enemy, who 'diligently seek to push their perverse doctrines down the throat of the common man: who write in Latin, translate, print, who are never still. No word that Luther utters in his cups but is immediately printed. Whatever in any way serves to maintain and advance their undertaking is set about without a moment's delay. What of us? We do absolutely nothing. We act as though Christ were our prisoner, who must do what we want. Verily, verily, dear brethren Christ's words make me deeply sorrowful: "I will take the kingdom from you and give it to a people who will bring forth fruit." As we fully deserve this scourge, raised above us in the schism of religion, so will unavoidable calamity force us to look about us for some improvement.'

Eck was perfectly correct, and was saying only what hundreds of others were saying, when in 1523 he reported to Rome that only very few bishops in Germany were rallying to the defence of the Church. The subsequent course of the Reformation only confirmed this statement, as we shall see even more clearly. Moreover, we see the direct apostasy of not a few bishops. Even in the west we see not only the direct threat of apostasy in Cologne and in Münster–Osnabrück–Minden but in Mainz, too, a largely indifferent chapter, who all but elected Richard Count Palatine as archbishop in 1555. Besides this, we cannot by any means point to all of the bishops who stood on the Church's side in the *Reichstags*, as proof of the thesis with which we are concerned in this context. All too frequently they were moved by political and economic self-interest. There were, however, as we have already discovered, a few episcopal rulers, whom we can count as a truly religious and ecclesiastical force.

The bishop of Meissen, whom Luther addressed with such contempt in 1520, applied himself zealously to preserving the old faith in all abbeys, chapters and parishes. The feudal margrave Philip, bishop of Freising (whom Eck found so arrogant), took his spiritual vocation very seriously. It is true that for political reasons he did not proceed very zealously against the Reformation. Christopher von Uttenheim (d. 1527), bishop of Basel, was a blameless, priestly representative of his class. Before the Reformation he had seen a moral and religious revival amongst his clergy. In the twenties he was defeated by the Evangelical town council. In Switzerland there was another influential cardinal, Matthew Schinner, who was even given a dwelling in the Vatican by the reforming Pope Adrian VI. Unfortunately he died in the same year, 1522. In 1523 Bishop Christopher von Stadion again became completely loyal. The loyal bishops also included Dietrich of Lebus, patron and friend of Wimpina, teacher and fellow-student of Tetzel. His successor, too, Bishop George von Blumenthal, a former colleague of Wimpina, threw in his lot manfully for the old faith.

As early as 1524, as we have learned, there had been an attempt to unite the Catholic bishops in a centre of restoration and resistance, and to carry out a reform of the clergy, in southern Germany. This took place through the important proceedings which Campeggi – having learned from Cochlaeus, Eck and Faber – initiated in Regensburg in 1524. Campeggi as papal legate, Archduke Ferdinand, Dukes William and Ludwig of Bavaria, the archbishop of Salzburg, the bishop of Trent, the

Administrator of Regensburg and the procurators of nine southern German bishops, agreed on the 'reformation which the priests should observe from now on'. In virtue of apostolic authority, these were declared binding on Germany. The content was strongly influenced by the *Gravamina* raised against Rome. Correspondingly, they dealt chiefly with the multitude of Church taxes and tried to remove those that were offensive. Once again a spiritual character must be apparent in the lives of priests, especially those having pastoral care of souls. Simony must go, taxes be regularised, avarice amongst parish priests and indulgence vendors restrained. An end must be put to the cancer of exemptions, all pastoral work be placed under the charge of the bishop, tithes must be reduced, as also the number of feast days. Frivolous and arbitrary arguments over holy scriptures should cease, and in its place should appear true study of scripture by the clergy. Subjects matriculated at Wittenberg were to be recalled. Heretics expelled from other states must not be admitted. Severe punishment should be meted out to runaway nuns and married clergy, and heretical literature must be destroyed.

There is no doubt that this was the road to restoration. An attempt was being made to form a new type of clergy by specially fostering the coming generation of priests. The principle that quality is the keynote of all reformation was accepted: better a few worthy and competent men than a large number of mediocrities.

All that was lacking was the creative spirit of renewal. It was not to be found in this highly significant and earnest document, which concerned itself too much with details, with symptoms. Nor were there enough zealous bishops, able to rouse that spirit into life. Likewise, there were too few princes, like Duke George, who had manifested its action. The only reason why this programme remained so important, was because it was the first official and public step towards Catholic ecclesiastical reform in Germany.

As well as in south Germany, where Eck, as professor and pastor in Ingolstadt, exerted his influence, in Mainz, too, which later was to play an important part as a place of refuge, and a gathering-point for Catholic forces, there were the beginnings of reform. In 1525 the cathedral chapters of the twelve suffragan sees of Mainz met to discuss measures against the Reformation.

What of the archbishop of Mainz himself, Germany's leading churchman? Already we have encountered him several times, and have not found his religious attitude particularly impressive – witness his action in the indulgence traffic of 1517, and in the early thirties in respect of his strikingly close relationship with Melanchthon. The way of life of this prince's son who became archbishop and cardinal, and who was loaded with benefices, was far from edifying. He certainly did not possess the moral power that was urgently required. If we may assume that the indulgence instruction was to some extent characteristic of his attitude to religion, then the outlook was indeed gloomy. In reality he wavered between the parties. He employed men who were suspect from the Church's point of view. As late as 1525 Luther expressed the hope that the cardinal might well marry. In 1532 Albrecht accepted Melanchthon's dedication of the Epistle to Romans, and sent presents to this systematic theologian of the new doctrines. At all events, he showed few signs of active endeavour in the Church's cause. When he – a relic collector like the elector of Saxony – once again made his collection of indulgences available to the public in Halle, Luther sent him a quite incredible threat, with a fourteen-day limit, on account on this 'idolatry in Halle' (end of 1521). The archbishop's reply was not very dignified: 'Dear Doctor, I have read your letter with all care and courtesy, but, unless I am much mistaken, the cause which has moved you to write has long since been remedied, and I intend to behave as befits a devout and priestly prince.'

Later on, however, even this cardinal began to realise the seriousness of the situation. Not only did he remain loyal to the Church but fulfilled the duties of his episcopal office more energetically, especially those concerning ordination. He celebrated mass devoutly – if we may believe the statements made by his subject Augustinus Marius, himself a blameless bishop. Albrecht became prominent, in fact, in a specially important way, in the work of genuine, vigorous Catholic reform. In 1534 he brought the first Jesuit to Germany. This was Peter Faber (see below, pp. 157 f.) who came to Mainz. It is true that the results of his efforts in Halle were discouraging. The church of our Lady in that town was planned as a centre of Catholic activity, but when completed it was taken over by the Reformers. Maurice von Hutten, later to be bishop of Eichstätt, filled his office with dignity and pastoral zeal. Unfortunately his attempts to elevate the moral standards of his clergy were unsuccessful. In 1548 he convened a diocesan synod. In addition, he was one of the conciliatory leaders. In 1546 he presided over the religious conversations at Regensburg. In Regensburg itself during the twenties, Berthold Pirstinger had vigorously sought to arrest religious and ecclesiastical corruption. He took a hand also in constructive literary activity. Another zealous man, loyal to the Church, was John VII von Schleinitz, bishop of Meissen (1535). His successor, John VIII von Maltitz, tried, after the death of Duke George in 1539, to maintain the cause in much more difficult circumstances. During the forties, Bishop Philip of Speyer worked hard to combat the colossal corruption amongst both secular and regular clergy. Eck praised as good bishops, Conrad von Thungen, bishop of Würzburg (d. 1540), and Melchior Vattli, bishop of Constance.

After the middle of the thirties, and in connection with the religious conversations of the forties, we meet with influential personalities, who were even more important in the movement for Catholic renewal: Faber of Vienna, Nausea and Pflug, Contarini and Hosius.

There is still no thorough study of this whole material. It is, of course, possible that a complete study might illumine the picture in the same way as research into the parallel fields of edifying literature and of popular and monastic devotional life in the same period has done. So far, however, we may not count on that; and the gloomy verdict of Catholic champions upon the majority of the bishops would not, in any case, be altered thereby. Germany simply did not have men of the genius and sanctity of More and Fisher; and such men would have been needed to cope with the magnitude of the task ahead.

A glance at the ranks of cathedral chapters produces similar results. Amongst these worldly men, too, there were true pastors who served the Church faithfully. There was Laurence, high steward of Pommersfelden, dean of Mainz Cathedral, who in 1524 supported Cochlaeus in his battle in Frankfurt; there was

Cochlaeus himself in Breslau, Eck in Ingolstadt-Eichstätt and Gropper in Cologne. In Meissen, Trier, Cologne and Breslau, there were a host of cathedral prebendaries who were faithful to the end. It is true that the interior motive was always the key to the real situation. Even within the cathedral chapters, who on the whole opposed the Reformation, there were too few who really threw in their whole energies and their material resources, or even – most important and obvious – their prayers, in the cause. How small was the number of those who consistently and permanently supported the tiny band that went on fighting to hold on to almost forlorn positions!

Very soon one centre of Catholic life began to stand out as particularly healthy. This was Cologne and the region of the Netherlands. This region was powerful, whether we have in mind the suppression of the Reformation by the emperor's officials in the Netherlands, or the university of Louvain with its loyal Catholic theologians, or the most important stream of moderate Erasmianism, which gave birth to such a sturdy flourishing of Catholic life along the lines of the *devotio moderna*, assisted by the spirit of the Cologne Carthusians (see below, p. 150 f.). In assessing the value of Cologne we must completely disregard the calumnies of the brilliant but quite inaccurate *Letters of Obscure Men*. Even those directly attacked were far worthier than this unrestrained pamphlet asserted. Arnold of Torgern, rector of the university, was held in high esteem by those who knew him. Later he was to assist in producing one of the first reform memoranda for Archbishop Adolf von Schaumberg. The Dominican, John Host of Romberg, a blameless priest, an indefatigable writer, a man full of a new and infectious zeal for the Church, described as 'one of the pillars of the Church in the Rhineland', praised Van Hoogestraeten his former teacher in Rome, who had been calumniated in the *Letters*. In Host's eyes he was the most modest and delightful of them all. It is true that this commendation does not cancel the harshness which characterised the man in his role as inquisitor, but it is in harmony with the evidence we find in his own writings of his ecclesiastical correctness and his corresponding theological soundness and honesty. In this prolix refutation of Luther he was not content with superficial criticism in terms of the scholastic presuppositions, hitherto taken for granted. He went back to St Augustine, for the most part. This proves that he recognised something of the true import of Luther's early published propositions. He blamed the emperor for the fact that most Catholics regarded the conflict as harmless. He displayed the same superiority he had already shown in the Reuchlin affair. He replied, quite unruffled, to the jibes in the *Letters of Obscure Men* about his bad Latin, saying that the substance and not the form was the important thing. The manner in which he said all this was friendly and sympathetic. With a forgiving smile he said, 'These boys do not know what they are doing.'

More important as a religious and ecclesiastical power was the collective effort of the university and the clergy of Cologne against the Reformation led by Gropper, and centred on the Charterhouse of St Barbara, for the Church in Cologne was already the fruitful centre of genuine revival. At this point we intend merely to indicate the foundation of the movement which was profoundly to influence the lower Rhine. The development will be described later.

The cells of new life found in Italy in the Oratory of Divine Love had their counterpart in the region of the lower Rhine in the circles practising the *devotio moderna*, the new devotion with its mystical piety, its humanist–religious language and the pastoral care of small groups – whether living in communities, or kept in touch by the exchange of letters. At the beginning of the Reformation the *devotio moderna* not only persisted, it gathered momentum and, in its own style, became a creative force. This was manifested, for example, in Herzogenbusch in the Netherlands. The prior of the Cologne Charterhouse once said that in that region there were living, both in town and country, 'a mighty host of devout men and women, leading a life of piety such as would be hard to find anywhere else'. These Carthusians of a humanist education loved to use superlatives, and so we must qualify this statement, but the religious zeal of speech and the demonstrable expression in action compel us to admit the existence there of a truly excellent state of religion. The Carthusian prior, Landsberg, in Cologne, had systematically encouraged the spread of such devout community life beyond the walls of his monastery. The Cologne Charterhouse became the centre of an important circle. Its influence far exceeded what was to be expected from its normal spiritual links with other provinces at the time of the Reformation. In this region we have already discovered, therefore, that devout and Christian form of humanism which was to form such a decisive element in the Catholicism of the sixteenth and seventeenth centuries.

Two important preparatory forces in the coming renewal are still to be mentioned. These are, in fact, two mighty events in the Reformation history of the twenties: Adrian VI's admission of guilt at Nuremberg in 1523, through Chieregati, and the Sack of Rome in 1527 by the Spanish–German troops. Adrian Floriszoon of Utrecht was himself of the *devotio moderna*, and one of those who laid the foundations, in this devotion, of the future Catholicism of lower Germany. As pope, he had looked back sadly to those places where its power was acknowledged: 'How much better it would be were we back in Louvain!' When he did make a confession of guilt at Nuremberg this merely provoked the Reformers and the Catholic estates to redouble their attack and their demands. Thus even on the Catholic side this confession has been declared useless. No verdict could be more unchristian, for this confession was no less than a courageous fulfilment of a fundamental commandment of Christianity. The long overdue guilt had been paid, and in some degree the Church's spiritual domestic economy put in order. At all events it was the first precondition of any thoroughgoing ecclesiastical reform. *The confession of guilt by Adrian VI was the real start of Catholic reform in Germany.*

The destruction of Rome in 1527 was an event of world-wide importance. The self-assurance of the Renaissance world was shattered. This was true of the frivolous as of the sinful forms of cultural optimism, and also of the culpable carelessness of the humanists. 'If only this terrible chastisement opens up the way to an improvement of morals and laws, then perhaps our misfortune will not have been so great' (Sadolet). It is obvious that this shock – the divine chastisement prophesied by Savonarola – prepared the way for the Italian, papal and Catholic, conversion. The elements of a new reform-minded religion spread from Rome

E

to the rest of Italy. The advance of the views held by the Theatines was accelerated. Those decisive Catholic and reforming
tendencies that were to be directed in the most varied way to
Germany under the succeeding popes, could now get under way.
In Germany, too, the fall of Rome was seen as a divine judgment,
and it helped to speed up a long overdue change of heart in
Catholic circles.

THREE

Dissolution goes on while a New Mind forms in German Catholicism

I

Whenever we examine the development of the Catholic reform of the sixteenth century, we are struck by the pertinacity of entrenched abuses. Even at the height of the century of saints, in the second half of the Spanish–Italian sixteenth century, and in the first half of the French seventeenth century, one is overwhelmed by a sense of the ineradicability of the spirit of this world from the sanctuary of the Church. How much more, therefore, may we expect to find dark blemishes in the period of the first beginnings of reform!

Let us take a report from 1529 as our starting-point. The earnest and blameless Wimpina from Frankfurt/Oder had castigated the general hypocrisy, avarice and ignorance, in short, the unspirituality, of the clergy, in the bitterest terms. 'These clergy have nothing in common with their sublime vocation but the name. Ignorantly they seek after position, in order to practise sheer indolence, avarice and lasciviousness.' Monks are the worst of all. 'If they knew exactly – as a result of their nocturnal dialogue with the Almighty – how much punishment long dead parents still had to undergo in purgatory, they would make good business out of it, extorting from rich and poor alike. They grab cattle out of the stall, fish, honey, wine, corn, wool, and money from the purse. Bit by bit they take away the necessities of life; they skin people until they are full as leeches. They have not the slightest feeling for the miserable lot of the country folk, even when they see before their very eyes a poor mother who is trying to suckle her child although she is quite famished with hunger and thirst. In their arrogance they imagine that this way of life is their right!'

Although Wimpina makes most important reservations and speaks of many monks who are full of zeal for perfection, who are very angels of humility and piety upon earth, the picture of the rest remains as ghastly as ever.

It was Wimpina, too, who at that time castigated the 'rotten pot-bellied' cardinals for their failure in the battle which it was their duty to fight. Because Luther's sword is raised against none so threateningly as against these 'fat steers, these provosts, prelates and bishops, I would have thought that these protonotaries and archbishops and incumbents of "reserved" dignities, these provosts and deans, would have been quick to rise in defence of their dainty dishes. Thus they could have saved themselves before the collapse, or if they were too incompetent to do so, they ought – so I think – to have handed over their seats and rank on the chapters to the theologians, who have so often enough warned them that they ought to support their groaning tables upon defensive writings' (1523–38).

We shall see that this state of affairs changed in the thirties. Even so, we must note that at that time the spirit of Catholics was not evenly developed. Their forces were not organised. Moreover, the real leaders in the battle were growing old. The immorality and religious weakness of the clergy of all ranks had not been remedied. Some fifteen hundred parishes are said to have been without a pastor. The cathedral chapters seem to have had little awareness of the fact that the Church was fighting for her life. When Morone came to Germany in 1542, the pope's plenipotentiary, bearing serious promises, to carry out, with the bishops, the reform of the clergy, the old archbishop of Augsburg told him: 'If his holiness or his predecessors had tackled this job twenty years ago, they would have been much more successful. Now everything will be fruitless, because even with the best will in the world the bishops are powerless to do anything. Even a council cannot be expected to provide means of correcting such vast disorders.' Albrecht of Mainz took up the same attitude at that time. He accepted the frightful corruption amongst his clergy with resignation: it seemed to be a self-evident and unalterable fact. Optimism was more or less dead even within reforming circles. On 13 March 1536 Sadolet called Contarini's hopes in question: 'Things are not at all what you think they are. Do you think that if there was the slightest hope of accomplishing anything good and wholesome I would not spend myself utterly – to the cross and death? This excellent pope is not stronger than the corruption of the times; for the whole body of Christendom is sick of a disease for which there is no present remedy.' Allowing for the excesses of humanist rhetoric, both in his blame and in his praise of exempting Christians in various professions, Sadolet's judgment is amply corroborated by others. This pessimism, which appears fatalistic at times, itself weakened Catholic power. Basically, however, it was valuable, for it conveyed the notion that this threatening collapse was the judgment of God, a punishment for our sins. Germany and England were already lost to the Church in 1536, and even Italy was rising against Rome.

It certainly cannot be said that in this period a sense of their own power and security characterised Catholics in the arrogantly sinful manner of the twenties. Now the danger was much more clearly perceived.

Pope Paul III himself expressed this sense of hopelessness. He felt that the common life of Christendom had fallen into the greatest and most urgent danger, and that daily the Christian cause was rushing towards disaster. He was right, for the religious and moral situation was catastrophic. We could say that in spite of important fresh starts, things were getting worse. This applied to papal Italy and also to Germany. The reform decrees of 1535, 1536 and 1537, exposed the well-known pre-Reformation sink of iniquity, made plain the various manifestations of disruption, the many-sided religious, theological, pastoral and human failures, and all the unhappy moral and theological distortions of Christian life, and of the priesthood in all its grades. The manifesto of the reform cardinals of 1537 saw the Church tottering beneath the wrath of God. This document openly declared that the basic cause of all the abuses in the Church was the arbitrary and capricious exaggeration of papal power, and the simoniacal sale of spiritual graces for money. The cardinals admitted the unadorned truth that the source of the whole trouble lay in the shameless excesses of the curialists. They also acknowledged in detail all the corruptions of the benefice system – including the special burden this laid upon Germany: the deceitful jargon of the chancelleries with its subtle artifice, exemptions, appeal from bishops to the penitentiary and the datary – where a man could often escape punishment by cash payment – the scandal of dispensations. Not only did they admit these things but demanded their abolition, as Eck had done some fourteen years earlier. Not only did they see that there was sin in all of this: they confessed it. Rome was in a state of sin and giving scandal to strangers. With every justification they complained of the neglect of divine worship – even in St Peter's – of the saying of mass upon mass by ignorant priests, and of public immorality.

Men of the stamp of Contarini and Aleander, who knew how things stood in Germany, had been able to make the curia see that the heretical apostasy in that country was no artificially engineered affair but a genuinely popular movement. To convince the Romans of that fact was indeed an accomplishment.

Since Eck had voiced his complaint and made his proposals in 1523–34, the Reformation had gathered a momentum that took Catholics quite by surprise. The pain of bitter experience thus altered the attitude of those loyal to the Church. Compare Eck's reform proposals with his letters written at the end of the thirties and the beginning of the forties. In the early twenties there still was fairly general hope that purposeful attack with rough and ready methods would overthrow Lutheranism. The world of papal might and right was still a reality. Even the existence of the university of Wittenberg seemed to depend upon that world. To prevent a man studying there all that had to be done was to cut off his benefice. One need only demand that the chancellor and vice-chancellor of every university take an oath against Lutheran doctrine. University privileges could simply be denied Wittenberg, and all courtesy required was a prior bald request to the elector of Saxony. At that time the only thing that Eck laid much store by was the attacking and persecuting power of the really zealous Lutherans.

How this situation changed for the worse! Bishop Marius regarded the spiritual situation as utterly hopeless. In 1536 Morone found the old faith in a state of complete disintegration in Germany. 'Not only in the territories of the Reformed princes, but also in Catholic lands, the people are utterly confused, not knowing which religion to follow.' In 1536 Witzel, who had little sympathy for official Catholicism, attributed this confusion to lukewarmness and despondency. Many were ashamed of their faith. They went to church only under cover of darkness. Hundreds of people had not gone to confession or received the eucharist for several years, and many had died without viaticum.

A catastrophic shortage of priests was reported by Aleander in 1538, Morone in 1536 and 1540, Eck in 1540, and John Fabri O.P. in Heilbronn in 1550. 'A few years ago a monk was as rare as a white raven; now there are none at all. The few priests left are disreputable and ignorant and hence hated even by the few Catholics. If a priest is in the least educated he goes over to the Lutherans. What desolation!' There were more monasteries than there were monks, and many had become dilapidated or secularised. When Peter Faber, S.J., came to Worms in 1540 and learned all about the pitiable condition of Germany, he reported to Rome that his only surprise was that there were not two or three times as many heretics. In 1550 Nadal and Canisius were amazed to find that the whole of Vienna was not Lutheran. 'What else could one expect when the clergy are so corrupt?' Nadal, the Jesuit, wrote from Austria in 1550 to say that the schoolteachers even in Catholic districts were normally Lutherans, and were teaching the children the Lutheran catechism.

The liturgical piety of the people was in harmony with this. Its core, the mass, had become very largely an external observance. The common practice was to leave before the end – after the Gospel, during the sermon, or immediately after the consecration. There were very many who never thought of visiting a church to pray. People brought birds and dogs, as if going to the hunt. Everyone chattered and moved about – canons, priests, sacristans and the faithful. The church had become a rendezvous and a place of entertainment.

Once again we touch on a delicate point: the question whether there is any real value in regular and frequent public worship. Even in the little parish of Hildpoltstein, served by the zealous Father May, where there was a special devotion to the Blessed Sacrament, in the form of the Mass of the Angels, we can gain little knowledge from this regular worship about the personal piety of priests and people, to say nothing of a sacrificial congregation gathered round the Lord's Table. Communion once a year seems to have been the rule. At a time when the number of masses was astronomical – Charles V had 30,000 said for the repose of his soul – it could happen that a visitator found consecrated particles being eaten by maggots, or damp and adhering to one another, or black with age.

Sad to say, such expressions of religious debility were not confined to the sphere of practice. People's ideas about the faith, too, had corrupted. The true doctrine of the mass as the re-presentation of our Lord's sacrifice was not to be found everywhere, nor were the graces that ought to have flowed from it into the lives of the faithful. The inordinate stress upon man's good works was not a matter of mere practice but had become fixed liturgically and in popular theology. Various reforming synods, such as had taken place relatively frequently, especially as a result of the imperial Reformation statement of 1548, all complained of the infiltration of inaccurate texts into the rite of the mass, and of superstitious notions concerning the efficacy of the mass. Many people saw in the mass a powerful instrument to guarantee, in a magical way, all manner of tangible and intangible results. Old extravagant doctrines of the *fruits of the mass*, had become fairly stereotyped. Looking at the sacred Host produced specially miraculous results, and so people crowded round the alter, or round the priest as he left the altar in order at least to be fanned by the corporal upon which the Host had lain. Attendance at mass gave protection against sudden accident, in particular against sudden death. Every mass released one soul from purgatory, converted one sinner and prevented one person from committing mortal sin. After hearing mass a repentant sinner died as though he had received Holy Communion. The mass assured that one would receive the last sacraments. All the time one was praying during mass for a soul in purgatory, that soul's pains were in abeyance. The food and drink taken after hearing mass were more nutritive than at other times. During the time of hearing mass one did not age. The mass made child-bearing easier, and brought prosperity.

As with the popular theological preaching of indulgences, so these fruits of the mass were proclaimed with astonishing certainty, and advertised with offensive clamour. Attention was one-sidedly turned to the effects of the mass, and religious conditions were pushed into the background. Moral earnestness was bound to suffer. This, too, gives a clue to the reason for the multiplication of masses, as it does to the discontinuance of the celebration of mass, once this sub-Christian concept of it had been exposed in all its emptiness by Luther, who for his part went to the opposite extreme of fatal one-sidedness.

In the sixteenth century there was wide open opportunity for the development of this externalised concept. Regular and systematic religious instruction of children by the parish priest was as yet unknown. It was not given even in school. Religious education was a matter entirely for parents and godparents. Catechesis for adults on Sunday or the specially interpolated instruction on Holy Communion at Easter must have been very scant. And so it came about that at the end of this period Witzel considered the religious education of children to be deplorable. Education was producing Turks, not Christians. In the same strain in 1540 Eck noted a serious decline in piety amongst both laity and clergy. Those who used to go to confession twice in Lent, now as a rule went but once. The rules of fasting were regarded as of no importance. Celebration of mass had become less frequent or had ceased altogether, as had the saying of the breviary. In short, the precepts of the Church were no longer taken seriously. Rules were tolerated no longer. With itching ears people listened to the novelties of those limping teachers who, running with the hare and hunting with the hounds, produced a mixture of Catholicism and heresy. In 1540 Morone reported to Rome that the bishops were prepared to make all sorts of concessions. They would have been content with the assurance that the Reformers would appropriate no more Church property. These were the bishops indicted by the cardinals' memorandum for living far from their flocks and handing over their charges to hirelings; these were the

bishops to whom their colleague, Hosius of Ermland, imputed
the sole blame for the state of the Church, at the same time painting a shocking picture of their way of life; these were the bishops
whose stubborn evasions concerning the coming council had to
be fought by Paul III. If any bishop, like Hosius, remained
faithful and true, he found none to stand by him on his chapter;
in his battle against the Reformation they all left him in the lurch.

The same state of affairs prevailed amongst the intemperate
and theologically ignorant lower clergy. In 1539 Cochlaeus
complained that nearly all of the parish priests in Saxony – and
they were a much better lot than those in the Rhineland – were
living in concubinage. He considered this evil to be, in general,
unavoidable. The priests could not do without housekeepers. In
the end of the day they preferred to give up their incomes rather
than the woman; the laity, however, would rather have married
priests than priests living in concubinage.

There were clergy, however, who had given up the old faith
so completely, that they only went through the outward motions of
celebrating. Others were arraigned for heresy and, more frequently, for fortune-telling.

Only with great effort could clerical life be restored to its
earlier honourable condition. The difficulty was greatly increased
by the bad example of the members of the curia, with their
courtesans and their traffic in benefices. There were men who
were not content with 'twenty, or even thirty, benefices, but
who were daily resigning benefices in return for pensions, selling
them with the right of resale, and who the very next day would
buy new benefices with which they once again began to trade . . .'.
Eck goes on: 'I knew of one in the time of Leo X, who enumerated
for us his thirty-nine benefices and provostries.' In the ranks of
twenty-four, thirty or forty canons, one might count no more
than five or six ordained priests. Eck knew of a case where there
were only five priests on a cathedral chapter of fifty-four men,
and the aristocrats amongst them held the fattest livings. Worse
still, in Eck's eyes, was the fact that many of them never prayed
at all, while the others very rarely observed the Hours. Many,
too, were Lutherans, possessed and read Luther's books, and
studied as canons in Wittenberg, in full sympathy with the Reformation. Very rarely did they reside in their livings, rarer still

were their visits to church, least of all to the choir. When money was being disbursed they came to collect their share, and then vanished speedily – *ut canis ex Nilo*. Very often the dean himself was not a priest, 'A few days ago I heard of one church where neither the bishop, nor the provost, nor the dean, was a priest.'

Danger threatened from another side also. Renegade monks tried to find positions in the service of the Church. Real or pretended papal dispensations to live outside the monastery made these attempts dangerous.

Such corruption in the clergy had quickly aroused the hatred of the people, and a serious shortage of priests resulted. From two opposite causes there came about a terrible decline of Catholic schools and theological faculties. Whereas on the Protestant side the leading educator in Strasburg followed the method of the Brothers of the Common Life – his own teachers – with its principle of unity, the condition of Catholic schools was almost hopeless. There was no reorganisation, and there were no new foundations. During the forties in Cologne there was only one master who taught occasionally, and at times the theological lectures stopped completely. Ingolstadt was better off on account of Eck. After his death only one professor of theology remained, and when he died there was no one teaching theology from 1546–48. In Vienna things were much the same. In Freiburg there had been only two professors since 1531. 'The Church's servants are all dying out, and no new ones take their place . . ., the churches are dirty and dilapidated – people would not keep a horse in such a place – broken images of the saints only arouse ridicule.'

We could say that the colossal process of clerical, moral, religious and ecclesiastical corruption had run the full gamut.

This condition persisted in all essentials until the very end of the period we are studying. In 1555 the Jesuit, Nadal, described the state of Catholic districts as almost hopeless. There were neither religious nor theologians, with the result that the Catholic princes and bishops did not know what to do. From sheer necessity, good Catholics tolerated married priests and semi-Lutheran preachers. All the inns were full of the writings of Luther and other heretics. Such writings were being read by women and children. This was all going on, moreover, in regions that still called themselves Catholic. Scarcely a Catholic in Germany was producing controversial writings any longer, and the older Catholic works were not being printed and were hard to find. Catholics were saying, therefore, that there was nothing to read except heretical literature. Catholic theologians everywhere were themselves reading these books and were getting into a state of utter theological confusion.

We must take note how these various symptoms of disintegration persisted strongly for many decades longer. Even after a great deal of Catholic reform had been accomplished, Catholic corruption was still being described, as, for example, in the memoranda during the seventies of the cardinal archbishop of Augsburg, Otto, Truchsess of Waldburg, whose deep pessimism in 1542 we have already noted. He pointed out that on the one hand the libertine and unchristian spirit of the Renaissance advanced with quite undiminished vigour, while on the other, the spirit of the heretical Reformation had become powerfully established in the ranks of the Catholics. The curia was still regarded as the enemy and exploiter of Germany. Its very name – especially that of the Roman curia – roused the wrath even of Catholics – and all the more because the vicious life of the Roman clergy went on and was well known in Germany.

Protestantism had made vast inroads into the lower and higher clergy. Not only were there many Protestant sympathisers amongst the cathedral canons but many were actually Lutheran or Calvinist heretics. This gave rise directly to another danger. These men would elect heretical bishops. 'This applies, as is well known, to Mainz, Cologne, Strasburg, Würzburg, Bamberg and other places.'

As formerly, the bishops took no care of their flocks. Once again Cologne was threatened by the uxorious Gebhard Truchsess of Waldburg. His Bavarian Catholic successors received no less exalted orders than he. The bishop chosen for Bamberg swore loyalty to Trent, it is true, but did not live accordingly and permitted his clergy to marry. Things were the same in the monasteries (especially in Austria and Bohemia) as a result of lay abbots. These men were not elected properly, but merely installed by the princes on making some kind of profession without asking for any confirmation or dispensation from Rome. The deeply rooted public corruption of the German secular and regular clergy still went on. Their lives were an enormous scandal, arousing nothing but contempt, hatred and revolt. The people, however, wanted priests; and if there were no Catholic priests, they turned to heretical ones. The records for 1562 show that in Bavaria, of a hundred priests, only three or four were without concubines. In 1568 Canisius estimated the figure at barely ten per diocese. All sense of the responsibilities of their vocation had gone. 'The evil of the German Catholic clergy and their ignorance have brought the plague of heresy to Germany.' And so the reforming activities of zealous bishops were crippled by the force of circumstances. Not one bishop but was compelled to deal with many simoniacal, depraved, criminal, concubinarist and drunken apostates, among his clergy.

In Germany the monastic system faced complete collapse. The number of monks had mightily declined; and those who were left lived more like denizens of the underworld than inhabitants of a cloister. There were whole monastic communities who had given way to luxury and unchastity. What a scandal this was to the people, and how the Church must thereby have become hated by Catholics and heretics alike. Harsh measures alone could have done any good. In 1523 Eck had proposed that completely or partially apostate Augustinian eremites should be treated as the Templars had been earlier: they should be completely suppressed and their houses turned into hospitals, or used for some other charitable purpose. In the seventies this method was in fact applied as a last resort to many spiritually corrupt Catholic monasteries.

Obviously, such priests could provide nothing at all in the way of pastoral care of the people. Hence the colossal ignorance of German Catholics of religion; hence, too, their indifference to religion and contempt for the Church. In the seventies one commentator considered conditions within the Church to be as big a danger as the Lutheran heresy without.

The worst German disease of all was the nobility's monopoly of high ecclesiastical offices. Hence we see the source of most of the evils. Unless this could be corrected, there would be no hope of Germany ever having good bishops, for they would be recruited solely from a wholly degenerate aristocracy. Amongst the members of the aristocratic chapters – which, moreover, were always at loggerheads with their bishops – were to be found neither morals, piety, learning nor virtue. The interest of these gentlemen centred almost exclusively upon drinking, hunting and women. They could not have set a worse example. Hardly ever could they be seen in church. If they did appear it was to carry off their share of some particularly lucrative tax, and then they would pass the time walking about outside the choir engaged in idle chatter, even while mass was being said by their vicars – no doubt with little enough devotion in any case. There were even churches where – at least on working days – the canons met socially in the chapter house during the time of the choral Office, in order to devise some pretext for being seen around the church.

'As well as the places in the chapters of the greater cathedral churches, they lay claim to all the best prelacies, prebends, parishes, and benefices throughout the diocese. They use the revenues to keep dogs, horses, loose women, and to provide a most luxurious way of life. The more avaricious collect benefices in order to enrich their relatives. And so there are no decent livings left for any devout and learned priest (from the burgess class).' Nothing was so rare as a worthy priest amongst the prelates. How could men of such birth be expected to sing an antiphon or recite a versicle? It was the money they were after. Divine worship could be left to the burgesses. It was said: 'The vicars go to church on behalf of the canons, and the canons represent their chaplains in hell.'

Without exception these are all Catholic voices.

True: in these descriptions we detect a certain painful lack of precision and some degree of unrestrained desire to exaggerate, despite an honest solicitude. Quite generally we can affirm, that the reform proposals, attached to the one-sidedly imprecise condemnations, paint a much brighter picture – equally imprecise.

None the less, the final score is undoubtedly much the same. On all sides in the seventies, within the lower and higher clergy, secular and regular, in the curia, whether in Germany or at Rome, amongst still Catholic people, the Church's existence was threatened as much as it was from heresy outside. We need not even begin to speak of any attempt to win back what had been lost. Particularly disastrous was the return – half a century after the storm had broken – to the old methods of covering things up and procrastinating. 'In the end one must dare to take resolute action. One must begin to act and cease endless and fruitless consultations. One ought, prudently and slowly, to remove at least the worst clerical scandals.' In 1573 the pope was again urgently advised to take these things seriously – especially prayer, sacrifice, the mass and fasting – to think of nothing except the salvation of souls. An end to hesitation and lost opportunities! Now is the time to awake and to get on with the work of Christ!

We can make what deductions we will: the state of the Church and of religion must have been unusually bad if in the seventies, after countless attempts at renewal, it could still be described in these terms. What might be called a good Catholic atmosphere, sustained from the richness of tradition, had largely disappeared from the people as from theology.

Where was Catholic self-assurance strong enough to survive, with power and creative energy?

The unexpected spread of the Reformation – thought to be impossible – and the knowledge of the incurable, apparently inevitably advancing, corruption within the Church, had shattered the self-assurance of Catholics. In order to understand the Catholic revival, it is necessary to observe how this salutary, if crippling, knowledge penetrated even quite stubborn people in a very special way. This effect was notably apparent, for example, in a ruthless, fanatical anti-heretic like Pope Paul IV. Even he was troubled by fear of the Reformation erupting in Spain, and even more by fear that heresy might approach the chair of Peter through the ranks of the cardinals. For a Catholic, there could have been no clearer expression of fear that the Church was collapsing, than this. This explains Paul IV's inhumanly harsh distrust of Morone and Pole, and his persecution mania. 'Truth to tell: we want to face the danger that threatened even in the last conclave, and take precautions in our own lifetime, that the devil cannot in time to come place one of his own upon the chair of Peter.'

Do these admissions not refute our assertion made earlier

(p. 95 f.)? Do they not justify the common view of Reformation history which we contested? That is not so, for we must not lose sight of the elementary fact, that in a large community healing and rebirth come about only very slowly, in the humble obscurity of a thousand small beginnings. We must remember also, that the long period of evil decay would have to be balanced by a correspondingly long period of restoration punctuated by failures. Genuine and powerful advance was bound to be surrounded on all sides by even greater corruption and decay. Such terrible collapse within the Church does not make demonstrable positive Catholic energies any less real. We must see both sides of the picture, and allow neither aspect to disappear from mind.

Many chronicles show us that throughout the Reformation period there was much strong, living attachment to the Church and to her doctrines – an attachment that was far from mere habit. Many monasteries provided, in all of their members, a shining example of true Christian life according to their vows. Individual monks in various orders displayed a zeal for piety and a mystical grasp of the facts of salvation, and this life was reflected in a considerable output of edifying literature. The creative originality of these efforts may not have been outstanding but it was extraordinarily widespread. It would be a denial of the plain facts to say that the intimate, practical and literary effort that went into the production of this contemplative devotional writing, was sheer externalism, for this work was itself a prayer in the deepest sense.

On the other hand, the colossal threat which we have described was the very thing that really aroused for the first time the undaunted courage of the Catholic champions and reformers, and the excessive confidence of the middle party. None of these men can be suspected of failing to recognise the real situation and the terrible difficulties facing Catholic reform. In so far as concerned assistance from outside – as with the Jesuits – any underestimation of the difficulties was soon dispelled. That is to say: they all possessed a spirit of faithful devotion, and the ability to go through with their programme to the bitter end. Public opinion was burdened with scepticism. First of all, faith in the future would have to be restored. The road out of the Church was the one claimed to be *modern* and self-evidently *better*. The overwhelming power of this public opinion would have to be countered, values reversed, men's respect regained. Gradually a *movement of minds* towards the Catholic Church would have to be initiated. A growing stream of conversions back to Catholicism must arise, and young blood especially would have to flow into the Church.

Which were the centres which still possessed enough Catholic life to attempt – not necessarily to accomplish – this gigantic task?

Obviously they were those we have already noted in the previous section of Part Three as centres of conservation and renewal: individual parishes and monasteries, which became the focus of a vigorous Catholic life, the literary champions, diocesan synods, the Roman nuncios. As we have said, however, in many places, as the sense of impending crisis grew, the work became more organised and more intense. That indefinable something emerged, that always dominated the revolution, that something which we call *novelty*. (Not for nothing is renewal in many forms a basic reality of the gospel of Jesus Christ.) This novelty created for itself new energies and new forms, or it was a new energy and a new form at once, and this in turn produced a new mentality.

Renewal of life always proceeds outwards from small beginnings in a few cells; but new growth breaks through opposition only when a number of these power nuclei coalesce to form a core. The renewal of Catholic life in the forties and fifties, which provided the foundation for further renewal, is a clear proof of this principle. Only the work of Bishop Hosius of Ermland rested very largely upon his own shoulders and no one else's. All other significant beginnings, which heralded a real change, were the work of an organised coalition of forces: the *devotio moderna*, the Jesuits, Trent.

Over and above this there was a specific Catholic force which elevated all activity in like manner. In its continuance, its fresh start, and in its blossoming, Catholic life was radically dependent upon its link with the Church – that is to say, all of the Catholic preachers, writers, pastors and people were closely linked with the Church. Their strength grew as this link grew firmer. Hence it was an expression of the power of anonymity, of objectivity, of loyalty. And so in the Catholic revival of the sixteenth century it was not just the frequently mediocre performance of individuals but the antecedently given doctrine and power of the Church that was at work. People stood up for a fundamentally traditional thing, not for something invented – as Luther did – or for a change of mind and heart based upon a rediscovery of the Word and one's private belief – as did the Protestants. The Catholic attitude was imbued with the irrational power of anonymous activity, of anonymous obedience. In antithesis to an often painfully ruthless contempt of tradition amongst the Reformers, we see the delightful strength of the sense of loyalty to what has come down from our fathers. This played an important part in the conflict.

Despite the continuing decay of the Church and even in the midst of that decay there were Christian and priestly souls amongst the clergy and laity – men like the magnificent Carthusians of Cologne 'who were horrified at the irrevocable loss of souls, who were full of pain at the contempt of God and consumed with the zeal of his house', men full of solicitude for the orthodoxy of their city of Cologne, and who sought new means of combating old evils. The longing still burned that the Church would be renewed in all her ancient purity and love. This thought was moulded into an urgent prayer by Landsberg, one of the Cologne Carthusians, who wished specially that the order would return to its original strictness, so that they would perform in deeds what they preached by word of mouth, instead of merely being men distinguished from others by their dress. Although still relatively few, the number of priests for whom prayer and the care of the faithful were urgent necessities, effectively increased.

How far all this was from a merely sceptical, negative criticism of the situation! We now find an attitude that was fundamentally religious. If both before and after Christian values were defective, at this period hunger after righteousness became apparent. Christian life in its true essence – to live in, and like, Christ' – was on the increase. Part of the work that contributed to this improvement was more and more directly connected with prayer. As St Theresa of Avila in Spain had explicitly included in her programme prayer for the defenders of the Church against heresy, for preachers and learned people, so the Jesuits announced a like intention at Regensburg in 1542.

Now we must describe this work of reconstruction as it actually progressed, in all its richness, and in its failures.

FOUR

Catholic Reconstruction

Catholic reform on any large scale in Germany could not be carried out without help from the south. This is the sad fact revealed by even the most superficial survey of Catholic collapse and of the beginnings of Catholic revival after, say, the middle thirties. The inner logic of the ecclesiastical situation in Germany and in Italy made it impossible for things to be otherwise.

I

The forces from the south were not the only ones in Germany, but they utterly predominated. To understand how these forces reached out beyond the Alps we must first sketch the beginnings of the revival of the Church in Rome and Italy.

It is one of the great facts of Church history that really comprehensive Catholic reforming energies did not by any means originate at the papal centre of things; equally, however, they bore great fruit only after they had been affirmed, unified and developed according to a uniform plan by the curia.

The growth of Catholic reform in the sixteenth century is a manifold proof of the fact. This growth, in so far as it merits direct world historical significance, began in Spain and Italy amidst the poisonous atmosphere prevailing there under Alexander VI. It began in small, insignificant non-official circles, which faithfully served the end of self-sanctification. The voice of Savanarola still resounded in the various forms of the Oratory of Divine Love. What mighty Christian power was there, how alive the Church was in these circles, were demonstrated above all by the Theatines who in 1524 had been born of this spirit (allied to the *devotio moderna* and to Christian humanism). The range of formative possibilities, from mighty inquisitor to Franciscan-like prayer, was shown in two members, Giampietro Carafa, later to become Paul IV, and Gaetano da Tiene. Many of its members clearly displayed a fullness of apostolic virtue. They made a clean break with Mammon and the immorality of the times. As bishops, they were no luxurious lords but faithful shepherds of souls.

As is well known these forces were very slow to make themselves felt at the curia. We have already learned from Aleander how little religion there was in that quarter. There was, it is true, an outstanding man at the curia – Cardinal Cajetan, whom we encountered, dealing with Luther in Augsburg in 1518. He was the most important Catholic theologian of the first half of the sixteenth century, and his literary polemic and his power as a reformer within the Church were of a much higher order than his performance in Augsburg in 1518 might lead us to suppose. It is not enough merely to stress his affinity with curialism. It was Cajetan who succeeded in having the German Adrian VI elected pope. This alone should give us food for thought, and indeed his fearless reform proposals, too, ought to win our sympathy. He was by no means the ranter that Luther made him out to be at Augsburg. He was a most modest man. That is why the fate of the German Franciscan, Schatzgeyer, overtook him also: in that coarse age his voice was not strong enough to be heard, certainly not above the din of Reformed polemics. His Thomist theological clarity was far removed from rigid traditional rigorism – as represented, say, by Ambrosius Catharinus Politus and Wimpina. This Thomist and curial cardinal had an open mind. He remained friendly with Erasmus, found the Vulgate inadequate, and upheld the rights of free criticism even against the testimony of the Fathers and tradition.

Pope Clement VII was, as we have learned, a hindrance to Church reform. None the less, even during this most disastrous

pontificate in the history of the Church the objective record can
show signs of the beginnings of reform. When in November 1523
this Medici came to the throne, Carafa obtained his influential
appointment, and Giberti, a man with eminent potentialities for
religious reform, became secretary of state.

The real change came with Paul III (1533–49). This scion
of the Farnese family who became pope at the age of sixty-seven,
was a product of Renaissance Rome at its worst. His elevation to
the rank of cardinal by Alexander VI was directly the result of the
shadiest goings on within the sanctuary. And yet it was he who
personally introduced Church reform in that age. Unfortunately,
he did not belie his pagan origin and become a converted sinner;
but he was a reforming pope. He found himself at a point of
transition. Nor was the change effected against his will, or merely
in small tactical regulations. The severe criticism launched
against him is supported by no direct evidence, although it is
made more plausible by the unapproachability of this pope,
and his unrestrained nepotism in the service of Farnese family
politics. But direct evidence is lacking. (Even his equivocal
attitude in the matter of the council can be excused, because the
chief opposition came from France.) In spite of all later lapses,
he confirmed the good opinion we have of his desire for reform;
he welcomed the forces of renewal that were surging within the
Church, directed these, in face of enormous difficulties, into the
most critical area of the curia, and kept them there in spite of
opposition. The convocation of the reforming cardinals, the
confirmation of the Jesuit order, and the convocation of the
Council of Trent, were three actions, each having world-wide
effects, and together altering the face of the world. Paul III's
unhappy retrogression into fatal politicising of the leadership of
the Church – especially towards the end of the forties – was unable
to destroy the ecclesiastical reform he had set in motion. The
very limited appreciation which the Protestantism of the time had
of this reform does not alter the facts. When the magnificent
reform decree of the papal commission of cardinals was published
in 1537, people would not take this intention to reform seriously.
A biting satire entitled *Beelzebub, To the Holy Papal Church*, was
being circulated (1537). Luther for his part poured scorn upon

men like Contarini, Carafa and Sadolet. They were 'liars, desperate boys, who were reforming the Church with foxes' tails. One ought to pray that the pope's name be dishonoured and cursed, along with his god, the devil.' In those days, Evangelical polemic displayed little of the true Christian spirit that is ready to applaud any sign of improvement. Worldly opposition at the curia itself adopted a similar contempt for the attempts at reform. But uncompromising Christian fervour had now manifested itself in great style at the centre of the Church. Then came the confession of guilt by Adrian VI and the change of heart within the Church, which he had initiated.

Suddenly we are surprised by the appearance of a host of important personalities: Carafa, Giberti, Morone, Cervini, Reginald Pole, and most important of all, Cardinal Gasparo Contarini. He had come to Germany, and had read Luther's writings. This layman is one of the most valuable illustrations of the widespread interest in theology that existed in those days far beyond the ranks of professional theologians. At an early age he became a man of great independence of mind, reading, with equal ease, the Latin and Greek Fathers and St Thomas.

When he was offered a cardinal's hat he considered whether he ought not to refuse it. This aristocratic Venetian had no interest in worldly position or pleasure. In the circles in which he moved, men had rediscovered the gospel in the spirit of the Church. They went back to the heart of Christianity (cf. the book *De benificio della morte di Christo*). Contarini, who, like Pole, Giberti and Cortese, advocated the use of peaceful methods against the Reformers, and who none the less wanted to defend the Church, were deeply possessed by the notion of the freedom of the Christian man. 'The power of the pope, as inflated into tyranny by the extreme curialists, is contrary to the law of Christ, which is a law of freedom. The rule of the pope is a rule of reason over freely created men. . . . It is the theories of the extreme curialists which have provoked such books as *On the Babylonian Captivity of the Church.* . . . If you (the pope) rule according to the rule of reason you will become "free in a pre-eminent sense".'

In order to arrive at a true estimate of the work done by these men of the reform, we must see clearly how deeply all the reforming circles were imbued with a spirit of earnest and increasing confesssion of guilt, and of the real intention to reform. The numerous memoranda concerning the necessity of reform in the Church, which none had dared to lay before Clement VII, now emerged in the light of day. Above all, there was Contarini's circle which embraced all of those who represented the power in Paul III's reform commission: Carafa, Cortese, Giberti, Sadolet, Fregoso, Reginald Pole, Aleander and Tommaso Badia. All of these men were able to distinguish between the essence of the Church and the individuals who embodied that essence. No matter how far corruption had eaten into the Church, it still remained their mother. 'I can see our holy mother, the Church, upon whom our salvation depends, has become so transformed that she seems to bear no mark of the gospel, and no trace of humility, austerity, continence, or apostolic power.'

It is specially noteworthy that much reform work was done by laymen. The above quotation is from the lay jurist, Giovan Battista Caccia of Novar. One of the prime movers, Contarini, 'the unique', as his contemporaries called him, and Reginald Pole, although laymen, were both made cardinals.

What has all this to do with the situation in Germany?

There can be no doubt at all that Paul III's reform measures were stimulated in part by the conditions prevailing in Germany. The German nuncio who was reporting in Rome in 1535 stressed the necessity of reform. Similarly, Aleander and Contarini, advocated reform on the first reform commission, as did Peter van der Vorst, the Dutchman.

On the other hand, the beginnings of reform in Italy reacted in many ways upon Germany. Schöneberg sent the cardinals' memorandum to Germany by a confidential messenger (Cochlaeus?). A special case is seen in the effect the reform had upon German (as upon Italian) humanism. Unlike Adrian VI, Paul III did not offend the humanists. He opened up the way for the highly significant diversion of pagan humanism into ecclesiastical channels – with all the attendant dangers. The unbelieving and frivolous Pietro Bembo, elevated to the rank of cardinal, slowly became converted. His case was typical of the transformation of similar influential figures, and their assimilation into the work of the Church. He exerted an influence upon humanists north and south of the Alps.

The personal influence of outstanding Italians upon Germany was extraordinarily important. Men like Aleander, Cajetan, Morone and Contarini provided a wealth of vital influence. Contarini, in particular, was a powerful force in the German Catholic development. Impossible as it is to understand Contarini apart from his lectures on Luther, it is equally impossible to disentangle him from the above-mentioned Italian foundations of Catholic reform. As early as 1522, as Venetian ambassador to Spain, he had come in contact with the young Charles V. In 1541 at Regensburg he was the true representative of the spirit of the religious conversations, and a man after the emporer's own heart.

In addition, the mighty unity of Catholic polemic, both in its theological, and in its humanist–intellectual, aspect overlapped all territorial frontiers. Luther's literary adversaries in Italy had many links – through the orders with their multi-national member-ship – with controversial theology in Germany, and vice versa. We repeatedly discover theologians on both sides of the Alps being forced to turn their attention to the Roman curia and to the pope.

It was the council, however, which became the strongest and deepest link between German and Roman efforts at Catholic reform, for the whole concept of a council was to be made a central point of discussion precisely in Germany, by the emperor.

II

It is the result of a propitious accident that parishes watched over by a capable pastor as at Ingolstadt, Hildpoltstein or Mainz, have become known to us in some detail. These may be taken, however, as representative of a number of such healthy and loyal parishes, and we may speak, therefore, of a sizeable amount of conservative and edifying activity in parishes that remained in possession of the ancient faith.

We would have to assemble the detail systematically, in order to construct this picture. It would be most important, too, for us to know precisely, at how many centres during the colossal apostasy a zealous preacher gathered thousands around him, Sunday by Sunday, to be instructed in Catholic doctrine – as, for example in the cathedral parish at Regensburg, where between two and three thousand gathered regularly to hear Paul Hirschpeck preaching.

In the not so very thin ranks of bishops who actively served the Church, there were at least two, who achieved more than average eminence by their important work for the reformation of the Catholic clergy. These were Otto Truchsess, bishop of Augsburg, and Stanislaus Hosius, bishop of Ermland. The first became a cardinal in 1544, the second in 1561.

The most important work of the bishop of Augsburg, who died in 1573, was done after the end of the period with which we are immediately concerned. None the less, the work he did from the early forties onwards merits our attention. The two diocesan synods of 1543 and 1548 plus a host of pastoral instruction to his clergy made his diocese a centre of practical Catholic reform. By his official connections with Charles V and Paul III he was able also to extend his influence further afield through the *Reichstags* of 1544, 1545 and 1555. He received encouragement from the most important Catholics of his time. His whole view of life was greatly deepened by the retreat which he made under the direction of the Jesuit, Claude Jajus. He also employed this man directly in his undertakings. He appointed Canisius cathedral preacher in Augsburg. He founded a house of studies for aspirants to the priesthood, which in 1554 was elevated to the status of a university. Real fruit came, however, after 1563, when the university passed into the hands of the Jesuits.

The most important individual contribution to Church reform in Germany at that time came from Stanislaus Hosius. His work, too, belongs, strictly speaking, to a later period, but it provides the purest representation of the Catholic reconstruction of our period too, both in its uniqueness and in its limitations. His pastoral work, his organisation of reconstruction, his resolute defence of the faith, his piety and his personal life, were all exemplary. His literary polemic, his ascetic edificatory theology, and his pastoral theological writings, were on an amazing scale. No one else in Germany at that time could come near him for sheer output. Nor did anyone reach a wider public – not even Eck with his *Enchiridion*. Hosius was a great personality in his own right, and completely the product of loyal, orthodox churchmanship. He introduced a fresh spirit, and remoulded everything. In all of the departments mentioned, however, we must allow our praises to stop short of the superlatives that are appropriate only to true creative genius. His literary work will enable us to return later to discuss his importance in another context.

We cannot possibly discuss here the mighty labours performed by the papal nuncios in the rebuilding of Catholic Germany during the forties and fifties of the century. We have already got to know what manner of man Aleander was, and the work he did. A man like Morone, however, made his influence felt far beyond the realm of politics and diplomacy. In harmony with the programme of the new cardinals made by Paul III, he achieved true reform within the Church. Of this we have many notable proofs: his conversations with Albrecht of Mainz concerning the reform of the clergy; his visitations in various German cities like Augsburg, Speyer and so on. We must admit that he was fortunate to have made the acquaintance of Peter Faber in Worms, for this man, in many ways, was the father of the emergent reform in Germany. Morone did not hesitate to request the unrestricted services of him and several other Jesuits for Germany. His instructions to Dr Vauchop and Fr Jajus, S.J., throw light on this co-operation.

Even in Morone's case this work displayed all the more power as he did it in ever-increasing knowledge of the almost hopeless state of religion in Germany. 'Germany inclines more than ever to Lutheranism, and one might think that God himself encourages this by every means.'

We can do no more than mention the discussions in the dioceses, especially the discussions about the operation of diocesan synods – following the *Reichstag* in Augsburg in 1547–48. The most important work done along these lines – at the Synod of Cologne – will have to be discussed later. Any exhaustive and comprehensive exposition of this subject would certainly reveal a host of small fresh enterprises, which prepared the soil for Catholic revival.

III

Let us be content with a more detailed description of that aspect of reconstruction in the Church in which can be seen a concentration of energies producing fruitful circles of renewal, or which most instructively reveals the course of events. The Jesuits exemplify the first category, Catholic controversial theology the second. In this period Trent provided a programme of union, and so will be discussed in its own proper context.

Without a doubt, to the Jesuits must be attributed the principal achievements in the Catholic revival – in Germany as elsewhere. These achievements did not come about, however, by this foreign Society of Jesus laying entirely new foundations. What happened was rather that the new energies of the disciples of Ignatius found important predecessors in late medieval forms of German piety, and made full use of those vehicles which they found ready to hand. The great contribution of the Church historian from Bonn, Joseph Greven, was to draw attention to this important link by highlighting the significant example of the Cologne Carthusians.

We all too easily forget that the humanist demand for a new Christianity at first came from Catholic voices. In many ways it remained a Catholic demand. After what has been said in Volume I about the unchristian elements in humanism, we are unlikely to misunderstand this statement. We must not, however, rule out the courageous reform proposals of Geiler, Wimpfeling, Trithemius, Peutinger and Aleander, just because for the time being they yielded no fruit. In retrospect we can see how they contained the germ of later mighty reforms. Even the spiritualisation of Erasmus, which has to be regarded primarily as disruptive of dogma, was closely akin to the efforts of the *devotio moderna*.

The encounter of the Jesuits with the Catholic forces of the age likewise took place through humanism. This happened in Germany in Cologne. More precisely: it happened through forces at work in the region of the lower Rhine, that is through the form of humanist piety which found its most productive root and most valuable expression in the *devotio moderna*. This means that the new piety and the pastoral work of the Jesuits made contact with the oldest forms of reform movement we know in the Church in the modern period, that organic unity was perfectly assured, and, what is more, within Germany.

This linking up reached into those reforming energies and endeavours within the Church, which were directly associated with the Reformation. These attempts at reform began officially with the Dutch pope Adrian VI. He had, as his trusted co-operator, van Heeze, also a Dutchman. As in Rome, so in Lüttich after Adrian's death, van Heeze laboured diligently for Catholic reform. From the point of view of the history of development, the most important thing was his link with the Cologne Carthusians; for these men became the most important focus on the lower Rhine of vigorous Catholic devotional life and conscious Catholic reform. In and through them the work of the Jesuits first attained real and permanent significance for Germany.

It was no accident that the Cologne Carthusians were the very people to be able to produce such a remarkably extensive effect. They were at once the architects and the fruit of a Catholic region. The city of Cologne was, and remained, Catholic. It was renowned for its loyalty to the Church. The city itself was proudly aware of this fact, and the Carthusians praised it in their edition of Dionysius.

The fact must not be disguised, however, that this 'unshakeable Catholic' disposition amongst wide circles in Cologne, had a political motive as well. A secularisation of endowments could have meant the destruction of the political independence of the city. 'Loyalty to the old Church' not only 'assured them of their freedom as an imperial burgh' but was a means to that freedom.

The Cologne Carthusians themselves tell us that at the beginning of the sixteenth century the order of St Bruno no longer stood at the high level of its original austerity; but, with the exception of a few individuals, who were punished as they deserved, their ranks were never sullied by the same sinful corruption that was apparent all around. The Carthusians were still in general blameless monks, although they may have interpreted their ideal differently from their medieval brethren.

For a long time a progressive movement had been at work amongst the Carthusians. Since the late Middle Ages this order had 'not only reformed individuals, but whole monasteries belonging to other orders; it had even initiated movements that had led to the foundations of new orders'. In the fourteenth and fifteenth centuries it had produced an astonishing number of writers. The *Life of Christ* by Ludolf of Saxony affected the great rebirth of the Church in the sixteenth century through its effect upon St Ignatius. The early Carthusian, John Rode, was the author of the formation of the Bursfeld reformed congregation. From 1503 until 1521 the eminent Francis Dupuy was prior of the Grande Chartreuse near Grenoble, and general of the order. The London Priory of The Angelic Salutation was one of the monasteries which distinguished itself by resisting the demands of Henry VIII. When Eck had to name a well-informed deputy for the papal reform legates who were to come to Germany, he chose Gregory Reisch, prior of the charterhouse of St John in Freiburg, Breisgau.

The fact that the veneration of that most world-renouncing of all medieval ascetics, St Bruno of Cologne, reached a climax at the height of the self-intoxicated Renaissance world, makes more sense than might appear at first sight. For one thing, there was a good dash of disillusionment at the heart of the cultural optimism of the Renaissance. Savonarola and Michaelangelo were, after all, true representatives of their age. Conversely, at that time the Carthusians, in Cologne at least, were beginning to take an interest in the world. This interest was shown by their openness to humanist forms of thought, and also by their turning from a purely monastic type of piety to a real pastoral interest in the wide world around them. Both of these developments were carried out in a truly Catholic spirit, and with real zeal for the perfection of their own lives.

We are able to follow this development as revealed in the charterhouse at Cologne through a host of small features and in many fundamental statements that were of the widest implication. This was the development of a genuinely Catholic milieu, in which the heritage of the Fathers was not only conserved but put to fruitful use; for these men had the capacity to mould something new out of what they had received from tradition. The beginning of this application to pastoral work was contained in the *devotio moderna*, which of its nature directed their minds beyond the walls of the cloister. Secondly, it was necessitated by the collapse of the Church. All around them the Carthusians saw terrible corruption going on in the Church, especially in the unspiritual lives of the higher and lower clergy. They could sense the victorious advance of the Reformation. Both of these experiences 'urgently moved them to undertake a mighty salvage operation upon the Church'. Increasingly, they carried out this work themselves. Amongst them we repeatedly discover the conviction that it was not enough merely to conserve and intensify the old piety but that the message of Christ must address men as they are in the concrete situation of the time – that is it is compelled to adopt new methods.

Obviously the Carthusians were well able to distinguish between humanism that was Christian in spirit, and humanism that was unchristian or antagonistic to Christianity. The general chapters of 1537 and 1538 forbade members of the order to read Erasmus. This did not signify a rejection of humanism. There is plenty of evidence from the Cologne priory, from the whole order and from the humanist circles themselves, that there was no such rejection. Humanism did not infiltrate the ranks of the Carthusians as a force that weakened Christianity. In this infiltration it was genuine medieval Christianity that mastered what was new – not the converse.

Under Prior Blomeveen the numbers of Carthusian monks in Cologne increased from fourteen priests to a much greater number. Blomeveen himself had published a reform document in 1527, and this expressed the fundamental attitude of all Catholic reform. We do not reform others but ourselves. This was in harmony with close attachment to the Church. The Carthusians always subordinated all their desires to 'out mother, holy Church, and to her teaching'.

They wanted to carry reform outside their monastery by spreading their spirit of prayer. Two professors of theology in Cologne placed themselves under Blomeveen's direction, so as to learn from him the practice of contemplative prayer. The experience gained from this was published in the Latin *Manual for Priests* which in turn exerted an influence on a wide circle.

Blomeveen was deeply disturbed by the problem of religious rebirth. His first chapter significantly asks 'why man was created and how he can be reborn'. The second chapter speaks of the renewal of the will and of the understanding. One precondition for any kind of devout renewal stands above all the rest: all mechanical prayer must go.

Blomeveen carried his efforts into the official world of the hierarchy. In his urgent letter to Clement VII (1532) we see how the recognition of decline only increased his zeal for reform. The manner in which he approached the pope shows that he was aware of the gravity of what he alleged. His soul was aflame: 'The pope avoids calling a council! He refuses to give up his pomp and play-acting. He lets the debauchery of the clergy go unpunished. The occupant of the chair of Peter does not care that souls are being lost.' The rot is to be found in all classes: 'The Church will never again flourish if people think that only this and that need to be reformed, but not the whole thing . . .'

The old asceticism was still alive. John Justus Landsberg, who, as a student in Cologne, had been moved by the spirit of the Carthusians, whom he then joined, has left us a description of the rigour with which the Carthusians observed their rule in Cologne at that time. What an austere spirit of penance! Landsberg, too, was shattered at the sight of the terrible corruption in the Church. He heard God's imperious call and said quite simply: 'Not to take arms with all vigour against such great evils, would be unworthy of a Christian.' Almost all of his vast literary output, including pamphlets, contained nothing but pastoral material, mostly of an edifying kind. Even his polemics were absorbed for the most part in this same kind of writing. He stood directly in the tradition running from St Bernard to St Francis. In every conceivable form of sermon and prayer he sang the praise of the God-man, our suffering Redeemer.

He manifested, too, an unusually warm interior freedom. It is quite astonishing, with what ingenuous assurance Landsberg propounded the notion that the rules of the order – and the order itself – were mere necessities of a particular age. He knew and declared with great effect, that the 'one rule of the gospel' covers everything. 'This leads us to true perfection. If we live by it we need no monastic rules, no fraternities, no vows. But because we abandon the gospel, the efforts of our religious founders have become necessary.' From man's failure, Landsberg drew conclusions exactly the opposite to those drawn by Luther.

The Prior Blomeveen had already engaged in polemic against Luther. This had not been a particularly brilliant effort. But whenever these Carthusians found opportunity outside Cologne of demonstrating their loyalty to the Church in a practical way, there the power of their religious life was manifest. (On the exemplary stand of some of the Carthusians in Mecklenburg, see Volume 1, p. 105 f.) The fate of Dietrich Loher exemplifies the details of such activities.

This Carthusian was driven out in the forcible secularisation of two charterhouses. With him, increased danger released greater energy. In 1546 he acquired authority from the general chapter 'to protect the German Carthusians from extinction'. In lower Austria he tried to 'purge the order from unreliable members'. His most important results were seen in the *Reichstag* of 1547–48 in Augsburg. We might say that here he saved the German Carthusians for good. This was undoubtedly a fact of the first importance for the health of the Church in Germany. To understand the whole power of this man we would have to examine somewhat more closely his labours in defence of the Church, in consolidating loyalty to the old Church, and in fighting for established rights in the political arena of the *Reichstag*.

Loher spent a year with Cardinal Otto Truchsess in Augsburg. The reforming zeal of the Carthusian from Cologne fructified this important centre of Catholic renewal, which, like Cologne, was to become fully developed under the Jesuits.

The importance of the Carthusians reached its climax in that they prepared the way perfectly for the Society of Jesus, with whom they entered into a 'unique community of labour', in which their share – on Greven's evidence – was much larger than was formerly supposed. Not only were the Carthusians in good order and able to provide shelter and a base for the first Jesuits to come to Cologne, nor were they merely an exemplary self-contained monastery; they were an important centre from which radiated out a mighty Christian energy. The combined efforts of the Cologne Carthusians and the first Jesuits represented a synthesis of two centres of activity. At first, however, the Carthusians were the more active partners. The road of development was marked out by Canisius, who came from the Carthusians, entered the Society of Jesus, and then, as their representative in Cologne, slowly built up the work of the Jesuits there, always relying upon the full support of the Carthusians.

The charterhouse in Cologne had become the gathering-point for mystics from the spiritual milieu of the *devotio moderna*, centred at a Begine convent in the Oisterwijk district. Their founder was the blameless, zealous pastor, Nicholas von Esch, their leader, a prominent lady, Maria van Hout (or van Oisterwijk), who practised mystical prayer, and burned with spiritual fervour. This leader along with two Begines and the founder moved to Cologne. Under the protection of the Carthusians in Cologne, the link between this order and the mystics became closer.

A circle of monks, priests, laity and Begines, typical of the humanist *devotio moderna*, was formed. This provided a vigorous beginning of universal monasticism and of the priesthood of all believers, such as was to be found in the fraternities of the Italian Oratory of Divine Love, and later of St Charles Borromeo and St Philip Neri. This circle practised a form of piety with a predominantly mystical slant.

About 1537 Esch introduced to this circle the seventeen-year-old Peter Canis, son of the mayor of Nimeguen. Within this circle he experienced his first 'conversion' to Christ. In view of the many false interpretations of late medieval or early modern Catholic piety it is instructive to learn that his spiritual director recommended no peripheral devotional practices, but, as Staupitz did for Luther, directed him straight to Christ the Lord. 'If you truly understand Christ,' Esch told him, 'all is well, even if you do not understand anything else.'

As in Cologne, so in the Netherlands there were other charter-houses – closely linked in many cases to Cologne – which were centres of similar devotional circles. As he himself tells us, Peter Canisius was closely associated with them.

The Cologne Carthusians took as their model the great German

F

mystics, whose writings they read and expounded. As Luther had done, Canisius threw himself avidly upon the study of this spirituality. He sought out the unpublished works of Tauler; and the first literary product of this, the first German Jesuit, was a study in German spirituality of the past: an edition of Tauler's works.

Then he began to hear reports about the Jesuits, and in these men he – a Carthusian in mind – saw an even better means for the sanctification of the world. He shared this belief with his friends, for when, at the beginning of April 1543, he set off to meet Peter Faber, the first Jesuit to come to Germany, he took with him an urgent invitation to Faber from Gerard Kalkbrenner, the prior, to come to Cologne. In answer Faber said of the educators of the young Canisius: 'Blessed be he who has planted this noble tree; blessed be those who have watered it.'

In the following year, 1544, at the general chapter in Grenoble Kalkbrenner advocated 'a close spiritual union with the Jesuits'. They then sent out that magnificent document which recognised and approved Ignatius and his followers 'wherever they were to be found in all the world'. In this they expressed praise and agreement, and offered their fellowship in prayer. In this we see that the rivalry between orders, which had been responsible for much of the contempt into which the religious life had fallen, was quite absent from the Carthusians in their attitude to this quite new congregation, whom they knew, indeed, only in one aspect. The Carthusians had a selfless sense of being obligated to the work of the kingdom of God.

This openmindedness, too, had always been a characteristic of the Cologne Carthusians. Other old orders, too, were represented in the zealous reform group that surrounded the Carthusians of Cologne. The important and indefatigable controversialist Dominican, John Host of Romberg, was a man of irreproachable morals, and the prolific author of new works as well as the editor of old ones. He was an avid reader of Erasmus, a cultivated Latinist, and a fearless critic of the age. For this reason he made many enemies. He was, however, a man who accomplished an amazing amount, and was a collaborator of the Carthusians in their edition of Dionysuis. He dedicated his commentary on the psalms to the Carthusians, Blomeveen and Loher.

IV

In the reform consultations under Paul III one of the proposals made was that 'all monasteries should cease to accept novices so that a completely new generation might be formed later on.' This method was not adopted. However, what the Church urgently required, was demanded: a new generation of priests; and the energies of the faithful members of the old orders were insufficient to supply this. Apart from the fact that their numbers were dwindling, they could not be expected to accomplish the necessary reconstruction, for they had lost the confidence even of Catholics, on account of the terrible contempt into which the monastic state had fallen. The general corruption of the Church, too, prevented comprehensive reform being carried out by the old orders. In this situation a revival in the Church had to come through a totally fresh approach.

The new power that was required came from the order founded by the Basque, Ignatius of Loyola (1495–1556).

Through its fruits, the religious development of this great Spaniard has dominated Catholicism throughout the entire modern period. This movement proceeded quite independent of the Reformation; none the less it is symbolic that Ignatius' religious conversion coincided with Luther's declaration at Worms and the consequent irreparable schism in Christendom. Ignatius with his work thus appears most significantly as the great anti-Luther.

It would be a misunderstanding of the nature and power of his work, however, and a misrepresentation of its results, were we to ignore the essentially positive attitude of this anti-Lutheranism. (a) It was deeply rooted in God, whose greater glory was always the avowed object of all the work of the society. This root was at once full of mystic ardour and practical efficiency. (b) It possessed an unrestricted missionary impulse that was ready for any sacrifice. Cost what it might, every individual soul in the world was to be saved for heaven.

It is true that even the first companions of this saint fell short of his creative genius, which manifested a synthesis of inexhaustible richness, whether in mystical prayer, in all manner of religious organisation, in self-sanctification, in spiritual direction, in the discovery of new methods of sanctification or in an infinite effort to win souls. None the less, the first Jesuits who came to Germany included men of outstanding gifts (Peter Faber and Peter Canisius, for example).

As might be expected, the majority of those who followed were not quite of the same calibre. All of them, however, exerted a decisive influence. Like Faber, Canisius and Jajus, all of these early Jesuits made their mark by producing an effect that was fresh and tinged with genius. The world-historical importance of the activity of St Ignatius was that he succeeded in embodying his revolution in an institution and in methods that were able to spark off creative action in other brilliant personalities. It is certain that the success of his enterprise was determined by the type of man who put himself at Ignatius' disposal. Just as decisive, however, was the permanent co-ordination, direction and fructification of energies, in the attainment of a logically conceived end. In a pre-eminent degree, what can be said of all genuinely Catholic activity, can be said of the work of the Jesuits: it must emerge out of the community; it must be a function of the Church.

This functional law applied in the highest degree to the Jesuits. All of them were agents of the whole order. This was the cause of the unprecedented uniformity of their work. This uniformity was achieved by a system and scheme that was operated by highly individual personalities, and a host of collaborators, whose functions were gradually more specifically defined.

This was a basic law of Jesuit activity in the early days of the order. Without observing this fact, we cannot understand the work of St Canisius in and for Germany. The mystery of that work is precisely this, that he was not himself but an agent of the order. This anonymity often took very strange forms. Whoever denies the value of this must be blind to the precious power of heroic obedience, and must be ignorant of the personal energy by which Canisius offered this obedience.

The transformation in the Church was not effected by scholars, not by theologians, nor by lawyers. It had to well up out of the life of men, from the fullness of believing, sacrificial hearts. When Fr Jajus announced that in Germany men would never be won over except by the way of knowledge, he meant this to apply to the external approach, to the matter of indispensable aids; but his statement in no way denies what has been said about more essential things. The theology of Canisius could scarcely be described as creative thinking – nor could the theology of the other Jesuits in Germany in the early days. But like Peter Faber and Jajus, he possessed other gifts. In the life of prayer and mortification and pastoral advance, we find a torrent of energy that immediately places him in the company of the great men of action. The increasing number of Jesuits who came to Germany always evinced enough of the impulse towards true piety and unstinted pastoral devotion, to enable the work of the few early outstanding leaders to continue to exert a decisive influence upon the age. The work of these sometimes inadequately educated, always overworked and constantly moving, Jesuits, may have had its defects, but if we observe the uniform stamp and the single direction of all of their work, far removed from any self-interest or luxurious living, we will see that it all bears the mark of true and unpretentious service. This was the impulse that moulded the new, emerging Catholic mind. 'If truth is reinforced by word and example, it urges people on – even against their will – to admiration, love, and devotion' (Jajus 1550). Those Jesuits possessed the mysterious power of good example contained in the identity of thought and deed – the exact opposite of the fantastic discrepancy between the ideals of Christianity, the Church, the priesthood and apostolicity, and their actual embodiment, which had been at the root of every evil in the Church in those days.

What was the substance of the novelty brought to Germany by the Jesuits? What was it that made them capable of setting reform in motion – although very gradually – whenever its necessity was indicated? Canisius, speaking of Faber, put his finger on it: 'He has nothing else in mind but to work with Christ for the salvation of souls.' This, however, was a disposition that permeated the whole being, turning this simple statement into an absolute demand upon life, in the spirit of the gospel of the Crucified, and allowing of no exceptions. The prior of the Carthusians at Cologne, Kalkbrenner, went into more detail: 'They are apostolic men filled with the Spirit and power of God, with fresh courage and a new power. Their words are leaping sparks; they kindle men's hearts ..., and they gather a rich harvest in the end, which the unseen Sower ripens in the hearts of men.' He himself hurried off to Mainz to meet Faber, and make a retreat with him. 'One ought to go and fetch such a treasure as this, even if one had to go to India to find it.'

The fullness of the love of God was once again alive in these Jesuits. They were consumed by a hunger of soul, were ready for heroic sacrifice in the service of the Church, and manifested true piety in every aspect of their lives.

In addition these new things were activated by logically developed new methods. The immediate result was a deep transformation in individuals (through the *Exercises*); then, co-ordinating their experience, they set about spiritual renewal at its roots (education); finally, fully aware – as at every stage – of their goal, the whole process was fully developed (colleges; pastoral work; catechism).

The *Exercises* of St Ignatius has come to be one of the great slogans of the Catholic revival. The various forms of the *devotio moderna* with its various modes of expression and devotional practices, still required some kind of systematisation. In the charterhouse at Cologne they were already speaking of 'spiritual exercises'. The Jesuit system went further and produced something new in one of the most fruitful methods yet discovered of realising spiritual energies, particularly of the will. In this sign the Jesuits conquered.

Allowance may well have to be made for the enthusiasm of youth when the twenty-two-year-old Canisius stated that he literally felt the grace of God flow through his body; but the fact remains that through the *Exercises* he experienced the miracle of a powerful and enduring new (second) birth. 'I can scarcely describe how my heart and mind have been transformed by these *Exercises*, and how I feel armed with a new strength, how I seem to be utterly changed into a new man.'

Real life grows in quietness. This had been the secret of Luther. This, too, was the secret of the decisive new Catholic powers at work in saintly or at least genuinely devout and spiritual men. It was most evident amongst the Jesuits. In the *Exercises* they all passed through a mighty school of silence where only 'God and the soul' stood face to face.

As with Ignatius' whole mission, so too the creation of the *Exercises* was in a deep sense a fulfilment of the times. More clearly and with a more masterly impact than any other pastoral methods, these *Exercises* represent the attempt to force the people of those days to face up to the problems of Christian life, to make them conscious of all that was questionable in their religious condition, and to lead them – almost to force them – beyond the practical relativism of the age, to a clear Catholic determination in theory and in practice. These *Exercises* and their foundation in St Ignatius' little retreat manual, once again went right to the heart of the matter. They touched men's hearts with a power like no other to 'transform in the spirit of the author' (Holl). In 1554 Ignatius himself commented that the capable men the society possessed had been produced in great measure by the *Exercises*.

To begin with (until 1554) the *Exercises* were chiefly designed for the élite. The object was to win over powerful individuals who could provide impetus in the reform, to educate individuals for the renewal. Even in the midst of the burden of ever-increasing pastoral responsibilities, Faber gave retreats only to individuals. Even men who had much in common, spiritually, like the Bishops Helding and Pflug, he dealt with separately.

It is not necessary for us to analyse the structure and technique of the *Exercises*. We must, however, ask why these methods were so much more effective than the many well-intentioned efforts that had gone before. We recall the confrontation of Luther and Eck at the Leipzig Disputation. The secret of Luther's power was reproduced in St Ignatius' *Exercises*, for these did not impart ready-made doctrines – not even received revelation – but insights that had been wrung from the depths of tested personal experience – as the preface to the first edition explains. In these insights burned freshly the restrained, but all the more permanent, interior fire, of a battle won. It is true that while the secret of their efficacy reminds us of Luther, the mode of operation was as different as could be. The element of subjective unrest had been completely sublimated into a mighty objective quality issuing in the praise of God. The eruptive, Vulcanic aspect had been mastered by asceticism.

Conversely, the *Exercises* were a concentrated presentation of

the whole effort at Christian reform. They were a quite extraordinary activation of Christian being and energy, most of all
of its innermost heart-beat: prayer. In general, Catholic decay
had been a process of atrophy of prayer-life: Catholic reform was
a gradual, and then an exuberant, blossoming of the life of prayer.
Ignatius and his *Exercises* were not just the first climax of genius
in this process but possessed a special charismatic unction of
stimulation and discipline. They were the creators of modern
activist pastoral care, with all its advantages, and with the
serious disadvantages, too, of a later moralistic attitude, which
so often lacked patience, and tried to rush the soul towards
salvation according to a fixed recipe, preferring discipline,
moralism, and self-assurance to growth out of mystery, and out of
the courage of faith.

Let us repeat: these first Jesuits in Germany – and it is only
of them we speak – were all men with an inborn or an implanted
desire to seek and save souls. They were fishers of men – but in a
very deep sense. Despite all the misdeeds they saw in their fellow-
men, still they loved their immortal souls. They thought it important, too, to be amiable amd trustworthy in the eyes of those they
sought; and in turn they extended their own confidence and love
to them, demanding nothing, but the whole man.

They desired nothing for themselves, for they were no prelates,
and sought neither honours nor riches. The suspicion of self-
interest, with which every reform-proposal put forward by a
member of the higher clergy was met, was not extended to them.
The rejection of prelacy and any advantage attached to clerical
position, gave these early Jesuits a special charm and their
efforts a special fruitfulness. In a man like Jajus, for example,
these qualities formed part of the deepest substance of his striving
for perfection, even before he entered the society. He had heard
the 'terrible word' of the Lord: 'Woe to them who seek the
highest places!'

Following the example of their founder, the first Jesuits in
Germany tended the sick, and in other ways, too, cared for the
corporal needs of their fellow-men. The Calvinist Seibert took
this amiss. During the seventies he recalled the work of the
early Jesuits in Worms and elsewhere, where 'they led many away
from the gospel; especially one, who led a hypocritical life,

spending half the day and night in churches or hospitals, eating and drinking and sleeping but little, and making no boasts of his deeds, so that many were taken in by his behaviour'.

At that time the part of Germany which had remained Catholic could boast very few priests who were worth their salt. The priestly qualities of the Jesuits, therefore, automatically impressed people deeply. In those few parts of Germany especially, where there was a fervent desire for renewal, their importance and power was immediately and instinctively recognised. The competition shown to obtain their services is proof of the dearth of available priests and the parsimony with which their services had to be shared out between the centres of activity – Cologne, Augsburg, Regensburg, the bishop of Speyer, of Passau and the nuncio.

The work of individual Jesuits in Germany during the period under review confirms this general assessment in every detail.

In the year 1540, when the foundation of the order was confirmed, the first Jesuit, Peter Faber, appeared in Germany. He came to Worms, accompanied by Peter Oritz, the emperor's Spanish theologian, one of the earliest and most enthusiastic patrons of the Jesuits, to attend the religious conversations convoked by the emperor. This occasion quickly acquainted the loyal Savoyard with the weaknessess of the Catholic position. He found the inclination to compromise solely upon the Catholic side. In addition, the representatives of the Catholic interest were impossibly divided; and, moreover, they lacked any religious zeal. There was far too much lukewarmness. He drew his conclusions 'As the great powers (pope and emperor) can do so little, and as ordinary measures are useless against the daily growing evils, so much the more must we hope that the Lord of the harvest will come to our aid.' Here was a new confidence. He believed in the power of the new method and in its special mission. He believed in the power of the ancient Catholic heritage, in the continuing Catholic life of Germany. He said to the Cologne Carthusians – by way of a reform proposal: 'Search in the corners of the city, and there you will find hidden treasures of sound doctrine and piety.' Here was the optimism that must characterise all true activism. Father Jajus confirms this view. He announced that even amongst

Protestants many were secretly longing for the sacraments, and even for a return to the Church.

In Worms and Regensburg Faber saw clearly that the Protestants possessed a sure sense of purpose. He measured their real importance; but their views did not affect his own in the slightest. His lively, Catholic confidence and instinct remained as robust as ever.

His attitude produced results. Raynauld's report to Paul III on 7 June 1541 clearly shows how Faber recognised the universal and open discouragement of Catholics as a serious evil, which had to be resolutely attacked on all sides. Faber saw the problem in all its depth; and ever and again we experience Faber's intense awareness of the mysterious efficacy of pure, religious, pastoral zeal, and of how he was able to kindle the spark of this zeal in others. In Regensburg so many came to make the retreat that he could not cope with them all. The initiate then gave the retreat to others. Once again the mighty power of infection contained in Christian truth and love proved itself. In Faber spoke 'one whose life of virtue was strengthened by the imitation of Christ'. What had been truly devout in the antecedent efforts of the Church was now stepped up into the realm of holiness. Here was the secret: 'His heart is constantly oppressed by the unbearable pain of beholding Germany, once the adornment of religion and the glory of Christendom, on the brink of ruin.'

Faber was one of those sympathetic souls, in whom clear-cut moral or dogmatic judgment does not destroy a higher sense of responsibility, which compels a man to pray for all. Faber never ceased to pray even for the apostates: the king of England, Luther, Butzer and Melanchthon. All his life long he wanted to pray for Wittenberg above all other cities.

We are accustomed to hear only of the sharp antagonism the Jesuits aroused in Protestants. Obviously this was their dominant reaction; but they also found certain sympathy on the other side. Faber's irenic, selfless and fervent Christian nature provides a happy proof of this. It is well to note, if we would properly assess the effectiveness of the first Jesuits in Germany, that their style of operation was far removed from the heavy-handed, scolding Jesuit imitators of the end of the century. At the human and personal level, the early Jesuits were very much more attractive than their later imitators. Hatred was little seen, love was much in evidence. 'If a man wants to be of use to unbelievers today, he must be marked first and foremost by a great love for them, and he must rid his soul of all thoughts that might lessen his esteem for these people. For they, too, are supposed to love us.'

As papal legate in Germany, Morone adopted this method. The authority vested in him by the curia facilitated its development. He instructed his collaborators, Dr Vauchop and Fr Jajus, 'not to quench the smoking flax'. Love and prudence were to be their guides, not blustering and threats. Jajus tells us that in Regensburg he went 'from house to house, associating with men of religion or of the world – happily, or unhappily'.

By far the greatest force in Germany in this period was Peter Canis of Nimeguen, after he had joined the Society of Jesus. The Catholic heritage he had acquired jointly from his father, mother, stepmother and then the Carthusians, was made to yield exceptional fruit under the tutelage of the Jesuits, especially of Faber and then of the founder himself.

In essence all of his energies were religious, and this is the key to a true assessment of his incredibly many-sided work. His diplomatic efforts and his administration all radiate this religious quality. For him – as with Luther – Christian religious values were uncompromisingly set above all other values, none excepted, national values least of all. He was distinguished from Luther, of course, by his deep pastoral activism.

It was not as a creative genius that Canisius performed this religious work. If we regard only personal idiosyncrasy as of value, we will be incapable of reaching a true assessment of this man. Canisius was tremendously gifted with a versatile ease of understanding, which, along with his equally great zeal, admirably equipped him for all manner of activity. He was fully competent – and in large measure with acquired powers – to evaluate a programme that he had not himself devised. As we have said, he was the pure expression of that power which we saw, diluted and alloyed, in all of the literary champions of the Church against the Reformation: he was completely an agent or function of the Church. He became this as a result of his Jesuit training – based upon his heritage and Carthusian education. Obedience in the widest sense was the substance of all his labours.

With him, too, through the love of God, the driving force behind this obedience was a hunger of soul. He describes his interior disposition, at the time of his profession in Rome, thus: 'I experienced an intense longing, that streams of faith, hope, and love would flow from you, O God, into me.' Terror over his own unworthiness was overcome by courage, 'so that I had no longer any doubt that I would be able to fulfil the commission which I was to undertake in your name' (1549). Prayer for Germany was never absent from his lips, and he was for ever urging others to offer up the same prayer. He even entreated Ignatius to lay the obligation of this prayer upon all Jesuits, and the founder granted his request.

The piety and pastoral zeal of St Canisius were, in fact, but the climax of long present energies. The climax, however, was such as to create something new. It produced more than a fresh accent; it composed a new melody, sustained by a mighty new harmony, which commanded attention, which attracted and overpowered many. It was nothing less than the fullness of a new Catholic apprehension of faith, bringing with it a new Catholic energy and self-assurance, that displayed not the slightest deviation from the truth of its own position, and presented the Catholic cause as the only cause that could be ultimately victorious. When Canisius wanted formally and publicly to profess his faith in the ancient Church, he made statements, the separate items in which closely resembled those of a hundred other propositions in the general polemical Catholic literature of the time. But coming from him, these had a fresh ring, and we would be hard put to it to find any real parallel in the first half of the century. Canisius wrote: 'I acknowledge you, O Father of heaven and earth, my Creator and Redeemer, my power and my salvation! You have never ceased, from my childhood, to nourish me with the holy bread of your word, and to strengthen my heart. So that I would not go astray with the shepherdless sheep, you took me into the house of your Church, educated me there and instructed me through those masters and shepherds, in whom, according to your ordinances, your own voice can be heard and must be followed. . . . I desire to remain true to the faith and doctrine in which I was instructed as a boy, confirmed in as a youth, and which I now teach and defend as a man. I am compelled to make this profession for the honour of your name alone, by the power of acknowledged truth, by the guidance of holy scripture, by the unequivocal testimony of the Fathers, and from the duty to bear witness to my brethren, from hope of heaven and the expectation of the blessedness that is promised to those who make an honest and true profession. If, on account of this profession, I am despised and ridiculed, in that I shall see and extol a special proof of your grace, O God. I will see that you are allowing me to suffer for righteousness, and that in truth is the lot of the blessed. On the other hand, you have prevented me from inclining to those who can never be your friends, for they resist your Church and the Catholic faith. Forgive them Father, forgive them . . . . For me you are the beginning and the end of every good. May I give honour and glory for ever and ever.'

The volume and variety of Canisius' work was so great as to appear almost chaotic. At times he was so overburdened that he could not say mass. He undertook a thousand activities in a hundred different places; he preached, taught in school, gave lectures, wrote reports, held consultations, heard confessions, was a diplomat, a popular missionary, a prison chaplain, a disputator, a university rector, an author of practical theology, and a founder of schools, colleges and universities. Yet in all this activity he never fell into the trap of externalisation. An interior fire set a light to everything he touched; and Canisius always aimed at quality. He knew full well that the decline of religious life in Germany had been caused not least by the multiplication of external practices. 'People prayed from habit, and not from devotion.' Hasty confession had to be replaced by earnest and more detailed recounting of sins. Any priest – like the Cardinal of Augsburg – who had cut loose from the sinful world and was a good shepherd of his sheep, still had to break with more refined forms of worldliness if 'we are to come closer to the ideal of our true Shepherd'. Although a sufficient supply of priests had become the key problem in the whole reform of the Church, Canisius had sharp enough eyes to see that a badly trained candidate for holy orders was a disaster.

This man, who was a product of the school of Tauler, Faber

and Ignatius, would be content with nothing less than real quality, no matter what it cost. He possessed a captivating eloquence that was free from all empty rhetoric, and that had been nourished and consecrated by his great love of God. How he prepared for his work! He practised almost complete abstinence; he meditated long into the night before he preached. He was devoid of egotism; he gave up his rector's stipend to the poor; he made a real fight to decline the thrice proffered See of Vienna. In Canisius dwelt the undiminished spirit of complete renunciation, as it had supported Ignatius in 'those years of struggle to unite the ideal of poverty with the ever more urgent educational task of the order'.

Naturally we are specially interested in the manner in which Canisius handled the polemic dispute with the Reformation. Comparison with Luther is instructive. The Jesuit frequently let reproaches cast upon him go unanswered, pondering them in his own mind in a spirit of charity. Luther, too, left many reproaches unanswered, but did so out of a proud sense of triumph. He despised his opponent. It is true that the idea of loving his opponent with the love of the Crucified was there, but it occupied only a small corner of his soul. A loving and humble disposition was lacking; it was driven out by defiant presumption on the power of God.

Canisius' unrelenting demands never led him into coarseness. It is true that Catholic apologists have often tried to water down the saint's utterance, leaving only what is mild and gentle. This is as stupid as it is false. Canisius could say hard things about the Reformers – as about the negligent in his own camp; and – unlike Ignatius – he recommended the inquisition for Germany. Above all he was a missionary, searching for souls. He frequently reproved Catholic heresy hunting – as practised, for example, by Lindanus: 'Truth must be defended with spirit, with dignity, and with sobriety.' Of Rome he demanded gentler treatment of the Germans, 'so that the smoking flax is not quenched'. For, he said, 'harsh cures without love, as advocated by most anti-Protestant authors, irritate rather than heal the Germans'. He asked for the spirit of gentleness, 'for in Germany we are sick of past bickering'.

Nor do we find in Canisius any of that *superbia*, that thirst for the power of the order, which would put the interests of one's own society before those of Catholic life in general. This weakness of the Jesuit order, as Cordara was later to describe it, was quite absent from Canisius. If one takes the fact seriously – to the point of exaggeration – that Catholic presbyteries and monasteries were corrupt, then one must admit, in logic, that it became a duty for ascetic priests to supplant the corrupt ones. For the rest, Canisius was not one of those who was ready ruthlessly to appropriate the property of the older orders. On the contrary, he seemed to impute some justification to the animosity aroused in the old orders against the Jesuits.

In the years 1545/46/47 the leading German Jesuits travelled to Trent. Hitherto their work had been predominantly that of itinerant missionaries, rapidly changing their place of activity, and with a paramount interest in direct pastoral work; but after the first phase of Trent the process of taking root and of organisation began. Three spheres of work were now developed: popular education; the education of children from the upper social classes; and the fostering of worthy recruits to the priesthood.

From many sources we know how much infiltration of Protestant ideas went on in those days through Protestant methods of instruction of youth. In 1547 Gropper declared that the newer Catholic catechisms were inadequate. In this very sphere Canisius displayed his ability and revealed his mission at its most powerful: he was able to proclaim Catholic doctrine forcibly, and to impart it to countless numbers. His catechism was quite different from many later catechisms, which became a collection of abstract propositions about revelation, in which the word of God itself was seldom heard. Canisius' first catechism of 1555 was an interweaving of words of scripture and patristic texts. It was a positive production in which Luther was never once mentioned. The first version was followed by two more, including the 'shortest'. Since then they have run to over four hundred editions and have spread everywhere. Catholicism in Germany since 1555 is unthinkable apart from this catechism of Canisius.

These catechisms, those designed for the priests as well as those for the laity, had an elementary, a rudimentary object: once more to make known to all, the Church's teaching and her prayers. They were aimed both at the fundamental evil of theological vagueness, and at crass ignorance. The same was true of his sermons. Whether delivered at the *Reichstag* or in populous cities, it was hoped that those who heard would spread their teaching by telling others. Many were amazed to hear what the Church really did teach. In an unusually acute form, a constantly recurring experience in the history of the Catholic Church was being enacted.

In 1546 when Ignatius sent Laynez, Salmeron and Jajus to Trent, he laid down this rule: no sermons should ever contain any point wherein Catholics and Protestants did not agree. People ought simply to be exhorted to lead a moral life and practise the devotions of the Church, by being brought to a more fundamental self-knowledge of the love of their Lord and Creator. Head-on attack only embittered and hardened men: the clarity and beauty of truth was what won their hearts.

Ignatius' starting-point had been the idea of a religious crusade. In Germany, however, the question of education had gradually become the fundamental question in all religious or ecclesiastical reform. Fresh roots had to be struck. The logic of the situation demanded that the education of a new generation of laity and of clergy become the programme of the new order. In terms of the conditions prevailing at the time, its original programme demanded just such a development. And so, compelled by circumstances, even the very earliest Jesuits in Germany, beginning with Fr Jajus in 1545, began to devote much more interest to schools than Ignatius had envisaged in his original draft of the constitution. The schools which they had most in mind were those that prepared men for the university, those that is which served to educate the new generation of priests. As the Jesuits soon learned to their cost, and frequently reported to Rome, the clerical estate was so much despised, hated and persecuted in Germany, that scarcely anyone wanted to become a priest or a monk. One consequence was the decline of theology. Learning, too, as the Jesuits recognised, was a precondition for the reconquest of Germany, now theologically divided. It is true that in the end the deciding factor was genuine piety; but in Germany, as Jajus reported, piety would be valued only if it went hand in hand with knowledge.

With these facts in mind, the Jesuits came to the rescue of several Catholic theological faculties in the universities (Ingolstadt temporarily in 1544; Cologne 1545 by Canisius). In 1548 Ignatius finally yielded to the insistence of Duke William IV of Bavaria and appointed Jajus, Salmeron and Canisius, who had just organised the first Jesuit college at Messina, to the university of Ingolstadt. In 1549 a most distinguished seat of learning appeared in that city. Unfortunately for Salmeron and Jajus, the work was short-lived. Canisius remained there until 1552. The situation was difficult enough: there were incompetent teachers, lacking zeal, most of whom secretly inclined to the new religion. Scarcely any religion existed amongst the citizens. Canisius thus became an apostle in the widest sense of the word. Day and night his whole mind was set on the pastoral care of students and citizens. To these he devoted all his strength. He did all he could for them, and, of course, gratis. He grouped together students and non-students in various ways. He preached in the churches, in the churchyards, in the streets.

The Jesuits were not deceived by the appearance of success, nor would they be content with small results. 'Our lectures in Ingolstadt have been of little or no use, because the audience was too small' (1550). In addition, as elsewhere, the Catholic atmosphere had become almost non-existent in Ingolstadt. It was a rare thing to find anyone at prayer in a church. Students of theology had not been prepared for the new style of piety, and were incapable of adopting it. It was a thankless task, to accomplish which Canisius prayed for patience and joy, and Ignatius had to encourage him often: 'the smallest effect we can produce in Germany is more important than large-scale success in other countries'.

There was only one method: to found free colleges for a number of poor but gifted students. Reconstruction had to begin with small cells, and had to rely on as little material support as possible.

In the teaching methods of the new college humane studies (in contrast to the notably neglected theological instruction on religion) often ousted all else. On account of the great shortage of priests, students were often sent out to parishes immediately on the conclusion of their study of the humanities. None the less the whole atmosphere of these institutions was Christian and ecclesiastical. The new power of the Jesuits to reform the Church was recognised not least in the mightily increasing work of their schools, and in their methods of teaching and of learning. It was evident also, how much wearisome effort had to go into the smallest details of thoroughly mastered practical pastoral work, if control was to be gained of the key positions.

Once the new style of college education had been seen to be necessary, the iron logic of the founder of the order could tolerate no return to the methods of earlier years. He pointed out emphatically to those in Cologne that they must not seek the easy successes of a general mission to the peasantry: 'We have higher obligations.' It was in Cologne, indeed, that there arose the Three Crown College directed by the Jesuits. Soon it became for Germany 'what the Roman college was for the order as a whole: a nursery that sent workers out in all directions'. It was in Cologne, too, that the Jesuits were to find their first and the greatest number of aspirants for their order. In 1549 they had fourteen, five of whom were sent to Rome.

This revival of vocations to the religious life was to prove one of the profoundest effects of the work of the Jesuits in Germany. Their example, their doctrine, the life and atmosphere of their schools, provided the first illumination for many Germans of the validity and worth of a healthy religious life. Old monasteries. too, acquired a new lease of life through the example, direction, retreats, schoolteaching, lectures and the hearing of confessions of the Jesuits, as well as through the entry into their ranks of ex-pupils of the Jesuits.

Through its founder, through the circle of its first members and the bulk of its early members, that is in the last fifteen years that concern our enquiry, the Jesuit order was a product of Latin Catholicism. Even in Germany in the early days nearly all of the Jesuits were Latins. This fact raises afresh the question as to the real value of their work for Germany and her people.

It is obvious that the Jesuits brought to Germany elements of Latin piety that had forthwith to be deeply integrated with the German mind. This posed the decisive religious problem of the Counter-Reformation in Germany.

On the other hand, we must not inject modern problems into past history. We have learned about the emergence of national conciousness before and during the Reformation. In spite of this, most of the personalities, who counted in the religious and political spheres, were quite unaffected by whether or not the propounder of a Christian doctrine was a German or not. It never occurred to Luther to think less of Calvin because he was a Latin. Only the ignorant, therefore, would assert that the cultivation of Latin in Jesuit schools in the sixteenth century was an un-German activity. To be fluent in Latin was a precondition of higher education for every German in the sixteenth century. In those days it is true that the Jesuits stressed the supranational character of allegiance to the Church.

This could become a disadvantage, and later did so become. This, however, in no way detracts from the colossal, selfless work the Jesuits did for Germany in the sixteenth century, just as outside Germany they had done similar work as foreigners – in Messina, for example, where Italians and Germans had worked together. Only one committed a priori to the view that a non-German from Rome could not possibly do any good work in and for Germany, can affirm the contrary. Even if we were inclined to discount many of Fr Faber's protestations, it remains obvious that this man's heart had become unusually attached to the Germans and to the Rhine.

A misrepresentation of the work of Peter Canis along these lines is possible only through complete ignorance. 'You know, O Lord, how urgently and how often you have commended Germany to me; and I continue to bestow all my care upon that country, putting myself utterly at Fr Faber's command to that end, for which I shall live and die. I shall collaborate with the guardian angel of Germany' (Michael). When in 1545, at the age of twenty-four, he confessed: 'If I am not ordered to leave Cologne, I will offer body, soul, time, studies, my whole being, in life and in death, for Cologne.'

We might be tempted to set aside all that has been said of the early Jesuit activity in Germany as unimportant, because too sporadic, too much in the nature of random preliminary soundings. It could be pointed out that all the important Jesuit strongholds in Germany were effectively occupied, or reoccupied, only at the very end of our period: Vienna, 1551; Ingolstadt, 1556; Cologne, 1556; Trier, 1560: Mainz, 1561; Würzburg, 1561 (1567);

Braunsberg, 1564. We must remember, however, that it is the pioneers of any great movement who deserve the most praise. The decisive thing had been to create a new confidence in the Catholic Church, to establish the first institutions that would be potential breeding grounds for a new generation of priests and laity, and to revive the Catholic spirit in Germany. All of these things, the Jesuits accomplished, beginning their work in 1540. Along various lines they set off a chain of effects in the spheres of religion, politics and culture.

FIVE

Catholic Controversial Theology

From the start of the Reformation the group most directly engaged in preserving the Catholic heritage were the Catholic controversial theologians.

We now know, through the organised labours of Joseph Greving, founder of the *Corpus Catholicorum*, that the literary effort behind the old Church at that time was much more imposing and extensive than was formerly supposed. In the interest of historical accuracy, the image of Reformation history must be rid of the notion, that Luther and his followers utterly dominated the literary field. In addition, a more precise picture of the Catholic resistance will do much to explain the religious conflict between the two parties, as it will give added weight to certain reproaches made by the Reformers.

It is true that hitherto we have been very badly informed about the Catholic literary efforts of those days. All that we really know are their directly controversial utterances. We do not know much about the deeper qualities of these men, about their more personal attitude to religion, to the Church and to the Christian way of life; nor have we been able to separate what was traditional from what was original; nor have we uncovered the exact motives which held them to the old Church. We do not know what it was that turned lukewarm, compromising members of the Church into capable, inspired, defenders of the Church, what it was that changed peace-loving humanists and world-renouncing monks into animated champions of the old faith. We are largely ignorant of their spiritual freedom or lack of it over against their opponents, and of their knowledge of Reformed writings, and of their human, personal qualities. Now that the magnificent work of Paulus, Greving and their circle has provided much more material on this period, there is no excuse for delay in producing a complete picture of the intellectual and religious energies at work in Catholic literature during the first half of the sixteenth century. This ought to be done in conjunction with a like treatment of the religious power at work in German humanism.

It is obvious that this work – to be successfully carried out we hope – cannot be done here, as it were in the passing. We can find space only for a few pointers and summarising remarks.

Let us return to the beginning of the Reformation period, so that we may construct a more concrete picture of a few of the chief figures, and from this angle, gain some understanding of the new Catholic mentality that was beginning to emerge.

I

There can be no doubt that the most important representatives of the literary defence were Dr John Maier from Egg – called Eck – and John Cochlaeus.

About Eck we have nothing more to say, except to maintain that his *Enchiridion*, that appeared in the critical year 1525, is to be regarded as a turning-point in the Catholic polemical treatment of Luther and his work. It summed up all previous work in the subject and provided a convenient discussion and assessment. In its eighty-two editions by 1600, it became one of the chief literary weapons used against Reformed doctrine.

John Cochlaeus was a man of a totally different stamp (see Vol. I, p. 295 f.). He was a schoolmaster, a scholar and a humanist, but, unfortunately, no theologian. That such a man should suddenly, as the storm was breaking, and then all through the Reformation period, be the one who for the most part assumed the theological direction of events, was a fact with far-reaching consequences.

There was no question of Cochlaeus entering into peaceable discussion with Luther in a spirit of understanding. His fantastic vocabulary of coarse and distasteful invective[1] indicates how little hope there was of any genuine understanding. This invective, moreover, was quite contrary to his demand that the people be presented with pure doctrine 'with gentleness and without defamation', as it was contrary to his early aim to convince Luther, and lead him back to the Church. Besides this, Cochlaeus was the old-fashioned type, who refuted word for word, and did not see that the revolution breaking out all around him was no theoretical affair, that stood or fell with particular theological proofs. It is true that by 1522 he had to some extent advanced beyond a purely defensive attitude, demanding of controversial theology some positive Catholic reconstruction; but he himself paid little heed to his own demands. He indulged, too, in a great deal of sophistry.

There was more to Cochlaeus than that, however. Although at the beginning of his theological career he had an unbridled desire to dispute with the renowned Luther, we must not exaggerate this motive. His association with men belonging to the Roman Oratory of Divine Love brought him deeply under the influence of the new Catholic spirituality. At an early date his central motive became the love of God, with no ulterior interests – 'to love as Christ loved us, with an eye to no material rewards'. He gave convincing proof that he was in earnest about this, by his faithful and unselfish love of the old Church and the old faith. All his life he spent the few pence he had supporting Catholic literary endeavour, and towards the end of his life he – a humanist – denied himself the honour of having his collected works published, to make way for the printing of books by a Conrad Braun. In 1547 he could affirm with every justification, that in the past twenty-six years no other man had devoted so much effort and money to the Catholic cause as he had done in his Latin and German books.

---

[1] Lying, traitorous apostate; filthy sow; dog of a priest saying mass for dogs; wild, death-croaking raven covered in poisonous, stinking excrement; warmongering, howling wolf; most accursed and desperate slave and tool of the devil.

He had been stirred by the sense of responsibility for the 'calamity threatening us all'. Anyone who could see this and withdraw, he affirmed, must have a heart of stone. He was deeply affected by the concept of the unity of the Church. Fervently he prayed to Christ for the reunion of all separated Christians in the one Church and the one faith. 'If he does not grant this result, we certainly will not achieve it by our scribbling.' He wrote that in 1544. He now upheld this view, so long forgotten by those holding important positions in the Church, but now coming into its own again: 'If there is the slightest possibility of healing those affected by heresy, it will only be by the example of a good and virtuous life.'

He desired, therefore, that Luther be remembered in the prayers of Catholics and that none despair of his conversion. 'We ought to, and we will, pray Almighty God, in whose hands are the wills of men, to have mercy on this stubborn sinner.' His deep veneration of the saints was a product of his belief in the communion of saints. Above all, he had a profound attachment to the Blessed Sacrament. This was the well-spring of his whole life.

He had a tremendous national consciousness, a deep attachment to his native land, and a strong sense of responsibility for it and what it stood for. In his earlier letters from Italy to Hutten he had ridiculed the charge that he had no national feeling because he supported the curia and corresponded with the papal nuncios and cardinals. On the contrary, it was for nationalist reasons that the Reformation must be suppressed, as he had pointed out in 1523 and frequently thereafter. Only thus could the glory of the empire be restored, for this depended upon the universalist concept of collaboration between empire and papacy, and upon the avoidance of the ruin threatened by Luther. He attacked Luther's Schmalkald Articles, 'for the honour of the German Nation', and to preserve that nation from shame and contempt at the coming council. He was constantly speaking of the well-being of 'the Fatherland', of 'the Holy Roman Empire', of 'the German Nation'. These terms flowed easily from his pen, and his concern was deep and obvious. As revealed in the scene in Luther's room at Worms, Cochlaeus felt deeply, the tragedy of Germany. He wept when he recalled the magnificent blossoming of piety in the empire before the days of Luther's assault.

Cochlaeus gave up a great deal when he decided to enter the lists in the defence of the Church; for 'he was a scholar, who lived and breathed scholarship, and took no delight in anything else; by nature, he was afraid of the bustle of a world, in which he felt very ill at ease. Cochlaeus had recently acquired a peaceful home and a sufficient stipend, so that he could live in quiet retirement. At one stroke he gave up all this, and stepped into public life, for which he was totally unprepared, in order to serve the Church that was threatened with death and destruction. "I have always loved the liberal sciences," he cried out to the Lutherans at the *Reichstag* in Worms, "and I still hold them in high esteem, but for me the Catholic faith is of even greater value than these." By this devotion to his Church, he accepted an intellectual martyrdom, which he endured for thirty long years; and scarcely ever did he complain of the theological activity which went so much against the grain, or of his life, frustrated through the faults of others' (Spahn).

Despite all his disagreeable traits, despite his hatred and his occasional comic excess of self-esteem, he was a loyal champion of the Church and one of those most worthy of our attention.

Catholic literary defence was not always purely theoretical. It sought points of departure for practical effect. Here, too, Cochlaeus played an important part. Indeed, we will probably find him more congenial than Eck, with his highly official approach to the bull of excommunication.

Cochlaeus had a clear idea about the critical nature of actual propaganda and the organisation of the defence programme, and also of the importance of gaining control over official places in state and Church. At the end of the thirties no other German had so diligently sent report after report to Rome as he had done; during the forties none had been more zealous in his support of the efforts of the new crash troops, the Jesuits. For the guidance of those who were to be the Fathers of the coming council, he had a whole series of his own and other men's writings printed. He persuaded the Polish bishops to adopt a hostile attitude towards Wittenberg; he sent a flood of books to Poland, and tried to have Rome annul the privileges of the university of Wittenberg. A growing number of the best of the Italians supported him:

Cardinals Contarini, Sadolet, Pole, Giberti, Madruzzo. He wrote to the three brothers, the princes of Anhalt, who inclined to Lutheranism, urging them to remain loyal to the Church. He translated and wrote works for the Scots and the English, and dedicated books to Englishmen; and because Henry VIII was beginning to be a threat to the Church, at his own expense, he sent two of his nephews over to examine the situation. He stood the cost of publishing the controversial works of Witzel, Haner and Mensing. He moved heaven and earth to win back Pirkheimer to the Church. He was constantly urging Erasmus to take up the cudgels against Luther; in the same manner he importuned John Fisher, bishop of Rochester. Some of his books he dedicated to the Protestant elector, in the hope of winning him back. He wrote to cities that were threatened by Lutheranism (Lübeck and Breslau); he sent special messengers to Bern to warn the people about Zwingli's doctrine. He prepared a fresh edition of the Psalter of St Bruno, 'as a substitute for heavier reading amongst the less educated clergy'. In 1532 in Mainz he helped Nausea to prepare a plan of visitation and to set it in motion.

As early as 1523 he had sent a memorandum to the curia setting out his views on how the Reformation could be systematically suppressed. The estates and the people ought to be treated with nothing but gentleness. The clergy must be made to lead a more deeply religious life. Pastoral work must be much more thorough: for example, edifying literature must be distributed. Literary work, too, must demonstrate how Christianity did not obstruct economic progress, but in fact encouraged it by its very nature. Error must be refuted from scripture and reason, so that the faithful understand the justification of the commandments. Not only should Luther's books be suppressed, but sound books must be distributed. Luther's preachers must be opposed, but not with brute force. Force should be used only against Luther himself, for his avowed object was total revolution (1522).

Like so many others, on this delicate problem of the use of force, in later years Cochlaeus changed his mind. After the rejection of the council in 1537 by the Schmalkalders and Luther, he admitted that the mildness hitherto shown towards the heretics was the cause of their defiance. No one in the curia dared try to punish Henry VIII for his fulminations against the council, nor to condemn Francis I because of his treaty with the Turks. Cardinal Sadolet sought friendship with Melanchthon; Morone and Giberti wanted to see Henry VIII treated leniently. The pope went so far as to offer his nephews as hostages for Lutherans if they came to the council. Alas! only fear and force would persuade their opponents.

Cochlaeus wanted to organise a regular campaign of defence and attack against Melanchthon. There was to be a team made up of Usingen, Vehe, Alfeld, Neumann, Crotus Rubianus (who had quietly come back to the Church) and a Dominican. Unfortunately the necessary financial support was lacking.

In view of the ardour of this man, and, indeed, of the other literary collaborators in the fight, this lack became a real tragedy. Amongst Catholics their work encountered a quite inexplicable stubborn apathy. Pettiness, egotism, fear and amazing irresponsibility, were the cause of failure, even in official ecclesiastical circles. They were simply left in the lurch.

In 1521 Cochlaeus, utterly alone, took up his pen in an ill-starred attack upon Luther. No one trusted him; no one would carry his letters; no one would print his books. He had no friends, and scarcely dared go into his own church. For whom was he working? After Adrian VI became pope the atmosphere improved; but the situation remained much the same: fear of the Lutherans was the dominant factor. Frequently, Cochlaeus' printers refused to print their names and addresses in his books. He was constantly in the ridiculous position of having to hunt for a printer. The cathedral chapter of Breslau were antagonistic to the Reformation, and they had Catholic books printed at their own cost; but in what mattered most – the labours of Cochlaeus – they were most unhelpful. Indeed, they were positively stingy. The bishop of Breslau, James von Salza ended up by wearily resigning (1539). Other bishops were quite unmoved by the literary battle. Not content even with failing to take part, they deliberately withheld support. Such disillusionments were all part of the suffering Cochlaeus had to endure. In general, Catholics were far too complacent. 'Instead of fighting, they pile up merit by endowing more altars, and meanwhile no one is able to save the mass.'

For a short time at the beginning of the Reformation controversy Jerome Emser played an important part. This man was a well-known and accredited humanist, chaplain to Duke George of Saxony. He, too, was burdened by the same defect as Cochlaeus: he had a theological battle to fight, and he was no theologian.

His opponents, chiefly Luther, used him ill. He may not have been free of moral faults, but at least he admitted them and that he deserved punishment. He looked with admiration at Cochlaeus' purity: 'O what a rare grace!' At the same time, with a clear conscience, he was able to rebut the exaggerations of his adversaries. Aged forty-one, he could say of himself, 'where sin had been in plenty, the passage of years has brought an even greater abundance of grace'.

His resolution, too, was on a large scale. He saw the corruption of the Church, which never had been in such a low condition. Should there be no improvement, 'then the Day of Judgment would have to come'. At first he had hoped that Luther might be the Church's reformer. The attack upon the mass showed him that Luther was concerned with more than just abuses. Then he began to feel responsible for the Church's fall. As the years passed, prospect of success faded. He, too, often found himself without funds; and he experienced the weariness of being quite alone. He was deluged in a flood of mocking verse and song. But he persevered.

He, too, suffered from the temptation to refute his opponents word for word – a fruitless method. Indeed, this became his settled principle, and he was indignant that Luther did not oblige by replying in the same style. 'I have compared your book with all the authorities, page by page, and expected you to do the same.'

As the battle developed he acquired greater theological skill. We can even detect the change to a more positive approach; but in essence his work acquired no greater theological depth (cf. below, p. 203).

Now we turn to a totally different figure, a man of first rank, who made much more impression than all the rest: the Franciscan doctor of theology and law, Thomas Murner of Strasburg (d. 1537).

He, too, when he took up arms against the Reformation, was a man of renown, an influential author and the most merciless of all the critics of corruptions in the Church of his day. As with Cochlaeus and Emser, his first concern was to win back Luther to the Church. He knew all about the Reformer's excitability, which laid him open to the danger of throwing the baby out with the bath-water. For this reason he proceeded in a most conciliatory tone in the *Christian and Brotherly Admonition* of 1520, which he addressed to 'our reverend and dear spiritual father in God and brother in the faith of our Lord Jesus Christ'. He was only interested in the truth. Fearlessly he acknowledged the right of the laity to take a hand in reforming the Church, if the clergy failed to do so. Now, however, the well-being of nation and people was at stake. Luther's approach was bound to lead uneducated people into revolt, as had happened in Bohemia; and the exposition of scripture could not be left to individuals. Scripture is a 'deep ocean from which some draw nourishment, and in which some drown'.

This approach of Murner's was no use. The sound of his voice soon died away. He, the acclaimed popular preacher, was smothered in a 'veritable cascade of filth and poison', a heap of scandalous inventions, and made the target for incredibly coarse ridicule. Many – Hausrath, for example – have constructed an image of this poor man from these vile effusions. Murner paid them back in full: 'I ask the whole world to forgive me for the undisciplined language I have used of these church robbers. I know full well how damaging this is to myself. But if I am silent, the villains spread lies about me, and the ignorant believe them. If I speak with moderation I impress no one; if I speak as no man should speak, then I am like those who fight with filth: whether I win or lose I am befouled.'

This, however, does not reveal the heart of the man and his real achievement, although he was a master of popular polemic. In his battle he was not urged on by passion or the desire to shine. 'God knows, it is no bishop or prince that drives me on and commissions me.' As earlier, so now he remained closely linked with the people, whom he did not want to be misled on matters of faith. As a preacher and doctor of sacred scripture it was his duty 'to preserve simple Christianity in all the piety of faith'.

He could not forgive Luther for disrupting the unity of the Church. His own guiding concept was the unity of the Church.

There can be no doubt that Murner far excelled all of his co-workers in 'intellectual agility, specific polemical gifts, and in depth of sensitivity' (Pfeiffer-Belli). His speech was alive and sparkling with religious richness and warmth. He was capable of fervent prayer – for example, to the mother of God:

> All praise and honour,
> O Mary sweet, to thee in faith we bring.
> You have saved Christendom
> from error and suffering.
> Help us to find unity
> through thy Son Jesus, O pure maid!

It is true that his moving polemic made use of other tones as well. On account of the growing animosity in his city of Strasburg, his moving complaints and warnings, which must impress any unprejudiced person, changed into fanatical outbursts and merciless scorn of the 'great Lutheran fools'. It should be noticed, however, that unlike Cochlaeus and Emser, he did not indulge in personal invective. At all times he was concerned about men's souls, and never about his own reputation. He bothered little about theology, except on fundamental points, like the papacy, for example, which alone safeguarded unity, and without which there would be no Catholicism. He always avoided the dry, tedious and oppressive style of the teacher. His polemic was always lively and striking, always ready with repartee. On one occasion Luther involuntarily confirmed this about the 'loquacious word-spinner': 'The Rhine will dry up before you do.'

At all events this Franciscan towered far above the dreary correctness of so many of his Catholic fellow-workers. His writings, like his preaching, revealed a lively personality. His efforts to disclose to Catholics all the treasures of their inheritance showed polemics at its best when given a positive slant.

Unfortunately there was no sign anywhere of a new over-all conception of Christian life. As we have said, one of the great weaknesses of the Catholic effort in those days was that, right up to Luther's death, this man's questions never elicited a new total concept from the defenders of the Catholic faith.

In the ranks of Catholic controversialists there was another Franciscan who, in spite of his frightful dog Latin, is a most congenial character: Caspar Schatzgeyer (d. 1527). This man was a true son of St Francis, as far as such a thing can be revealed in theological writings. He combined staunchness with a dislike of bickering. To the end he maintained an unbiased judgment, and searched in charity for truth. He fought according to the rules of his opponents – proof limited to the text of scripture, but proof in plenty. He kept at sufficient distance from a problem to see its true essence. He kept sufficiently to his own ground in order to maintain the autonomy of his refutations. Thus defence and refutation word for word was happily expanded into something positive and more like preaching.

This was already expressed in the foundation of polemics: it was dutiful responsibility for the Church, for men's souls, that urged him on in a specifically religious manner. 'Woe to me if I do not preach the gospel.'

He may have seen hell filling up as a result of the new heresy, but he saw also the joyful fruits that were ripening as a result of the appearance of this self-same Luther. 'For a long time I have been troubled and sorely oppressed to see Satan with so much power against the word of God. I thought I saw God being utterly dishonoured by the deception of the ignorant and the ignominy and persecution to which true preachers of holy scriptures were being subjected. But now I see how God is so good and almighty that no evil can come, for he is going to bring forth better things out of all this – as St Augustine has explained. I see much good fruit now emerging from the Lutheran error.'

In the central theological dispute over the doctrine of the mass, we will see this positive orientation coming fully into its own.

Schatzgeyer, as representative of a small section, is, unfortunately, a conclusive proof of how ineffectual was the praiseworthy, the obligatory, attempt to be objective. The fulfilment of a supreme requirement reaped tragic consequences: truth and efficacy, which ought to coincide, ran counter to one another. The tragedy of Schatzgeyer and other lesser minds was that they lived in a stormy, belligerent and intolerant epoch. In those days any man in the typical crowd, who was larger-hearted, more spiritual, and of broader vision, would have had to possess genius to survive and to exert a decisive influence upon a wider world. If he lacked this quality, his other qualities only earned him contempt as a weak irenicist. Coarser minds even regarded him as a dishonest compromiser. In the battle his voice was drowned in the din. Speaking gently now to one side, now to the other, he only excited ridicule. All we can say is: did such a man come too late, or too early? Certainly he came at the wrong time. The gentle flame of the irenicist is quite ineffectual in polemics. He accepts a task for which he is quite unsuited. His method would be to extol the glories of his faith, and bring back life to the frigid by the gentle warmth of his mind. But if he is thrown into an atmosphere of vituperation, he is bound to fail; and when, as with Schatzgeyer, he unfortunately lacks popular appeal and a lively style, a certain dullness results and he cannot possibly exert a wide influence on the world around him.

Schatzgeyer was an extraordinarily pleasant and noble religious, imbued with the spirit of the gospel. Any modern Protestants who are inclined to take at its face value all that Luther said about the total corruption of religious orders and of Catholic piety at the end of the fifteenth, and the beginning of the sixteenth, century, need only read the short rule of life for religious orders, which Schatzgeyer wrote for his monks in 1526. It is imbued with a truly interior and free spirit. His efforts, too, to harmonise the dogmas of the old and the new religions breathes the spirit of Christian brotherly love. The coarseness that characterised the literature of the time is quite absent. This Franciscan, who was so severe upon himself, was full of the true missionary spirit, which does not seek its own in the cause it espouses, for it is primarily concerned with the good of its enemy's soul. This is the spirit that is spiritually superior to the scolding rage of the adversary and of its own party.

In his writings, Schatzgeyer discussed every religious question of his time: grace and free will; faith and works; merit and works; penance; the sacrifice of the mass; priesthood and celibacy; communion under both kinds; baptism and Christian freedom; vows and religious orders. At all times he displayed the same excellent attitude that meets its opponent with due respect and an understanding of the problems he poses. Schatzgeyer was free from all the externalism associated with work-righteousness. His spiritual mind and love of God on the one hand, the sovereign will of God on the other, were the keynotes of his life. By one act of generous love for God, a man earns more merit than by a thousand good works, done always with an eye on reward. The freedom of the Christian man and the true kingdom of Christ do not arise out of, or consist in, ceremonies, rites, seasons, food or drink, or such things: they are interior realities.

We will shortly have to mention one or other of the many Catholic literary champions, as we investigate their work according to its theological content – as antidote to the mighty assault of the Reformers. In addition to these we would have to search through the further three hundred Franciscans, Dominicans, Augustinians, secular clergy and laity, who more or less constantly wrote in support of the Church, bearing witness in many parts of Germany to the existence of Catholic life, while the Reformation rolled on to victory. We do not by any means propose to take refuge in easy over-estimates. A survey of the entire Catholic literary effort, gigantic as it was, allows us to break into no triumphal song. There is no star of dazzling brightness. The Catholic literary front knew no consummate, outstanding, leading genius, whose voice spoke for all, and who prepared the way for their words, as Luther did on the side of the Reformation. There was no one who clearly outshone all the rest and created something really new. There was no Catholic whose spiritual dawn brought new and living light even to his own many faithful camp-followers. There was none who had created striking, inflammatory slogans, brimful of the riches of revelation.

Even so, when all has been said, we must admit that these little heard of names and their work represent moral and religious values that have to be included in our estimate of the general spiritual climate of these decades.

II

In those days of the awakening masses, of an emergent public opinion that made its influence felt far and wide in the Church, in theology, and in the schools, in that time of general revolution,

G

the correctness of a doctrine was taken much less seriously than it would have been in more peaceful times. The element of popular appeal, evident in Protestant literature of the sixteenth century, carried much more weight than it would have in other periods. This popular element in theological writing was, in fact, the very form best adapted to addressing the laity. Theological questions were at stake; and in those days an enormous number of people were interested in such questions. As the substance of the new theses pushed the clergy into the background, so the form in which it was expressed had to be 'laicised' if it was to be effective – it had to use non-specialist language. The Reformation became an ecclesiastico-theological lay movement – a popular movement. Its victory would be quite simply decided by whether or not its leaders knew how to put across its theological content to the people. Correct notions, ingeniously embodied in the scholastic formulae of a 'clerical' system, accessible only to the professionals, were no longer of any use. Those things with which Cochlaeus and Emser reproached the Protestants – that they filled their writings with everything that might rouse the passions of the common people – were the very things calculated to bring victory to the new beliefs. The Catholic response was the resolute refutation of each new doctrine, and the demonstration of the evil consequences for Church and state: revolution, the disruption of society, the decay of morals, the destruction of the German nation. Luther was shown to be the collector of a thousand already condemned heresies; his self-contradictions and changes of view were laid bare, as were the disputes between Protestants. But all of these expositions were bedevilled by the ponderous intellectualism of the scholastic tractates.

In spite of invective and coarseness, there was no real bite in the Catholic attack – except in the case of Murner. And so, on the Catholic side, coarseness became a real evil, and damaged the Christian spirit. It became so much a habit, that its absence was regarded as sheer dissembling. For example, the Dominican Pirata was accused of such dissimulation in Constance in 1524 by three Protestant preachers. For their part – as they assure us – they preferred to hold on to and use their rich store of insults. It is true that Catholic coarseness in this period – like Luther's, and like most theological anger in all ages – was rooted deeper than in mere personal passions. As a rule, however, dogmatic intolerance was marred and devalued by personal resentment. Cochlaeus went so far along this path that he could not look for a courteous response from the heretics, nor did he show courtesy to them. He directly damaged Christian charity and also what small prospects there were of making any impression at all upon his opponents. Here we see the vast problem for Christian anger: how to maintain missionary zeal in face of passionate indignation. In those days little attempt was made to seek the erring in love, while feeling violent animosity towards error.

The damaging quality of such invective was felt in those days, although it was frequently excused in Catholic writings. 'No wonder we throw insults when we are compelled to suffer insults daily!' 'I have paid him (Luther) in his own coin and given him measure for measure' (Sylvius; Pirkheimer; Murner).

The great service done by the conciliatory theologians was to draw the poison from this polemic. These men so combined humanistic relativism with understanding Christian charity that all acrimony died away. Aleander had on occasion reminded Cochlaeus of the spirit of charity. With much more spiritual justification, Contarini set the model for dispute at a high intellectual, moral and religious level. He wrote magnificent words of Christian peaceableness. He was a staunch, loyal Churchman, who had the courage to make public confession of his own guilt as a Catholic, and who did not applaud every action simply because done by a Catholic. He wished that 'many Catholics had not written against the Reformers, for they did more harm than good' (1541). Aleander (1523), Erasmus and John Faber of Augsburg had long been of the opinion that many rushed into theological polemics, who only made matters worse by their misguided and badly informed zeal. Pighius and Hoffmeister discovered that there was far too much indiscriminate polemicising, the sheer incompetence of which was calculated more to induce doubt than faith amongst Catholics.

From all that has been said we may conclude that Catholic controversial literature in those days kept a positive end in view also: instruction, encouragement, reconversion. Unfortunately, however, this was the smallest element in its composition. It was chiefly concerned with defence – a secondary activity. Decisive, however, for this and, indeed, for much later theological developments, is the fact that the Reformation period viewed Catholic activity as essentially defensive in face of an aggressive new faith.

In very great measure the Catholic defence was content to go limping along behind Protestant literary production. To begin with there was some reason for this, but soon it betrayed sheer failure. Paris and Louvain were half a year behind developments with their verdict. In 1531–32 Cochlaeus refuted a writing that was already more than a year old; and in that fast-moving period this meant a lot. Wimpina left a manuscript lying for years in order to publish it *post festum*, in an unsuitable form. Hoogestraeten took three years to complete something which should have been written on the spot . . .

Very rarely did Catholic polemic succeed in producing even an *apologia*, let alone something on a grand scale that turned defence into a powerful new confession of faith. In vain we look for a fresh formulation of the old unchangeable truth, at the stimulation of purifying pressures. Certainly the simple exposition of Catholic doctrine in the usual forms was more impressive than it had been; none the less, it was not enough in those revolutionary days. It could but imperfectly penetrate the confused babble of voices, and gain the ear of those now so firmly enchained by novelties, and then keep their attention and support. The same words and formulae do not make the same impact upon men's souls at all periods in history. Only some kind of rebirth could have weighed down the scales against the revolution. Energies were dissipated by too much attention to particular problems. An unintelligent attachment to logic-chopping blinded men to the originality of holy scripture. Too many measured Luther's world – the very opposite of the scholastic world – by purely scholastic methods. As a result the crucial presuppositions, wherein the essential difference lay, were completely ignored. The disputants were talking at cross purposes. This was true of those who had risen to eminence in the scholastic world – Eck, for example – and also of those whose true home was in humanism – Cochlaeus, for example. Very often the whole breadth and depth of history and life was pathetically oversimplified. By far the majority of those swept away by the Reformation had no idea that they were subscribing to a totally new interpretation of Christianity. On the other hand, in method and form the adversary was pursued far too much on his own ground. The Reformers called the tune, and in this period the Catholics were never able to regain the initiative. The Lutherans prescribed the methods and the mode of proof. They demanded proof from scripture, and they proclaimed a new historical perspective. The commendable attempt of most Catholics to comply with this demand and to prove all they possibly could from some text or other in scripture, led to many blunders that made an impression on no one, and often earned ridicule and loss of confidence for Catholic theology.

The Catholics who were reluctant to be led into disputation were the ones who first displayed sensitivity to the dangers of the defensive approach. Aleander adopted this attitude (in his instructions to the German legates). Thus he vehemently opposed the Leipzig Disputation and Luther's hearing in Worms. In 1521 in Worms Cochlaeus had to promise him that he would act merely as a reporter. This, too, was the view of Nicholas Herborn at the synod called by Philip of Hesse in Homberg in 1526. He refused to dispute with Lambert. Eck's *Enchiridion* has one chapter devoted to the very topic, 'that one ought not to dispute with the Reformers'. Bishop Fisher declined to take part in disputation; Hosius saw it as a ruse of the devil, for the procedure seemed to imply the view, that the Church and its doctrine are capable of essential alteration. 'Disputations flourish, schism thrives.' Pighius, too, clearly saw the danger. 'If only most of our Catholics writer had kept out of argument about texts of scripture!' It would have been better to assert with Tertullian, that the heretics have no claim to the Bible. In 1524 the bishop of Constance petitioned the imperial government to act in terms of the imperial bann on disputations and prohibit the 'conversations' for which the town council of Constance were preparing; but the town council went on with these conversations in 1526.

On this point, however, the attitude of Catholics, even of those mentioned, was not uniform. The two great Germans, Eck and Cochlaeus, were both consumed with a desire to dispute. They were both strangely and powerfully influenced by the

Erasmian view, that a storm like this could be ended – like a scientific question – by arbitration. As late as 1540 Cochlaeus could assert during his long conversation with King Ferdinand, that the Reformation could have been stopped had Luther disputed with him in 1521. We discover the same error in Hosius. Although a man with a deeply pastoral approach, he possessed also an exaggerated trust in the power of dialectical proof to settle religious questions.

The result was, therefore, that almost everything depended upon a thorough knowledge of Luther's writings and of his real interests. Superficial refutation was not enough. As we have seen, Luther's personality and writings contained hidden depths. Did his opponents have sufficient understanding of these things to ensure the success of their refutation?

Amongst Luther's literary opponents were men who knew his writings well, who had gone to the trouble of getting to know the Reformer thoroughly. These men wanted to persuade him: Murner, Schatzgeyer, Hoffmeister, Contarini. The same cannot be said with equal confidence of Eck and Cochlaeus. Eck *knew* all that Luther had said – as he *knew* everything indeed – but he did not really know. 'These so-called Christians (Leonard Käser and company) had always lied until now, and I am amazed that intelligent people have not seen what they say is utterly childish and, indeed, proceeds from the devil, the author of lies, the avowed intention of which is to overthrow truth from sheer malice.' Cochlaeus admitted in 1526 that he had not read the whole of *The Babylonian Captivity*. Such defective knowledge of the opponent's writings was all too common. Not only in his youth but in 1545, after he became a bishop, Hosius felt such contempt for Reformed writings, that he could not bring himself to read such *spurcitias*. He was quick to correct this error, however. Catholic literary defence was much marked by a striking underestimate of the power of the enemy. German Catholicism of those days lacked any complete and deep understanding of the Reformation movement. A thousand bitter rejections of Luther's views did not prove that he had been understood. All his life long Cochlaeus waged a selfless and heroic war against Luther; and in the end of the day he completely missed the religious relevance of Luther.

Most certainly, as the years passed, understanding of the world of the Reformers grew. Fisher of Rochester was probably the first to display this wider vision. Others were Bartholomew Latomus, Contarini and Gropper. Hoffmeister, too, correctly applied the Catholic concepts of invincible ignorance and the extraordinary means of grace. All in all, however, on both sides literary dispute was a chain of misunderstanding. Catholic controversial theologians did not do justice to Reformed interests. The moment they found themselves face to face with the violent, damaging, dogmatically false assault of Luther, they forgot how far many of Luther's assertions coincided with Catholic demands for reform. As was necessary and right, they saw what divided them; but very often this was all that they saw. What they had in common was ignored.

It is sometimes said that in a battle the stupidest thing one can ever do is to concede something to one's opponent. This may be true of politics and every kind of material warfare. It may be true in general also if, through a formally false operation, one's own strength is damaged. But it is radically wrong when applied to the battle for intellectual and religious values. Most of all is it wrong when Christianity is concerned. In this case the distinction between polemics and enduring apologetics, between refutation and real persuasion, is a matter of life and death. In this battle one has to lose in order to win. Spiritual victory depends upon one recognising the justice in one's opponent's cause, and his right. The courage to do this is the essence of spiritual warfare, and is a central demand of Christianity. In general, the literary champions of the Reformation, on both sides, mostly ignored this demand. And so with the best will in the world, the Reformation situation was darkened at the centre, and its healing became difficult, became impossible on these terms.

Correspondingly there was a colossal failure of people to admit their own guilt. But such frankness would have demonstrated real spiritual heroism, and a fundamental precept of Christianity would have been perfectly honoured. Complaints sent to Rome about abuses in one's own house or amongst one's own people were no substitute for this frankness. On the contrary, the Catholic position was much weakened, because men, who complained of the moral and intellectual defects of the clergy and the bishops, were silent about the most obvious public corruption of the Church, when face to face with their opponents. They weakened their own position even more by pointing to the emaciated figures of the ascetics as the true representatives of the clergy, by denying the financial exploitation of Germany by Rome, and by refusing to admit any kind of degeneration in the cult of our Lady. Cochlaeus was right: 'The Church now needs people to defend her, should she have to fetch them from the gallows.' At the same time, it was necessary that the defence should be successful. Let there be no mistake: confession of one's own guilt is not the same thing as a lack of self-confidence. The latter ought to be more, not less; pride in one's Catholic heritage ought not to grow dim but become even brighter. But this confidence has to be allied to a sense of freedom and spiritual depth which knows the riches one possesses and is able to put them into currency that is not frozen in dead formulae. Such pride in the gift of divine truth is well able to live alongside consciousness of one's own guilt.

Sad to say, things did not improve with the passage of time. The number of Catholic voices dwindled, as a result of the complete collapse of solid theological study. This collapse had two causes: first, the indiscriminate rejection of scholasticism, and the scientifically and religiously pernicious exaltation of Erasmus; second, the loss of Church property. By 1537 even Eck's voice had lost much of its brilliance and attack. He repeatedly spoke of decline: 'Our numbers are slowly dwindling; and the new men are not so reliable.'

With the passing away of the first generation by about 1550, polemic was largely silenced. In view of the position established by Protestantism, this was an expression of Catholic weakness. Contrary to Eck's affirmation, the new men included some of great quality. However, thirty years later, at the height of positively slanted Catholic reform, the critical, if gloomy, historian of dogma Alphonsus Pisanus, S.J. (for years professor at Ingolstadt and Dillingen), still portrayed the situation as though Catholics were negligent in resisting the Reformation, while Protestants were zealous in spreading it. We know the complaints of Eck and Cochlaeus: 'The Catholic printers and bookbinders are still poor.' 'Wherever one goes to study one comes across heretical books. The heretical printers and publishers triumph and grow rich, for the heretics have all of their ideas printed. Catholics frequently read forbidden books, unwillingly, indeed, for they have nothing else. Meanwhile the Catholic presses print deceitful soothsaying and other nonsense.' 'It is true that many Catholics have written against the Reformation, but not nearly enough. It is not so very easy to write controversy. So far no one has really done it properly.'

From the late thirties onwards we find more frequent sceptical estimates of Catholic theology from the ranks of Catholic writers themselves. People were beginning to see the problems of the age, and thus their own faults, more clearly. They saw how powerless the polemics of the past was to arrest the process of schism. These were the years when the variation in Catholic effort began to settle down into fundamentally different methods, as the situation in Germany and the methods of dealing with it came to be more logically and thoroughly examined, not least, in Rome.

We have already learned that many Catholics did not think much of Eck, and that, for his part, he said harsh things about the controversial writings of Pigghe. Nor was he satisfied with Gropper and Pflug. He himself was so rigid that he had no sympathy at all for any changeability: 'in matters of faith I never quite trust them, for I know what they used to think'. It was not as though Eck never praised anyone at all. He thought that Dr Melchior Vattli, bishop of Constance, an outstanding man from the moral, theological and literary point of view, had been unjustly neglected. He could achieve more than four or five other theologians and still be liked (1541). He admired Bishop Fabri of Vienna, and doubted whether there was another like him at the Viennese court, who could so well serve the cause of the faith.

Contarini provided a marked contrast to Eck. We have already seen his spiritually freer method. His criticism of many Catholic faults was far exceeded by the ever-dissatisfied Witzel, who was utterly pessimistic. We will hear more of him later. He rejected the fatal whitewashing that still went on in Catholic literature. In general, he asserted, the whole of controversial theology was deceiving itself. Its books only provoked new ones. (Pighius said the same thing.) The art of persuasion worked well enough in its own sphere; but in religious controversy all labour was in vain. Witzel complained also, very properly, that 'the Catholics unfortunately defend, not only use, but abuse'; but, 'to want to justify modern practices (in the curia), is to strengthen heresy and bring ruin to the Church'.

Ever since the many literary feuds between the humanists and the schoolmen (we recall the *Letters of Obscure Men*), men had been aware of the burden borne by one attacked by a strong group. Luther's ruthless victory had heightened this experience and the fear it engendered. In 1523 Eck confirmed that many learned German Catholics had written books against the Reformation, but had not risked having them published, out of fear of the slanderous broadsheets of their opponents. The competent and educated humanist, the indefatigable Cologne Dominican John Host of Romberg, publisher of so many works by other Catholics, admitted that hitherto he had not published his anti-Reformation books for fear of the vile attacks he would provoke. The coarsest and basest insinuations were the order of the day. One lampoon depicts the Catholic leaders in a row: Murner – 'ready at all times to protect shame and vice'; he wrote for money, being bribed by Henry VIII. Cochlaeus, too, was bribed, but by the pope. He lived with his smart Anna for concubine. Eck was the worst of the lot: the most indefatigable liar, and insatiable in all sins against the sixth commandment . . .

Not everyone could be intimidated. The work that did get printed proves this. At the end of this period, John Fabri of Heilbronn replied on behalf of all calumniated Catholics. Luther had called him the prince of fools, an ass and a whoremonger, and Justus Jonas the 'whores' patron'. Fabri was a Dominican of nimble wit, a humanist by education, and one who followed the road to reconciliation with unerring step. He was an author of noble and powerful style, and always ready for the fray. In 1558 he added up the work done by the Catholics. He knew of only a part of this work. However, he mentioned briefly thirty-five names of champions of the old faith. Because Flacius had accused him of an immoral life, he replied pertinently in a manner that was both meek and frank. 'I do not deny that I am a sinful man; I confess it, and hope, with God's help to be able to do so with a humble heart in the hour of my death. What Illyricus says, however, about bathing with maidens, I can utterly deny with a good conscience, to the honour of God and the truth. Before God, who shall come to judge the living and the dead, I say that you,

Illyricus, are a dishonest, Godless, perjuring villain, liar, and heretic.' Fabri possessed the inner freedom and outward adroitness that was so lacking amongst Catholic polemicists of the twenties and thirties.

There was, however, a technical reason for the ineffectiveness of Catholic polemics. It arose from the general attitude which we have described as correct but unfruitful and pedagogic.

An important proof of this is the personally unimpeachable Wimpina, from the days of his early disputes until his death in 1530 in Frankfurt/Oder. His correctness and conscientiousness were above reproach; and his writing was marred by no personal coarseness; but he was stiffly conservative. He aimed at knowing all the Fathers and schoolmen by heart, but he had no ability to create anything new. All he would recognise was tradition. This in turn was a characteristic weakness of the intellectual attitude of many Catholic controversialists of the sixteenth century: it was the obverse of a not fully assimilated objectivism. Educated to be mere followers, they were too little aware of the fact that they lived in a new age with its own laws, and that the task had fallen to them of grappling independently and creatively with the problems assailing the Church.

We must not forget, it is true, that the effort thrown in against the Lutheran tide could at first have no prospect of success. Public opinion was dominated by a deep-rooted discontent with Rome. As a result all Catholic effort was deprived of lasting effect. It could count on no sympathetic echo, which would amplify a thousandfold a slogan or the words of a sermon. The Catholic preacher's word was sown on hard and dry soil. The Reformed preaching could count on tropical growth. It is always very much more difficult to give lively and undiminished expression to a total, naturally binding (and even burdensome) tradition, than daringly to preach one-sided truths that one has struggled for oneself (cf. p. 96 f.).

We must probe deeper. Luther's attack was sparked off by a revolution that was essentially religious. He was concerned with the most burning truths of Christianity. If then the Catholic response was conceived as a literary–polemical exercise, rather than as a pastoral action, how could it be other than ineffective from the foundation upwards?

This aspect of the affair in Germany is illumined by a symbolic event: in 1540-41 the old champion Cochlaeus made a retreat with the Jesuit Fr Faber in Worms. As a result Cochlaeus came to see that the schism could be healed only by a return to genuine piety. Here was the formula that was valid in every period of the Church's decline: we will be saved by saints.

III

Let us not bear in mind only what is negative in the picture before us. There was great value in this mighty effort; and we have to define it more exactly, but, obviously, without dissociating it from the inadequacies we have described.

What were the chief functions of this work? First of all the Catholic defence programme prevented the complete collapse of the self-confidence of German Catholics. This was a great danger in face of the enigmatic advance of the Reformation. Theology achieved the protection of the minimum of Catholic life.

Second: as the personal work of Eck, Cochlaeus, Hoffmeister, Witzel, Faber, Gropper, Contarini, etc., this effort was a function of the Church. Like every genuine revolution the Reformation was able to attribute real value only to its own vehemence, its own opinion here and now, its own characteristic way of thinking – which was made to appear miraculous. This subjectification was all the more dangerous as it worked itself out in the sphere of religion, and attacked the inviolable foundation of all human order, given in revelation. In spite of Luther's unconditional attachment to the Word, boundless disintegration threatened – a sinking down into chaotic unrestraint. In opposition to this, the work of Catholic theologians was part of the mighty salvaging of Christian revelation, and of the intellectual and religious heritage of all mankind. The preserving of the objective and of tradition, represents the chief value in the Catholic defence programme. In the midst of far advanced theological vagueness, there were quite clear signs of a unified Catholic foundation, very much along the lines of what Trent was to lay down as definitive.

Berthold Pirstinger, bishop of Chiemsee, had felt this problem of theological uncertainty, with some intensity as the Jesuits did later. Therefore, in his *German Theology* he wanted to demonstrate from St Augustine and the scriptures, 'what at last they were to accept as certain truth'.

The Franciscan John Wild, an upright man, was the only one to remain loyal, when all of the clergy fled from Mainz before the troops of Alcibiades of Brandenburg-Culmbach. (His fellow-religious, Conrad Kling, similarly was the only one to continue Catholic worship after the general apostasy of Erfurt.) He was prevented from preaching only for a short time. When he was allowed to resume his activities, this was his programme: 'God's grace and mercy, shown us in Christ, are what I have preached, and will preach. I have preached the word of God and the gospel of Christ. . . . At all times I have comforted myself with faith in Christ. . . . I will resume my preaching with these things, so that you can see, that all that monks and priests preach is not so evil, perverse, and diabolical' (1552).

In that, we hear the same words set to the same tune as was struck up much earlier by Catholic theologians. In 1527 the Dominican Hermann Rab (d. 1534), who has left us three volumes of sermons (1504–21), turned to resist the indiscriminate verdicts of the Protestants. He found warm, appealing formulae. Hitherto preaching, he affirmed, had not been entirely devoted to the doctrines of men and to human pomp. Naturally his opponents, those who reject mechanical works, 'all walk about in the spirit like supermen or perhaps angels; perhaps they have become wholly angelic or pure spirits. They drift about in the spirit and anything they do not like is vain human doctrine and show.' 'What use to me is the cowl and the monastic life? What use was the desert to John the Baptist, whom Christ praised so highly for the austerity of his life?. . .' 'The pope has coerced us! Utter nonsense! I have done this of my own free will.' 'We read the Old and New Testaments, although the learned little monk says we do not.' If an apostate nun had 'promised as much to some peasant, as she had to God and her bishop, she would have to keep those promises if she did not want to be reproached with unfaithfulness'.

Such general correctives as these are happily supplemented in the treatment of particular controversial theses. Over and over again as we read them the question arises: how was it possible for the Catholic position to be so universally misrepresented on the Protestant side? The saddening discovery is confirmed, that the Reformation schism did not *have* to come.

Let us begin with the principal reproach about work-righteousness. In 1523–24 John Dietenberger of the Dominican order had reiterated the ancient Catholic doctrine about the impotence of man's will, as expounded by the typical representative of Catholicism – St Thomas. 'No man dare trust in himself . . . but only in the mercy of God, from which we derive our good works and not from ourselves; and him alone we should praise in our works.' Good works are meritorious only in so far as they are performed by God's grace, and, indeed, by faith, without which there can be no good works.

In 1530, Peter Rauch, also a Dominican, wrote on justification: 'We are supposed to have taught, that man is able to be justified by his own power and works apart from grace and faith; but good Christians have always known that without prevenient and assisting grace men can do nothing about their own blessedness. This is ordinary Christian teaching.'

Another Dominican, Michael Vehe, expressed the same view in even sharper form at the religious conversations at Leipzig in 1534. 'Righteousness is achieved without the preceding merit of repentance, faith, love, hope or other works, but is given us purely by God's grace. . . . They teach correctly, who say – in this sense – that faith alone justifies, meaning that from justification they exclude what is merited through love or other works.'

Conrad Köllin of the same order, in his commentary on the *Summa*, Ia IIae (1512), teaches that for justification, 'faith above all is required, a lively faith, with repentance of past sins, trust in God's mercy, love and a true purpose of amendment. Justification is attributed to this lively faith. Merit only comes in dependence upon grace, and then, only because God has promised us a reward out of sheer kindness.'

This doctrine was expounded incessantly, indefatigably and in every possible context. To Catholics it was self-evident. We must not forget, however, that the opposition declared the exact opposite to be Catholic doctrine; and, what is more, they very largely justified their break with the Church by this assertion. In the Augsburg Confession itself we read: 'The scholastics wrote not one word on faith – how terrible!'

Specially dangerous were the Reformer's misinterpretations of the Catholic doctrine of the mass, which to them had become an abominable and idolatrous invention of Antichrist. Oecolampadius and others had asserted that, according to Catholic doctrine, the purpose of the mass was to atone for actual mortal sins, Christ's death on the cross having atoned only for original sin. According to Mensing, apostate priests went so far as to declare from the pulpit that 'to offer the sacrament in the form of the mass is such a terrible sin, that they would rather have debauched as many virgins as they had said masses'. Mensing told them, correctly, that it was 'as if they spoke about colour to a blind man'. The correct view, as expressed uniformly by him, or by Rauch, or by the cathedral preacher at Basel, Bishop Augustinus Marius, was that by his sacrifice Christ had blotted out the sins of the whole world. We receive the fruits of the sacrifice of the cross through *means*, the first of which are faith and baptism, then faith and penance and the mass, which is nothing other than a 'fresh representation and memorial of the bloody sacrifice of the cross. Atonement of sins is merited solely by the passion of our Lord Jesus Christ, which gives power and sufficiency to all the other attendant means.' 'The mass is not a sacrifice in the sense that by it fresh satisfaction is made, as though there were some deficiency in the sacrifice of the cross, that had to be supplied by the mass; nor is it an act that is of any use on its own apart from the faith of those who offer it or for whom it is offered.'

Admittedly we soon sense a certain vagueness in the terminology used; and this is confirmed as soon as we examine the polemics about the mass and the sacrifice of the mass more closely.

Cochlaeus, who himself exaggerated the superiority of the papacy beyond all measure, once stated, that it was short-sighted of most Catholic theologians to concentrate all their attention upon the primacy of the pope. To him the attack upon the Blessed Sacrament and the mass seemed much more important; for 'by this Luther threatened to tear the heart out of the body of the Church' (Spahn).

As we have noted, Cochlaeus himself lived by the eucharist. This devotion set the tone of his description of the holy mystery: 'With St Gregory and all of Christendom we believe, that at the time of the sacrifice, when through Christ's words the priest changes bread and wine into the true body and blood of Christ, the heavens open, the angelic choirs are there to greet the mystery of Jesus Christ, the highest stoops down to meet the lowest, and the earthly becomes joined to the heavenly.' 'Hail thou living bread, who art truth and life! In thee is all sacrifice perfected, through thee the Father receives infinite glory, through thee the Church stands firm, for ever unshaken.'

This does not mean that his exposition of the Catholic doctrine of the mass was successful from every angle. He was apt to dismiss the theses of opponents as so much woeful sophistry. Cochlaeus failed to see that Luther held fast to the real presence, regarding him as a Zwinglian and an argumentative rationalist.

The controversy became really sharp, however, over the question of the holy mass as a sacrifice. The opinion put forward on this point by Cochlaeus did not achieve complete clarity, even in his own mind. Isolated elements seem rather to crop up almost accidentally on the fringe of his mind. Or, again, an extraordinarily cut and dried superficial theology is offered. Sometimes 'the rough and stupid laity' were regarded as mere onlookers, who were not supposed either to hear or understand the words of consecration. But when the idea was expressed, that the laity co-operated in the sacrifice, the 'we sacrifice, we return' was suspiciously loudly emphasised.

None the less, Cochlaeus displays at least the elements of a correct theory of the sacrifice of the mass. A valid sacrifice to God can be made only with the fellowship of the Church (for is not holy communion the sacrament of fellowship?). But the one who sacrifices is Christ. It is Christ who presents his body through the Holy Spirit, and who changes the wine into his blood. As he once offered himself for us upon the cross, so it is he who makes the daily sacrifice, and thus is he a priest for ever. 'We firmly believe that our sacrifice in the mass takes place *principaliter* through Christ the Lord, and that the priest is only his minister.'

And so there can be no question of the priest having power to command God. He has authority humbly to entreat God on behalf of the faithful departed, who rest in God's hands, not his.

Murner was the first to see the significance of Luther's central attack upon the mass. To this theme he returns in all his controversial writings. His first remarks bear traces of an inner struggle, and Luther gave him credit for being in earnest in the dispute. 'I smell no lies about you, as about Emser.'

For Murner, too, faith is indispensable with the mass. It is no magic: 'Thank God that you have again discovered that faith and the mass go together!' he said to Luther. 'Catholics have never been short of that commodity.' 'We know every bit as well as Luther, that the mass does not consist in our works and merits, so that it is not even our sacrifice, but Christ's.'

Emser's views were the least adequate. For him, too, eucharist and mass were the main theme. His proof of the sacrificial character of the mass, however, was notably absent. It is true that Emser correctly relied upon the Church and the concept of the Church, but he did not see how this fact really affected his theme. The dominant thought was that 'we sacrifice'. There was no trace of the fact that, as on the cross, so here, Christ is the real offerer. Nor did he see the sacramental unity between Christ and the faithful.

This narrow theology arose from the popular notion of the fruits of the mass. 'Has anyone ever seen, or heard of, someone assisting devoutly at mass and suffering any hurt on the same day, or if he did, failing to be miraculously healed?'

Emser could have learned better from the book written by Henry VIII on the seven sacraments. He himself translated this book in 1532. This sharply accentuates the objectivity of the action of the mass: what happens at the altar is so far beyond human strength that it cannot be diminished by any sin of the priest. Obviously, faith is presupposed, just as Christ saves no one apart from faith. In the mass Christ himself is both priest and victim.

Amongst the controversialists of those days were those also, who could cope with the task in hand. These treated this mighty theme on the grand scale it deserved, approaching it with real religious depth. This can certainly be said of Caspar Schatzgeyer. With a clarity that left nothing to be desired, Schatzgeyer expressed views in all of his works, which would have completely altered Catholic devotional attitudes, had these ideas not been allowed to fall right into the background for centuries. The basic thesis, which he never ceased repeating, was this: the mass and the sacrifice on the cross are one. The sacrifice of the mass is the sacrifice Christ himself made to the Father, on the cross, and which is made present for us in the mass, not just as a memorial, that is in mind, but as a real event – 'a glorious and true making present'. The sacrifice of the mass is more the sacrifice of Christ than it is that of the Church or of the priest. It is not our action and our sacrifice in the sense in which we make other sorts of offerings of our own. The minister of the Christian Church does not perform the act as though he wanted to give something of his own to God the Lord, or as though what he gave were a personal merit of his own or of his own or of someone else. 'The priests of the new covenant do not take Christ's place, and acknowledge no other priesthood except that of Christ himself, just as they know of no other sacrifice.' 'Christ alone is priest and sacrificer, the others are simply ministers.' 'Christ is both priest and sacrifice.'

Again, the concept is magnificently deepened when Schatzgeyer introduces his basic conviction about the unity between Christ and the Church: 'The one who makes the sacrifice is the whole Christ – Head and body,' . . . 'the Church, including all its members.' For these members are all 'priests and a royal priesthood, and therefore possess the power to offer sacrifice'. But 'what is it that the members of Christ offer in their sacrifice if it is not Christ, their Head, who lives and works in them, and in whom, in turn, they live and work, and through whom all their sacrifice is acceptable?' The sacrifice is wholly referred back to Christ. In this deep sense the mass is 'a sacrament of the community of all Christians', and hence, 'all members of the Church, living and dead, share in it, for even the dead live within the unity of the body of Christ.'

It is a plain fact that where the concept of the mass is expressed in terms of the priesthood of Christ and of the idea of the mystical body of the Lord, there we find a living centre of Catholic Christian life. When we assess the disposition of power and try to see this whole period in true balance, it is essential that we should be aware of these views.

From the beginning of the literary dispute Catholic theologians accommodated their methods to those of their opponents, and tried to prove their theses solely from the scriptures (and the Fathers); but it is remarkable that very many of them, while tactically acquiescing in this method, were well aware of the inconclusiveness of the method, and in fact rejected its validity, 'because each party claims the support of scripture, Catholics and Protestants'. There are numerous examples from the disputations. In opposition to the radical Anabaptists, however, the Lutherans, too, appealed to the traditional usage of the Church. If nothing can be accepted save what is in scripture, what scripture proves the canonicity of the Gospels? 'Where is it written that we must believe the Gospel of Matthew, of John, or the others? If it is not written, why then do you believe the Gospel of John?' (Mensing; Ambrosius Catharinus; Pelargus).

This, too, was a reinforcement of the idea of the Church and its authority. There was only one way open: to preserve true doctrine and hence unity, that is attachment to the Church. The same Dietenberger, who in 1530 had constructed his *Questions* purely upon scripture proofs, demonstrated the fundamentally correct method in his *A Muzzle for The Bible-Thumpers*. Before taking up separate points at issue, he defined the Church and her authority. This was, in fact, the heart of the matter. Without a clarification of views on this point, everything else was bound to end in confusion. For this reason Hoffmeister, who had worked until a late date to achieve a reunion of the parties – while tolerating no ambiguity – and who was a frank critic of curial excesses, submitted his book on the Augsburg Confession to the judgment of the Church. 'We seek harmony in the Church; we love the Church; we have devoted ourselves utterly to the Church.' At the time when the religious conversations were beginning, Cochlaeus frequently returned to this theme: every discussion of particular tenets of faith is unprofitable if there is no agreement on the concept of the Church. Is there or is there not a visible Church with a final court of appeal in the living teaching authority of the pope and a council?

The topic itself and the historical evolution of the quarrel, including its long preliminary history, resulted in the question of the primacy of the pope being specially violently disputed (see p. 226). At this point it will suffice if we point out that by no means all of the strictly Catholic theologians were in favour of exaggerated curialism. In 1522 John Heigerlin-Faber, later bishop of Vienna, contributed greatly to the clarification of Catholic thought by his frank criticism of curialism allied to loyalty to the Church. In 1523 the Dominican Conrad Köllin and many others declared that the pope, as an individual, could err and become a heretic, but not in his capacity as teacher of the Church. Aleander believed that Luther's early theses on the pope could be discussed. Thomas More believed that Henry VIII, in his defence of the seven sacraments, had exaggerated the power of the primacy.

Above all, however, it was the courageous attitude of the reforming cardinals under Paul III, that demonstrated how the widespread and justified anti-curialism of Germany could be allied to an undiminished acknowledgment of the primacy of the pope.

Basically, in their doctrine of the Church and of the primacy, the Catholic theologians simply developed the fundamental distinction between the person and the office – the distinction which, unfortunately, Luther missed altogether. As John Host of Romberg said: 'Had he only striven for reform in and through the Church! The whole world would have flocked to him. However, by the goodness and power of God, even Luther's heresy will help bring about true reform according to the precepts of the apostles and the Fathers.'

The correct and orthodox theology which we have mentioned was, however, frequently bedevilled by the unhealthy vagueness of Catholic theology. This was almost entirely overcome by the Council of Trent. The defined doctrine of unity began to take effect: the present common Catholic basis became a thorough reality.

The new situation had very little effect upon the period with which we are concerned. Catholic confidence had been mightily reinforced by the fact that the final great remedy had been applied: a general council had met. The solemn decrees produced a sense of possessing the ancient apostolic tradition, and of being joined by an unbroken chain to one's divine and apostolic origins.

This was an experience that brought extraordinary power. The universal Church was speaking far too late; but her voice had far deeper resonance than the voices of all the countless disputants on both sides, if only because men had grown so unaccustomed to hearing her voice. Moreover, when this voice really began to be audible north of the Alps, the loudest tongue in Germany was for ever silent: Luther was dead.

Simply through the knowledge of Catholic truth, the Council of Trent eminently advanced the positive elements in Catholic controversial theology. For, what was thus imparted was the very opposite of arid, merely correct formulae. The decrees were genuinely theological, were profound and arresting; they really mastered the problems, speaking from the fullness of scripture and tradition, and for the universal Church.

The beginnings of this change in controversial theology from a negative defensive approach to a positive approach lay quite far back in time. It lay, in fact, in the special and quite indispensable sense of religious and pastoral need.

We have already shown how this applies to Eck and Cochlaeus. Wimpina, too, moved slowly away from technical polemics to the awareness, that it was more important to educate the clergy and educate people in positive religion. The manuals of dogma were a product of this movement. Religious warmth is specially noticeable in the *Dogmatics* of Berthold Pirstinger. Most important of all was the production of sermons and catechisms. Eck produced his model sermons based on scripture by commission of the Bavarian dukes William and Ludwig. He himself set great store by this part of his work. With pride he referred Aleander to the four-folio volumes of his sermons: 'there you will see what Eck is capable of in this field'. It is a fact that he did much useful work by these German models, which were then translated into Latin.

By contrast, Eck had very little success with his horribly uncouth translation of the Bible. No wonder! The gulf between this and Luther's linguistic masterpiece is appalling. On the other hand, John Dietenberger's translation compares very favourably with many others. His was the most read Catholic German Bible. Dietenberger had learned a lot from Luther; and he acknowledged his debt to Luther's work. No less than fifty-eight editions of the whole work are known, and fourteen of the New Testament. Dietenberger was also responsible for a catechism (1537), which was entirely positive in conception. In it Nicholas Paulus found 'no trace of bitterness' but 'the calmest and noblest language, the most charming instruction', and amongst other qualities, 'excellent discussion of the simple faith, that God is, and of faith in that God'.

John Fabri, O.P., from Heilbronn, learned from Dietenberger, when, in 1551, he wrote his catechism, in which he actually incorporated a few propositions from Luther's Shorter Catechism. In 1549 he compiled a biblical concordance of doctrine and practices for the assistance of preachers.

At this time Frederick Nausea was working as a preacher at the Viennese court of King Ferdinand. His sermons were distributed far and wide. This man was an ascetic, and his words produced a deep impression. Unfortunately his Larger Catechism – a comprehensive exposition of Catholic doctrine – became a symbol of the absence of sacrificial spirit amongst Catholics: its publication was delayed because funds were not forthcoming.

The composition of this class of literature was completed by a series of confession manuals and hymn-books (the hymn-book of the Dominican Michael Vehe: fifty-two hymns with tunes, for use inside and outside church, including not one ribald song). These gained great authority and enjoyed wide distribution through the backing of Hosius, Canisius and the Catechism of the Council of Trent.

There can be no doubt that the chief result of the Council of Trent was the gathering together of forces. Catholic endeavours were retrieved from isolation. The call for organisation and concentration, for uniform direction of Catholic energies, had found a very special response.

By this time the concentration of Catholic energies had become a prime necessity, just as hitherto its neglect had been inexcusable. Blame had to be laid not least upon the curia, who took far less care of loyal Catholic theologians in Germany, than of dubious benefice-hunters, even those with Lutheran leanings.

We already know about the efforts and bitter disillusionment of the indefatigable Cochlaeus, which he reported to Pole, after twenty years experience. Eck, for his part, had affirmed in his reform proposal to Adrian VI: 'The Lutheran cause relies upon books. For this reason, if one were to provide twenty of the most learned men in Germany with benefices of a sort, so that they were not so much despised, the battle would be half won already.' He also demanded that scholarly work be organised: the pope should arrange for the printing of the proceedings of the ancient councils; scholars should be appointed who would prove the falsity of Luther's basic doctrines from ancient sources (scripture, the Fathers; the councils). Fabri, too, in 1525 demanded of Clement VII that Luther be refuted by a combined effort of theologians chosen by the German bishops. Likewise, in 1524 James of Salza, bishop of Breslau, asked for the centralisation of the work of controversy. The previous year Aleander expressed radical views on the prerequisites of a proper Catholic controversial theology (the first curialist to do so): the work to date did not impress him in the least; it had done more harm than good. He found reason (as had Bishop James of Salza) to demand expert knowledge of Catholic disputants. The nuncios must know Luther's writings thoroughly. He suggested the production of a register of Catholic literary opponents of the Reformation, according to dioceses. In 1536 John Heigerlin-Faber made the same demand in his memorandum for the council. It was necessary to know the Reformers' writings thoroughly; and the curia would have to support the defenders, as yet totally unprovided.

The first more or less official recommendation of the organisation of the literary defence in the broad sense was made when the Catholic princes, bishops and theologians met in Cologne on 5 January 1531, for the election of Ferdinand I as king of the Romans.

As we know, however, all proposals, entreaties, demands made to Rome at first accomplished nothing, and later very little. What else could one expect of Clement VII and his court? All that counted there was diplomacy. No one had any understanding of the importance of intellectual discussion. Indeed, they despised such things. Even the support of individual theologians was shamefully parsimonious. Some of these never gained actual possession of the livings allotted to them, because members of the curia or Lutherans disputed them. Complaints became more numerous. The ex-Dominican Peter Sylvius, filled with an exemplary love for the Church, was forever complaining of how his anti-Lutheran labours were hampered by sheer penury: he had neither money nor sufficient opportunity to print.

In 1525 Eck was complaining that the curia did not support him against Gotthard Wackinger in his benefice dispute, and let the living go to the heretics. Even if we regard this and similar occurrences as private affairs, the fact remains that the curia showed hardly any interest in one of their most indispensable champions within Germany. Certainly it is not true that 'all scholars would regard the neglect of Eck as typical'. It may well be, however, that Eck was unable to keep a secretary and clerk, on account of Roman stinginess – as he himself asserted. 'How hard up we are, who labour for the faith!' He received no recognition for the 'disputations, books, sermons, and dangers I have undertaken for the reputation and honour of the apostolic see, while the ignorant are abundantly provided for. Eck, the defender of the faith is placed lower than the pope's cooks and coachmen.'

He was still uttering such complaints in 1540 and 1542; and these complaints were in harmony with those of Pighius to Paul III: it was a rare thing for a pope to reward a scholar.

It may well be that as the tide in Rome turned towards reform under Paul III, literary theological work began to be more highly esteemed. Morone demanded, that the few theological scholars still to be found in Germany ought to receive financial support (admittedly he adds – 'as in the past'). Correspondingly his instructions told him to support Fabri, Eck, Cochlaeus, Nausea, Witzel, Hauer, Marstaller, Köllin, Herborn, Dietenberger and Bernard of Luxembourg. But even the curious assortment of names on this list, ranging from loyal churchmen down to doubtful starters like Witzel, and from Eck and Cochlaeus down to the utterly insignificant Bernard of Luxembourg, inspires little confidence. The assortment certainly matches the success, or rather the lack of success, of the enterprise. It is a fact that the reform memoranda of the seventies – even in respect of literary defence and edification – give the impression that hitherto nothing, or very little, had been done, and that no one in Rome had a correct picture of the state of affairs in Germany. They did, however, acknowledge the importance of Catholic controversial theologians[2] and were willing to describe them as collaborators with the truth. In every country such theologians were to be assembled to support the German defenders of the faith. Because of the great Protestant literary activity, and the great threat this was to the faith, the apostolic see was to appoint outstanding men to plan and supervise the defence by refuting the most damaging writings. (How Eck, Cochlaeus, Faber-Wien and Hosius had all exerted themselves in this way!)

It is against the background of this curiously uncomprehending attitude in contemporary official circles, especially in Rome, that the loyalty of the Catholic controversial theologians begins to shine out in its full worth.

This controversial work was amazing both for its unshakeable conviction, and for its indefatigability. On close inspection we see a marvellous richness of labour, devotion, docility, passionate conviction, too, and powerful eloquence. It is most moving to see how poor wretches, despised and lonely, sometimes exiled, often in ill health, doggedly persisted in their defence of the old Church for ten, twenty, thirty years and more, throwing all their resources into the cause, using their own books, and paying for the printing of foreign books, until they had not a penny. 'In spite of opposition, in spite of the hopelessness of winning back the heretics, like a servant who owes his master a hundred bushels of wheat or a hundred measures of oil, they offered their hundred chapters in the name of God' (Pirstinger). Compare with them the careless, drowsy prelates. 'Had these wealthy prelates possessed the same zeal for the Church as these poor priests, the state of German Catholicism would have been quite different.' 'But when so few prelates take any interest in defending the Church, what can such as I do, oppressed by poverty and distress, to save the Church?' (Peter Sylvius).

Pessimism? It is perfectly true that the firm conviction that truth was possessed in the Church, the unwearied effort to refute Luther, and the ultimate increase of positive religious instruction

[2] Canisius considered that in Germany one author was worth ten professors. Therefore he recommended the setting up of a special Jesuit writers' college for the production of controversial literature in the German language.

of Catholics, did not go hand in hand with a feeling that victory was imminent. On the contrary, the feeling that one was defending lost positions filled the hearts of many Catholic champions. Even a man like Cardinal Hosius spoke more than once of the 'declining Church'.

This fact makes the loyalty of the man all the more admirable. In 1528 Wimpina announced that in face of the failure of so many theologians he wanted to carry on working even if there seemed to be no prospect of rooting out the heresy. In the same year Berthold Pirstinger admitted that hope of winning back the heretics must be abandoned: the devil would never let them go. Bishop Fisher of Rochester was the first to express the notion of abandoning Luther personally, and saving every effort for those whom the arch-heretic had led astray. This was the most important Catholic form of the notion of reunion.

One of the consequences of the low quality of the cathedral chapters and of the episcopate in Germany until the forties was the absence of any controversial writer in any episcopal see – with the one exception of Berthold Pirstinger. Another consequence was that the bishops, for their part, only very rarely placed such men in influential positions.[3]

A man like Gropper had influence because he was vicar general of Cologne. The same was true of John Heigerlin-Faber who was a counsellor of Archduke Ferdinand, then vicar-general of Constance, then bishop of the small and poor diocese of Vienna (from 1539); and it was true of Nausea. The opposition knew this and exploited the fact. The work of Eck, Emser, Cochlaeus, and then that of the participants in the great literary and oral discussions in Augsburg in 1530, and in the religious conversations of the forties, even the work of the monastic superiors and the provincials of the orders, was raised above the purely private level only in a very limited degree. None of it was allowed to exert a wider sphere during a reasonable period of time. What significance did Eck's lecture-room have for public opinion in those days? On account of his unwearying literary output it had

---

[3] Bishops like Marius Augustinus and Leonard Haller (in Eichstätt), men of modest intellectual stature, were effective only to the extent that they knew how to use their pulpits.

some significance; but his speech and personality certainly had not enough weight to attract a stream of youth to Ingolstadt. Only on rare occasions did he have authority to coerce public opinion by direct intervention in public institutions. His three missions to Rome, his reform proposals to the curia and his work in Germany as promulgator of the bull of excommunication of Luther and his followers, were important. But how little autonomy he was granted, how small the recognition he received from Rome for all his labours! His intervention in Memmingen, where he was invited by the clergy, and in Constance, where he was invited by the town council, was of little significance. Aleander recommended him to Rome as a suitable candidate for a bishopric; but this came to nothing. And yet we must consider what Eck might have been able to accomplish, had he been given adequate power to intervene in affairs; for he had closely observed the activities of his opponents in their literary spreading of the Reformation, he knew how to assess the importance of the regions according to their population densities, and he had carefully weighed up the possibilities of resuscitating the Swabian League (1535). In addition he proved himself an adept in all manner of wire-pulling. He gave the nuncio, Vergerio, advice, which revealed a knowledge of human nature and a gift of handling men. He could say of himself, that he knew almost all the personalities of the day, great and small, clerical or lay, Lutherans, Zwinglians, Catholics and semi-Christians.

Had there been about half a dozen theologians like Eck and Cochlaeus occupying German bishoprics from 1520 onwards, the course of the discussion, that was so decisive for the nation, would have been notably relieved of the lamentable burden of Catholic apathy.

IV

Advancing, or even incipient Catholic reform had a good effect even upon controversial theology. It grew in a noticeable measure, intellectually and spiritually, and extended its effective radius. Episcopal sees were conquered. Figures of greater and broader stature appeared, able to exert a more powerful effect upon the wider stage of history.

An outstanding representative of this transformation in Germany was Stanislaus Hosius, a controversial theologian of high standing, and also a bishop of blameless and devout life, a model of devoted pastoral activity. Because, in addition, he was a typical representative of the methods, the aims and the intellectual outlook of a large section of Catholic controversialists in this period, it is worth while examining his work more thoroughly. His ideas form part of the total store of Catholic thought, in a higher degree than his specifically literary work indicates.

Following occasional and insignificant polemics against the Reformation in 1526 and 1527, from 1545 onwards he took up full-scale practical and theoretical battle to 'protect the faith'. The definitive crisis in his life – the transformation from humanism to theology, more precisely to St Augustine – had provided a thorough preparation for this work.

Hosius stood in the tradition of orthodoxy as typified most clearly, with all its advantages and disadvantages, by Eck. Hosius was the end of the line, the point where it was consummated in genuine Catholic reform and the Counter-Reformation. He was the consummation through his religious depth and also through his episcopal and prince-episcopal status.

How did Hosius assess the situation? He saw the Church in the utmost danger of destruction. Hence there could be no talk of waiting. The issues at stake were neither insignificant nor innocuous. The Church with all its doctrine and life formed an absolute unity. Nothing may be wrenched from her store without the whole thing collapsing.

The most blatant expression of this threat to life from within was the well-known abuses, the indifference of bishops and the incredibly far-reaching theological confusion. The clearest indication of this was the craze for disputations. According to Eck, Herborn, Catharinus Politus and Schatzgeyer, Hosius reiterated Jerome Stoszseufzer's complaint, that of all arts, biblical exposition alone was regarded as an open field wherein anyone might romp around without any previous schooling. This was the pernicious implication of the quite untenable scripture principle.

Hosius saw the terrible corruption in the Catholic ranks. Unfortunately even he lacked the spiritual freedom to confess this publicly, in writings designed for publication. In this he fell behind the frankness shown by Hoffmeister and Schatzgeyer. He even indulged in deliberately tendentious representation. In this sphere trust in the intrinsic power of truth was very small indeed. In this he acted the politician. He was at war; and in war it is imprudent, damaging, impossible, to hand over an advantage to the enemy in the form of an admission of one's own weakness.

Nor is it true that Hosius felt these abuses in the Catholic ranks as a personal spiritual burden, no matter how severely he condemned them, and no matter how alien they were to his own priestly qualities. He lived by a profound belief in divine providence: these abuses were God's punishment for the sins of his people, and thus did not come about apart from the will of God. What did they mean in respect of heresy? Truth enjoys absolute primacy, and so he regarded a single heresy, a single case of schism, as much more serious than all moral turpitude added together.

Hosius took no more to do with Luther personally. For him the Reformation was already a fixed historical structure. He knew Reformation literature better than any other Catholic. We may not say, however, that as a result he came to a deeper understanding of the aspirations of the Reformers.

In Hosius' eyes, the essence of the Reformation was uproar, rejection of authority. The threat to the special priesthood implied a threat to special princedom – to the state. The essence of the Church was her unity. Hence the Reformation stood condemned – all the more because the motives which gave rise to it were so base. Hosius goes so far as to assert that the Augustinian monk Luther revolted to begin with out of sheer envy of the Dominican Tetzel, who was preferred before him as the indulgence preacher. This envy turned to pride, which dared to reject all of the Christian past – theology, councils, popes and the saints. Thus there was nothing religious about the Reformation, as far as he could judge. If Luther did not see things in a different light before he died, he would be damned.

He applied the same judgment to all Protestants. Hosius shared Catharinus Politus' opinion, that more or less all heretics were culpable. He scarcely even hinted at any theoretical 'invincible ignorance'. As a rule his condemnation was expressed positively and unconditionally. The Reformers had simply ceased to be Christians. There was only one Christianity – Catholic Christianity. Anyone who apostatised was a heathen and had no right to call himself a Christian. Catholics ought to have no dealings with the Reformers, but should keep strictly and utterly apart from them. This conviction was fundamental for Hosius. Christianity is an indivisible whole. This unity is a precondition of Christian life. 'Were you to accept every article of faith, but refuse submission to the Church, you would have no kind of fellowship with Christ.'

These few points allow us to see Hosius' intellectual and religious disposition: spiritually integrated, but lacking intellectual breadth, quite static, a hearer of the word only. He took up Catholic doctrine in direct contradiction of the Reformers, and carried the antagonism further, so that there would be no danger of his doctrine suffering damage or loss. In a deep sense Hosius was incapable of appreciating alien values. He lacked all understanding for what we might call justifiable relativism (a recognition, for example, of the capacity for development in what remained the same in essence, the recognition of subjective variation in the appreciation of the same object). This was striking enough in a humanist. On only one point did he show any flexibility: he of all people, strict churchmen that he was, replaced the rigid Catholic catechism of Filippo Archinto by that of Erasmus.

He never knew what tragedy there could be in seeking for and holding fast to truth. Until his dying day he read and learned almost without interruption. But his mind never developed. His intellectual outlook never changed. He never reshaped the idea of the Church in terms of a new style of preaching. As he had never wrestled for, but merely learned, what he knew, he remained essentially a conserver. This was a primitive Catholic attitude. Hosius was the predestined vessel into which the rigid Catholic system could be stuffed quite objectively without noticeable breakage, and then used to determine the Catholic mind of his time.

The work and effect of this man display the irreplaceable value of this absence of complication, this simplicity, this integrity. Hosius had made Christian *serving* mean *serving and nothing more;* but that is what was urgently needed by Catholics at that time. They had to experience and grasp the value of perfect unity and of an absolutely fixed foundation. They had to grasp in all its fullness that reality, for which Catholicism must be the vehicle, and without which it would cease to exist – the Church.

As might be expected, the notion of the Church stood at the centre not only of Hosius' theology but of his whole thought. This, and the religious depth arising from it, revealed the true and definitive function of this man within the Catholic restoration.

Hosius was powerfully possessed by a sense of the uniqueness and sacred authorisation of the clerical office in contrast both to secular and state authority, and to the general Christian calling. There was no justification for Protestantising princes or town councils meddling in questions of doctrine. The authority of the priesthood, of the episcopate in particular, alone conferred that right. Hosius was indignant that the bishops' sense of their own spiritual power had grown so weak. 'There was a time when even mighty rulers showed great reverence and fear for the words of the bishop. Today it would seem as though we bishops were afraid of our own shadows. The bishops no longer appreciate their own dignity.'

The power of the bishop is seen at its height in the pope. Going further than Contarini, who showed some hesitation in his doctrine of the primacy, but avoiding the exaggerated curialism of the anti-episcopal Pigghe, Hosius exalted the pope's juridical primacy above the status it had in the common Catholic view of the time, and made the pope centre of unity in an absolute sense. All unity depends upon him; whoever is not subject to the pope is no Catholic. The pope alone guarantees that fellowship within the Church, upon which all infallibility rests. In contrast to Lutheran or Protestant individualism – his deadly foe – he held fast to the notion that revelation is no private possession. The truth is never found with the individual but always in community. To be rooted in the Church, to live with it and out of it, is not one important detail – it is everything. 'Whoever utters the word of scripture on his own and not in union with the Church, advertises his own little private property; even while using the very words of scripture he is lying; it is the devil who opens his mouth.' This is fundamental egotism – Satan's great objective, or 'throwing oneself down from the pinnacle of the temple'.

The question becomes quite urgent: what, then, did the

Reformers mean by their demand for the 'clear word of God'? Over and over again came impressive proof that 'the word of God is not plainly given as soon as a sentence of scripture is quoted'. The word of God comes when its true meaning is understood, and that is by the Church. 'Not every word of God is God's word; that is not everyone who utters a word from scripture is telling us what God is.' Proof of this lies in the mass of various interpretations there have been of scripture, especially since the appearance of the Reformers. Had not Luther himself, when fighting the fanatical sectarians, had to call the Bible the heretics' book? And wherein, had the Church not spoken, would be the distinction between canonical and uncanonical books?

For this reason Hosius and the adherents of the old Church fought this mighty battle. It was not in order to advance their own personal opinion but to defend the Church. On this issue Hosius was spokesman of the essential point of view of Catholic controversial theology: it knew that it was a function of the Church.

The Church's superiority lay in her essentially objective and hence inviolable, holy, sacramental and teaching authority. Separation of person and office is essential to the Catholic viewpoint. Once again, history provided the apologia for theory. Hosius, following Augustine, pressed the affirmation that no pope was ever a heretic, and asserted that whoever does not accept Judas the betrayer as an apostle of the Lord, does not accept the Lord. This was applied to the contemporary situation: the Lord slumbered even in his unworthy episcopal representatives.

In his own activities Hosius realised this requirement in a high degree. Scarcely any other controversialist of the sixteenth century felt so deeply and expressed so well the sense of the total *otherness* and inviolability of revelation. In a degree hitherto never achieved he was unexceptionably orthodox. He kept a firm hold on the total content of scripture. He was the perfect hearer of the word: the institution of the Church preserved faith. Only one institution was justified and stood firm – the Catholic Church. For Hosius the *sentire cum ecclesia* had become the substance of everything – in a most productive form. It grew, not least, out of the sense of a mighty inherited and obligatory tradition. He was filled with deep reverence and enthusiasm for this patrimony. This was what he demanded, and this was why he fulminated against the self-assertion of the Reformers of yesterday and today, whom he considered to be blasphemers.

This complete unbroken attachment to the Church provided the objective basis for radical polemic against Luther and the Reformation, a polemic which ran to the severest condemnations. The colossal coarseness indulged in by Hosius, and his frequently unintelligible polemic, are quite free from personal passion or base hatred. This was due in part to the balance and habit of obedience which controlled this man's whole behaviour. He knew nothing of fanatical, overwhelming ardour. His warmth never flared up into a furnace. This, too, was why his positive work of reconstruction did not mature completely. On the other hand, it was what marked out his polemic as so superior to that of his opponents and to that of many of his colleagues.

The extent to which this polemic exhausted itself in sheer defence against the Reformation, is astonishing. Hosius' *Confessio* contains the most comprehensive Church dogmatics written before Trent. It was written with a polemic slant. Occasionally he had seen the whole work of Trent itself from this angle, and tried to give it a practical application. His testament was no exception. Filled with a spirit of devout prayer a sense of deep responsibility, this document, written as a solemn profession in God's sight, yet turns into a polemical definition and defence of Catholicism against Protestantism.

In this polemic we find again all of those themes which gradually came to form the stock in trade of the Catholic defence programme in the Reformation period. The chief theme was the fact of intra-Protestant schism. (In the fifties Hosius could provide ample evidence of this.) This was stressed over and over again, and demonstrated to be the result of the scripture principle, which was self-destructive. Luther's own self-contradictions were used similarly.

It is obvious, however, that we have not got far beyond the isolated polemics of the early Reformation period. The manner of treatment of themes had expanded; wider contexts were evident, and the dispute had moved to more fundamental issues. This did not mean that a more intellectual and creative theology was emerging. The theology was primarily pastoral and homiletic. It

H

was even essentially rhetorical. It is true that Hosius wrote in Latin that was on a par with the best models of the age for clarity, measure, 'theological majesty', and for variety and impressiveness. Hosius shared Eck's and Fisher's belief that in practice the forcible suppression of the Reformation was necessary and permissible. It could even be regarded as a duty of charity. In view of the situation it was even admitted that apart from the power of the scepter, all labour was in vain. He himself had experienced this in his attempts to bring back to obedience to the Church those cities over which he had spiritual, but not temporal, jurisdiction. The arguments which in the end persuaded his political subjects, were ineffective with those who were merely his spiritual subjects. The Reformers should be exiled. Only, indeed, if it were possible to expel them all. If this were impossible they should all be allowed to remain, so that they might destroy one another. Strife amongst the heretics means peace for the Church!

Supported by the above-mentioned episcopal and priestly self-confidence, in the essential form of a sense of pastoral responsibility, Hosius repeatedly and tenaciously returned to attack the Reformers. The organisation of the work, the uniform direction and logical execution, which he demanded of the bishops, he himself performed in an exemplary fashion.

His experience in the chancellery of Bishop Tomicki and the connection he formed there enabled him to use a variety of ways of exerting his influence, including that of direct legislation. Tirelessly he admonished the bishops and the court: 'Perhaps on one occasion, one of these many words will touch somebody's heart!' He incessantly sent letters to scholars, officials, to the king's physician, to preachers, to the queen, to the legates and to the irresolute king himself. He never tired, even when they ceased replying. From the fifties Hosius was a living centre of Catholic controversial theology for the whole of Europe. His literary works magnified his effect. His *Confessio* went through thirty editions in as many years, and was translated into several languages.

In spite of this, on account of the lamentable weakness of his episcopal colleagues, and of the nobility, and in face of the victories of the Reformation, he had a profound sense of standing alone. But he thrived on this; the feeling did not paralyse him but moved him to perseverance. Measured in time and quantity, he performed an enormous work under the most adverse circumstances. His energy never flagged. He was a genius of effort. In a more propitious atmosphere what might he not have accomplished! His life's work was not the fruit of a brief creative outburst. Hosius' unusual gift was iron concentration and noble pertinacity. He kept on working at full capacity until a ripe old age: the Church must remain; the Reformation must not win.

Hosius' personality and work were utterly imbued with the one spirit that did have power to heal that age: the spirit of true religion. His work arose and grew as a response to the religious need; and it was sustained solely by deep interior religious resources. Hosius made little attempt to gain material power and property; in terms of his own age, he was a model of virtue on this score. He never sought money. In 1539 he declared his programme: the kingdom of God; Christ; abounding charity. A bishop is merely steward of earthly possessions, not their lord. 'What we possess belongs to the poor.'

His vivid, magnificent sermons – which, unfortunately, made him an exception amongst the prince bishops of his day – impressively proclaimed salvation. Christ crucified was their beginning, middle, and end: the cross alone is our redemption, the grace of God is all our hope. His supreme righteousness of the spirit leaves no room for any idea of *work-righteousness*.

His testament is a natural and abundant stream of devotion from a true worshipper to the Father of mercy, through his crucified Son, who alone is our justification. It breathes the spirit of the scriptures and the liturgy. On his death-bed Hosius still maintained this same spiritual disposition in an extraordinary manner.

His whole life bore this stamp. Even his polemics are deeply characterised by the thought that grace is everything, and all our striving and virtue but the work of an unprofitable servant. In the very heat of battle he always returned to this avowal: God demands our most strenuous co-operation; but all our hope is in him alone.

All of this is relevant also to Hosius the statesman. He was the very opposite of a Machiavelli. He was a statesman with a rigid, awake and devout conscience. In this sphere, too, he was the pastorally minded servant.

This central growth of personality out of Christian piety

reveals to us the real, ultimate end of all the work: the refutation and defeat of the Reformation, absorbing though that activity was, was but the beginning. The existence of the Church was threatened but it would survive. And its survival would not be merely external. Hosius' polemic always aimed at the conversion of his opponent. With extraordinary patience his missionary heart went out towards the souls of the Reformers. He had no desire to use hasty severity with them. In this was shown the practical operation of his basic motto of peace and love. Those Reformers, to whom he denied the Christian name and whom he refused to greet, he still called brethren. In the separated he recognised his brethren, whether they liked it or not. Only when they ceased to pray the Our Father would they cease to be brethren.

To the extent that we are able to disentangle the complicated objectives from the obscurity of the situation we recognise how rigid exclusiveness on fundamentals was supplemented by an extraordinary effort in the cause of union. It is true that in this respect the true heresiarchs were completely excluded from all considerations: they were hardened heretics. Like Fisher of Rochester, he wanted to help the weaker vessels who vacillated and did not know where to turn. These were the people to be helped by the production of a completely clear doctrinal foundation. In a deep sense, polemics were ultimately pastoral in aims – for Catholics as well as the others.

This bishop was filled with longing for the return of the vacillating and the apostate – even if there was going to be a permanent schism. His moving language reminds us of St Paul. In his pastoral letter on unity he breaks into a moving, fervent prayer. Hosius hoped to see Christendom once more united. Not to hope for this seemed to him to signify a lack of faith and trust in the mercy of God.

It is quite obvious that Hosius' work for unity was not carried out in a spirit of accommodation. There could be only one aim: return to mother. The only thing which could prevent one being blown like a reed in the wind was a stubborn rigidity in the truth of faith. Compromise was in vain. The interim was pernicious, threatening to destroy the Church. Awareness of faith and a sense of responsibility for every individual soul were what made this bishop at once dogmatically unrelenting, and patient and hopeful in practice. At times hopefulness clouded his vision, as, for example, when he thought that he detected in Melanchthon a vacillation that was leading him back, step by step, to the point from which he started.

And so this labour, so utterly defensive and polemical in origins, ended up quite positively. In those days it would have been quite impossible to rise completely above the defensive approach; but calm security in possessing the Catholic faith could be regained. 'At least we are not beginning to totter!' For the Reformation was nothing new; it had long since been refuted. The Reformation was but a repetition of Satan's battle of temptation against Christ, characteristic of all time; and so the outcome could never be in doubt. In addition, one thing stood out in relief, something for which Hosius had always striven energetically: the revival of Catholicism. This was the really decisive thing. By his powerful, world-wide work, Cardinal Hosius is entitled to be numbered amongst those spirits who gave a fresh stamp to the age by this revival. The last decade of Reformation history proper was already marked by this Catholic restoration.

Attempts at Union : The General Council

I

The aims and desires of those who remained in the Church, of those, above all, who actively fought for her in the political and theological spheres, are not so easily brought to a common denominator as is usually supposed. This is most clearly demonstrated by the literary champions, whom we have just been discussing. Two types evolved. The first was intellectualist, rigid, dour, dogmatic. We might say, with some reason, that these were men who, as theologians, had remained completely untouched by humanism, whose minds had not been fructified by a wider vision of the variety of the subjective conditions of human knowledge and action. Setting aside the burden of moral weakness and abuse of administration in the Church, they saw no problem at all in the Reformation revolt. To this type belonged a host of smaller minds as well as more distinguished, chief of whom were Eck and – with the qualifications explained earlier – Hosius.

A very different type embraced those who had been affected by humanism. Their very separation from scholasticism brought them into direct contact with the problem of the spiritual justification of many ecclesiastical positions, and gave them a deeper understanding of the aspirations of the Reformers. It is significant that at first a whole series of representatives of this type – that is before they found their way back to the Church – were more critical of the papal curia, and sat more lightly to Catholic doctrine, than was consonant with loyal churchmanship and staunch faith. There were others, it is true, of notable freedom and breadth of mind – like Contarini – who never had to find their way back. And there were others again, who – like Witzel – never got past vacillating, and who ultimately followed a middle course, not wishing to become Protestants but who were Catholic only with qualifications.

The understanding and humanly sympathetic type of orthodox polemicist, however, included some who had never been affected by humanism. These were the scholastic irenicists. There was a truly missionary type of apologist and polemicist, for whom peace was a more urgent spiritual necessity, who wanted to persuade their opponents, who were open-minded enough to refrain from hastily ascribing base motives to the apostate. We have already come across one of the best representatives of this type in our much-applauded Caspar Schatzgeyer, the Franciscan, a man of kindly humanity and deep concern for the unity of Christendom.

It is illuminating to note, that the representatives of the last group held more firmly on to the notion of *reunion* in its authentic sense than did the representatives of the first-mentioned group. None the less, however we may describe the objectives of the former group, for them, too, the condition into which Christendom had fallen, as a result of the schism, was untenable, and the healing of that schism seemed an absolute necessity.

All groups, with the exception of a few individuals, saw in a general council the one universal means of restoring health.

We already know about the clamour of Christendom for a general council since the days of Basel (Vol. I, p. 25 f.). We know, too, that the Lateran Council (1512–17) made almost no impression, not only in Germany but in Italy too, and that France had in fact appealed against it. To the mighty task of reform, which the whole of Europe expected a council to undertake, was now added the question of faith, posed by the Lutheran schism. Never had a council been so impatiently awaited in all quarters, as in the decades since the outbreak of the Reformation. Once already, so it seemed to many, a general council – under Germany's leadership what is more – had ended in worse division of Christendom. It was to be hoped that the old power would once again prove itself. If only the egoism of the curia could be eliminated, the old true Church would seem to be capable of regeneration. In 1534, after sixteen years of the deepest division in doctrine and in life, a well-informed man like Cochlaeus was found speaking of the council as though it were a magic charm that could conjure up peace in an instant.

This sort of example shows us how much the notion of a council even, had been affected by the current theological confusion. (In judging all ecclesiastical affairs in Germany in the fourth decade of the century, this must be kept in mind.)

As representative of the curia, in 1521 Aleander defined the situation: the whole Lutheran controversy turned on the authority of the pope. The emperor, however, declared at the same time: 'under no circumstances can we permit discussion of papal authority and the legality of decrees'. Aleander believed that one might very well discuss the primacy with Luther.

Most theologians in this period had upheld the infallibility of the pope. Admittedly, they had defined infallibility in various ways. The starting-point had been the Lateran Council (1512–17) when, in the presence of the ambassadors of Spain, Venice, Florence and later of the emperor, and of Roman noblemen and senators, the bull *Unam sanctam* was renewed, the pragmatic sanction of 1438 was condemned, the pope, with hyperbolic rhetoric, was declared a 'God upon earth', and the Pisa convocation of renegade cardinals was utterly overthrown, along with their protectors, Louis XII of France and Emperor Maximilian. At that council the view had again triumphed: 'As in the Ark of the Covenant the rod and the manna lay close to the tables of the law, so in the breast of the pope knowledge of divine law lies close to the sword of destruction and the sweetness of grace.'

Silvester Prierias – who derived the authority of a general council from the pope – and Cajetan were strict papalists, but shared the open-mindedness of Fisher of Rochester, and Contarini – Cajetan a little uncertainly, it is true. The one who expressed himself most sharply of all, and most logically, was Pigghe. He attributed indefectibility as well as infallibility, to the pope. He almost welcomed the reproach that he was flattering the pope of Rome, and making gods of men. He denied that a pope could fall into heresy, although every jurist thought that he could. Not content with that, he also taught explicitly that a general council was not infallible, as history proved.

There were, however, others beside jurists, who thought that a pope could become a heretic. Alfons de Castro concluded that any man can err in matters of faith, even if he is the pope. He proved this by reference to Pope Liberius, Pope Anastasius and Pope Celestine, who had erred, and not merely as private persons. For him it was only the whole Church that was infallible. Tetzel, too, and Emser, a Gandavo, Köllin, Ambrosius Catharinus Politus and many others, limit infallibility in the case of a pope who turns heretic. The pope has, indeed, all power over the whole Church, even over councils; but if a pope turn heretic, a general council has power to depose him. It is against this background that we must see Paul IV's fear that a heretical pope might allow heresy to take possession of the see of Peter.

The most dubious thing, and that which constituted the biggest obstacle in the way of understanding with Protestants, was the unrestrained exaggeration of curialism. This in itself, at the height of the sixteenth century, was grotesque. In view of rising anti-Roman feeling, it had become a threat to the Church's existence. Prierias described the pope as 'the father of all temporal majesty, head of the earthly orb . . .; the power of the emperor and of all earthly rulers are merely delegated by the pope; he may directly elect an emperor on his own initiative, and hence he may depose princes . . .'. Hoffmeister corroborated this curialist view, but more in respect of religious matters. He said straight out, that with the papacy, people had paid more heed to the laws of men than to the word of God (1538).

We have already observed how there can be no question of the conciliar idea having died out. These very exaggerations were bound constantly to provoke reaction, and this had to come from below, for it was directed against the primatial peak. It was those exaggerations, too, that were the very thing to destroy any Protestant interest in a council, or at least to provide Protestants with a welcome excuse for declining to attend a papal council. The popes, for their part, were terrified of a recurrence of Constance, or even of Basel.

And so the struggle for a general council, which went on all through the Reformation period, was marked on the one hand by the passionate desire of Christendom for this means of healing, and on the other by resistance from two opposite extremes – curialism and Protestantism. Gradually the emperor made himself prime mover in the council, and thus it became a rock of offence for all of the emperor's enemies – France, and then England, in particular.

Medieval councils had never been purely theological and dogmatic affairs; they had sometimes been political as well. This was specially true of the council upon which so much hope and fear now centred. It became an expression of the struggle for world power between Charles V and Francis I.

The idea of the power of the emperor within the Church, and the concept of the emperor itself, had noticeably developed since the Council of Constance (1414–18). In calling the Council of Pisa in 1511, Maximilian had appealed more to the failure of the curia than to his own office as steward of the Church. After Pavia in 1525, Gattinara had invited his imperial master to call a general council, in his capacity as steward of the Church, the pope having refused to do so. When Clement VII in Cognac abandoned the emperor for the second time, Charles invited the cardinals to call a council on their own initiative. By 1530 – when many around him wanted a national council – Charles V had become quite convinced that a general council was absolutely necessary. A council, and only a council, could save the situation, he told the pope – otherwise Germany was lost. Thereafter he never changed his mind about this. The indolence of the pope forced him to test how far he could go in carrying out the plan on his own initiative. In the instruction for Matthew Held which he sent to the German princes in 1536, the question of the autonomous activity of the emperor in Church affairs was raised. Should, for example, a council be held without the pope and without France? In January 1538 Henry VIII informed Charles, that he did indeed reject a papal council, but not an imperial council. In 1545 the actively anti-Protestant confessor Pedro de Soto reinforced the emperor's self-confidence by suggesting the possibility of an appeal, against the pope, to the judgment of scholars. In 1547 in his rage over the withdrawal of papal troops from the scene of war, and over the transference of the council to Bologna and the pope's refusal to call it back to Trent, Charles became more hardened in this view: in the end he would call a council himself, rescind the decrees already promulgated at Trent, and carry out the reform of the Church. In Bologna and Rome in 1548 he put forward similar ideas.

The emperor, however, was not completely in earnest about this. In 1548 Charles set down these thoughts for his son and heir to the throne: in the midst of all human vagaries there is but one universal rule – 'trust in the help of the Almighty'. . . 'to gain this one must defend our holy faith. After all my efforts and schemes to win back the apostate in Germany, I have come to recognise that the council is the only means. . . . You can see Paul III's unreliability in treaties and his lack of zeal for Christendom, especially for the affairs of the council. All the same, respect his dignity!'

No wonder Paul IV – the Neapolitan hater of Spaniards, racked by pathological fear of heretics, yet blindly trusting the allies of the Protestants and the Turks in France – was highly suspicious of Charles' churchmanship. This, however, is no proof that his suspicions were objectively grounded. Nor may we ever lose sight of the ecclesiastical dignity of the Roman Emperor and of the dire distress of the Church, quite uncompensated on the other side by a dogmatically firm definition of papal power. It is unhistorical and superficial to conceive Charles' attitude purely in terms of power politics. He was guided by a deep, churchmanlike sense of solemn responsibility before God for Christendom and the Church.

The political resistance of France, and the political and ecclesiastical resistance of the curia prevented the emperor from accomplishing his desired aims. This was highly significant. Within the Church the papacy achieved a freedom of movement, which, under pressure from Protestant doctrines and ecclesiastical schism, enabled it to mould the nature of the council, when it finally became a reality. No matter how deeply and variously both the interior and outward course of the Council of Trent and its effects were permeated with politics, Trent was primarily a dogmatic council, and one of the most important stages on the Church's long, long, road away from politics.

II

From Worms in 1521 Aleander had reported that the imperial chancellor considered it useless to proceed against heresy without a council. Moreover, everybody in Germany – not just Luther's followers – was clamouring for a council. In 1522–23 the *Reichstag* at Nuremberg countered Chieregati's demands with their demand for a council on German soil. This had a conciliarist ring about it. The same was true of the 1524 *Reichstag* in Nuremberg with its demand for a national assembly to satisfy the desire for discussion of religion, for the sake of the empire. Many thought that the demand was amply satisfied by the counter-proposal: the emperor forbade a national assembly, and instead proposed holding a council in Trent, an Italian city, but regarded as German. In Speyer in 1526 Ferdinand declared that Charles was going to discuss the matter of a council with the pope. The resolution of the *Reichstag* expressed the hope that there would be a council in German territory within a year or a year and a half. The imperial declaration for Speyer in 1529 announced that the council was now a certainty.

It was in character that the great conciliatory action represented by the *Reichstag* of 1530 should have stressed the question of a general council. The emperor was well aware of the difficulties; but he feared that without a council there would be a general apostasy from the Church in Germany. It was unfortunate that his counterpart in Rome at that time should have been Clement VII a man who curiously changed from 'imperial' state secretary to 'French' pope. 'Ought he to oppose the blood of Christ to a few drunken Germans?' The emperor ought to consider 'how readily the old question of conciliarism could raise its head and precipitate a schism'. The emperor would at least have to be personally present all the time, like the emperors of old at the early ecumenical councils. There must be no risk at all of schism emerging. To ensure this, France, England and Scotland must be represented. The pope's dealings with France had already made him suspect, that France would not welcome a council.

However, the idea of a council had too thoroughly taken possession of the universal imagination, so that the curia certainly could not refuse out of hand to have one. It is to Clement VII's credit that the decision to hold a council was made during his pontificate – on 28 December of that fateful year, 1530. Under Clement VII, too, in 1533 Peter Paul Vergerio set off on his first journey to Germany to discuss the council. On this occasion he visited Wittenberg. On the other hand, the German demands became so insistent that in the *Reichstag* of 1532 at Regensburg the Catholic estates, led by the anti-Habsburg chancellor Leonard von Eck, moved that the emperor 'should call a general, or at least a national, council on his own authority, if the pope did not quickly call one himself'. In February 1533 on the second meeting between Charles and Clement in Bologna, the two agreed on the question of sending a legation concerning the council to France and to the Protestants.

In spite of the many difficulties and vacillations which it brought, the change of pope did not assure the victory of the proposal to hold a council. Thereafter, no matter how much opposition came from the Church or from political interests, the council was safe. On 13 October, the new leader of the Church, Paul III, enlisted the most influential men he knew in the cause of the council. Morone was the prime mover behind all the ideas that for years had been leading towards a council.

In Germany, too, hopes of salvation grew. A man like Cochlaeus became more hopeful. Apart from a few early uncertainties, he had always been a staunch supporter of papal infallibility. Now he told Paul III that at this quite indispensable council all conflict over the relation of pope to council, whether from the conciliarist or curialist point of view, must be utterly avoided. The head was indeed higher than all else, but it, too, was part of the whole body. Duke George and Witzel expressed similar views, but their desire for peace made them ready for greater accommodation. They belonged to a group in whom dealt the spirit of religious indifference. In the proper context we will return to this later.

Eck, too, was now of this party. He had revised his view of the effectiveness of diocesan or provincial synods. Paul's elevation to the see of Peter aroused hope in a general council – 'according to the universal opinion, the one indispensable means of rooting out heresy' (1535). Later (1537) he went even further and said that without a council all that Germany, England, Denmark, Sweden and Norway, could hope for was a universal scourge. When, indeed, would apostasy end? On this occasion too, the level-headed Eck did not indulge in facile optimism. He knew the curia. He dared to remind Paul III of the dishonesty of the late pope: 'For twenty years we have been accustomed to such legations, burdened with mandates and articles and a tissue of obscure words, riddled with controversial points and conditions, couched in a labyrinth of equivocal phrases, so that the Germans have been laughing for years at fine promises about a council.' Now promises must be honoured. If the Germans see that the pope is scarcely in earnest about the council, then all hope is lost.

Eck never lost this fear that the council might come to nothing. He repeatedly voiced his fear. He urged Vergerio to move heaven and earth to prevent the present project from fading out. He impressed upon Aleander that 'the Protestants fear nothing so much as a general council'. Duchy after Duchy, imperial city after city, one nobleman after the other, was lost to the Church (1538): 'our sins have mounted so high that the world no longer deserves a council, and so the whole structure of the Church will collapse'. Meanwhile the Lutherans scoffed, saying that the pope had never been in earnest about calling a council, neither after Mantua nor after Vicenza; and many simple Catholics took offence at the lack of zeal shown by their supreme pastor. And yet the council was the only means left. Either a council would be called, or all human ingenuity would be in vain.

In those days the slogan 'Council' covered many aspirations. Eck thought primarily of the reclaiming of apostates. The question was, however: would the reclaiming of the Reformers succeed? It was still assumed that the Protestants would be invited. Vergerio's second visit to Germany represented the great attempt to achieve this. A second time he visited Wittenberg, staying at the elector's castle, where he invited Luther and Bugenhagen to dinner. He was impressed by Luther's 'demonic eyes', and deceived by the reciprocal invitation he received from the heretics. With naïve haste he reported that the Protestant princes and the Reformers agreed to attend the council, on certain conditions. The degree of confusion which distorted the judgment of this curialist is quite amazing.

It is true that a contemporary need not have felt the prospect of union to be so hopeless as in reality it was. Today we can see that in 1514–16 Luther's split with the Church was already past repair, because the basic concept of the Reformation was quite irreconcilable with the Catholic concept of the Church. None the less, the Lutheran view of Christianity still held firm to the unconditional unity of the Church and the essentials of sacramental life. The differences, on the other hand, basic and divisive as they were, were defined with extraordinary theological ambiguity. Every exegesis of Luther's provides proof of this. It was this very ambiguity which allowed both Protestants and Catholics to assume that efforts at union made sense. On the other hand, the many demands for and attempts at reunion from the Evangelical side, prove how much they felt the necessity of the unity of the Church. Many in those days believed that for the sake of unity almost all theological differences might be overruled. An outstanding example are Melanchthon's verbal transactions with the representatives of the emperor and the pope in Augsburg in 1530, and the way he held for years on to the hope of having a reunion council. Certainly the humanist Melanchthon was no Luther; but in 1530 Luther was no longer identical with Protestantism, or even with Lutheranism. On the other hand, in 1530 Luther had praised Melanchthon so highly, and the latter was now so much the classical exponent of Protestant dogma, that one could accept his judgment and action as a valid expression of Protestantism in that period. If at times Melanchthon seemed ready to sacrifice everything, short of the marriage of the clergy and the cup for the laity, then desire for union on the Evangelical side seemed considerable indeed. There was possibility of union perhaps not with Luther, but with large sections of Protestantism.

Seen as a whole the conciliatory forces in Protestantism were ultimately victorious only in the sense that the dogmatic element was softened. The victory was not enough to effect the restoration of unity. Following renewed negotiations, which the emperor – having defeated the Turks in the Mediterranean in 1536 – carried on in Rome, on 2 July 1536, a bull was issued (*Ad dominici gregis curam*) calling a general council to meet on 23 May 1537 in Mantua. The chief aim of this council was to stamp out heresy. When this was announced the Protestants immediately refused to attend. Luther, now a sick man, poured out invective against the pope and the council. All the prefaces to his many works written in 1537–38 are in the same tone. The political supporters of the Reformation, too, the Schmalkald League, rejected the council, at the diets of the league in 1537 and 1538.

Thus the emperor and the pope faced a new situation. The council was prorogued in 1537 and again in 1538, and on 21 May 1539 it was adjourned indefinitely. The crisis came, on both sides, in the following decade: the emperor tried to solve the religious question by conversations, then by war and the Interim; the popes, however, in the end held a purely Catholic council without any Protestants. This was called on 15 March 1545, to begin at Trent on 13 December.

The fact that the Protestants succeeded in hindering or frustrating the working of the council does not mean that they were not interested in its progress of its decrees. A general council was still something to be reckoned with in Europe, if not quite in the same way as in the fifteenth century. Not only England but Protestant Germany, too, feared what a council might achieve. The important sessions of the first phase of the council in Trent and Bologna were followed with the greatest interest by the Protestant groups. They wanted to be able thoroughly to justify their refusal to attend.

The Protestants found themselves in a different situation when the victorious emperor held his armed *Reichstag* in Augsburg in 1548, and ordered the expedition of the council. All the same, although at that time the Schmalkald Leaguers had quite lost their power of political resistance, although much Protestant energy had been expended to expedite the council – until just before the betrayal of Elector Maurice of Saxony – and although the council, so recently rejected, was now greeted with suspect enthusiasm, this did not mean that a large part of Protestant Germany was really in earnest. The true face of Protestant religious power was shown in the way they reacted to the Interim. The political correspondence of the period proves that they were solely interested in evading the immediate grasp of the emperor and in gaining time.

In addition to the rejection of the council by the Protestants, rejection by France and England was also decisive for the papacy. Both of these factors had repercussions in the Schmalkald Diet of 1538. Without these countries, or rather in opposition to them, an ecumenical council could not take place. Francis I made common cause with schismatic England against the council, and even after the truce of Nice in 1538, still refused to adopt a more accommodating attitude. When at last the council was summoned at Trent, this was the result of a reconciliation between France and the emperor accomplished at Crépy in 1554. Both had then declared for the council and promised to support its decrees by armed force.

There was another obstacle in the way, and we must not ignore it, because it is specially instructive concerning the mood in Germany and the alignment of religious and political forces. Not all of the German bishops hailed the council with joy. Some showed tough opposition.

The proceedings of the Council of Trent need not be extensively discussed now.

With unerring Roman instinct for what was critical, the questions of reform were not dealt with first. First on the agenda were the contested articles of faith. This did not please the emperor at all. His view was that the doctrines of the Church had long since been adequately defined, that heresy had simply arisen out of abuses, and that hence these abuses ought to come up first for discussion.

There was real perception in his view, and it found theoretical and practical support in loyal Church quarters. Certainly the chief danger was theological confusion amongst Catholics, and the doubt that was powerfully nourished by the Reformation. The efficacy of this theological confusion, however, the real danger of infection, largely resided in the practical disintegration of the priestly ideal, manifested in the unpriestly lives of so many of the clergy. Conversely, the liberation in those days of many priests from the bonds of concubinage almost automatically conferred orthodoxy upon their doctrinal views. The first and last touchstone

of Christianity is the Christian common life. One might think
that it was here that improvement ought first to be sought.
Actually this was where the work of reform did begin – in Germany as everywhere else. When Fr Claude Jajus, along with
Canisius and Salmeron, was sent to the university of Ingolstadt
at the request of the Bavarian duke William IV, his task was 'to
encourage the improvement of degenerate morals by good example
and scholarly lectures'. Elsewhere, too, living example was
always represented as the primary reforming influence. Did it not
even seem, that the reform labours of Paul III since 1536, and
much in the memoranda of the cardinals and their attempts at
reforming themselves, corroborated this attitude? For the German
public at large, at all events, the redeeming power of the council
depended entirely upon its dealing with the question of reform.
If this question was not attended to first, the council would
appear as the last in a long line of disappointments. The Protestants would then point to the order of the agenda to justify
speaking of deceit.

The question had a political angle too. It is doubtful whether
the emperor still hoped for a reconciliation in doctrine in 1545–46.
We may not ignore the fact, however, that this advantageous
position *vis-à-vis* the Protestants largely depended upon their
good faith in the honesty of the irenical *Reichstag* of 1544. The
'Christian and friendly agreement' there envisaged was bound
to be formally declared impossible by the dogmatic decisions of
the papal council, and the Protestants thus set in opposition to the
emperor.

This deep-rooted contradiction in the notion of what the
council's purpose was resulted in the first phase of the Council
of Trent being overshadowed by an antithesis between pope and
emperor. To begin with the emperor's policy kept the legates in
Trent busy. The emperor was represented by the ruthless Machiavellian politician, Diego Hurtado Mendoza. His verdict on the
council at the end of 1546 clearly shows that he did not believe
at all in the supernatural reality of 'this insignificant company'
in which 'more trouble was created than ever Luther caused, and
where all are only seeking the interests of the curia, and each man
his own'. Charles' view cannot be said to coincide with his repre-

sentative's; but it must have greatly distressed the emperor, who was labouring for the unity of Christendom, to see how at Trent the most important dogmatic definitions were promulgated, without the slightest heed being paid to his wishes or to the situation in which he found himself. In the midst of all this, occurred the inexplicable withdrawal of papal troops from the scene of the Schmalkald War. Charles may be excused for suspecting that more than purely ideal reasons were behind the pope's method of running the council.

However that may be, feeling between the emperor and the curia ran so high, that the latter used a mild epidemic as excuse to move the council in 1547 out of the emperor's sphere of influence to Bologna, where the non-imperial fathers continued the diet. This transference was nothing less than the sabotage of the emperor's work. His animated protest against the legality of the 'so-called Council of Bologna' was registered immediately. But the stubborn Paul III was now impervious to anything the emperor did.

It is hard to decipher what the result of this situation was for German history. Dogged by this contradiction, the council could not produce a quick effect upon German affairs. On the contrary, the open split in the highest Catholic authorities could do nothing but strengthen the position of the Protestants, and tempt the emperor to make muddled concessions in matters of religion.

Paul III died in November 1549, having suspended the council in September. His successor, elected by the 'French', was Julius III (del Monte). This pope became such an emperor's man, that the second phase of the council can be called the imperial phase. On 14 November 1550 the pope reconvened the council. On 1 May 1551 it moved back to Trent. In the autumn of 1552 the first Germans turned up: Mainz, Trier and later, Cologne. Procurators came too from Protestant princes and imperial cities. But now it was too late – even the emperor thought so. In its first phase the council had pronounced on basic issues, in sharp contrast to every form of Protestantism; only a fresh approach to the same material could have changed the original flavour of the council. We must not forget to take into account the almost unimaginable theological vagueness of those days. Even so deeply religious a

man as the Spanish imperial secretary, Francis Vargas, wanted a
resumption of the material already settled. That he was a firm
opponent of curial abuses is not enough to justify calling him 'an
antipapalist' – as Pastor has done.

And so it ended with the Protestants merely protesting and
putting up unfulfilled conditions. The council was powerless to
alter anything in the political and ecclesio-political schism in
religion in Germany. Its effects operated purely within the Catholic Church; but these were, indeed, extraordinary.

III

When it opened in 1545 the council was attended by only thirty-
four prelates, most of them Italians. In addition, the papal legates
were at their post from the start. These, and the order of business
which they set out and executed with easy superiority, turned the
council into a mighty embodiment of the Church's teaching
authority – a clear contrast to Protestant subjectivism. In spite of
all the curia's fear of the resurgence of conciliarism, this became
the most papal of all councils, a veritable precursor of Vatican I,
and without which Vatican I could never have been conceived at
all.

From modest beginnings the council grew, and, under theological guidance, that emerged with amazing power, it reached those
great and fundamental decrees of the first phase, concerning
justification and the sources of faith. In the sequel the council
developed into the most important event in modern Church
history. It created a new Catholic self-confidence, in marked
contrast to the fearfulness and uncertainty at the beginning. But
it took time for this surge of new life, and the new dogmatic
insight, to break through to Germany. As late as 1559, many
years after the second phase of the council had ended, Canisius
spoke of the council still having to begin, as far as Germany was
concerned. He saw the hopes of good Catholics in Germany still
unfulfilled, and the careless bishops still unaffected by the work
done at Trent. It seemed to him – as to the papal bull announcing
the council – as though the utter destruction of the *respublica
christiana* was still threatened, and the council, which alone could
save it, was still to come.

SEVEN

Attempts at Union :
Theological Solutions

German history at that time was more directly affected by attempts at reunion initiated by German theologians and by the emperor. The effect of these is, moreover, more easily measured. These began earlier than the council, reached a climax during the imperial Interim in 1548, and, in a sense, in the attached reform work of the emperor.

I

Towards the end of his life Eck had made the demand that Rome should measure the reliability of those who defended the Church by their constancy in one conviction. He believed that many of the new Catholic men were not entirely reliable, just as he had to affirm that the curia were accommodating semi-Lutherans in a not very reputable manner. 'Witzel, who is favoured by the apostolic see, holds views in matters of faith, that are suspect and plainly erroneous. Is it not a scandal that the Church yields to heretics? In spite of my dissuasion, cardinals like Sadolet write letters to Protestants, which these exploit to the detriment of the faith. The emperor is guilty of the same weakness. Had he listened to old Brandenburg, to the Bavarians and to

Duke George, instead of to time-servers and compromisers, things would not have gone so far. The Regensburg Book, the overthrow of such conciliatory attitudes, is a dead letter.' 'Religious conversations with Lutheran princes are useless. It takes a heavy axe to split this block: besides the council the only useful thing is the armed might of the emperor. There is nothing else that the numerous Protestant princes fear' (1540).

That is how Eck saw the situation. There are many today who still see it in that light; but these too often confuse resolute clarity with inflexibility. Even if we accept Eck's firmness and uncompromise as indispensable for Catholics, and even if his views proved correct, his manner was not universally helpful. It would be a sad day for dogmatic truth and the possibility of intellectual breadth, if more critical as well as more intelligent ideas were denied their due place in the total scheme, just because what was safe and rigid was alone allowed to stand. No matter how much we concede Eck's correctness, his particular censures clearly display a certain unjustified narrowness. It is certain that the mediatorial attitude, which Eck rejected, manifested that fundamental characteristic of the epoch, which we have described as theological confusion or vagueness – almost unimaginable by us today. Frequently it was accompanied by a blindness, which in retrospect seems to tinge the later attempts at understanding the Reformers with tragedy. That, however, does not alter the fact that they were amongst the meaningful historical forces of their own time, and contributed to the heritage we claim today, even although they never reached their goal in reunion.

To begin with we must make it clear that there were many conciliatory-minded men, and many ideas about the realisation of reunion that were in no way tinged with any disloyalty to the Church. It was simply that in these men of strictest churchmanship, the pain and exasperation of schism had grown into a desperate complaint at the dangerous condition of Christendom, had become a burning longing to remove this scandal. These were men, whose unwavering dogmatic orthodoxy had not driven solicitude completely from their hearts, and who were determined to use every means available to repair the schism.

Let us not make unfair demands of pre-tridentine orthodoxy.

It is enough if we recall that there were most important articles of faith that had not yet been defined (on justification, the constitution of the canon, the value of tradition), and that theological certainty, especially on the concept of the Church, had been radically weakened by the conciliar theory and the attendant endless discussion, and also by exaggerated curialism. It is from this angle especially, that we must form our judgments, keeping in mind the almost incomprehensible freedom of dogmatic opinion at the end of the Middle Ages, whether expressed in sermons, by professors, or by authors.

And so, when Gropper, Pighius, Contarini, Pflug and Seripando, proposed the doctrine of double righteousness – although differing amongst themselves – that is of a transforming, and an imputed, righteousness, this was in no way a defiance of the Church, as long as the Church still had not decided otherwise. These men, in fact, must be regarded as true pillars of the Church – of the Church in Germany, what is more.

The real problematic of the theology of reunion only starts with those whom we might call the expectant party. These were men, brought up in the school of Erasmus, who in some way or other shared his a-dogmatism. Their number included members of the hierarchy, for, unfortunately, it was precisely amongst those men that the practical understanding of dogma was most popular. The a-dogmatism of Erasmus found fatal parallels in the practical attitude of popes like Leo X, Clement VII and even Paul III. Certain Germans shared this attitude. These men regarded the problems of the troubles in the Church primarily from a juridical and political angle, being concerned most of all for the unity of the fatherland and for its military power against foreign foes. Such men were to be found around the emperor at the *Reichstags*.

Morone, himself no learned theologian, but deeply involved in attempts to defeat the Reformation, recalled having found himself in a very difficult position as a result of this fact. Writing from prison he had drawn the attention of the Inquisition tribunal to the fact, that before the institution of the Roman Inquisition one had been allowed to express oneself much more freely on matters of faith. 'Discussion of dogmas went on everywhere and religious books were bought without any restriction. Anyone could play the theologian, and say whatever he liked.'

In their intellectual method, the irenicists resembled the conciliatory minded, although dogmatically they differed. The irenicists included Schatzgeyer, Hoffmeister the Augustinian eremite (who, as vicar general for Germany, had tried to carry out the reform of the order resolved in 1539), the Franciscan Wild in Mainz, the Dominican Matthew Sittardus (1522–66) and John Faber. All of these men wanted to avoid unnecessary harshness and set themselves against misdirected zeal. They were intelligent men who wanted, wherever possible, to understand their opponents and convince them, rather than simply refute them. 'Against apostasy severity is of no use – only love.' 'Not to want utterly to destroy adversaries, even when they are heretics, does not mean giving up any part of one's religion' (Sittardus, 1526).

It is true that many of these men underestimated the dogmatic danger in Lutheranism. First they would have to clarify their own minds. There was, for example, the Franciscan, Quiñonez, later a cardinal, who visited the Saxon province of the order in 1522, and who, in contrast to Pellican, the dogmatically imperilled guardian at Basel, approved of Luther's cause, with the one exception of *The Babylonian Captivity*. Something the same might be said of the emperor's confessor, John Glapion, also a Franciscan, who thought that *The Babylonian Captivity* was something quite new and a contradiction of the earlier Luther. We have seen how the Dominican John Faber, friend of Erasmus, underwent the same disenchantment.

Amongst the men who best displayed the value to the Church of this open-minded theological attitude, was John Gropper (1503–59), a native of Soest. He had always been a jurist. The theological vacillation manifested in the negotiations at Augsburg forced him to study the foundation of the problems. In a short time he acquired amazing theological knowledge – as had Hosius and Pflug. He became the outstanding man at the provincial synod in Cologne in 1536 – probably the most important German synod before Trent. In his *Enchiridion* he provided a full-scale textbook of dogma. He attacked clerical corruption. He then became the centre of resistance to his feudal superior, Hermann von Wied, who was trying to Protestantise the electorate of Cologne. Later he carried out catechetical work. He recognised the tactical necessity of producing a counterblast to evocative Protestant popular literature, and to their catechisms, pamphlets, sermons and the like. He wanted to cater specially for the youth and the ordinary person. He saw, too, what this work demanded: to speak as much as possible from the holy scriptures, and not in one's own words. In harmony with this outlook, he welcomed the great new forces of Catholic revival – the Jesuits, and the council, in which he, too, saw the only power to save the Church. This man, what is more, won the respect of the suspicious and doctrinally hyper-sensitive Paul IV, who offered him a cardinal's hat in 1555, and when he was dead, staunchly defended him against suspicion of unorthodoxy.

This non-professional theologian was so much activated by hopes of reunion that he made it a focal point in the religious conversations, but his life's work proved how much solid churchmanship could be latent in such conciliation. It proves even more how necessary it now is to form a proper notion of conciliatory theology. It is certainly true that Gropper's notion of reconciliation was entirely free from any improper compromise.

A whole circle of the conciliatory minded of various types grouped themselves round Duke George of Saxony, the strongest prop of Catholicism amongst the princes. By his declaration to Luther at luncheon in 1519 he had already displayed his theologically muddled large-heartedness. Around him we find (after Emser and Cochlaeus) Witzel and a whole series of statesmen, jurists and humanists, including his advisers, Caesar Pflug, the duke's 'faithful knight', and his son Julius, who later became a theologian and then a bishop. These men, like the politically motivated mediators, Granvilla, Seld and Zasius, were not deeply interested in dogma. What was the significance of a slight divergence in theological formula, especially when in many things, 'part of the other person's opinion does not make sense'? They saw bitter distrust growing out of the religious schism. 'When people who form part of the one community not only distrust each other, but do all they can to keep apart, and even rejoice in each other's discomfiture, how can such people unite against a common foreign foe? Only unity can save the empire from calamity and destruction.'

Admittedly there were vast differences amongst these men.

It would be unjust to Julius Pflug if we linked him with genuine mediatorial theology. Julius Pflug did share humanist adaptability (like Helding and Billick), but he held firm to Catholic dogma, although dogma was not one of his chief concerns. The concessions he was willing to make did not affect dogma. His object was to strengthen the Church against the enemy, Luther. The fact that he asked for concessions from his territorial ruler was no proof of weak churchmanship but only of how used people had become to direct interference by a secular power in Church affairs. 'You are the man of God. You are aflame for the unity of the Church, you shudder at the thought of schism. This was said in a true Catholic sense – even if it happened to be Witzel who said it.

At times even a man like Cochlaeus worked out principles which were similar to those of Gropper and Pflug; and his activities, too, were often turned in the direction of mediation.

Like the rest of the irenical theologians, he was moved not just by concern for the unity of the Church and the faith but also by patriotism. They are a proof that one need not be a poor Christian to be filled with deep concern for one's fatherland. It is mostly of the Protestants that we hear the reproach that they were bringing ruin to their country; but the reproach applied to others as well. Because of the Schmalkald War, John Wild in Mainz complained of the one-time proud and imposing Germans, who were now destroying themselves, while the rest of the world looked on in derision. 'May God forgive all who hitherto have caused us to resist unity. . . . I cannot bring myself to incite Christians against Christians . . .' This is in harmony with the mood of the much-mentioned Dominican John Fabri of Heilbronn, from whose widely read book on the mass, written in 1555, we take the following quotation: 'Behold dear brethren and see what is the doctrine which moves you to encourage such hurtful, miserable desolation! Have pity on your fatherland which is on the brink of collapse. See what has come about through false doctrine. . . . Foreign rulers, whom we must support, to the prejudice of the peace and prosperity of the German nation. We are the laughing stock of all nations. Behold brethren the Tower of Babel you have built. I exhort you with all my heart to return to your Father's house!'

The real problem of conciliatory theology in that period centred upon humanism, more precisely, upon Erasmus and his relativism, his underplaying of dogma. Erasmus had no part in real Catholic revival. We have already acknowledged his efforts to deepen Christian piety and to purify the administration of the Church from many abuses. But we saw, too, that these efforts were so bound up with an a-dogmatic and relativist basic outlook, that there can be no talk of Catholic reform instigated by him. In particular, this basic outlook poisoned all that Erasmus sought to do for the peaceful settlement of the Reformation dispute. His zeal for peace and tranquillity was not Catholic, was not even religious, but rather relativist. He was very little interested in the doctrinal aspect of the reunion of the two parties. His ideal was education, not religion. His was a flabby, not a tense, 'both this and that'.

There were few places where this relativism established itself as a practical attitude within Catholic circles in Germany. It appeared perhaps in the form of the partially politically motivated state-Church of Charles V, which was expressed in the religious conversations, in the Interim, and amongst the jurists we have mentioned. It appeared also in the shocking weakness of those theologically incompetent bishops, who did not want their tranquillity or their property disturbed. In their circle there were, however, a few who could understand the finer points of dogma. One of these was Tiedemann Giese, a canon of Frauenburg, from 1537 bishop of Kulm, then of Ermland (d. 1550). His treatise against the central point in Luther's doctrine, justification, won acclaim for being the clearest and most definitive exposition of the Catholic position in literature. By contrast, however, in theory and practice he was such a conciliator, that Hosius, his successor, was able to impute the most hair-raising heresies to him. He had let his nephew study with Melanchthon, and in 1536 had sent one of his works, by this nephew, to Erasmus for perusal, and then to Melanchthon. For a Catholic, theologically educated bishop in the mid-thirties of the century, this may well have been a sign of dogmatic uncertainty.

Anywhere at all where we encounter real relativism amongst bishops, we find that fundamental Catholic attitudes had been abandoned. There is no need to prove that Hermann von Wied, archbishop of Cologne, was one of these, as was the Brandenburg bishop Matthew von Jagow (d. 1545). In 1539, the year of the truce of Frankfurt, when it was resolved to hold religious conversations the next year, this bishop had distributed Holy Communion under both kinds.

As well as these men who plainly went over the score, there was a host of 'still' Catholic forces that were no longer firmly rooted in loyalty to the Church, and who therefore favoured a prejudiced compromise. They were openly of a divided mind. Because many, laity and clergy, were no longer quite clear what pure Catholic doctrine really was, they took up a vague middle position, theologically, in worship and in the administration of the sacraments. At the end of the period we are studying there were a great many who fell into this category. Theological compromise proper was paralleled by the impossibility in practice of giving the straightforward title of 'Catholic' or 'Protestant' to many parish clergy. Even at the end of the forties in many districts the clergy could not be precisely divided up into Catholic and Protestant groups.

Amongst conciliatory theologians were some who changed their allegiance. There was even a man like James Micyllus, who anticipated the *cuius regio* with its nonsensical consequences, and changed his religion according to where he happened to be. Again this mood fitted well the incredible religious vacillation of Biberach which more or less chose to have its religion determined by purely external contingencies – Lutheran, Zwinglian or Catholic.

Of quite a different stamp were the 'expectants', who simply awaited the definitions of the council and only then decided in line with these. There were many such in Protestant regions, and in Catholic regions, too, according to Morone's testimony.

There were even more flexible characters, who thought they could be Catholic and Protestant at once. In 1536 the pastor of the Lutheran parish of Rod/Weil was at the same time Catholic parish priest of Hasselbach. He tried to satisfy both places, by preaching in the one, and celebrating mass in the other. At the Lutheran visitation he blamed members of the parish who had forced him into this duplicity. At all events he was left to officiate as a Lutheran.

All this is less surprising when we remind ourselves of how disguised the decay of Catholic public worship had been. Even in the radical Reformation in Hesse many Catholic ceremonies were retained to begin with – Latin hymns, surplice and stole at the distribution of Holy Communion. At first the Latin tongue still played a big part everywhere; and the practice of aural confession was continued; celibacy, monastic life, the Divine Office and Communion under one kind, were allowed to go on. Clerical excommunication, too, was left to function. As a young man, Pole found the ceremonies scarcely altered, when he visited Wittenburg in May 1536. Not until 1542 was the elevation of the Host entirely discontinued in Wittenberg. It went on just as long in Thuringia. In 1552 Melanchthon found it necessary to produce a memorandum about its abolition. Not until the beginning of the sixties had they got that length in the Palatinate. The Saxon Ordo of 1539 provides the Kyrie eleison and Gloria in Latin for Sunday worship. On feast-days the Preface, Sanctus and Agnus Dei were to be said in Latin. A missal for Osnabrück of 1543 kept even closer to the Latin mass. Alb and mass vestments, too, were prescribed – to avoid giving offence to the people – and there is evidence of their continued use. Luther had a hand in this method of disguise. For example, he paid heed to the neighbourhood of spiritual territories – the ceremonies were not to be too unlike old-established custom.

Such details are more important than would appear at first sight. All of this, along with the growing scarcity of priests, gave rise to a feeling of helplessness and loss of orientation. An atmosphere of practical relativism developed. This must be kept in mind if we would appreciate the full potential of the conciliatory action of the princes, of the emperor in particular. This, too, gives the necessary frame of reference for a complete assessment of the real dangers in conciliatory theology. We need name but one representative of this theology: George Witzel, the vacillator. On the Catholic side, he was the counterpart of Capito, like him an offshoot from Erasmus, fructified by Luther.

Whatever Witzel (d. 1573) may have done against the Reformation and against the excesses of curialism by his criticisms, and whatever he may have done to the fundamental structure of the sacramental papal Church by his profession and for its purification and the healing of the Reformation schism by his restoration proposals and his co-operation, his middle of the road position placed him outside the Catholic sphere.

George Witzel can boast a colossal life's work. Urged on by a profound patriotism, he set himself the endless task of removing the unhappy schism in religion and in the Church.

He had been deeply influenced by Erasmus, and he was a product of the Erfurt humanist circle. He was a pupil of Luther and of Melanchthon. All the same he became a priest, but then apostatised to Luther. The study of the Fathers led him away from Luther once more. But he only half came back to the Church. He did not want to fight alongside the rest of the Church's champions, but deliberately followed a middle course. He was, in fact, the middle course.

His ideal was contained in the old slogan: 'Back to the simple apostolic Church!' By this he meant the Church as it was, say, in the eighth century, professing the doctrines of the first four councils. This provided the foundation for the unity of the parties, and then reform could become a reality. All his life he never gave up hope of reunion. He was an enthusiastic supporter of Charles' attempts at reconciliation, especially of the Interim. He was bitter about the Council of Trent: it had made far too few concessions.

Witzel illustrates the extent to which theological confusion could run amongst Catholics in those days. He had parted company with Luther because he believed in the 'common worldwide Church of God (which we believe and call Catholic), which has been victorious over a hundred schisms; has always stood firm against the gates of hell'. The Lutheran Church is not this Catholic Church; nor is the Roman and papal Church, for with regard to it some reservations have to be made. At the foundation of his thought is the conviction that the authentic Catholic Church could essentially be destroyed, as is presupposed by the theories of the *Defensor pacis*, of Occam and Gerson. Witzel and these others supplemented this view by the doctrine that only a general council can save the Church. It was not for nothing that Witzel so explicitly called for an ecumenical council – according to his own special formula. In it he saw the 'one place of refuge for wounded religion'; and he fervently hoped that it would lead back the bulk of the Reformed to the Church.

At the time Eck had judged Witzel correctly, but not completely. Eck saw the danger and the ennervation of this inadequately supported type of mediation. Little as he appreciated Witzel's long list of wholesome, critical theses, yet he was correct in pointing out the danger of this vacillating man. Eck had spotted the spirit of Erasmus. Certain bishops, who knew nothing about theology, had been impressed by Witzel's writings, and wanted to have him working near them. They had heard that this man 'follows, so to speak, the middle of the road, is neither a convinced papist, like Faber, Cochlaeus, and Eck, nor completely a Lutheran, and so they consider him to be the very man to bring about an understanding. They imagine that one can negotiate over the holy faith like neighbours over a piece of land, legal arbitrators and friendly bystanders offering advice, refusing this, conceding that . . .' This is the kind of man upon whom Rome has settled a pension! It may well be that Rome has also given him a dispensation to remain a priest and marry. In the many writings 'which this man brings forth into the world oftener than the rabbit her young', he avoids the main articles which the Reformers attack, in order to establish his opinion – with one exception: he maintains that faith is insufficient and good works are necessary. Eck tells us that when he reads the arrogant and theologically inexact babbling which the vacillating Witzel had learned from Erasmus' *Adagia*, 'my spirit burns within me, not with anger, but with zeal for the faith which this man is destroying'. The pope ought not to make decisions from purely tactical considerations, but like a true pastor caring for a flock. If bishops find some tenuous excuse for letting a Catholic cleric remain married, loyal princes will then ask if the bishops are going to find another Lutheran thesis equally plausible tomorrow. Would Catholic opinion not tend to think that such bishops were Lutherans?

In Witzel Eck thought he detected the Lutheran autocracy, which disregarded important pronouncements of the Church; and he failed to see true religious zeal in Witzel. Most of all, he saw equivocation. In his *Conversations* he had three characters: a papist, a Lutheran and a true believer. He pictures the pope on the right, but beneath he lists points which the pope must concede to Luther. In the centre he depicts his own patched-up opinion, foolish and arrogant, in harmony with the inexact babbling he learned from Erasmus. This sort of thing is neither hot nor cold.

When Witzel set peace and unity as the supreme goal, and identified this with the goal of Christ, the ancient Fathers and the councils, his approach was utterly different from that of Hosius, for example, who, under the same watchword, laid the blame for schism upon Luther. Witzel was so preoccupied with the externals of unity that he damaged the solidity of the foundation upon which it rested.

All the same, we have to admit that Eck was far from appreciating all there was to Witzel's irenic influence, and what was truly Christian about it. A single page in the introduction to his *Conversations* proves this. For Witzel, the unity of the Church and harmony within it were truly a great ideal. With moving impressiveness he proclaimed his longing and the longing of others for this ideal; and he fought with ardour for its realisation.

He seems to have counted himself as one of that middle group who lumped together the pope, the cardinals and the originators of the Reformation, in respect of fallibility, and who were in love with neither party, preferring to hold fast to the gospel of the Lord, and showing a readiness to become progressively enlightened in their understanding of that gospel. This was indeed Erasmian relativism. How right he was, however, in his sarcastic rejection of the excesses of curialism ('where the pope seems to be worshipped like a God'), or of certain externals attached to the cult of the saints, or of the ghastly evils of hypocrisy ('this kind prefer to abstain from flesh-meat, than to abstain from touching a virgin'); and how right he was to see the root of all the trouble in the refusal to admit error: 'No one will say, "I have erred!"' Witzel preached the absolute necessity of confessing one's guilt. By this alone he did the Church a great and charitable service. Through the confession of sin, he added a power of insight and resolution, and by these qualities gave impetus to the revival of Catholic Church life. The proof of this is found in his reform memoranda. These were amongst the most important that age produced.

The value of a reform memorandum, and the possibility of its being put into practice, are not assured by its having noted particular faults and suggested the corresponding remedies. As often before, in the sixteenth century there was no lack of analysis of and complaints about faults. These complaints had become stereotyped; the same old formulae were repeated so often, that men lost sight of the reality and lamentable extent of the decay. The quality of reform memoranda was decided much more by their having emerged out of a fresh and original total impression of the situation. In particular, their efficacy depended upon whether or not the author could see past the isolated faults to the fact that the whole of Christian life was being called in question.

None of the memorandum writers of the first half of the sixteenth century came near Witzel in this respect. He possessed the necessary human understanding and a refreshing naturalness, combined with sufficient spiritual freedom and insight to perceive the relativity of certain non-absolute definitions.

His memorandum on reform for the Church in Fulda in 1541–42 resulted in the production of the reform mandate of the abbot of Fulda, a document that commanded much attention both in Germany and in Rome. Witzel's memorandum displays in equal measure a solicitude that nothing of the Church's store of doctrine be lost, and a profound striving for the restoration of ancient values.

He also produced a simple and lively instruction on how best to follow mass. He knew full well that upon this depended the prevention of further leakage from the Church and from religion. For this reason he constantly tried to understand the laity, the 'ordinary Christian people', and to touch their spirit, weaning them all the while from sheer externalism. Very intelligently he allowed German hymns and a German translation of the mass to play an important part in this scheme, 'so that the people may have some idea of what is sung, read, and prayed, day by day'. 'For, in truth, the lack of good Catholic preaching is so serious, that one sends feverishly to every collegiate church and monastery to find someone with even the rudiments of learning. Anyone at all who can, must preach. . . . If necessary, we have to choose and ordain married men and lay citizens who have studied a little' (1548). The complaining people simply do not know the pertinent doctrines of the Church. Not least the 'accursed lack' of religious instruction of the youth must be put right. 'We are

bringing up young Turks, not Christians!' These are our princes
of the next generation. Schools are the nurseries of the reviving
Church. These are what will determine the height of this mountain
(the reform). Talented children of burgesses must be educated,
fed and clothed, free, so as to produce pastors, preachers, deacons,
choristers, clerks. The only condition should be that they work
in their native country. There are enough defunct monasteries,
the revenues of which might well be applied to this purpose.

In order that the people may be filled with the Spirit of Christ,
one should be free to administer baptism either in Latin or in
German – for there is 'no danger to faith or the Church' in that.
If the priest prays in German, as at extreme unction and at
weddings, then the men who at present lean on the wall outside
and yawn, might come in to the font and join with the priest in
asking for grace and the Holy Spirit. 'Satan invented haste: a
quarter of an hour for the baptism – four full hours for drinking.
Then everybody thinks that his Christian duty is done.'

The Blessed Sacrament ought to be treated with much greater
respect than it has hitherto received. 'To say mass against one's
conscience is a terrible thing. To do the same for money is even
worse. Most horrible of all is to be guilty of blatant fornication and
still to say mass.' All monetary offerings attached to ecclesiastical
institutions must be voluntary.

'The heart of the mass for the people is the confession of sins to
God, prayer for the main needs of the soul and for all Christendom,
commemoration of the passion and death of Christ, and thanks-
giving to God the Lord; and at this it is permissible for the people
to go up to the altar and receive the sacred food and drink with the
priest, if they so desire.'

Disedifying muttering of prayers and hateful hurrying over
of words at the psalmody must stop.

Anniversaries must be commemorated for rich and poor alike,
out of brotherly love, and there should be an explanatory sermon
on the liturgy of the dead and on death itself. Let there be no sort
of money-making, so that 'the cynics will have nothing to say about
devouring the dead'.

All of this revealed a basically profound concept of the Church.
There is much appeal in the way that Witzel not only showed the
clergy their faults but did the same for the laity, without adopting

a superior priestly tone. He conceived the Church as a whole comprising both clergy and laity,[1] without in the least detracting from the special priesthood. The good of both required their spiritual unity.

Witzel may have thought that 'Christianity was in such a bad way that it could scarcely be raised up again', that the Turkish war and the plague were like two divine plagues sent to chastise German Christendom, but he never gave up tireless pleading that at least 'something might be improved and purified within the house of God'.

II

Even after Luther's early disputations within his order, and the Leipzig disputation in 1519, and also the many religious conversations organised in the twenties by individual cities (Zürich, Baden, Nuremberg, Basel), attempts went on all through the history of the Reformation in Germany to settle the dispute once and for all by theological contests ending in a verdict, and, later, through theological conferences.

In the course of this disputation the attempt to attain theological agreement within a broad framework had been set in motion, first at the *Reichstag* at Augsburg in 1530 and then at Leipzig in 1534 during a conversation attended by theologians and statesmen delegated by Cardinal Albrecht of Mainz, Duke George of Saxony and the elector of Saxony. Agreement no longer sought a final settlement but only a rapprochement. At Leipzig in 1539 the attempt was renewed by delegates from the two Saxon rulers and the landgrave of Hesse. Butzer and Witzel took part. They avoided decisive questions and so were able to produce a list of formulae that pleased both sides. On this occasion the Church made no statement. A representative of the Catholic duke dared to express his viewpoint thus: 'The priests and the see of Rome have turned the apostolic Church into a whore; this Roman Church means nothing to us.' In this he repeated fundamentally the same view which he had expressed a year earlier: that the power

[1] He advocated the charitable care of the laity in an exemplary fashion. He demanded hospitals and homes, even for servants and foreigners. Employers were to provide in their wills for servants, instead of leaving all their estates to monasteries.

of the pope gave him no more than the right of supervision over the bishops, and this ought therefore to be curtailed.

It was in the same year, 1539, that these attempts were invested with the greatest possible significance by the emperor – as we are about to learn.

From the Protestant angle religious conversations were something quite natural. They were perfectly in harmony with the Reformation's starting-point: the application of the subjective opinion of the individual to the content of a religion of conscience. It was perfectly logical that the most active centres of conciliation should have come to be – on the Protestant side – those territories where the a-dogmatic standpoint inherited from humanistic relativism, was most in evidence: Zwinglian Hesse; then Brandenburg. For Philip of Hesse, for whom politics had always ranked first, this way had long been indicated. In Brandenburg it was opened up after the death in 1535 of Joachim I who all his life had been the unswerving protector of Catholicism, in collaboration with the bishops, most of the monasteries and the university. By his labours he had established such a strong tradition, that even the Reformation now beginning under the irreligious and compromising Joachim II (at first with notably unresolved and sometimes dishonest juxtaposition of Catholic and Protestant elements) maintained a mediatorial position, which it was able to exploit fully in the sense of creating agreement between the emperor and the Evangelical princes. The transition was completed by the election of the elector's grandson as bishop of Havelberg, Lebus and Brandenburg. He brought the bishoprics into the control of the territorial ruler.

Historically, the religious conversations appear as in some measure a substitute for the constantly postponed council – in 1539 adjourned until an unspecified date. This was an exchange of immense significance – an essential transposition of the question. The objective authority of the Church, speaking imperiously in God's name, receded; theological authority, human and searching for the truth, came to the fore; and supreme leadership was supplied by political power – the emperor. The critical consequences are at once obvious: the truth can no longer be regarded as absolutely fixed; whether consciously or unconsciously, it has become in some degree the object of negotiation. Applauded by Catholic and Protestant theologians, the emperor introduced the typical spirit of humanist relativism and of human irenicism into the discussions about dogma. For a few years this spirit dominated the proceedings.

Which predominated: religion or politics?

It is not easy to answer this question. Every answer requires qualification. To do justice to the religious conversations it is necessary most of all to be aware of the complexity of the forces at work behind them, and of the complicated problematic which characterised them,

The religious conversations were also an expression of the ecclesio-political partial balance of power achieved between the Schmalkald and the Nuremberg Leagues, as represented in the truce of Frankfurt of 19 April 1539, and which seemed to make it improbable that power politics would settle the issue decisively. We must remember, that the numerous attempts and the complicated events of the past twenty years had caused the prospect of a mutually agreeable smoothing over, to dim on both sides, little as anyone wanted to admit it. Prospect of a council had vanished. It is true that there were princes who believed less than others in a religious or ecclesiastical settlement of the dispute, and who therefore behaved as though the schism were a fact, to be accepted, but regarded as politically incidental, so that political settlement could be attempted 'as though we were united in faith'. On the other hand, the religious conversations were a last attempt to side-step a definitive power-political settlement. This fact does not, however, deny that the attempt was motivated also by an honest religious search for unity. On the contrary, the religious conversations were a truly shattering phenomenon in this very respect. Their separate stories do not make much sense, but the spirit which guided them does. For, in the midst of a split in the German Church, a split such as none had ever known before, and following a period of bitter strife and of many failures by Rome – most of all the delays over the council – they represented the desperate attempt to achieve this impossible unity by a more or less private path.

We have constantly to make clear the significance of the effort which loyal churchmen and papalists like Cardinal Contarini and

Gropper and others of similar moral and religious calibre devoted
to these attempts. Those we have named were notable forces on
the side of the Church and the pope, and their power was rooted
in the Christianity of the Crucified and his sacramental Church.
If, from deepest conviction, they openly sought agreement through
religious conversations, it follows that these attempts were supported by a Catholic impetus that must be taken seriously. It was
not as though the people concerned knew nothing of Lutheranism,
or were lukewarm Catholics.

There is another thing which prevents us from declaring
Charles V's religious conversations and the tendencies under-
lying them, or the practical proposals which accompanied them,
to be contrary to the policy of the Church. This was the attitude of
the curia. How little clarity and unity was to be found there!
In Rome itself they had not yet come to see the incompatibility of
the two doctrinal systems. We recall the hopes which were
entertained there in 1530 of the possible conversion of Melanchthon and of the elector of Saxony. It is true that Melanchthon's
wavering attitude about 1530–31 occasioned all sorts of reports
about the Lutherans veering towards the old Church. These
came from Protestant sources too, from Wittenberg, for example –
reports of Catholicising reaction everywhere, that various Christians were requesting the services of priests ordained by Catholic
bishops, and were observing the papally decreed fast-days and
feast-days. Clement VII himself believed in 1531 that concessions
could be made to the heretics if that proved a means of drawing
them back. In 1532 he presented his theologians with the Augsburg Confession for examination. It seemed that agreement was
not impossible. In 1532, despite the dangerous attitude of the
Protestants, he caused the emperor to try to keep up negotiations
with them. 'They may be Lutherans, but they are still Christians.'
At that time, Rome, too, was seeking a middle course (Pastor).

Much of this was, of course, tactical. People were accustomed
to haggling. For example, Clement VII requested the emperor to
be cautious in granting concessions, lest he offend the rest of
Christendom, or in case other nations might make similar demands.
However, the curia consented somehow to the first religious
conversations. Explicit approval was given for the conversation at
Regensburg by the active participation of Contarini, and by the

retrospective consent to the Interim. In 1542 did they not send Morone to Germany with important concessions concerning the cup for the laity, marriage of the clergy and benefices, concessions hitherto rigidly refused, so that the way to reunion might be prepared?

The religious conversations of the forties were thus politically motivated and orientated theological events. In them were manifested religion and politics, honest convictions of faith and calculating tactics. They were a changing interweave that matched an essential feature of their real director – the emperor. As far as their attitude to the doctrine of the Church was concerned, he regarded them with a quite untheological mind. His Catholicism was a matter of sheer tradition. In spite of this we must admit that at least in those years the emperor was less preoccupied with the irreplaceable value of unyielding dogma. To him the Catholic faith seemed so simple and clear as not to require any supplementation by dogma. For this reason, at the conversations, there would be no dangers hidden in transactions over theological formulae. Basically that was an ideal that approximated the ideal of Erasmus – only the emperor did not accept the rationalism of Erasmus, but by his firm attachment to the Church and her sacramental institutions, reversed the direction of this ideal and used it as a force for Catholic reform. Clear proof of this fundamental reserve is the fact that in all his settlements with apostates the emperor always had in prospect the decisions of the general council.

This impression is strengthened when we take into consideration those who worked with the emperor and those who affected his judgment. The part they played in the religious conversations was important (Granvella, Naves, Lund). Their influence went back to 1526, and at the start of the forties it became so strong that the proposition put forward by the imperial party could not by any means be assumed to be simply the views of the emperor.

When the magnificent victory of Pavia was followed by the 'deadly' League of Cognac, on 27 July 1526 Charles mentioned in a letter to Ferdinand, for the first time, the possibility of accommodating the Protestants in matters of religion – provided the coming council corroborated everything. This letter was based literally upon a draft by Gattinara; and Gattinara was an exponent of the great state-Church. The philosophical and theological foundations of his thought are also known to us. He was an Erasmian and regarded the followers of the great humanist as the only reasonable men, the only ones who had not lost their sight, as a result of the present conflict between the pope and Luther. He was surrounded by a whole group of influential Erasmians, who by various means had the ear of the emperor or were able otherwise to influence the public.

The recipient of this letter, Ferdinand, was the very one to suggest the idea of religious conversations during negotiations with the pope in 1528 – before the peace of Barcelona; and it was his theologians who were specially prominent at the religious conversations in the forties.

This means, therefore, that from its inception the idea of religious conversations were strongly imbued with the spirit of Erasmus – and with the political slant indicated. At the conversations in Regensburg in 1541, when Granvella, diplomat and politician, took over the leadership, this attitude became a determining factor in the proceedings. It may have been through Granvella's influence, that the emperor then confused the Church itself with abuses in it – in a quite untheological fashion.

Granvella offered the Protestants a straightforward settlement of religion, and, by reason of this, the emperor should not ask too many questions either of the pope or of the Catholic estates. This was an unveiled expression of that view which Eck attacked mercilessly: 'This is no use, and no words will help matters; whoever wants to unite in faith with the Roman Church must accept the pope and the councils, and believe what the Roman Church believes. Anything else is hot air, supposing we were to argue for a hundred years.'

One or two comments on the course of the religious conversations will illustrate even more clearly the complicated nature of the problems.

At the reconciliation negotiations between the pope, the emperor and the king of France in Nice in 1538, Charles had been able to get no assurance from Francis I concerning the council. At this very time, however, he received news of certain tendencies and moves towards reunion in Germany. He felt justified, therefore, in slackening his own unfruitful efforts to achieve a council, and in trying this new way. On 22 September 1538 he wrote to Ferdinand saying that 'he wanted to meet the Protestants on certain particular points which did not affect the substance of the faith and would cause little offence'. In 1539 even the Schmalkald League adopted the view that a religious conversation was perhaps the only way. To the pope's dismay – although he was quickly appeased by territorial concessions regarding Camerino – and to the annoyance of the Catholic princes, Charles approved the celebrated truce of Frankfurt on 19 April 1539. This was the real starting-point of the religious conversations. In the next year a clarification of the religious question was to take place, by the totally new method of agreement reached through conciliatory theology. In the same year Cochlaeus in Germany defended the memorandum of the reforming cardinals – the most definitive proof of a will to reform within the curia – against the misunderstanding of over zealous Protestants. He did this, moreover, in collaboration with Sadolet and Contarini, the leaders of the Roman reform party and moving spirits of the Roman Catholic desire for understanding.

The emperor's approval of the truce of Frankfurt was in line with the conciliatory attitude he had adopted since the religious peace of Nuremberg in 1532. The only jarring note had been struck by the dogmatically more correct, and autocratically abrupt, demands made at the diet of the Schmalkald League in 1537, by the imperial representative, Matthew Held, a native of Arlon in Luxembourg.

According to plan, the series of religious conversations was begun in 1540, not in Speyer as arranged but in Hagenau, in June. Nothing came of it. In November of the same year there was a meeting in Worms. Granvella had taken charge. He saw that the emperor's political activities could not succeed in any direction, if the German princes were not united. On the other hand, he believed that it was impossible to force results entirely by means of power politics. Correctly, he saw that the ultimate seed of contradiction lay in religion. The conclusion he was driven to accept – being primarily a politician – was that a religious peace must be reached unconditionally. Granvella's leadership meant that there would be theological unclarity. The composition of the delegation pointed in the same direction. The theologians included Faber, Nausea, Cochlaeus and Eck. The Catholic party even contained representatives from electoral Brandenburg, electoral Palatinate and Jülich. No tenable theological decision could be reached in the presence of such 'Catholics', who were scarcely Catholics in reality any longer. The reaching of a proper decision was made even more difficult by the personal intervention in the disputation of princes of both parties.

At the height of the proceedings the meeting was adjourned until 1541 in Regensburg. At the *Reichstag* in Regensburg the emperor appeared in person. Now he was at peace with Francis I. Contarini accompanied him as papal legate. Charles had given the Protestants plain proofs of his readiness to compromise. He told the landgrave of Hesse that they had, after all, one and the same gospel. The religious conversations going on simultaneously manifested the same warm desire of the emperor for agreement. In short, the picture contained very many reassuring features.

But things had changed very little since the last time Charles had come personally into direct contact with the theological views of the Protestants at Augsburg in 1530.

The negotiations at Worms had apparently produced a secret ancillary fruit in the form of a kind of common basis for Protestants and Catholics, as a result of discussions between Butzer and Capito on the one side, and Gropper and Veltwyg (secretary to Granvella) on the other. The Regensburg Book containing their theses became in part the basis for the religious negotiations. It is of prime importance to our assessment of the Church's atitude, to remember again that the curia did not stand back but was represented by Contarini. Representing German theology we see Cochlaeus and Eck together with Gropper and Pflug, who stood in the foreground.

Eck's presence is enough to tell us that attempts at agreement would have very doubtful success.[2] He was quite opposed to the idea – to the annoyance of Contarini – as was Nicholas von Amsdorff on the Evangelical side. This man regarded agreement

[2] Since 1540 Melanchthon had shown more dogmatic rigidity than before. Now his meeting with Calvin in Regensburg seemed to have influenced him enough to make him appear a Calvinist in the eyes of his Lutheran opponents.

as vain deceit. None the less, agreement was reached on many points – man's original state, original sin, free will. In particular, acceptance of double justification seemed to open a prospect of a more far-reaching understanding. But on those articles which touched directly upon the Catholic concept of the Church (sacraments, transubstantiation, the priesthood, the Church), sharp antagonism remained. Nor were matters helped by Charles' readiness to send an embassy to Luther to gain his support for the agreements reached, nor by the suggestion that everyone wait in patience until a council settle the points left in disagreement. Luther remained as intolerant as Rome. Both rejected the suggestions at the same *Reichstag*, as did the estates. Unfortunately, Contarini died in the following year.

In Germany the dogmatic situation began moving towards a dangerous climax. In direct contrast to the Roman development, characterised by the Inquisition instituted in 1542 through the collaboration of Carafa and Ignatius, the resolution of the *Reichstag* of Speyer in 1544 arranged for the religious question to be settled by a religious agreement reached at a free German council. It is true that the formula used in the resolution was ambiguous. What did it mean by 'a common, free, Christian council within the German nation'?

It looked as though an ambiguous formula had been chosen deliberately. The failure of the religious conversations at Regensburg had sobered the emperor. He saw now that the situation could certainly not be clarified by religious conversation alone. And so he proceeded to seek assurance in the methods of power politics.

At the *Reichstag* at Worms in 1544–45 the religious settlement was postponed for a year, and so another religious conversation was held in Regensburg in 1546. Maurice von Hutten, bishop of Eichstätt presided. Luther died while this meeting was in session. On the Catholic side, two leaders were now dead: Eck and Fabri. Cochlaeus was the sole survivor of the old guard. Now he took his place alongside the younger men: Hoffmeister, Billick and Malvenda the Spaniard. The latter sensed danger. If union were achieved, the council was finished. He stepped into Eck's shoes, and opposed agreement. For the most part the Protestants, too, for different reasons, opposed agreement. The conversations never got off the ground. The mighty attempt to have religious conversations ended in open disaster. In the nature of the case, with no final authoritative court of appeal, the mind of man remained incapable in practice of achieving spiritual unity.

Charles for his part now tried to find such a mandatory authority in armed force. In 1548 he was to carry out a decisive religious settlement in the form of the Interim, as a fruit of an armed victory. Then the whole thing was to collapse.

After Passau 1552, Charles had been completely defeated, politically, in Germany; and yet, he still remained loyal to the idea of a religious agreement. His belief, that patient discussion would reduce even further the number of articles over which there was disagreement, never faltered. (At first there had been thirteen or fourteen, then in Worms five or six.) The problem, as it affects these last years, must not be viewed in isolation but seen as part of the whole stream of political life. Within this framework the reversal of the Reformation revolution, and the fulfilment of the emperor's hopes, still seemed possible. With the death of Edward, Mary became queen of England, and married Charles' son, Philip. Was the maritime kingdom not about to return completely to the Church? Would the total encirclement of France and of the Papal States not make the house of Habsburg the unhampered architect of the fate of Christendom?

As we know, these hopes were never fulfilled.

III

The emperor's efforts were not totally fruitless. If his religious conversations were unable to effect a union of the parties, the imperial Interim at least resulted in a highly important reform action in the Catholic sphere (below, p. 305 f.).

The emperor's demand of the pope, that the council must first of all set about a reform, was anything but a question of the order of business. Charles wanted to take away from the Reformers what he, like many others, erroneously imagined to be the most important reason for schism. He did not demand simply their return to the Church, but their return to a reformed Church. As the emperor saw it, the Council of Trent did not satisfy this necessity, and so he tried, after his victory over the Schmalkald League in 1547 (see below, p. 300 f.), to solve the problem himself in connection with the Interim, by his 'imperial formula for reformation', published on 9 July 1548. In the shortest possible time diocesan and provincial synods were to discuss the reform document and turn its demands into realities. This and the emperor's successful efforts to bring the advance of the new doctrine to a standstill in the Rhineland, Gueldres and Cleves (below, p. 284 f.), formed an important part of the Catholic revival that was now beginning.

We have already heard of the Protestant leanings of the elector and archbishop of Cologne, Hermann von Wied, who had crowned both Charles V and Ferdinand. At first, a supporter of the Edict of Worms, he had persecuted the Reformation. Catholic theologians, including Hoogestraeten, had dedicated their controversial treatises to him, and hailed him as a zealous devotee of the saints. Then, weakened by Erasmianism, and having no theological education, he changed over to Lutheranism. From 1539 to 1540, very soon that is after the very important reforming synod of Cologne in 1536, he became the ally of Melanchthon and Butzer. He had never, in any case, been a spiritually minded man. He had not celebrated mass more than thrice – for the simple reason that he had never mastered Latin.

The plans for Protestantising were opposed by Gropper, who developed in the opposite direction from his episcopal master; by Adolf von Schaumberg, who had been coadjutor of the archbishop since 1535, and who remained loyal to the Church in spite of all the defection at the court; by the Carmelite provincial, Eberhard Billick[3] – a most important man in the work of Catholic restoration; and by the suffragan bishop of Cologne, John Nopel, who did valiant work as preacher in Cologne, and was the first to confute Butzer there. These men became a centre for the opposition of the majority of the town councillors, of the clergy and of the university. This augments the picture we have already formed of Cologne as an important centre of Catholic forces.

[3] He took part in the religious conversations at Worms-Regensburg in 1540/41, at Regensburg in 1545 and in the negotiations at Augsburg in 1548. He appeared at Trent in 1551/52, and from 1556 was suffragan bishop of Cologne. He died in 1557.

This work of defence was significantly supplemented by the emperor's political move against Gueldres–Cleves in 1543. Finally, the archbishop's sympathy for the Reformation, by which he gained the support of the Schmalkald League, made him a threat to the Netherlands; and so the emperor was spurred on to use armed force against the Reformed princes (below, p. 284 and 294).

Hermann was forced to abdicate (1546), and his successor, Adolf von Schaumberg, immediately put a stop to all Reformation activities. Melanchthon and Butzer had to give up all Protestant propaganda in the electoral church.

The question is: how much real regenerative power was there in this defence effort?

In respect of Gropper, we already know the answer. Billick, too, was a real religious force. These two were the very men entrusted by the emperor with framing the reform proposals at Augsburg. The result was the imperial reformation formula. What was the significance of that formula, and how effective was it?

In conjunction with the Interim, the imperial formula was conceived as no more than a provisional attempt at reform. That is to say, a real solution of the Reformation problem was to come from the council. (The papal legate at the *Reichstag* of Augsburg in 1547–48 had raised no objection.) The value of this proposal for improvement was not least that its author had learned much from the failure of earlier attempts. As we have said, the complaints against various abuses had been repeated all too often in the past centuries; they were as much part of the total picture as the abuses themselves, so that people had grown deaf to them. What was missing was a vigorous new idea that would provide religious energy. Complaints, like reform proposals, even those of synods and those contained in diocesan statutes, had always been too much concerned with externalities and particular cases.

As was only natural, the imperial reform scheme included much that was well known. In view of the persistent decay it could not be otherwise. It closely resembled the demands of the princes' committee of Speyer in 1526, for there, too, it was not the bishops and the clerical estate, that set about the eradication of abuses, but the committee of princes themselves.

This reform document, however, was more comprehensive in design than any previous memorandum. In addition, its demands were supported by the highest authority, the emperor himself; and it expressed a more vigorous will to reform than had been officially expressed anywhere in Germany before. Its importance lay, not primarily in its particular demands but in the sense of real danger with which it was permeated – the awareness that much of Catholicism had lost all of its Christianity, and had retained nothing but the empty form; and it contained the conscious desire once again to dig down to the authentic, wholesome substance of Catholicism.[4]

Once again the objective that was given priority was the reform of the clergy. The document enquired closely into the motives which made men seek ordination; and the correct means to correct abuse was found: strict examination before granting admission to holy orders.

The only problem was how to carry out this wholesome prescription. The authors of the memorandum well knew how often similar proposals had been put forward. The powerful reforming energy behind this document was proved by the fact that the whole stress was laid upon putting the thing thoroughly to the test in practice. It was to be done despite all circumstances. No sort of dispensation, or legal title bought from Rome, was to exempt anyone from these requirements.

The concept of the clergy – including the prince bishops – as pastors, was once again given due prominence. They were the shepherds of those redeemed by Christ's blood. The collection of a number of benefices by one man was prohibited. At the same time they were sensible enough to advise the augmentation of the income from a benefice, where necessary, so that a priest could live in reasonable comfort from a single benefice. This was an important move in solving the problem of the clerical proletariat, who were such a chronic focus of decay within the organism of the Church.

There could be no proof of the competence of recruits to the

---

[4] Specially worth noting is the attack upon mechanical prayer as a result of the over-repetition of the same forms of prayer.

priesthood until the standard of theological education was raised. To create this standard, the memorandum made far-reaching suggestions affecting all of the clergy, secular and regular. In particular, a revival of scripture studies was demanded. This was something of supreme importance.

It was in harmony with the whole tenor of this document, that the value of preaching was stressed at every possible opportunity. The bishops were explicitly mentioned in this regard. The function of the sermon was defined in strictly pastoral terms. There was to be no carping polemics: in general, earnest irenicism characterised the whole formula.

By contrast there are other passages which plainly reveal the limitations in the psychological understanding of these reformers, as in their theology. They did not think that the use of German in the liturgy would be helpful. The words of the liturgy simply cannot be understood by everyone; and 'men, in general, have much more respect for that which is incomprehensible and mysterious than for what they understand with no difficulty'. Administered in everyday German, the Blessed Sacrament would become an everyday thing. It would be sufficient if parts of baptism and the marriage service were read in German, as by ancient usage, and that on Sundays the epistle and gospel were read likewise in German, and that, above all, there be a sermon in the vernacular. The vivifying effect upon religious life of various blessings was described with some restraint, and the limits of these blessings was pointed out.

The life moulded by pastoral care ought at all times to be officially regulated. To that end there should be visitations. No church should be exempt from episcopal visitation, not even the cathedral church. Synods were given even greater importance. They were, 'the health of the Church, the terror of adversaries, the pillars of faith'. The ecclesiastical rights of the ordinary man were recognised in some degree: the laity must have opportunity of making known their complaints.

Everything depended upon the extent to which these ideas could be turned into realities. We have learned about the efforts in that direction within the region around Cologne – the city of the two chief authors of the formula, and a city in which at that time the question was emerging with the most fateful urgency: 'the Reformation or reform?'

In Cologne it was not so easy as it might seem to distinguish the imperial reform from the changes of the Reformation. Here, too, the new doctrine had serious and fervently religious supporters When, for example, the Reformed preachers had retreated from Bonn, great numbers of the citizens made pilgrimage to Busch-hoven to hear Protestant sermons and receive the cup of the laity. The Catholicism even of the clergy in Cologne was not absolutely certain either. Proof of this is the course of the struggle between Hermann von Wied, who became a Protestant, and Adolf von Schaumberg, supported by the majority of the cathedral chapter. In the deanery of Medebach there were parishes with married clergy who, along with their flocks, had long ago broken away from the authority of the archbishop. By contrast, the city parish priests without exception ranged themselves behind the imperial and archiepiscopal work of reform. They were supported by the town council, the university and the majority of the cathedral chapter. This did not in the least signify that there was not a great deal wrong in various groups of the Cologne clergy, who remained loyal to the Church.

As always, everything depended upon the spiritual strength of the leadership. Gropper had already passed the test; and now he had a zealous reforming archbishop for superior. Adolf von Schaumberg's loyalty to the Church sprang from deep conviction, and was no mere expression of a coadjutor's opposition to his reigning superior and prince. His anti-Protestant activity – influenced undoubtedly by his loyalty to the emperor – was essentially supplemented by positive reforming clergy, devoted to rebuilding the Church.

His work acquired a serious and most congenial quality at once, by the fact that he knew the limits of his strength. He did not want to be the sole support of the reform. He knew the ineffec-tiveness of one-sided authoritarian regulations. Accordingly, all of the courts of the Church within the province were to take a hand in the reform.

Quickly, therefore, in the autumn of 1548, he convened a diocesan synod for Cologne and made his suffragans at Lüttich, Utrecht, and Münster–Osnabrück–Minden, set the reform work in progress at diocesan synods, on the basis provided by the imperial formula, and prepare the way for dealing with the matter successfully at a provincial synod.

The work of the archbishop and of the diocesan synod in Cologne was easy. The formula was immediately accepted. The regular clergy, too, showed themselves inclined to reform. Gerard von Hammer, prior of the Carthusians in Cologne – as we already know – was the most resolute of them all in putting the reform into operation. Unfortunately there is little evidence of any follow-up to this fine beginning.

The synod of Lüttich acted more independently, although politically this diocese was utterly dependent upon Charles. Examination of candidates for the subdiaconate and the diaconate was immediately and energetically taken in hand.

A totally different mood was evident in Utrecht, where a tough defence of the abuses rooted in clerical privilege, was attempted. Most of all there was to be no episcopal interference with exemptions. Nor was there to be examinations for candidates for holy orders. In Utrecht they even dared to offer as a reason, that there would be too few candidates who could satisfy the moral requirements. They agreed to one reform: insistence upon attendance at the Divine Office. How was this to be achieved? By increasing the stipends.

Most thorough in his resistance was the weak charactered bishop of Münster–Osnabrück–Minden, Francis von Waldeck (1491–1553). He had been terrified by the battle of Mühlberg, and the violent revolt of the cathedral chapter at Osnabrück. On 12 May 1548 he had promply 'vowed loyalty and protection to the Catholic religion before the estates of his territory at the High Lime of Ösede'. He assented to the holding of a diocesan synod as required by the archbishop of Cologne, in terms of the formula, and appeared in person, canonically attired, at the autumn synod in Münster. His edict, however, did no more than slavishly follow the reform document sent him: it revealed not even the slightest intention of positive participation. What else was to be expected of this man, who lived in open concubinage, was divided in his innermost soul, and whose nature was vacillation and unscrupulous compromise? In the end he earned his desserts: the contempt of both sides.

The lamentable result of his diocesan synod need not surprise us therefore. The bishop had tolerated and encouraged Lutheranism for so long that the clergy of the state, who for even longer had regarded themselves as Evangelical, now put up direct opposition. As a condition of obedience to the bishop they demanded the cup for the laity and the right to keep their wives. If this condition were not granted they would abandon their pastoral responsibilities and move out, taking their wives and children with them.

The difficulties in the way of reform were first seen in their true light at the provincial synod held by Adolf von Schaumberg in 1549. As at many of the *Reichstags*, the princes had not been present, so at this provincial synod none of the five suffragan bishoprics was personally represented by its ordinary. The same thing had happened in Cologne in 1536. Their threadbare excuses made depressing reading.

A host of resolutions were passed: against the sale of spiritual jurisdiction; against the leasing of incorporated churches by monasteries or chapters to the highest bidder; concerning the obligation of residence at collegiate churches and abbeys; concerning convents of nuns and canonesses; concerning the removal of abuses associated with the mass; concerning preaching;[5] concerning the revision of the breviary, the application of alms to the poor, the supervision of the schoolmaster, and the hospitals; against the cup for the laity; concerning the pastoral training of monks; and against simony.

But the opposition, too, showed their hand, especially in Utrecht. In Cologne the zealous attempts to improve theological teaching at the university met with astonishing obtuseness in the ruling courts; and the collegiate churches, the real opponents of reform, clung tenaciously to their privileged exemptions. They were violently opposed to any visitation by outsiders.

The reform resolutions in Cologne were executed with wise caution. It was realised that this was a long-term programme, and that the reformers required here a brief, there a long and tedious,

---

[5] The number of sermons the city parish priests were required to deliver was unusually high. For Advent, Lent and during a further total of six weeks in the year, they had to preach daily (in the country on Monday, Wednesday, and Friday). Specially chosen priests were to deliver controversial sermons.

period of preparation. It was easy to determine which were to be holidays of obligation, and which books were to be proscribed or avoided for the time being. Everything, however, that concerned the examination of people, monasteries, churches and schools, required time. On 11 January 1550, obedient to his commission, Gropper had prepared a visitation scheme for the abbots, prelates and rural deans: 'an exhaustive compendium of detailed questions concerning the secular and regular clergy, hospitals, schools, the way of life of the laity, which will be thoroughly examined at a later date during visitations in many dioceses'.

In spite of all the preparations, visitations were not carried out everywhere, not least, because the great opponent of autonomous Church life put forward his own demands. This great opponent was the territorial Church system as embodied in the person of Duke William of Jülich–Cleves–Berg, who effectively obstructed archepiscopal jurisdiction and visitation within his territory, in order to keep the Church and its jurisdiction completely in his own power.

Even in the parts of this archdiocese that belonged to the electorate, visitations proceeded very slowly. The reports from the deans were a patchwork, and their contents often suspect.

At the provincial synod the archbishop had spoken most persuasively and skilfully in support of the ideals proposed in the reform. Most of the participants in the synod had reacted with honourable zeal and lively interest, and had set about the execution of the scheme with a right good will. Adolf von Schaumberg had done all that he could to enlist the whole-hearted support of all the clergy in an all-out religious and ecclesiastical action, and the majority of the clergy had responded. But the whole scheme was an *imperial* reform. The archbishop's work was weakened as the imperial power declined, and as a result of persistent opposition from the Netherlands. The driving force had not been sufficiently religious in inspiration to overcome the juridical and political opposition of the territorial Church system. Nor may we overlook the fact that this work was hindered also, as the emperor's effort so often had been hindered, by the estates of the realm: these men had no spirit of sacrifice at all, but haggled all the time over their own immediate, petty interests. The reform was never able to gather sufficient momentum to sweep all before it.

In a tragic fashion the determination for reform shown in Cologne was further seriously obstructed in 1549–50 by the delegation from Rome of three bishops to Germany, bringing the far-reaching indult bull of August 1549, concerning apostate or renegade monks, nuns and secular clergy, and concerning the cup for the laity and fasting dispensations. This dispensation was another manifestation of the impossible state of affairs that had come about, and which men were trying to improve by purely external means. Adolf von Schaumberg, very properly, was horrified; for this extraordinary compromise took the whole punch out of the Cologne reforms. With good reason, Adolf von Schaumberg reported to the pope on the circumstances in Germany. In fact, the delegation accomplished very little. The dispensation was asked for by few, and meanwhile the churches became emptier and emptier.

The poor results achieved by the Cologne reforms were most plainly seen in the territory ruled by Francis von Waldeck. In 1551, in connection with the Cologne resolutions of 1549, he had accepted a thoroughgoing mandate. This was a purely external show, matched by no spiritual transformation; and its effects lasted only while the power of the emperor was there in the background.

Failure once again? Not exactly. A genuine change could not come from this angle because reforming zeal was not backed up by the brightly burning flame of heroic religious endeavour. None the less, the imperial reform formula of 1548, viewed as a whole, was a remarkable piece of work – as was the provincial synod of Cologne. Looking back we can see another of the centres of power that gave evidence of the continuance and increase of Catholic life, and from which energy laboriously but courageously radiated to combat unending decay. The steadfastness of these power-centres was ultimately rewarded by the emergence of a regenerate Church.

PART FOUR

The Military and Political Struggle
Settles the Issue

ONE

The Foreign Political
Account Settled

Political developments within Germany resulted in 1539 in
the emperor's position being directly threatened, as a consequence of the business over Gueldres (see above, p. 81 f.). If the
Protestants succeeded in claiming this addition, the ecclesiastical
electorates of the Rhineland would be opened up to the Reformation. Already Westphalia was well and truly threatened by its
own bishop. The Netherlands would be thrown wide open to the
infection. The majority of the college of electors would become
Protestant. (A few years later the full gravity of this danger became
evident for the first time, when Mainz got a new archbishop and
elector, whose loyalty to the Church was not at first quite certain.)
It might well be, that no Catholic state would be left in Germany,
except Bavaria and the Habsburg hereditary estates. For the
electoral ruler of the Palatinate had Protestant leanings; and in
1542, Brunswick-Wolfenbüttel, the last buttress of Catholicism
in the north, finally collapsed. The duke Henry fled to Bavaria
where he sought in vain for effective support from the mighty
Leonard von Eck. Bugenhagen led the Reformation to victory in
Brunswick. In 1543 Hildesheim, the last Catholic position, fell.
In the midst of general Protestant advance all around, it had held
out bravely to the end.

On the other hand, it became evident that the truce with France (Nice, 1538) did not provide much assurance of peace. It is true that in 1539 France meditated a truce with the Turks on behalf of the emperor; marriage plans between France and the Habsburgs were reopened in 1540. But by 1539 Charles had realised that he would have to look upon friendship with Francis I as a brittle affair. In this same year, without any feeling of embarrassment, Francis incited a serious attack upon Artois in Flanders. In 1540 he renewed his alliances within Germany in a way which seriously threatened the emperor: he made alliance with Cleves against the emperor. He married his niece, the twelve-year-old heiress of Navarre, against her will, to Duke William, who would now become ruler of Cleves, Jülich, Berg and Gueldres.

Once again Lombardy became a chief bone of contention between the emperor and Francis; and once again Charles allowed this affair to take a most dangerous and irrevocable turn: on 11 October he feued Milan to his own son Philip. A breach with France was now almost unavoidable. The assassination of the French ambassador at Suliman II's court by German soldiers, France's formal alliance with Denmark, Sweden, Scotland and Cleves, and the support Francis gave to what was going on in Gueldres and the Netherlands, were but symptoms and forebodings. In 1541 his most Christian Majesty declared war: in the north, supported by Denmark and the mercenary leader Martin van Rossem of Gueldres; in the south, against Navarre and Roussillon. In the east the French were able to cause the Turks, on the death of Zapolya, to fight for his son in place of Ferdinand. Ferdinand's army was destroyed, and Hungary as far as the Tisza fell to the Turks; Vienna was threatened. A storm destroyed Charles' fleet when he attempted a second campaign against the North African Mohammedan pirates. Chaireddin Barbarossa was able to threaten Nice.

The growth of the new religion outside the empire was important also for the situation within Germany. In Geneva Calvin began to organise his Church government; in Scotland Knox led the Reformation to victory.

The immensity of the difficulties now facing the empire once again illumines the short-sightedness and the meagre national interest of the German territorial rulers. It seemed perfectly right to them to exploit this very situation in their own petty, cantankerous interests, regardless of the terrible dangers to which they exposed the empire. The cause was partly secularisation, as exemplified in the dispute between the two Saxons over the bishoprics of Meissen, Merseburg and Naumburg. Like the curia, Bavaria pressed the emperor to take harsher measures against the new religion in Germany, but Bavaria itself was not prepared to collaborate.

All of Charles' varied political and theological undertakings, from the truce of Frankfurt in 1539 until 1545, must be seen in this framework. It provides the background which alone makes evident, and partly intelligible, the curious interweaving of politics, religion and theology, of honest struggle and Machiavellian deceit, of Erasmian broadmindedness and magnanimous daring.

It was in the years after 1539, however, that important assistance came to the emperor from the Protestant Schmalkald front, in the person of the landgrave Philip of Hesse.

When this prince (1537) and Melanchthon sabotaged the draft of the so-called Schmalkald Articles (see above, p. 80), the prince was not interested in a purely theological issue. There were signs in him of a deeper transformation which, if skilfully directed, might have led to most surprising results, might even have completely changed the further course of Reformation history. His manifest activity as leader of the Schmalkald League began to be less vigorous. More than this: he began to incline towards the emperor. In 1538 he made alliances with the emperor's regent, Queen Mary, in the Netherlands. He felt obliged to affirm that the Schmalkald League had a purely defensive aim; and he demonstrated his sincerity by declining to be drawn into a private war with electoral Saxony.

This was the turning-point in the alignment of forces in Germany; and for the first time the emperor gained an opportunity to attempt a solution of the German problem by military means. For Philip kept to the course he had indicated, although with many equivocations. At the Frankfurt diet of the Schmalkald League in 1539, it was he who initiated discussion on the question of a private war. At the same time when the emperor was trying to

drive a wedge between him and electoral Saxony, and the supporters of the Confession of Augsburg were inclined to break
loose from the Hessian Zwinglian, Hesse offered his services to the
emperor against all foreign enemies, including Gueldres. He would
fight any except Germans.

The emperor did not spoil the opportunities that were maturing,
through over-zealous acceptance. He let things take their course,
for Philip needed the emperor – on account of his notorious bigamy. Personal passion became a serious threat to the Reformation.

On his mother's and on his father's side Philip was hereditarily
disposed to sexual excess. His father died of syphillis and his
mother was known as 'Lady Venus'. Although he had ten children
by his wife, the daughter of Duke George, he lived a life of more
or less uninterrupted debauchery. He himself admitted that he had
been faithful to his wife for no longer than three weeks. He gave
no hint of any scruples of conscience. The only time such a thing
was mentioned – by Philip himself indeed – was when he met with
serious difficulties in satisfying his sensual desires. Margaret von
der Saale, daughter of one of his sister's ladies in waiting, whom he
desired, and this lady's mother, insisted on a regular betrothal –
a second marriage; and Philip agreed to their plan. He had no
religion, although since the age of fifteen he had been an ad-
herent of the Reformation. Occasionally he had personally taken
part in theological discussions. But now he began to consider
religion: those much reiterated affirmations of Luther about the
bad consciences of monks and clergy who fell into sensuality because
they were not allowed to marry; or what Luther had written to
him in 1526, that in case of need a man might keep several women
– the words of St Paul 'for it is better to marry than burn'. In
The Babylonian Captivity Luther had also said that bigamy is better
than divorce. Similarly, in 1531 Melanchthon had explained the
case of the king of England: 'Without in any way burdening his
conscience he may beget posterity by polygamy, that is he may
take a second wife without putting the first away.' Butzer had
come to a similar verdict: auxiliary marriage was nowhere forbidden in scripture. At an early date, about 1522, the sixteen-year-
old Philip seems to have been specially impressed by Luther's
preaching of the new idea, that a man has the right to demand the
satisfaction of his sexual impulses.

Margaret's mother laid down the condition that the marriage be witnessed by important members of her own and the prince's family, and take place in the presence of leading theologians – Luther, Melanchthon and Butzer. Butzer's views were closest to those of the landgrave. His support was won for the plan, and he undertook to bring over the theologians from Wittenberg. The thing was to be kept secret, however, to avoid giving scandal. Things went wrong, for the weak Butzer tried to square the unsavoury good turn he was doing the landgrave, with the old worn-out pious formulae. Why should the thing be hushed up? 'For the mighty advancement of the glory of God. Let the Lord Jesus give us his grace. Amen.' Equally hypocritical was the reason Philip gave in his appeal to the Wittenberg men. He, once so unscrupulous, now felt great fear that he might die in battle, burdened by his present adultery and unchastity – which he admitted – and so fall into the hands of the devil. The remedy was a second marriage. Thus the words about a 'glad conscience' and the 'gospel' had become unscrupulously abused and contaminated. A great source of power had become suspect and devalued. One asks: which displayed the greater lack of basic Christian outlook? The many princes who in those days fornicated without a qualm, or the fake qualms of conscience of the landgrave? Very soon Melanchthon, who at first fell in with the scheme, was to describe the whole affair as a deception of hypocritical piety.

Philip wanted the Wittenberg theologians to supply a written testimony, that bigamy was permissible for him as a Christian. He seasoned his request with political threats. In the end he might feel compelled to support the emperor. As we have seen, he had made solid preparations for that possibility.

The statement from Wittenberg, i.e. from Melanchthon, with Luther's consent, was framed the day after the request arrived (10 December 1539). It contains all the vagueness and lack of definition that we might expect in an attempt to buttress an impossible situation with Christian justification, for political reasons. To the present day this statement has remained open to many interpretations. It stressed, however, that 'no law' was being set up, but a 'dispensation' was being granted. If, then, Philip could avoid fornication and adultery in no other way, he might take another wife; but this must be kept secret, 'that is to say, your Grace and this same person will be known to certain trusted people, as under seal of confession'.

The elector of Saxony whom Philip had likewise asked for help through Butzer, gave more space in his reply to an exhortation to remain faithful to the first wife; but in the end he fell in line with the opinion of the theologians, but insisted on the new marriage being kept utterly hidden from the public.

The disgraceful doubleness of Luther and Melanchthon – who so often exaggerated the antithesis between the Old and New Testament, but now relied one-sidedly upon the Old Testament for justification of polygamy – found support from other preachers in Hesse; but there were a few who displayed more courage than their leader.

The landgravine gave her consent, and the wedding took place on 5 March 1540 in Rothenburg/Fulda. Butzer, Melanchthon and the representatives of the elector of Saxony were present. The marriage certificates again declared that this bigamy was 'to God's greater glory'. Butzer wound up his address: 'The Lord will help, so be it we do and suffer all for his kingdom's sake.' The landgrave gave Luther a present of a tun of Rhenish wine.

Obviously the affair could not be kept secret. It gave great scandal to the people, as to many theologians. It was the leading theologians especially who ended up in trouble.

How could publicity be avoided? Butzer, Schnepf, Brenz and Osiander were for denying the whole affair. Butzer himself made this demand of the landgrave. His Old Testament reasons for this, and his suggested emendations (Margaret was to describe herself, legally, as a concubine, 'such as God has allowed his special friends to have') are again an evil mixture of pious jargon, hypocrisy, and sophistry, ending in sheer blasphemous lies. 'The world often had to be kept from the knowledge of the truth by the intervention of angels or saints. The Bible is full of such things.'

Sad to say, Luther's point of view was similar. The cunning landgrave had asked for Luther's and Melanchthon's advice about what to do, now that the cat was out of the bag. They might well consider that eventually he might be forced to produce their own signed counsel. Luther asked for a denial: 'What is Yes in secret cannot be Yes in public, otherwise secrecy and publicity would be the same, and that neither is nor can be. Therefore the

secret Yes must always be a public No and vice versa.' This is a
shattering kind of argument from the lips of the undaunted monk,
discoverer of the 'pure word' with its: yes – yes, and no – no.
'What of it if one were to tell a resounding lie for the sake of a good
end and for the Christian Church?' In the end he was prepared to
say: 'Luther made a fool of himself' (in the advice he gave about
this marriage). The full dishonesty of Luther's behaviour is
finally revealed in his assertion that he wanted to act 'like Christ
in the Gospels (the Son knows not the day or the hour) or like a
devout confessor, who must declare before a court that he knows
nothing at all about what he has heard in confession' – as if it
were a question of the self-accusation of the sinner, Philip, and not
of the justification of an action that was said to be no sin at all.

Philip of Hesse, whom they had helped, now hit back vigorously at the 'holy people', to the shame of the theologians. 'If the
matter is not of conscience in the eyes of the almighty, eternal,
immortal God, what has it to do with the accursed, sodom-
istic, usurous, and besotted world? . . . If you are so concerned
about the offence of the gospel, then sweep out the filth in earnest,
so that we can see you are in earnest and not joking.' 'I will not lie,
for that is bad, neither apostle nor Christ himself has taught it;
Christ has indeed strictly forbidden it.'

In ancient law and in Charles V's penal code, promulgated in
Hesse by Philip himself, bigamy was a serious crime. The elector
of Saxony's rebuff of Philip in the event of the latter being appre-
hended by the emperor, and the unusual opposition in Evangelical circles, showed the landgrave the danger he was in. The remedy
lay in drawing closer to the emperor – and this worked.

On 13 June 1541 Philip made a pact with the emperor at
Regensburg. He promised to support the emperor and Ferdinand.
He undertook to make no alliance with any foreign power, France
in particular. Moreover, he would oppose French agreements
within the empire, that is in the Schmalkald League, and aid the
emperor in war against France. He would work for the exclusion
of the duke of Cleves from the Schmalkald League. Conversely,
he would support the emperor in his claims in the Netherlands
(Gueldres). In return the landgrave was to receive the emperor's
friendship and forgiveness for all that he had done, publicly or

secretly, against the emperor, his laws, or against Ferdinand – with the general reservation, that now gave a hint of the emperor's real purpose: 'unless a general war on account of religion broke out against all Protestants'. For his part, too, Hesse had made an exception of the religious question and of the Germans.

This treaty was but part of a comprehensive plan, which the emperor was carrying out in the years 1541–44, parallel to the ironing out process of the religious conversations. He won to his cause, not only Philip of Hesse but also Elector Joachim of Brandenburg, and Duke Maurice of Saxony, Philip's son-in-law. Joachim, too, promised help against France and Cleves, and in addition wanted to renounce the Schmalkald League. However, the strictly Catholic emperor paid a high price: he confirmed the Church order that the Protestant elector had decreed. In addition, Charles won over Count Wolfgang of the Palatinate, the margrave John of Brandenburg-Küstrin (brother of the elector of Brandenburg), and the margrave Albrecht Alcibiades of Brandenburg-Culmbach (1543), of whom we shall hear more.

These settlements were events of prime importance. They directly crippled the Schmalkald League, and were the start of the settlement of the problems of foreign policy. They contained nothing less than the possibility of a later defeat of the Schmalkald League, and so of the Reformation in Germany. They are a clear proof of the emperor's political and strategic competence. Politically, ecclesio-politically and theologically he had prepared in a masterly way for a final settlement with the Reformers, upon the widest possible basis. It is true: he performed his masterpiece on a grand scale; but he failed in the humdrum school-work after victory. Thus the victory was thrown away.

All of these things and the interplay of forces came most plainly to sight, and received an expression that was of the utmost significance for the course of German history, at the *Reichstag* of 1541 in Regensburg. It was here that the treaties with Hesse and Brandenburg were made. The emperor displayed a quite extraordinary readiness to make peace. In opposition to a proposal by the dukes of Bavaria, he declared that military suppression of the Reformation was unnecessary. The Catholic estates impatiently urged the full imposition of the sanctions attached to the resolution made at Augsburg in 1530, but the emperor thought otherwise.

The acute Turkish threat, the conciliatory proposals of his counsellors, and the insistence of the elector of Brandenburg, led to that hitherto unheard of, vague, secret declaration of 29 July – of which the Catholic estates were not informed – which weakened the firm resolution of the *Reichstag*, entirely in favour of the Protestants.

The resolution declared, that the peace of Nuremberg should stand until a general or a national council; if neither was held, until a *Reichstag*. This in itself constituted an abrogation of the Augsburg decrees. The secret declaration promised protection to the adherents of the Augsburg Confession and to their preachers within Catholic territories. Their princes were promised nothing less than a 'Christian reform', i.e. a Protestant reformation, of still Catholic monasteries and collegiate churches, which were tenanted. Even the emperor's joining the Nuremberg League of the Catholic estates, now accomplished after a delay of three years, fitted into this general pattern; for he brought no additional real strength to this alliance. It had been laid down that no member of this alliance was to make war on any Protestant state.

In return for this compromise in the declaration, the Protestant estates promised help against the Turks, help that turned out to be most unreliable. In the very next year Ferdinand was forced, by the opposition of the Protestant princes, who ruthlessly exploited the direct threat of Austria, to extend the term of the declaration to five years. In 1543, at the *Reichstag* in Nuremberg, the Protestants repudiated the specific agreement in the resolution concerning help against the Turks.

It was in that very year, 1543, that Charles had thought the preconditions of a definitive clarification of the political situation were assured. France had unleashed a storm against the Netherlands and made an alliance with Cleves. But the emperor's military preparations had long been in progress on a grand scale. Within a short period the political situation was to change many times. This time it changed in favour of Charles, who in 1543 returned for the last time to Germany, where he remained for the last twelve years of his reign.

The die was cast. The superior toughness of the emperor had beaten the greedy rapacity of the princes, in spite of the emperor's and Ferdinand's obvious powerlessness. At last things were bound

K

to come to a head. The emperor began with the overthrow of Cleves.

The union between Gueldres and Cleves under Duke William was supported by German princes of both parties. On the other hand, the Habsburg efforts to unite Gueldres with the Netherlands went back into the previous century. The cession of the territory had been assured to the empire by treaties, in various ways. Geographically, from the point of view of the Habsburg Netherlands, it was a sheer necessity, to close up a vulnerable gap. Charles least of all, who sought to make of his Netherland possessions, a well-rounded unity, could give up this part of the Habsburg programme. In 1541 he sought a solution in one of those odd, yet characteristic, coalitions. The danger from Cleves was to be overcome through a political marriage. Thus the emperor's position would be strengthened and the Schmalkald League broken up, for there was a dynastic union between electoral Saxony and Jülich-Cleves, the duke of which was the elector's brother-in-law. In this way Saxony had a direct interest in the political set-up in the lower Rhine. This, and Duke William's love of the Reformation, made the Cleves-Gueldres question really serious. And so in 1541 Charles had the idea that it would be a good thing if the electoral crown prince were to marry Ferdinand's daughter. The dynastic union between Saxony and Cleves could then be recognised without hesitation.

This coalition obviously did not possess enough weight. In the same year, 1541, Charles had already thought of a sounder scheme. He had told his sister Mary that he would come back to the Netherlands in two years, to solve the question of Gueldres by military force. His assessment of the situation then, proved correct. In 1543 he returned from Italy. He came down the Rhine, past Bonn, and stopped before the town of Düren. The duke of Cleves had witnessed the terrible assault against the Habsburg Netherlands by the French from the west, and by Van Rossem from the east. At the Nuremberg *Reichstag* that year the imperial and royal power had been so weak that no one could speak any longer of unity in the *Reichstag*. Only the year before, in Nuremberg also, the political dissociation of the Protestants from the national alliance had gone so far, that the proposal was made, to send a separate Protestant army into the field against the Turks. In 1543 the two parties faced one another in the *Reichstag*, like two alien powers, with whom Ferdinand had to negotiate separately. No wonder, then, that the duke of Cleves thought that his prospects were good, and never dreamed of any reverses.

Meanwhile, however, the emperor was straining every resource. His agreements with Brandenburg and Hesse had proved lasting, in spite of Philip's duplicity. Cleves had not been accepted in the Schmalkald League and now faced the emperor on its own. The Danes and the French left their ally in the lurch. In two weeks the power of Cleves was broken, and William came in person to surrender to Charles. William repudiated his alliance with France and Denmark, Charles' enemies, and returned to the Church. A year later, having broken off ties with France, he married a daughter of King Ferdinand.

The consequences of this short campaign were unusually important, not only politically but for the religious question. Reformation activity in the west of the empire received a decisive, if not deadly, blow. In spite of the overthrow of the Anabaptists, these efforts and their prospects of success depended upon the secularising and marriage-minded Bishop Francis von Waldeck, bishop of Münster–Osnabrück–Minden, and upon the Reformation-minded Elector Hermann von Wied, archbishop of Cologne. The declaration of the resolution of the *Reichstag* of 1541 seemed to open up the way for the secularisation of the principle endowment in Cologne, through the free 'Christian order and Reform' that held sway there. Against the views of the cathedral chapter[1] and of the town council, the archbishop had set the Reformation in motion in 1542. The sermons of Melanchthon and Butzer, a Church order prepared by them, the indolence of the state diet, and the support of electoral Saxony and of Hesse – of the whole Schmalkald League, indeed – would finish the job.

This situation, even, accentuated by the progress of the Reformation in Jülich–Berg–Cleves, was turned to the advantage of Catholicism by the speedy victory of Charles.

---

[1] Here the situation was the reverse of what it was with many Catholic princes who let themselves be led by their Protestant councils. In Cologne leadership lay not with feudal and often Protestantising canons but with the Catholic priest-canons, who were doing the work, led by Gropper.

In spite of terrible pressure upon Ferdinand by the Turks, and the crippling exploitation of his distress by the self-seeking Protestant estates at Nuremberg in 1542 and 1543, Charles' grand design moved on towards its logical ends. In 1544 the harvest was gathered. First of all Charles had to indulge in a deceitful tactic that was not entirely above reproach. As Catholic emperor, he went further than what was agreed in the secret declaration of 1542. The way to victory had to be bought, it seemed, by a complete renunciation of this victory. Charles was compelled, using whatever means were available, to keep his hands free to settle his political foes abroad. He succeeded.

The scene of these events was the *Reichstag* at Speyer 1544. Charles proclaimed that France was the great enemy, worthy of the same contempt as the Turks. This idea still had weight. Despite the occasional unscrupulosity of Venice and the pope, and despite France's systematic unscrupulosity on this score, Europe still felt that an alliance with the Turks was unnatural. Francis I did, in fact, write to the *Reichstag* to explain the reason for his alliance. But his sophistries carried no weight. Charles had better weapons. Using an intercepted letter, he was able to reveal Francis' duplicity to his friends in the Schmalkald League. Francis had offered help against the Protestants – when he inherited Milan. But above all, Charles consented to a resolution of the *Reichstag* concerning the religious question, which seemed to amount to full capitulation: the Protestant princes gained their Reformed secularisation objective. For his part, as the resolution of 1530 had never been carried out, Charles had replied through proceedings in the Imperial High Court, which had contested the legality of secularisation. A stop was now put to all of this, and secularisation recognised. This amounted to the surrender of all hitherto firmly held fundamental claims. The real religious question, so said the resolution was not to be solved by force, but by goodwill and a 'Christian compromise'. The same old remedy appeared: a free council, national assembly, or a *Reichstag*. It is worth special note, that the council was to be *free*. In the language of the Reformers, for whom the text was intended, a papal-Catholic council was not denoted.

The emperor made this resolution on his own supreme authority, because the Catholics, obviously, were not in agreement. In substance it was a solemn reiteration of what the secret declaration had said in 1541, in a more basic form.

On this occasion the estates voted for the emperor. The encouraging rejection of France by all the estates persisted. Even Bavaria turned its back upon France. 24,000 foot and 4,000 cavalry were voted, to take the field against the Turks in six months; and they were to be held in readiness for defence against France.

It is all too understandable that the pope should have repudiated this resolution (24 August 1544). Once again Luther fulminated against this papal interference, as he did, in the filthiest terms, against the pope's December announcement of the freshly called council: *Against The Papacy in Rome, Instituted by The Devil* (1545). A crazy flood of insults followed: murderers, arch-clowns, traitors, liars . . . all on the road to the devil. It was a small thing to take away the pope's land: he and his court should have their tongues pulled right out of their throats, and hung on the gallows in a row, like seals dangling from papal bulls. Let them hold a council there on the gallows – or in hell amongst all the devils. Because words failed him to express his rage, Luther produced the pathetically vulgar picture of the 'papal sow' and the 'birth of the papacy'.

It is deeply symbolic that in his last labours Luther should have returned to attack the papacy. The denial of the papacy, of the living, infallible teaching and pastoral office, a denial that was an expression of a revolutionary new concept of the Church, had been the latent, unconscious presupposition of his own interior change, the ultimate objective of his indulgence theses. Ever since the Leipzig disputation in June, the great and decisive opponent had been the see of Rome, becoming more and more identified, in his eyes, with Antichrist.

But the living expression which Luther gave to his opposition is symbolic also, in an equally lamentable way. He expressed himself with boiling hatred, which has no equal in all the coarseness of his time. With uncanny irresponsibility he carried this to an extreme of distortion. In this way Luther damaged his own work seriously; the fine ideas, which even this last pamphlet contains, became diabolically repulsive. In 1541, in his introduction to

Hans Worst, Luther had complained of the dirty methods employed by Brunswick in his fight against the electoral of Saxony, and his strictures were perfectly just. 'He curses, blasphemes, babbles, rends, screams, and spits. If he were to be heard at it in the flesh, people would run after him with sticks and chains, thinking him to be possessed by a legion of devils, ready to catch and bind him.' Just before that, Luther had acknowledged himself as 'the most distinguished teacher of the age'. Did that not lay very different obligations upon him, than those implied by the title of the duke of Brunswick-Wolfenbüttel?

We are not concerned with justifying this sort of thing. Whoever does not condemn it harms his own, and Luther's cause. A popular book about Luther, written recently, affirms that the fury of the book on the papacy reinvigorated Luther. Of the belligerent imagery that accompanied it at the time it is said: 'He wrote a few dozen lines on Antichrist – popular, fierce, coarse, obscene.' The conclusion is that Luther's hatred of the papacy was the most powerful force radiating from his life (Thiel). These are woeful words for any Christian to hear, who feels the pain of the schism.

This imagery again shows how badly the atmosphere was poisoned, and how it was almost impossible for anyone to gain a clear vision of his adversary, and assess him justly. This in itself suggests that Luther was misrepresenting his opponents, and that there might well have been much more of positive value in the Church of those days than Luther and those who spread his teachings were able to see.

Charles knew that a crisis was imminent. He extended his rear defences as far as Denmark. In 1543 he had already made a secret treaty with England. After the campaign against Cleves he had spent the winter preparing for war. Now a conflict with France had to come. Having settled a dispute to his own advantage in northern Italy, he personally mustered his army outside Metz – with that self-reliance and personal superiority, which Butzer openly praised. There followed a victorious attack upon the Marne and Paris, during which negotiations between the emperor and the king were never broken off. This ended in victory, crowned by the peace of Crépy. On 18 September 1544 Charles did not repeat the mistake he had made over the peace of Madrid. He made no territorial demands upon France. Upper Italy, however, became his. A wedge was driven between France and the Turks, and the French returned to do their European, Christian duty. They agreed to fight against the Turks. More than this: they broke with the Protestants in Germany. By a secret treaty they undertook to join in a common effort to advance Church reform, through a council. Above all, they declared themselves ready to suppress the Reformation, ultimately by use of force.

This was an overwhelming success for the tough perseverance of the emperor. His mighty foreign political struggle had ended in victory. He stood free, the *sacra caesarea majestas*, confronting heretics and infidels alike. Now it was possible for him to face his task in Germany as he saw fit.

We would have a very one-sided picture of the disposition of forces were we to look only at the assent of the French, of Hesse, of Brandenburg and of the duke of Saxony. Even the petty jealousies and lack of purposeful initiative within the Schmalkald League do not signify that they had given up the fight and passively resigned themselves to fate. The years 1544 and 1545, too, were filled with a notable and varied Lutheran offensive. Hesse and the French, in spite of their promises, never ceased to undermine the emperor. The appetite of the Protestants had been whetted by the concessions granted them in 1544. At Worms in 1545 they showed no restraint at all in their claims. They proceeded straight away on the assumption that attack is the best defence. First, they rejected the Council of Trent in any form, and asked the emperor to do the same; then Hesse, Saxony, Sleidan and finally Luther, dared to call for armed attack upon the pope. Luther included this demand in the pamphlet *Against The Papacy in Rome*, which the elector of Saxony had distributed at the *Reichstag*.

The Catholic estates saw through these tactics which, in view of the vast and varied reformation of the past decades, represented a distortion of the facts; but they could do nothing, because their party had completely lost what little striking power it ever had, through the hypocritical duplicity of Bavarian policy. The radical, political egoism of Leonard von Eck even led him to say that it would be a better thing if the Catholics turned Lutheran than if the emperor were victorious. For according to the Protestants the Catholics would then be destroyed by the emperor. As well as this, Duke Ludwig of Bavaria died early in 1545. This meant that there was now no prominent leader to set over the Catholic League.

And so the year 1545, too, stood under the sign of Protestantism. Luther's insulting pamphlet on the pope to some extent betrayed the hope that the pope and the council – and the emperor – might be destroyed. The last secular Elector Palatine, Frederick II, who for so long had vacillated, now went over to the Reformation, and joined the Schmalkald League at the Frankfurt Diet of the league in 1545–46. Hermann von Wied sought admission to the league, and appealed against Rome – which took proceedings against him – and against the emperor's summons to a free German council in Brussels. The Schmalkald League for the second time drove out Brunswick-Wolfenbüttel, who tried to win back his territory. The duke was made prisoner by Hesse (21 October 1545). The reformation of Brunswick was assured.

When the Reformation seemed to be rolling on to total victory in Germany, Luther died, on the night of 17/18 February 1546, naturally and peacefully, in his birthplace of Eisleben.

His weariness of life had become acute. 'Pray fervently that the Lord will take away my soul in peace. May God grant me a blessed hour, and may his day of glory come soon, very soon, right soon! Amen!'

He felt himself to be constantly in the hands of God. It is true he valued the care given him by his wife Kate; but he wrote to her in the same gruff tone as before: 'You are going to provide – not God? As though he were not almighty and could create ten Martins where the old one is breathing his last in the room, or in the chimney corner. Leave me in peace with your worrying. I have a better one than you or all the angels to take care of me. He lies in the manger, and sits, too, at the right hand of God the almighty Father' (7 February 1546). 'I worry that you never cease worrying that the earth might swallow us up. . . . . You pray, and let God do the worrying!' (10 February 1546).

In the last week before his death he knew a great calm, without a trace of fear for his end. We must not put a false, sublime interpretation upon this. God and prayer had their regular place in his life. But his interest in much extolled eating and drinking was still as strong as ever. A mood or disposition that had progressively left earthly interests behind and become lost in deep thoughts or longing for God, in the style of the saints, or even in Luther's own style when, in 1537 in Schmalkalden, he longed to be released from his suffering body, was not Luther's mood at this time. With a perfectly natural resignation he accepted the prospect of death. He was inspired by an utterly peaceful and *natural trust in God* – if we may use such a phrase. The hour of his death, in so far as he himself was able to disclose it to us, was full of deep religious devotion.

On his table was found a note with his final profession of faith A truly moving summary! 'We are beggars – that is the truth!'

Outward victory for the new Church order had not deceived Luther concerning the moral and religious decline within the empire, that had accompanied the Reformation, had been its consequence in fact. There had been a universal decline in moral discipline and religious fervour.

Only a miracle could have prevented this; for Luther's principal work had been the revolutionary overthrow of the great old authorities. The inevitable consequence had been that many were soon utterly free and prepared to acknowledge no restraints whatever.

All the same, if this was Luther's work, it did not represent what was deepest and most characteristic in his thought – in his *faith*; and it was the exact opposite of what he wanted.

TWO

Crisis Precipitated by the Schmalkald War

When the emperor made concessions to the Protestants at Speyer in 1544 he had already been in conflict with the curia since 1541. It was not the emperor alone who failed to understand why the pope did not support him in his sharp accusation against France. Brandenburg, too, complained that the pope ought to deprive Francis I of the title 'Most Christian Majesty'. Ferdinand thought that Paul III was still ordering a council, although that was an impossibility. True: the inner tragedy of Reformation history, seen from the Catholic angle, lay in those years 1543–44, and in the incomprehensible failure of the pope. His neutrality was fundamentally nothing else than 'grasping family politics' (Brandi). In effect, however, it amounted to support of the French, who were in league with the Turks; and at this time, moreover, the threat came not only from the east but also from Chaireddin Barbarossa who was snatching away thousands of Christian slaves from the coasts of the Mediterranean. What a triumph for Luther! 'The news now is that there is a league between the pope, the French, and the Turks, against the emperor' (8 March 1544).

Accordingly, Charles V thought that the pope would hardly help him in his stand against the German Reformers, if it came to a hard fight. And yet, only if things were cleared up between him and the curia could there be any hope of reorganisation in Germany, after the failure of the theological attempts at reunion. Charles showed his greatness by the way he persevered, through all the disillusionment and bitterness caused by papal policy, in seeking an alliance with the pope, as a means of achieving far-reaching action within the empire.

An additional precondition was, that the emperor be able to operate within Germany unhampered by threats in the rear. The experience of many years had shown, however, how ready Bavaria was to prejudice a Catholic solution of the religious question, in the interests of egoistic territorial politics. Bavaria's rejection of the French in 1544 and their turning towards the emperor had not been an unambiguous action. Leonard von Eck was still his old unscrupulous self. In 1545 when, for the first time, the emperor was on the brink of war with the Protestants, Bavaria was again one of the uncertain factors in the reckoning. Eck remained a foe of Habsburg and a sympathiser with Hesse.

On the other hand, following the final defeat of Brunswick by the Schmalkald League, and in view of the attitude of the elector of Cologne, Bavaria was the only state in Germany – apart from the Habsburg estates – in which the old faith and the old Church system were still completely accepted. An alliance with Bavaria was the one thing that could safeguard the rear of the imperial front.

The emperor achieved both alliances.

As complete victors, the Schmalkald League held its diet in Frankfurt in 1545–46. They had rallied powerfully to the cause of Hermann von Wied, and had asked Francis I to take arms against the emperor. At a further diet in Worms the bishop of Münster sought admission to the league, but was refused.

At the same time the second religious conversations had begun in Regensburg and ended unsuccessfully.

The *Reichstag* met in Regensburg in April 1546. It was abominably badly attended. Even the princes' ambassadors were absent – very sensibly; for the power of the Schmalkald League had so increased that any regulation along the lines of the old religion could have been enforced by arms alone. In addition the landgrave of Hesse had had a conference on 28 May in Speyer, when he got to know enough about the emperor's plans for war. At all events, he immediately influenced the other participants.

Until he entered Regensburg the emperor had known how to keep his plans for war secret. In March he put the mind of the suspicious elector of Saxony at rest, and boldly demonstrated his peaceableness to the whole world, by travelling through the dangerously tense land with only a small escort, to the *Reichstag*. Only then, having seen that the Reformers intended to abandon him, did he let the veil drop, bit by bit. Then came a series of war treaties against the Protestants.

The treaty with Bavaria – i.e. between the emperor, Ferdinand and Duke William – against the Reformed party was signed on 7 June 1546. This assured only the required rear cover. Bavaria refused to become obliged to participate in aggression, but was prepared to supply artillery and rations; above all it was to remain neutral and the treaty was to be kept a secret. In this way Bavaria was able to maintain its confusing alliance with Hesse even during war. This alliance was, however, a last security in the event of the emperor being defeated. But things went well for the emperor, the treaty became an important turning-point in Bavarian politics. It marked the change from a Catholic territorial, to a Catholic imperial, standpoint. In its further effects, it represented, therefore, a move towards the Habsburg imperial policy of the counter-Reformation. In return Bavaria received hopes of acquiring the Palatine Electorate (in the event of the elector, now negotiating with the Schmalkald League, making war on the emperor), King Ferdinand's daughter was promised to Duke Albert, and thus there were hopes of Bavaria one day having heirs in Bohemia.

The change in the outlook of the curia was revealed at the *Reichstag* of Worms in 1545. It came by surprise and somewhat turbulently. In a few days, at the end of May, firm agreements between the emperor and the papal nuncio, Farnese, led to war against the German Protestants. In great haste the nuncio personally procured in Rome the explicit consent of the pope. To the 100,000 ducats he had brought with him to Worms as much again was added, and 12,000 infantry and 500 cavalry were promised in four months: almost a million ducats were voted out of the funds of the Church in Spain. This was a magnificent offer. The curia set about at once to equip the army.

Unfortunately the emperor was not equipped for battle. The war was put off for that year. Thus the curia began to mistrust the emperor, and not without reason. Was he in earnest about going to war? As the pope had taken care to publish the agreements with the emperor, the Protestants now knew what they had to reckon with.

After several months' negotiation, during which the emperor kept falling back on the idea of a religious conversation, on 6 or 26 June 1546 an alliance was again made with the pope. In July Paul III had already despatched his troops to Germany. It was like a crusade. The leaders were the pope's two grandsons Alexander and Octavius Farnese. There was no doubt about it: the curia were plainly concerned about religions questions.

The work was crowned by a third treaty. The emperor succeeded in well and truly breaking up the Schmalkald front. He did this by means of a fresh agreement with Duke Maurice of Saxony, the coming man on the Protestant side. Following much negotiation, on 19 June the emperor had tied down this equivocal man by a treaty.

As good fortune would have it, in March 1545 the politically short-sighted elector of Saxony had rejected Duke Maurice's dangerous plan to prepare for a settlement of the dispute between the emperor and themselves by a close alliance between Hesse, electoral Saxony and Maurice. Otherwise there would perhaps have been an end to the spiritual estates of the empire. But both of them – the elector and Maurice – had their eyes on the important regions of Magdeburg and Halberstadt. Now the emperor dangled the prospect of these ecclesiastical endowments before Maurice (by treaty, but still very vaguely), and recognised his right to the state of electoral Saxony, still to be conquered. Because of the Saxon electorate, however, he did not make any definite promise. The recognition of the council was a precondition; but approval of clerical marriage and of the cup for the laity was given. Maurice was already an unscrupulous Machiavelli. Ten days after his declaration of submission to the emperor, he pledged his protection to Hesse.

The margrave John of Brandenburg-Küstrin, who was enraged at Hesse because he was keeping his father-in-law, Brunswick, prisoner, also made useful agreements with the emperor. However, on 18 June contracts of service were made with the princely robber-knight, Albrecht Alcibiades, and with Eric von Calenberg.

296 THE NEW EPOCH: THE REFORMATION IN GERMANY

Things had now reached a stage when the emperor could offer that proof, at which he had ambiguously hinted, in reply to the complaints of the pope concerning the Speyer agreements: at a certain point he would provide definite proof that it was not he who was responsible for the ruin of Christendom. The Schmalkald League – who were arming themselves – now asked him to declare the purpose of his armament. He replied: 'The emperor desires to restore unity, peace, and justice, in the empire. He will deal with the disobedient legally and as befits his authority.'

In all his public utterances the emperor held firm to this statement of aims. He avoided saying that his motive and aim was the overthrow of the Reformation as such. But he stressed the fact that certain unauthorised persons had used the Christian religion as an excuse for unlawful acquisitions within the empire. He told his son Philip and the Queen-Regent Mary, that his true motive was religion, and that the political reasons were only the pretext. 'If we do not intervene now, the whole of Germany would be in danger of falling away from the faith.' We cannot simply dismiss his attitude as dishonest. For this dispute had long since become a supremely important imperial political affair, not least through the Schmalkald League and especially the activity therein of Philip of Hesse. It is true that his opponents might reply, that the emperor was now contradicting the assurances he had given since 1539, particularly those at Speyer. They would have made this objection more loudly and with more justice, had they known of the secret treaty of Crépy with the king of France. This leads us to ask: how sincere was the emperor when he made those assurances? Once again we cannot say that he was being dishonest. We can say, however, that he had been deliberately vague. This vagueness had been almost a necessary product of the double character of the whole situation and of its fundamental cause: the inextricable confusion of political and religious factors.

In 1544 the Jesuit Bobadilla had tried energetically to explain to King Ferdinand by letter, and to the emperor through his confessor, how serious the implications of these concessions actually were. He was told in reply that the thing would not last long. The action had been necessary in order to avoid civil war, and one had only been awaiting the moment when everything would be restored along Catholic lines. Besides these there were a host of other inconsistencies in what Charles had said concerning his intentions during those years. One thing is certain: the emperor was in deadly earnest about securing peace and unity in Germany. In past years, in exceedingly difficult circumstances, he had given ample proof of this. After the end of his victorious campaign he proved it again by the Interim. Even the Schmalkald War proved it; for he did not use it to bring about a brutal destruction of the whole of Protestantism in Germany but rather to create the preconditions of a peaceful restoration of the former Church order. His recipe was false, because dogmatic insight was weak. But he meant well.

It may well be impossible to ascertain quite unambiguously the emperor's final opinion about the German question in the years 1543–46. The reason for this certainly lies most of all in the dominance of politics over religion in the schemes of Paul III. Had the pope been clearly on the emperor's side, not from 1545 but from the start, as it was his duty to have been, and had declared himself against Francis I, ally of the Turks and the Protestants, the alignment of forces would have been much more definite.

War had become unavoidable; but the Habsburgs still had time to solemnise the projected political marriages. On 4 July the duke of Bavaria married Ferdinand's eldest daughter, Anna; on 18 July the duke of Cleves married his second daughter, Mary.

Much, if not everything, in this war, depended upon which side had the better leadership. Unity was assured on the Catholic side. The emperor alone directed the campaign. The Schmalkald League, however, were not clear about the manner and objectives of their opposition, nor about their organisation. Petty jealousies were not lacking between Saxony, Hesse and the cities. In particular the elector of Saxony distrusted the landgrave, and this had a devastating effect. By universal consent, Philip was the only competent one to lead the Protestants to victory. The one comparable political leader in the league, James Sturm of Strasburg, was never given nearly enough influence. His clear-sightedness never prevailed. (Granvella recognised his activity – and objected

to it – in 1548.) And so it came about, that the military preponderance, with which the Protestants started off – because their troops
were ready – did not save them from defeat, although they were
far better armed for psychological warfare than were the Catholics,
through the moral support of a deluge of pamplets,[1] and from a
mighty incitement of anti-Roman feeling by the preachers.[2]

The elector John Frederick and the landgrave Philip of Hesse
joined forces on 3 July 1546, at Erfurt: 16,000 infantry and 5,000
cavalry. They outnumbered the emperor's forces many times
over. The emperor, with smaller protection, was at Regensburg.
But he was not caught; nor was the way barred to the papal troops
coming from Italy, although Schertlin von Burtenbach and the
army of the south German cities in the League had taken the
Ehrenberg gorge. Nor were the imperial troops coming from the
Netherlands halted below Büren. The two sectors were not united,
however, until 15 September, when the campaign on the Danube
had been in progress for some time.

The tide of battle was turned in the emperor's favour by
Maurice of Saxony. Having been promised the Saxon electorate,
he broke into Saxony with Ferdinand. The elector was thus
forced to leave the long-drawn out campaign on the Danube –
prosecuted by both sides with an excess of hesitation and caution –
and move north. It was now November. With logic and a profound symbolism the political battle moved to the place where
the root of the dispute lay: to electoral Saxony, the birth place
of Luther's Reformation.

The elector having departed, the emperor was left in command
of the situation. South Germany was his.

Immediately he demonstrated that he was not interested in
the sheer destruction of his enemy. It is true that he exacted
heavy dues from the defeated cities, to pay his troops, and to
prevent them supporting enemy troops. But he neither took back
Würtemberg from the Habsburgs, nor did he simply compel the
Protestants to return to the old faith. The necessary conclusions
would be drawn and expressed by the estates at the coming
Reichstag.

[1] 'No Walloon will rule over us; nor yet a Spaniard!'
[2] Bugenhagen spread the grisly tale that the pope and the emperor had long
been hatching a plan to murder everyone from the age of two upwards.

The real crisis came in 1547. Elector John Frederick of Saxony had gained an advantage over Maurice. The political dangers which this war had undoubtedly brought so near, weakened northern German Protestantism. The north, therefore, attached itself to electoral Saxony. Ferdinand and Maurice asked for assistance. The emperor was very ill and came slowly, carried in a litter, bringing troops with him; but in the end of the day he was victorious.

Admittedly, at first, i.e. at the beginning of 1547, the emperor's power suffered a dangerous loss, at the very moment when he could least afford it. On 22 January the pope recalled his troops. In 1545 Pedro de Soto, the emperor's confessor, had urged him to get rid of all mistrust of the pope and make a treaty with him. He said: 'The pope could not be so diabolical as to want to destroy the Catholic faith by urging the emperor into a great venture, then leaving him in the lurch.' This was the very thing that now happened. It is difficult to regard it as other than a betrayal of the common religious cause. It is so, even if in Charles' settlements with the pope, the stress chiefly lay upon Charles' obligation to make the Protestants recognise the council. It was impossible for anyone to assert in 1546 that Charles would not try to fulfil that obligation; but it is certain, however, that in January 1547 the purpose for which the pope had made this treaty with Charles, had by no means been accomplished. Mistrust of imperial policy was no minor detail in the motivation of the curia but the central thing, especially in connection with Paul III's nepotism, which drove him to contemplate supporting the Protestants (Janssen). The reaction that was expressed here is intelligible only in political terms, and all that it meant to the pope must be fully and calmly taken into account. However, no matter how much we take into account the pope's fear of Charles' encroachment in the ecclesiastical sphere in Spain, Germany and especially in Italy, beginning at Milan, this does not alter the fact, that in this the cause of religion and the Church was being greatly endangered from political considerations. The withdrawal of the troops was not the whole story but rather the sign of anti-imperial coalitions in Europe. In this we can already detect a far-reaching point of departure for the coming rapid change of political alignment in Charles' disfavour.

Our verdict, however, must always be decisively affected by the fact, that the vicar of Christ, protector of the true faith, has to be judged in an essentially different way from the political head of Christendom. Undoubtedly, Charles had done great things for the restoration of the unity of Christendom. Paul III, by contrast, after an impressive start, had failed. He simply ought not to have removed his troops from the scene of war in Saxony, justifying his action by the sheer letter of the treaty – admittedly under foreign political pressure. The conclusion is unavoidable: in its critical years, Protestantism found no greater assistance than was given by several measures taken by the popes, who from the point of view of religious conviction were Protestantism's deadly enemies, and from the king of France.

This is an oppressive fact for Catholics, and one which clearly manifests the calamities inherent in the improper fusion of religion and self-interested politics. The question constantly arises: was the schism in the Church not a divine punishment for the practical inversion of the world order – for the primacy of dynastic policy over religion, at the central see of the Church? The fundamental attitude of the Roman central authority had become utterly worldly.

Charles, usually so self-controlled, broke into a fury: he knew how to distinguish the papal office from the man who held it and, at a council, would set things to rights in Rome.

In spite of the reduction in his military strength, things turned out favourable for the emperor. During the campaign on the Danube he had declined to negotiate with Philip of Hesse. Now he declined to do so with John Frederick. At the end of March he joined forces with the combined troops of Maurice and Ferdinand, and marched against the elector. At Mühlberg and – after the elector's retreat to Wittenberg – on the Heath of Lochau, he gained complete victory. The brave elector, who stayed with his infantry to the end, was captured (24 April 1547). This happened only a few months after the emperor had learned of the death of the king of France, and the death of the king of England.

This victory had extensive repercussions. On 16 April, Hermann von Weid had been ruled out of account by excommunication and deposition. Now the elector of Saxony was the emperor's prisoner. Hesse surrendered unconditionally. The imperial cities in the north, that did not submit, were powerless anyway. By the Capitulation of Wittenberg on 19 May the electoral dignity and status of Saxony were transferred to Maurice. Finally, on 19 June, Charles obtained, through Ferdinand, a five-year truce with the Turks as well. He was master of the world.

Once more the emperor did not know how to exploit his victory – neither politically, nor ecclesiastically. In the first respect, the death sentence on John Frederick, 'one-time elector', was a quite fruitless burden. Then the somewhat underhand imprisonment of Hesse and, later, the unnecessarily vexatious delay in liberating both princes, aroused increasing opposition, especially from Philip's son-in-law, Maurice. Not least: the emperor left Magdeburg unsubdued in his rear. The victory of 1546 in south Germany, and that at Mühlberg, and its consequences, left Charles in command of the situation; but it did not invest him with complete power. In those days war was something quite different from what it is today. In those days a genuine army was assembled for a specific campaign, and when that campaign was over it was disbanded. In addition, as soon as he was powerful, Charles became the political adversary of every power in Europe, with the exception of the Habsburgs and one or two allied minor princes. As soon as his foreign political opponents and those within Germany were more or less in checkmate, he should have exploited the situation. But the marvellous perseverance, which he displayed again at this time, was permeated by carelessness and also by contempt. It was not that the emperor needed to take vengeance; but he should have acted promply and established definite positions of strength. He failed to do either.

Nor did he establish a clear-cut ecclesio-political front. What we might call the Erasmian in him, played too big a part in his decisions. Political action was destroyed by conciliatory religiosity, and religion was damaged by a too weak policy. Charles' Interim (see below) could satisfy neither German Catholics nor the pope. It stirred up the Reformers to protest, and welded them together. Charles had no clear idea of how deeply the power of Evangelical belief had already struck root in the people. Besides this, the widespread, colossal hatred of 'papistry' ought to have taught him that even if he had taken some decisive step, his work would only have been beginning. His memoirs tell us the same story as his deeds: as he saw things, what now had to come – the resolution of schism by 'means of kindness' – was a mere corollary.

Charles' behaviour plainly shows that his primary concern was the peaceful inauguration of order. His assurances in this respect, in the midst of military preoccupation since 1545, had been no hypocrisy.

THREE

The Outcome. The Interim and its Consequences

In the autumn of that auspicious year 1547 Charles opened his 'armed' *Reichstag* in Augsburg. It began punctually on the appointed date, 1 September; but it was not carried through to its end in the following year with anything like the same energy. The emperor's curious irresolution on political issues, and his disagreements with the pope, threatened to precipitate a schism; his singularly muddled and tactically obscure theological viewpoint in the midst of the unusually licentious ongoings of the hard-drinking princes, made this *Reichstag* a source of fresh confusion leading to a definite split, instead of being the start of unity and peace.

The political development turned out to be a gradual collapse of the front which the emperor had created. It began with the victor's *Reichstag* itself. Bavaria's disturbing influence could be seen at work everywhere. Because the elector Palatine had voluntarily surrendered, he was left with his vote. Bavaria saw its dream shattered, and so returned to join the opposition.

As always, there was another source of trouble: the selfishness of the princes. They were all the more anxious about their privileges, because the mighty victor was trying to consolidate the imperial power on every side. Appointments to the Imperial

High Court[1] were to be more in accord with the emperor's wishes, and the court was to act more in line with his plans. Charles wanted to have an Imperial League, which would facilitate the direction of the government by the emperor, and provide a standing army that would be directly at the emperor's disposal, and independent of the views of the estates at the time. This was the most vital part of the whole programme.

Here Charles had put his finger on the fulcrum of any permanent administration. On countless and painful occasions he had savoured to the full the critical weakness of his position within the empire – the lack of a standing army which would have been able to protect the empire against its two perennial enemies: the Turks and the French. Only this could have put an end to the senseless ebb and flow of war and peacemaking, of success and fresh threats to life. It is true that this army would have been directly at the disposal of the Habsburg dynastic power in the Netherlands and in Austria. Charles had a dynastic mind. This does not alter the fact, that this dynastic advantage stood or fell with the interests of the empire, although not with the interests and centrifugal desires of the princes. An Imperial League was the only form in which in those days the empire could have found unity, and have asserted itself against France then and in later centuries; and Charles alone could have led it.

Unfortunately – but understandably – the estates set up such a successful resistance to all this, that only an insignificant residue of the great plan remained. As well as this the estates bound themselves to support the council then reopening at Bologna.

Not least, it was the Catholic estates who brought their weight to bear. Was it not the Catholic cause which the emperor had led to victory? And so they made their demands. Unlike the emperor, they were not concerned with a great universal issue. What moved them was not an earnest, utterly religious solicitude, which was aware of the presence of deeply and strongly rooted difficulties that had to be overcome. No – what they wanted was the restoration of episcopal jurisdiction and Church property.

The importance of political measures becomes evident only

[1] The enfeoffment of the new electors of Cologne and Saxony, the creation of the Burgundian imperial circle, the improvements of the Land Peace and of the monetary system have to be mentioned.

when seen in conjunction with the religious question, that is as part of Charles' vast conception of a secular–spiritual monarchy, in which not only the Protestants but in a certain sense the pope, too, was to show obedience to the emperor. In this connection the *Reichstag* represented an uncommonly tough fight by the emperor for a religious settlement. The devotion with which he constantly renewed his attempts to carry through even a single part of this plan, is significant. His hopes were bound to be dashed for they were built far too much upon relativistic presuppositions.

The outcome of Charles' efforts was the Interim which he proclaimed as law at the *Reichstag* (*interreligio imperialis*). This was to apply to all the estates, and only later was it limited to the Protestants (on account of the invincible Catholic opposition). This 'imperial interim religion' – the 'explanation of how religion is to be conducted within the holy empire until the decision of the general council' – did not come about by consultation with the estates of the empire (which were never finished), but was composed by a commission nominated by the emperor: Julius Pflug (bishop of Naumburg), Michael Helding (bishop of Mainz) and Agricola (court preacher of Joachim II, elector of Brandenburg). The Spanish theologians de Soto (the emperor's confessor) and Malvenda, as well as the provincial of the Cologne Carmelites, Eberhard Billick, exercised a decisive influence; and finally, in an advisory capacity, there was Butzer – not entirely unambiguous. The Interim is a Catholic text including a statement of the doctrine of justification, designed to accommodate the Protestants, a vague definition of the mass, the granting of the cup to the laity and allowing the marriage of the clergy, in force until the decision of the council. The work was to be completed by a special imperial reform of the clergy – of which we have already heard.

The Interim was not ecclesio-political in the sense that it reflected the preoccupation of the thirites with the problem of secularisation. There was no mention of any restitution of the Church property appropriated by the Protestants. This in itself was instructive; for it came about in spite of an unsuspected contradiction. Hardly anybody was satisfied, neither the protesting pope not the Catholic estates. Above all, those most concerned – the Protestants – were dissatisfied. The new faith made a great advance in self-awareness.

There were many on the Protestant side who did, indeed, welcome the Interim, because they hoped to see it result in the moral and religious elevation of the people through the reintro- duced ceremonies. They hoped that the universal licence and lack of respect for preaching and the sacraments would be checked. Some throughgoing effects, were in fact, produced. The Interim restored full Catholic life to a whole series of southern and central German towns. In those places, too, there arose the com- plete parity of the confessions sanctioned at Augsburg in 1555, and prevailing to this day.

Accordingly, a significant transposition took place in the interior structure of Protestantism. Wherever the Interim was effective, Protestant preachers had to leave their sphere of opera- tions and carry on in other districts. Magdeburg now exerted an even greater attraction, as the 'chancellery of God'. Butzer left Strasburg, where a tough battle was developing between the city and the bishop. The city eventually became Lutheran. He went to England where the schism was just then advancing into heresy. Osiander moved from Nuremberg to Königsberg, a move that was important for the intensification of contradictions within Protes- tantism.

On the whole, however, the scheme failed.

The Interim was highlighted by the conflict between emperor and pope, a conflict that in turn became more acute through differences over the council. In the conflict the Interim represented the emperor's autonomous attempt to accomplish something, in contrast to the dogmatic decrees of the Council of Trent, and to the council in Bologna in particular.

In his memoirs, Charles described the Interim as a *modus vivendi* until the council. In spite of that, it was more than a merely tactical measure. Its conceptions cut really deep, and showed the interplay of many motifs. First of all: Charles had never any sympathy for a thesis that would have prohibited him in all circumstances from autonomous intervention in the affairs of the Church. In a very real sense, he felt himself to be a second head of Christendom, a true steward of the Church. Nor was this concept a purely passive one. Not for nothing was Charles the king of Spain, where for a very long time the Church had always been for the most part subservient to the will of the sovereign. In addition, he embodied the great tradition of the emperor, according to which the autonomous intervention of the emperor in ecclesiastical affairs was quite normal, having indeed, on occasion, been the very life and saving of the Church. Moreover, since the reform memorandum of the cardinals in 1536, the curia themselves had recognised extreme curialism as an abuse. And so on both sides there had been a failure to define clearly the limits of competence which each possessed. For his part, Charles suffered from the general theological vagueness, which the curia had done so much to aggravate during the last generation – most effectively by their protection of Erasmus, by delaying punishment, by their temporary consciously equivocal attitude to Henry VIII's marriage, and by their political approach to the religious question in Germany. For the rest, in Augsburg 1530, the curia themselves had contemplated allowing the cup to the laity and marriage to the clergy, and they retrospectively justified Charles' autonomous action, by recognising the Interim in 1549. In short, it became evident, that the Interim was truly a serious fixation of the spirit of the religious conversations of Regensburg. It would be superfluous to emphasise how much Charles' political goals were interested in this renewal.

Just as we may little imagine that Charles ever gave a thought to the possibility of a schism. There was no need of that in his awareness of politico-priestly activity. Charles had been completely in earnest, too, when in the resolutions of the *Reichstag*, he had constantly represented the council as the *ultima ratio*, and sought constantly to bind the Protestant partners in the contract to accept it also. Charles was unconditionally loyal to the Church.

It is true that he constructed a picture of the coming council which was different from the reality of Trent. Was it the early influence exerted by his teacher Adrian, himself brought up by the Netherland Brothers of the Common Life, whose spirit was so much in harmony with the optimistic and irenic Contarini? Was it the practical relativisation of dogma, by the political treatment of the religious question by the curia? Was it his many theological contacts with the efforts at reunion in both parties? At all events, in those years a humanist underplaying of the dogmatic points of controversy seems to have appealed to the emperor. He had enough confidence in his political and diplomatic skill, to imagine that he could settle the issue, without any harm coming to Christianity. In fact, Charles might well have thought, in those years, that he had calmly mastered the colossal problems of administration as they arose, with dogged competence. He had solved almost impossible problems. Besides – Luther was no more; the Catholic princes certainly had not distinguished themselves for their power; the Protestants were his prisoners or his allies. Would it be such a fantastic thing if he, a loyal son of the Church, thought he could settle matters of faith? His brightly variegated empire could find unity only if it proceeded from a spiritual source. This spiritual unity could come only from religion – the Catholic Church. Quite apart from any personal ecclesiastical and doctrinal loyalties, Charles' imperial plans were bound to see the Protestant Reformation of Church and religion as nothing but an irreconcilable enemy. On the other hand, the most pertinent expression of these plans was compromising – but Catholic – theology.

The most important element in the analysis is still lacking: the emperor misjudged the times in which he lived. The age of relativism in all of its forms was past, never to return. The Interim was a well-intentioned but confused compromise, hence intrinsically feeble. Thus it was unable to release true religious energies; it could raise no preachers to proclaim it with authority. It was backed by no absolute religious demand; accordingly, an answer had still to be found to the religious question. The so-called Leipzig Interim of 1548 – framed by Melanchthon and the new elector – aroused as little response as that of the emperor. The religious contradictions had completely disentangled themselves, but had hardened in the process. The authentic expression of the age was the dogmatic decrees of the Council of Trent, and the rigidity of the Lutheran theologians – of Flacius Illyricus in Magdeburg, and of the unbending inhabitants of 'the chancellery of our Lord God'. The dogmatic weakness of Melanchthon's *Adiaphora* had no punch. After the Catholic estates had rejected the Interim at the Augsburg *Reichstag* in 1548, the Protestants displayed the same attitude almost everywhere in the country – nobles and people alike. John Frederick – unlike the broken down Philip of Hesse, – still in prison, showed a commendable power of religious resistance.

There is no need to stress how much political interests were expressed in every act of secret resistance to the Interim. None the less, it was precisely those days after the collapse of the political Protestant power that provided proof of the profound effect which the religious Reformation had exerted. It had become an essential element in many regions. This was to be seen in the south and even more in the north of the empire. The substance of the Reformed religious formulae on the one hand, anti-Roman feelings – involving the emperor, too – on the other, came to life in many popular forms of the sung and written word – professing faith, and deriding the adversary.

'Beware of the Interim – there's a rogue behind it.'
'To me, Lucifer, a child is born – the delight of my wife,
Mrs Pope, – and his name is Interim.'

This sentiment ran all through Germany.

At this point another mistake of the emperor becomes evident. Not only did he make no move against the sharp attack to be expected from the opposition but he also failed to insist on his military diplomatic victory being recognised outside the cabinet. The emergent people and the opinion of the ordinary man may not have been the power which called the tune but, in conjunction with the religious ideas of the Reformation, they constituted the only power which could have given permanence to a resolution such as the end of the Schmalkald War proved to be. Alternatively, the emperor should have maintained a permanent armed force. Charles had not even reckoned with the mood of the people. It was left to the opposition to exploit that.

The German princes automatically took the initiative in the opposition. Germany had long been accustomed to hearing jibes about bestial servitude (i.e. to Spain or France). Now the princes had got the better of the emerging power of the peasants, and exploited the revolutionary religious idea in their own interests. Having got thus far, were they going to allow the emperor to snatch away their independence? *Religion* and *Liberty* were the slogans under which opposition to the emperor gradually formed and consolidated in various circles of quite different tendencies. Even the old Cochlaeus saw that the emperor's victory was not going to be decisive. In fact the imperial front of the Schmalkald War broke up even more. What is more, out of this there emerged a new anti-imperial party. Interests that at first had been opposed, now combined to form a new core of Protestant political opposition, which was to grow into a genuine confederacy against the emperor and the spiritual territories. The growth of his confederacy was itself permeated with pathetic strife between the princes, princely neutrality and unprincelike cowardice. Helped by the robber knighthood of the margrave Albrecht Alcibiades of Brandenburg-Kulmbach, it led to an unworthy condition in the nation, to dissolution of the body politic. All the time the hand of Henry II, the new king of France, could be seen at work with the princes. Henry gladly used his money to set the Germans at war with each other, chiefly through the instrumentality of Elector Maurice of Saxony. As of old the French were again at their posts ready to attack the emperor.

Maurice's betrayal of the Schmalkald League had done much to bring about the emperor's victory in 1547. Now it was the emperor's turn to be betrayed by Maurice. On this occasion he and his partners in the deal not only betrayed the empire but also, in return for French money, handed over imperial territory to the king of France: Metz, Toul, Verdun.

By the time that this goal was reached in 1552, things had already developed very much further.

Magdeburg, still unsubdued, stood as a symbol of unbroken Protestant opposition to the emperor. It had been outlawed. At the Augsburg *Reichstag* of 1550–51, when the opposition was already proving more powerful, Maurice was commissioned to put the ban into effect. After the proclamation of outlawry there had been dangerous unrest in the city. On the other hand, as a reflection of the Schmalkald League and of the Interim, in north Germany defensive groupings emerged everywhere. Maurice, the authorised imperial field marshal, craftily exploited both. He had considerable funds voted for war and subdued the city in November 1550. But he made a secret treaty with the city on his own account. This campaign against Magdeburg enabled him to keep away from the *Reichstag*, and from the emperor, and to hold the army in readiness, which in the end was used to put the emperor to flight.

The margrave John of Brandenburg-Küstrin was the first to make a move towards forming an anti-imperial league. On 26 February 1550 he had made a pact with Prussia and Mecklenburg. At that time Maurice was still their enemy. A common opposition to the emperor then brought them together. Maurice was successful in overcoming, at home and in France, the understandable mistrust of himself, former ally of the emperor, and now imperial field marshal. By May 1551 mutual preliminary negotiations were so far advanced, that they were able to proceed with the founding of an anti-imperial league of princes. At Torgau on the Elbe the following banded together: Elector Maurice, margrave John of Küstrin, Duke John Albrecht of Mecklenburg the landgrave Philip of Hesse. The contract they made with one another – as with France later – stated the cause of their dissatisfaction: the mean imprisonment of the landgrave Philip 'for close on five years – an affront and mockery to us all'; the threat to the estate of 'bestial, intolerable and everlasting servitude, as in Spain'; and the threat to true religion. In many variants, and in every situation of total war, pillage and extortion, of all the three points that about the protection of religion was put first, with incredible frivolity. The sublime concepts of 'the word of God alone' of 'fervour' and 'true doctrine', were mercilessly debased – especially by Albrecht Alcibiades. In 1552 when the margrave of Küstrin once again broke with Maurice, he cast up their hypocrisy to these princes: 'It is not religion they have in mind, and they do not consider the word of God worthy of their attention.'

Peace with France had been an indispensable precondition for setting things in order in Germany. For this reason war with the Protestants could only be waged after the peace of Crépy. But before the emperor's army had even set off against the Schmalkald League, this precondition was once again destroyed, and in its place there emerged the one condition under which the Schmalkald League were able to pay back the emperor. In 1545 the duke of Orleans had died, the peace of Crépy thus losing one of its chief securities. On 6 June 1546, when the emperor signed the new anti-Protestant treaty with the pope, France had won back its freedom of action through the peace of Guines. Now France was a partner much more to be reckoned with. The militant princes now exploited this situation.

As various individual princes had already done in 1548 and on several subsequent occasions, now the league turned to France in May 1551 to encourage Henry II to make a speedy attack upon Charles. Negotiations were made with Denmark, England and Poland.

This all happened in a despicable and traitorous way. Still holding office as imperial field marshal at his hunting lodge on the Lochau Heath, Maurice signed the treaty which, on 3 October 1551, formulated a league of aggression against the emperor, between the princes' league and France, and which Henry II ratified in Chambord on 15 January in the presence of the margrave Albrecht Alcibiades. In return for 240,000 talers for the first three months, and 60,000 for each subsequent month, 'to protect German freedom' the king was to subdue the three cities which had belonged to the empire from time immemorial, but where German was not spoken, and to possess them – 'jurisdiction being reserved to the holy empire'.

In addition the German princes in the league promised to help the king win back Flanders, Artois and the free duchy. As in this affair the king was treating Germany 'not as a friend but as a loyal father', in future they would elect no emperor, who was not a friend of the king and ready to swear good neighbourship to him. Were the king himself disposed to accept such an office, 'we would be more pleased with him than with any other man'.

This was a shameful act, having no legal justification, and based only upon a complete absence of all national feeling. It was the outcome of unrestrained territorial self-interest. It involved an association between Protestant princes and a man who persecuted Protestants in France not only with severity but with cruelty. Although France was not to be satisfied with the way the revolt was carried out, and was disappointed in Maurice; although the German princes again abandoned Henry at Passau, nothing was altered of what had already happened, in particular, the appropriation of the bishoprics was not reversed.

As well as betraying him, Maurice unflinchingly professed loyalty, and expressed gratitude, to the emperor, and agreed to support the Council of Trent. Until March 1552, that is until the princes had laid down arms, he played a thoroughly double game. The margrave of Küstrin had parted company with the insurgents. He wanted, no doubt, to defend himself against imperial attack, but had no desire to take the offensive against the supreme head of the empire. The electors, Bavaria, and Würtemberg were restrained by similar considerations.

The troops of the princes joined forces and marched towards France, while the margrave of Brandenburg-Kulmbach prosecuted his terrible war of plundering on his own account.

The French king attacked on the west, and his allies, the Turks, attacked on the east. A letter of Suliman's makes it appear, that the Grand Sultan, his true friend, Henry II, and his allies the German princes, were all striving in the same direction. Henry saw what his goal was, and stated it: the German Rhine. Ferdinand, threatened by the Turks, needed peace. He remained neutral, and thus worked against the emperor.

Since more friendly relations had been established between the emperor and Paul III (at the end of 1549), and Julius III having shown himself well disposed towards the emperor, and having recalled the Council to Trent, the council once again became a principal and immediate concern of the emperor. In order to have more influence in it, Charles moved to Innsbruck. As at Regensburg in 1546, he had an insufficient escort. He still did not believe what the whole world knew and many had told him long ago: that he had been betrayed by the elector of Saxony. The far-flung coalition, and sheer hatred, now endangered not only the emperor's freedom but his life. He made his own position much more difficult – and to no purpose – by still refusing to set the landgrave at liberty.

On 19 May 1522 Maurice stormed the Ehrenberg Gorge. Charles fled across the Brenner, carried in a litter on account of his gout. Ferdinand accompanied him, as did the former elector of Saxony, now at liberty.

A catastrophic fall from the heights of 1548 to the depths of 1552!

The partial dishonesty with which the emperor had treated the Protestants since 1544, and the moral weakness inherent in his association with Maurice of Saxony in 1547, had taken their revenge – through Maurice the betrayer himself.

This elector was an Evangelical, and by his leadership of the princes he undoubtedly saved the Reformation. He died an Evangelical. Was, then, the desire to save the gospel the motive behind his actions? No! The securing of territory and the electorate was his driving force. This soon becomes evident when we compare his activities in Germany with those of Charles V. In 1553 Charles described his opponents correctly: 'Maurice is personally interested in neither religion.' It is difficult to discover higher and more universal vision behind his actions. He wanted to ascend and assert himself against the still considerable rival Saxon power. To do this he made use of universal demands – as at Passau during the preliminary negotiations and after the emperor's flight. But he only used these things; his true goal was his own personal, political advantage.

The most interesting thing, from the human angle, was the understanding between Ferdinand and the elector. For Maurice this formed his strongest reserve in securing what had been gained by arms.

Throughout the whole of their lives, the brothers, Charles and Ferdinand, had gone through the most difficult situations in harmony, and Ferdinand had maintained a truly extraordinary loyalty to Charles. The emperor's over-estimation of what had been accomplished in 1547, badly damaged their brotherly friendship.

Charles' empire was – as we have seen – a most precarious combination. All the more, therefore, did the emperor think, that the universal aims he had set for the empire – aims that were implicit in the empire – could be permanently achieved only if the whole empire remained together. And so he wanted to make his mighty dominion, including the imperial dignity, hereditary. Precisely because of the instability of his complex of states, however, Charles would never have risked this burden, before he had, it would seem, completely secured domination over the powers in the empire and settled the religious question in 1547. Not content with that, Charles wanted to put his son Philip first in succession, followed by Ferdinand and his son, Maximilian. In the end Ferdinand, urged on by his sister, Queen Mary, fell in with the plan. But dislike of the Spaniards, and of 'servitude' was too powerful, and Ferdinand, naturally, had no enthusiasm for the cause. The plan failed, but it did leave a wound behind: inwardly, Ferdinand had broken away from Charles. His son Maximilian, an anti-Spaniard, had done this long ago. The coming years were full of measures designed to strengthen and assure private, Austrian power. This antagonism of interests between the two brothers in the end facilitated the victorious prosecution of the princes' rebellion; for part of the assurance of power, just mentioned, was the understanding with Maurice. The fact that Maximilian inclined strongly to Protestantism did not in the least diminish Ferdinand's loyalty to the Church; but it shows how far away was any spiritual balance of religious forces in favour of the old Church.

The struggle between the princes and the emperor was temporarily resolved by the Settlement of Passau, 1552. The negotiations there took place in an atmosphere of threatening war. In fact, the margrave Alcibiades was still waging war at the time. The rebellious princes used their power quite differently from the way the emperor had used his in 1548. Unfortunately there was no peace: 1552 was the worst year of all for war and bloodshed.

The following persons were assembled in Passau: Ferdinand, Maurice, the ambassadors of the other electors, Albrecht of Bavaria, the bishops of Salzburg, Passau and Eickstätt; in addition, representatives of Würtemberg, Küstrin, Jülich. The emperor's representatives had no authority to settle. Charles wanted to make his own decision. Negotiation went on, in fact, between the two military parties. It was the warring princes or their spokesmen, Maurice, against the emperor. Ferdinand and the other princes mediated.

The demands of the warring princes were aimed at realising the substance of the election capitulation of the emperor. Once again they wanted to curtail the monarchical rights that had emerged. The princes, the prince electors in particular, were to be the normative factor in the empire. The emperor and his hereditary state, as a foreign power, was scarcely to have any more voice within the empire.

However, the emperor's toughness in negotiation, the loyalty of the city of Frankfurt/Main, which defied the assault of the

L

princes, funds voted from Naples and from the Fuggers, and the emperor's and Ferdinand's armed forces, had already changed the scene. He demonstrated finally that he had been in earnest with the proclamation in Worms in 1521, when Luther refused to recant. Ferdinand may have thought that one might accept the Reformation as a permanent feature, with a clear conscience: the emperor did not.

The part played by the Catholic bishops at the Passau assembly of princes – most of whom were Catholic – was not very edifying. Once again they displayed a predominance of political egoism over religion. In particular they gave evidence of colossal religious indolence amongst most of the prelates. Truly, within the prince-episcopal territories the old religion was not saved, for the most part, by loyalty to the faith, but through acquisitive secular instincts. The prime concern of these bishops was their liberty as princes, and for that reason they supported the double betrayer and the saviour of Protestantism, Maurice of Saxony.

The draft of the agreement that was finally accepted (15 August), represented real progress only in so far as the Interim was settled and religious peace assured, at least until the coming *Reichstag* – as in 1544. Admittedly, this time the consent of all the important spiritual princes and of all the electors had been given; and in that sense the empire had consented.

With the Schmalkald War, the Interim, the princes' revolt and its conclusion, and Passau, an approximate balancing up of the forces in Germany was reached at last. All that had gone before, important as it had been – much more important indeed – may be regarded as temporary. The eruption of the new religion with its corresponding structure of life up to 1545 may be considered as provisional. The three phases of the years 1546–52 reveal the opposite. In the life of the nation as a whole, within every stratum of society – princes, the cities, the nobility, the educated, merchants and peasants, the Reformation had become a real force.

Very soon the party of the militant princes was divided within itself as a result of private egoism. Mecklenburg and the margrave of Brandenburg-Kulmbach, Albrecht Alcibiades, did not sign the treaty. The latter of these men proved what little power a treaty amongst the princes had in the Germany of those days. The split in religion had shattered order too severely. Terrible confusion had been let loose.

To the accompaniment of grandiloquent slogans about German freedom and the pure gospel, this unbridled, licentious and frivolous prince overran the Rhineland (Mainz, Speyer, Worms), the Mosel valley (Trier, Wasserbillig, Grevenmacher, Remich), murdering, burning and plundering. His worst assault was along the Main, where he desolated or impoverished Nuremberg, Bamberg and Würzburg. This margrave became the great scourge of the empire. The confusion became unbearable as a result of the incredible amount of plundering that went on, and the ensuing starvation and plague. Bitterness amongst the despoiled people against the arrogant princes reached a dangerous level. King Ferdinand was reminded of the Peasant's War: even worse might happen now. Brandenburg persisted in his unscrupulous ravaging. He was bent on 'punishing the papists as long as one peasant remained'. At last he found himself face to face with the French defender of Metz – the duke of Guise.

Meanwhile many forces and much sympathy had returned to the emperor; and he had never ceased arming. He began with the most obvious target: France. He marched on Metz, but he was inadequately equipped and prepared. Besides this, he burdened himself with a morally disreputable ally. He did his own moral credit serious harm by winning the robber Alcibiades away from De Guise (24 October 1552), and by recognising his quite illegal and oppressive treaty against Würzburg and Bamberg – a treaty the emperor had in fact sharply condemned.

In spite of the baneful assistance of the margrave, Charles failed to take Metz. This long-drawn-out, stubborn action before this city on the Mosel was shattered against De Guise's brilliant defence. The whole enterprise ended in cold, wet and sickness (January 1553). This attack bore no fruit; but its effect upon Charles was critical. This had been his last attempt to turn the tide of fortune, to take up the whole battle of his life afresh. Failure finished him utterly.

When the emperor handed over the Saxon electorate to Maurice he endowed the Ernestines with a power that could be used against Maurice. Maurice's power in the state was not completely assured. The unrestrained plundering campaigns of Kulmbach contained incalculable possibilities of revolution. The Ernestines, with whom the emperor had been in alliance ever since the surprise attack at Innsbruck, naturally welcomed an opportunity of regaining their former position of power. Still a young man, Maurice had known a tremendous leap into power: at Passau he had been the representative of virtually all the princely interests against 'servitude'. It is understandable that he should have tried to remain at the top.

At the end of March, princes from the south and west had associated themselves in the so-called Heidelberg League, in order to be able to resist the threats of the margrave. When this man resumed his plundering in Franconia in April, an even stronger defensive league was formed, to which both Ferdinand and Maurice belonged. The margrave advanced: Maurice's army attacked him. On 9 July 1553 the great battle of Sievershausen was fought. The margrave suffered a serious defeat. Maurice, however, reaped the reward of his earlier faithlessness: he was mortally wounded and died two days later on the battlefield.

In December the emperor severed all connections with the robber knight. The treaties he had made with him had been entered into in utter desperation, only to avoid even worse things happening. These were now 'completely annulled, revoked and dissolved'. The margrave himself was outlawed.

The situation in Germany had now become seriously out of hand. Political, economic and social conditions, and – mixed up in all of these – the religious and ecclesiastical structures had been ruined.

On the other hand, it seemed as though every possibility of reaching a definite decision by means of the available forces had been exhausted. Peace was wanted everywhere; peace was now a necessity. A practical solution to restore peace and order at all costs now emerged. Once again men sought to achieve this modest but so vital objective through a *Reichstag*. This was held, after much vacillation, in Augsburg in 1555 – without the emperor.

Charles, indeed, had been the first to draw the conclusions from all that had happened so far: he would leave the stage of world history to be managed by other powers. In this way he could remain true to his fundamental views. He would not admit that his work had really collapsed, that he had been defeated. More than this: he would not directly do anything that was contrary to 'beloved and much desired unity in our Christian faith'.

In the end Charles withdrew his opposition, which had long delayed the *Reichstag*, and the way to peace was thus opened. Ferdinand was appointed to preside – but in his own right as king of the Romans. Charles told Ferdinand in no uncertain terms, why he would not attend the *Reichstag* in person: because of religion. After the Passau agreement and the ill-fated attempt at Metz, the result of future transactions over religion seemed more than ever likely to be a foregone conclusion.

Although Augsburg saw an abundant variety in the desires of the princes, this *Reichstag* became in fact the concluding formulation of the Passau *Provisorium*. A universal, permanent religious peace between the old and new faiths, was more than an antithesis to the plans of the emperor at that moment. It was a contradiction of the essence of his office as the second supreme head of Christendom. Charles had been made aware of this office and its obligations at Worms in 1521. When the exercise of the office became impossible, he did not withdraw, he resigned. On the day the Augsburg *Reichstag*, which inaugurated 'lasting religious peace', ended, the imperial ambassador brought the news of the emperor's abdication to Ferdinand in Augsburg.

The *Reichstag* was opened on 5 February, and its closing resolution was dated 25 September. The pope was represented by Cardinal Morone and Cardinal Otto Truchsess of Augsburg. On 23 March Julius III died. The new pope, Marcellus II (Marcello Cervini, like Del Monte, formerly a legate at Trent), made way for yet another pope on 23 May. This was Paul IV – Carafa – the typical inquisitor of the Counter-Reformation. His self-assurance, and his suspicion of anything that seemed to diminish papal power, his sometimes hysterical, exaggerated fear of heretical infection, would not allow him to take part in Augsburg. This made sense; for Augsburg, being based upon an irreversible foundation, was bound to produce results that the pope could neither approve nor reverse.

The religious question was not Ferdinand's first concern at this *Reichstag*. He was more interested in countering the tendencies towards political and social dissolution. The whole empire must be carefully regulated. Efforts to achieve this end went on throughout all the months the *Reichstag* was in session. The most basic theme, however, was and remained the religious question. Augustus of Saxony rightly demanded that this should be disposed of before anything else. It ought to be done, moreover, through an 'everlasting religious peace'. It was highly significant that the spiritual electors, too, were behind this move. There was a proviso, however, that peace would apply only to the confessional groups that had been represented at Augsburg: all other new religions were to be excluded. The standardisation of the Reformed faith in terms of political alignment was frankly and officially declared.

The estates of the empire were, as always, far from showing a complete understanding of the situation, and far from being prepared to make any sacrifice to improve it. To the very end the German princes, both Protestant and Catholic, maintained the compromising attitude which had earned them Charles' contempt. By this they clearly demonstrated how unfitted they were, for the most part, to cope with the mighty tasks of the time. They did not return to the *Reichstag*, although the general confusion made their presence more necessary than ever before. The work done by the Protestant delegates, however, showed how deeply they were imbued with a sense of victory, and how much the initial defensive attitude of the confessional, Protestant principle had given way to a more aggressive mood. In both committees they attracted the Catholics, especially the clergy, to themselves – not always without threats. The Catholics always suffered intimidation by Albrecht Alcibiades and others. The Protestants, full of self-confidence, sometimes reversed the roles: they suggested that the legality of Catholicism, not of Protestantism, was in question, that Protestants had the right to suppress all that was Catholic in the empire, and to appropriate all Church property, that Catholic subjects of a Protestant prince should be allowed, only the private practice of their religion, while Protestants subjects in Catholic regions should have complete religious freedom.

Both of the ecclesiastical princes displayed the same old uncertainty. Both lacked theological clarity as much as political courage. Most serious of all was the absence of courageous commitment to a clear goal. There was reason for their vacillation. Few scenes

so impressively reveal the absence of a genuinely religious Catholic sense amongst the bishops, as do these discussions. This came right out into the clear light of day, when the Protestants demanded that the lords spiritual be allowed to come over to the Reformation while retaining their territorial sovereignty. This would make it very easy for bishops who wanted to marry, to hold on to their endowments and make them hereditary – as Duke Albrecht of Prussia had done. The danger was doubly great, because the political and dynastic ambition of Protestant princes had led them to fearful perversity and breaking of their oath in respect of the Catholic outlook of their episcopal candidates. In 1540 Luther himself had refused to acquiesce in such a scheme of Duke Albert of Prussia, concerning his brother the margrave William of Brunswick, secretly a Protestant sympathiser, and elected bishop of Riga. The Duke, however, had a more flexible conscience. His brother was quietly to go through with this 'mummery' for the sake of spreading the pure word. This is to say, his brother was to receive episcopal consecration without professing the corresponding belief, and to take an oath to the pope, which he had no intention of keeping. In the same way the convinced Protestant canon of Meissen, John von Haugwitz, with the active collaboration of the new elector Augustus of Saxony, was elected bishop of Meissen, and sought papal ratification, solemnly vowing to use all his power to maintain the clergy and people in the profession of the Church's faith.

Proceedings like these reveal, even better than the unscrupulous violence of people like Albrecht Alcibiades, the terrible confusion pervading all departments of life, the state of dissolution, the spiritual uncertainty of men and, once again, the vagueness in wide ecclesiastical and theological circles.

Amongst the bishops at the *Reichstag* there was only one who had any theological perspicacity: the bishop of Augsburg, Cardinal Otto Truchsess von Waldburg. He refused to give up the notion of *one religion* – as 'a faithful Christian and a born German', as a man and as a prince of the empire, bound in conscience by faith and by an oath to the pope and to the emperor. Thus he would persevere until death. On the other side the same attitude was adopted by Duke Christopher of Würtemberg, who would be satisfied with nothing less than the abolition of the papacy. The death of Julius III caused the cardinal and the legate, Morone, to be recalled to the conclave in Rome.

In the end it was solely with regard to clerical reservation that the Catholic estates refused to yield. Had the lords spiritual been left their territories, while their subjects were forced to profess the new religion, this would have been the end of Catholicism as a significant factor in the estates of the empire. It is true that the reservation was included by the king in the final resolution, 'by virtue of imperial authority'. After frequent, if not completely sincere, appeal to the dictates of conscience, the Protestants contented themselves with having their rejection explicitly recorded. This did not prevent the vigorous annexation of endowments in northern Germany after the peace was made. This reached such enormous proportions in the seventeenth century, that the edict of restitution turned into a declaration of war.

On the other hand, Ferdinand yielded in respect of ecclesiastical areas situated in Protestant states. This was the price paid for complete freedom of religious determination for the secular Catholic estates. A miserable deal! But Ferdinand thought it better to lose this than perhaps much more. The secularised Church properties were to remain in possession of the Protestants – as things stood in 1552.

On 25 September 1555 the agreement was signed. In the same year, in his catechism, Canisius provided fatally confused Catholicism with the vital and sure guide-book it so badly required.

The religious peace had been agreed upon, in order to 'put an end to the serious uncertainty' which had arisen in the empire as a result of the 'split in religion', and to 'restore peace and confidence amongst the estates and their subjects, and to protect the German nation, our beloved fatherland, from ultimate division and imminent collapse'. For this reason, under pain of the Land Peace, it was agreed to abstain from violent, military oppression, on account of the old religion or of the Augsburg Confession, on any pretext whatever, in any form or in any degree whatever.

In this way those Protestants who derived from the Augsburg Confession, and the Catholics, achieved all that was possible at the time: a compromise. It was a wearily concluded, and in many ways confused, transaction, between unresolved and often contradictory forward surging forces. A lull in hostilities was achieved – nothing more. But it lasted for half a century.

All the same, the religious peace of Augsburg was the first full and legal definition of the *cuius regio, eius religio*. Each state was to have only one religion – that of its prince. Subjects had the right to move elsewhere. The principle was created in favour of the Evangelical estates, but applied to the Catholic estates also. Seen as a whole, these operated the method of expulsion exactly as did the Evangelicals.

A pagan principle was acknowledged; and Christianity was bound to suffer as a result. The fatal schism which was to damage the life of the nation to its roots – as it had done in past years – was indeed not ultimately definitive; but its effects were all the worse for that very reason. The idea that unity could be restored by force led to the devastation of Germany in the Thirty Years War.

The peace of Augsburg, 1555, was not a settlement between the emperor and the estates, as Charles and Maximilian wanted it to be. It was a peace amongst the states. The Land Peace, too, that was negotiated at the *Reichstag*, was not to be maintained by a central power but by the territorial princes. The evolution of sixty years was reversed – small as its result had been. At the close of Charles V's reign territorialism won in the empire. It would be inappropriate to say that Charles had brought this about. It was brought about, rather, by that power which made rising territorial princedom autonomous, mightily increased its self-assurance, and aroused new particularist forces: Luther's Reformation. But this was not its sole cause. Catholic princes, too, had always supported the territorial Church system. The real root of the Protestant State Church went back long before the Reformation. The universal emperor himself was a Catholic prince of this sort. There had, indeed, been a certain contradiction between his imperial demands of the lords spiritual, and the practical imperial administration in the Netherlands. In the Netherlands Charles did everything he could to secure for the territorial government, power to exclude the ecclesio-political power of the bishops.

The *Reichstag* of Augsburg in 1555 thus set the seal on the dismemberment of Germany. That is to say, the nation was now less of a unit than it had ever been. Made up of small units, it was left out of direct responsibility for the great political events of the world. Its political government became small-scale and petty. Augsburg, 1555 – the victory of the territorial princes over the emperor – cut the Germans off from political thought in the wide sense, and thus struck down their national consciousness. Charles V was no German; but in those days he represented the only possibility that the Germans had of remaining, or rather of becoming, a nation. This possibility was tied up with the Catholic faith, the rejection of which at that time meant the rejection of nationhood. In this sense Luther, running counter to awakened national energy, became the destroyer of the German nation-state, as a result of the chain of events which he inaugurated.

The old spiritual–secular *imperium* continued; but the spiritual power of the pope was no longer one of the partners. The religious peace of Augsburg was made without the emperor, without the pope. 'The most perfect expression of the dawn of a new age' (Brandi). When Ferdinand became emperor he was not crowned and anointed by the pope, and thus a further secularisation and nationalisation of the emperor's office had come about. The disintegration of the medieval, universally based concept of the emperor, had been completed. Charles' thought and action had still been rooted in a highly modernised universalism. It was symbolic that it was not he who closed the *Reichstag* of 1555, and that he abdicated. He had been the first to recognise the political import of the religious schism. He had begun the act which was not completed until 1806. From 1555 there was, in fact, only one head of Catholic Christendom – the pope. In a highly significant manner, the Reformation schism had helped fully to establish the pre-eminence of the clerical state in the Church. Most of all it was significant in that it helped towards that realisation of the essence of the Church which led to Trent, and was then consummated in Vatican I, when the unity of the Church was so thoroughly and securely perfected.

The emperor was fifty-seven years old when he signed the act of abdication on 25 October 1555. In an address – which, like his memoirs, gives evidence of his mania for figures – he gave an account of his reign, as he had so often done in writing and by word of mouth. In the following year he handed over the rule of Germany to Ferdinand, and that of Spain and the Netherlands to his son Philip.

In 1556, the year that Ignatius of Loyola died, Charles returned to the vicinity of the Jerome Monastery at Yuste. He lived there neither in the wilderness, nor all the time in religious meditation. He had long conversations with the monks, meditated on the sinfulness of the love of fame, read a Spanish, Erasmian, devotional introduction to the Christian life, and also a novel of chivalry. Above all, he remained in touch with his own past and with contemporary world-political interconnections. In 1554 exciting new possibilities seemed to emerge through the marriage of his son, Philip, to Mary Tudor, heiress of England – again Catholic. But these were hopes that quickly passed, and nothing about them could alter the sum of this great life, which all added up to disappointment – disappointment for which he himself was not to blame.

Charles V died on 21 September 1558.

Who was Charles – the real, the only true opposite number to the religious Reformer, Luther? Was he the inheritor and recapitulator of a long series of traditions, the representative of the historical in face of an innovator, who was setting up his own ideas against tradition?

First, we ought to state, that much in his life was of a high moral standard. His marriage was blameless, even if now and then we are reminded of the laxer principles of those days. Charles – like Ferdinand – towered high above most of his princely contemporaries in moral Christian living, no matter how loudly they proclaimed their wars in the name of the pure word, or in the name of the Catholic faith, as did Francis I and the German bishops. He was disciplined above all in drinking – and terrible drunkenness amongst the German princes was one of the worst features in the miserable life of the states. Luther well knew why he had pointed to excessive drinking as a special fault of the Germans. Evangelical Christians, like the fearless, biblical Frau Argula, who were sincerely concerned with the word of God alone, were deeply disturbed by this blatant contradiction of the gospel by the unrestrained drinking of princes, assembled to discuss the most important religious affairs. The scandal became much worse, for the poor people were the ones who were fleeced to pay for this debauchery.

Was Charles a religious man? He was, but his Catholicism was not very deeply based, theologically or intellectually. He was undoubtedly sincere in his belief. Baldassare Castiglione, papal ambassador to Charles for years, said that Charles was the best Christian he knew – layman or priest – and that verdict stands.

Charles wrote much, and in all of his writings the recognition of the honour and glory of God, and obedience to his will play a big part. In this we see a link with Gattinara. It is true that his phrases sound a bit formal and hackneyed at times – the repetition of traditional platitudes; but he meant what he said, and his words were a true expression of his nature. He had a genuine solicitude for the preservation of the kingdom of God on earth that had been entrusted to him. Likewise he was solicitous for his own soul and the souls of his children. Only a firm hold upon the faith of the Church, and a high sense of responsibility before God, could move a man to write such exhortations as are contained in his instructions to the infante, Philip, date 4 and 6 May of the critical year, 1543; and in his last testament of 6 June 1544; and in the words he spoke – in tears – at his abdication. One must love God and his grace above all things, treasure the soul as the most important thing in all creation, so that one may reach paradise and win eternal glory. 'All things are in the hands of God; it is he alone who can and will help us.' 'God will dispose things so that we do serve him.' The mercy of God is bound to accept us. These were the thoughts by which Charles lived. His final demand of Philip, on the occasion of his abdication, touched the central point: hold fast to faith in God and the Father.

As the years went by the emperor's mistrust of the pope grew. In later years his statement of loyalty to the Church did not perhaps have the absolute ring about it that it had in his reply to the university of Vienna in 1522; but in substance that loyalty did remain unshaken throughout all his later life. Even when he was warning the infante about the abuses and unreliability of the curia, he added an exhortation to respect the pope all the more as he became despised by others.

Within the ecclesiastical sphere, Charles' power struggle was unmistakable as it was natural; and it had wide repercussions.

It was free from all personal pettiness and self-interest. Throughout his whole reign it was deliberately and clearly directed towards saving the Church and its unity and purity. He prosecuted his designs with a pertinacity for which there is scarcely a parallel. A sense of his office and of his life's task supported him. He was the secular ruler of Christendom in distress, the responsible co-leader of the Church, in virtue of the rights and duties conferred by the Church upon the consecrated emperorship. He was steward of the Church, whom Gattinara saluted immediately after his election to be emperor, as the coming one shepherd of assembled Christendom. His great and chivalrous privilege would be to fight for the Church and win glory for her; and it was his right, in this emergency, to call a council – so the jurists taught. This consecrated dignity was matched by his outstanding personality. In 1553 he weighed the claims of conscience put forward by the Protestant princes, against his own conscience and – as he affirmed – his own greater responsibility, and the salvation of his soul. He had a mighty sense of being the ruler.

These facts were proved from time to time by the contrast, seen when Ferdinand had to handle ticklish situations on his behalf during the thirties. Ferdinand was not the man to chain 'the brood of German princes'. When Charles left the empire, the lack of power became very obvious. At Passau and thereafter, the towering peak had gone.

The quality which placed Charles above the other contemporary actors in the scene – not excluding the popes, Clement VII and Paul III – was his faithfulness. For him this was a fundamental disposition of mind. At times it turned into harmful obstinacy. At all events, it was the antithesis of petty personal greed. His goal was always something great. He was the servant of a predestined and obligatory task – even in matters of honour.

In the religious and ecclesiastical dispute, too, he was loyal. In spite of all the crafty moves of the thirties, in spite of the alliance with Albrecht Alcibiades, he remained firmly based upon a medieval, universal and unified Christendom – with the dogmatic reservations we have mentioned. Charles V was a man of honour. Various popes on several occasions surrendered religion to the interests of politics, and became actual promoters of the Reformation. The emperor never even approximated to this kind of action. In the eyes of saints and of the devout, Charles was the best servant the Church had in those days.

Was Charles a German? That question is easily answered, if we are thinking of *nationality* – although it is doubtful if such a question meant much in those days. Obviously he was not a German.

The question becomes more pointed, however, if we rephrase it thus: was he a German or a Latin at heart? Certainly no one could call Charles an Italian, a southern Frenchman or even just a Frenchman. At the same time he was not what is commonly described as a Spaniard – not by any means. His sense of sovereignty and his absolutism were basically different from those things as conceived either by Ferdinand and Isabella before him, or by his son Philip after him. In contrast to these he was marked out by a profound inner struggle always to come to a just decision.

This sensitivity of conscience was the very thing that matched so well his loyalty, and gave him an affinity with a moral attitude characteristically associated with the Germans. None of his contemporaries had this quality in anything like the degree that he had. The best qualities of the German and Habsburg blood were preserved, strengthened, directed and ennobled by Spanish faith. Upon these was constructed a great life, built around the dominant concept of the emperor. In a higher sense, Charles was the legitimate inheritor of the German empire, and certainly no 'Spanish alien' upon the imperial throne.

Charles was more closely connected with the whole Reformation event than was any other person, except Luther. The span of his life coincided with its full course, and formed a normative part of the whole event.

The connection was further deepened to become an identity of destiny. Charles' life was not just a part of the Reformation, in a specific sense it became its symbol. For Charles, representative of the Catholic tradition, ended up in failure, as did the victorious Reformation. The religious peace of Augsburg, 1555, proves this: the representatives of both power complexes admitted the impossibility of an unequivocal solution, by accepting a compromise. The Reformation had become really strong; but the old Church remained, and then flourished again. The attempt to win the whole Church for the new gospel failed. Augsburg, 1555, legalised a spiritual schism.

This fundamental failure casts a deep shadow over the history of the Reformation. What had been the meaning of those colossal sacrifices, of those victories, those defeats? There had been much that was petty and weak; but beyond these things mighty forces had struggled for lofty goals in the sphere of religion and the Church, and in the closely interwoven sphere of politics. The outcome had been a confessional schism, the rending asunder of the Church, of Christendom and the nation. Whatever gains be attributed to the Reformation, the result was primarily negative: the destruction of unity.

Merit and guilt seem to devour one another in this mighty drama, wherein a new world was painfully being brought forth. No human skill is able to disentangle the threads, to close the account. Now, after our long journey through those decades, we can see why this is so: the question of who was and who was not to blame does not arise concerning what is deepest in what can be historically grasped about the Reformation. For us men the story of the Reformation stands, for the most part, under the sign of tragedy.

This is true of those also, who call it a heroic age. It applies also to Charles V. It was not in his power to prevent or to heal the schism. Protestants can endorse this verdict of a Catholic. For Charles' struggle against that which emerged out of Luther's battle for conscience, was the product of an obligatory loyalty to fixed legality, which dictated his designs and his actions. But then, just as the battle was a duty and a necessity, its failure, too, was profoundly predestined. Luther's Reformation had not happened by accident. And yet here, in the Reformation, Catholics and Protestants can meet, although the two may have quite different notions of what constituted the *necessity* of the Reformation. Catholics and Protestants can meet in this Reformation, which changed the faith, the ideas and the life, of a large proportion of humanity and profoundly influenced the conditions of life of all Christians nation, including Catholic nations; in the Reformation, which introduced a contradictory variety of faith and prayer into the Christian world, and critically altered the basic conditions of the way of salvation for many hundreds of millions of people; for in this event ultimately we are brought to a halt against the mystery of the living God of history. This experience shakes the thoughtful student of history to the core.

CONCLUSION

Tragedy and distress of mind are not the last word. Today Catholics, and many Protestants want to ask further questions, as they try to assess the Reformation. The answer to these questions have been hinted at, more or less plainly in this book. A few more explanatory and more precise indications are, however, desirable.

In this second part of the book we have seen how from the end of the fifteenth, and during the first half of the sixteenth, century, the Church was striving to bring forth new life within herself. In spite of this, Church history of that period on the whole presents a disedifying and depressing picture to the Catholic. In the life of his own Church he sees much that must be condemned by the very standards which that same Church professes. On the other hand, the battle fought by those who separated themselves from the old Church did not produce much of value, and showed few results. In this book I have tried to fulfil this task, true to the admonition of Leo XIII, to speak nothing but the truth, and the whole truth, even if it proves an embarrassment to the Church and the papacy.

It is true that Leo XIII's courageous love of truth has been accepted in theory everywhere by apologists and theologians; but it has not yet become the universally accepted rule in practice. As a result it could happen, that a Catholic reader, who is unfamiliar with the sources, might be moved, on hearing of the mass of corruption in the Church of the sixteenth century, to ask if Catholic weaknesses have not been accentuated and the blame due to the Reformers somewhat softened, if there has not been too great a readiness to praise the Reformation whenever possible.

The suspicion that lurks in such a question is utterly false.

Readers who might be inclined to pose such a question ought to reflect that views need not be false because they are new and unfamiliar. Opinions must be controlled by the facts, not facts by opinions, no matter how much we have come to like them and regard them as inviolable.

If we now turn from the assessment of the power embodied in the Reformation attack, and study the question we have raised purely in terms of the problem of the *human* element in the Church, there is nothing about the facts that requires discussion. As has frequently been said, the massive evidence was supplied by loyal Catholics, testified by the official complaints of loyal Catholic churchmen, and any attempt at excuse is doomed to failure, and would only damage the Church even more. Even the foregoing chapters have pointed out no faults that had not already been stated by loyal Catholic contemporaries, or else directly confirmed by their complaints. They can be found almost in their entirety in the works of Janssen and Pastor also.[1]

Indeed, the problem of weak human nature in the Church, in so far as we regard it historically, cannot be solved either by general phrases or by the mere theoretical knowledge that there are bound to be corruptions in the Church. Only he has the right to pass a verdict, who knows the concrete cases of corruption; only he who has the courage (and the authority) to assume this burden in all its weight, can evaluate its gravity. The conviction that abuses do not diminish the essential holiness of the Church, is an inalienable part of the Catholic belief. But this tells us nothing about the historical burden carried by the men who have had to find their way to eternal salvation through these abuses, and nothing of the power of evil they represent, and which goes on working centuries later.

The suspicion we mentioned is false in another respect also. I must admit that I have searched with particular keenness for expressions of continuing loyalty to the ancient Church. In addition, to comply with a demand of compensatory justice, I have dealt with those things in greater detail than their proportion in the life of their times merits (cf. above, p. 95 f.). If, in spite of this, Catholics still find the picture depressing, that unfortunately only demonstrates the truly deplorable state of affairs.

[1] I do not want this remark to be misunderstood. They are more concerned with abuses in the narrower sphere of morality. For me the theological problem, 'theological vagueness', has been the critical thing. For Janssen and Pastor this was not so. Moreover, they mostly overlooked the specific effect of the erosion of priestly and pastoral ideals, the undervaluing of religion as against politics by leading churchmen, and then the questions about the correct or faulty structure of the Church.

If, then, corruption in the Church had gone so far, and if, on the other hand, there is much of value to be found in Luther, must Catholics admit that Luther was right in revolting against the Church?

This question becomes important for the community as a whole only when understood as the attempt to find an absolute, fundamental standard, by which one can measure the value and justice, or the worthlessness and injustice, of Luther and the Reformation.

Let us mention the determining factor first. Christianity and the Church go beyond the merely historical and reach deeper and higher regions. They are revelation, the object and content of faith. In this sphere there can never be any kind of justification for rebellion at all. Luther himself affirmed this at the Leipzig Disputation in 1519 (Vol. I, pp. 251 and 454).

Considering the deplorable state of the Church in the first half of the sixteenth century, the question might be asked: on such a view, where was the glorious picture of the Church to be found, that was supposed to inspire the faithful? First let us comment, that it is not one of the functions of Church historical research to go into such considerations; all it has to do is describe *things as they were*. First and foremost, however, the questioner must be exhorted to assimilate the facts thoroughly before he tries to judge them. We may answer, however, (*a*) that in the epoch we have described, the glory of the Church, as a historically recognisable state, for the most part, simply was not there – it had become historically invisible; and (*b*) that this fact did not in the least diminish the substantial, divinely rooted glory of the Church. This glory does not manifest itself completely in history, even in the outwardly most glorious epochs of the Church. Rooted in ontic holiness and truth of a divine sort – although shining through the criteria of divinity in the Church – it is primarily a matter of faith. (*c*) The attitude of the Catholic champions of the sixteenth century was in complete harmony with this affirmation. None of the many, competent to judge and whose reports have come down to us, and who at that time remained loyal to the Church, did so because they saw in the visible Church a healthy, powerful, resplendent and glorious organism. On the contrary, a thousand times over they tell us that in the face of the Church, their mother, they saw scarcely anything but wrinkles, and nothing but weakness in her whole life. Many of them, like Cardinal Hosius, and Paul III in the bull calling the Council of Trent, spoke of the imminent collapse of the Church. All of these loyal church-men affirmed in no uncertain terms, often with weary hopeless-ness, that all 'form and beauty' had vanished from the visible Church. They remained loyal, however, because in spite of abuses they believed in her essential, invisible glory.[2] They proclaimed faith in the one, holy, Catholic and apostolic Church ruled by the pope and the bishops, and possessing a special, sacramental priesthood. They had unshakeable faith – the supernatural virtue of faith – that objective, divine holiness and inviolable truth dwelt undiminished in this decayed Church; that the Lord was present – if slumbering – even in his unworthy bishops. They lived by the faith that the whole Christ dwelt undiminished only in this ancient Church; that all the essentials that the Reformers demanded – holy scripture, salvation as a free gift – were present in this very Church, and always had been; that, conversely, the Reformed doctrine was bound to damage and falsify the fullness and the assurance of revelation – directly or indirectly. In Charitas Pirkheimer's confession, and in various prayers, of which we have heard, this was all movingly expressed. Murner, Schatzgeyer, Gropper, the Carthusians and, above all, Eck and the Jesuits, made professions of faith that were brimful of absolute loyalty; but there is a certain flatness in all that we read; most of these defen-ders of the Church possessed their faith without seeming to derive any power to proclaim the hidden glory of the Church with any creative, moving fire. We do not for a moment forget the occasional sparks of inspiring devotion within the Church, especially as witnessed by Catholic popular devotion, and its accompanying literature and art, just before, and during, the Reformation.

The only conclusive attitude which the present-day Catholic can adopt towards the Reformation is that of a believing Chris-tian. Obviously he cannot represent Catholic loyalty to the Church in the sixteenth century as richer or more inspired than in fact it was.

On the other hand, this level-headed loyalty, this not always very impressive attitude, was enough to allow men to gain a

[2] Cf. above, p. 143 f.

334 THE NEW EPOCH: THE REFORMATION IN GERMANY

solid standpoint from which to make a judgment. In all of the incipient Catholic reform of the sixteenth century we discover, that one prime principle was accepted: in respect of office within the Church, the office must be distinguished from the person holding it. Conversely, this is where a basic error of Luther's becomes evident: he felt that the abuses in the Church fully justi-fied his revolt – after he had become the Church's dogmatic opponent. That is to say, he was unable to see past the pheno-mena of decay to the inviolable substance of the Catholic Church.

Having chosen their ground and taken a stand, those who remained Catholic received help from certain effects of the Reformation, and from certain complaints the Reformers them-selves made against the adherents of the new doctrine. We have heard of Luther's displeasure at the way his 'spiritual' freedom was being 'carnally' abused, at the indifference with which many people in Evangelical states treated the purely restored sacrament, and neglected its use, and at the ingratitude of the people, that made him tired of preaching. 'Since the pure doctrine of the gospel has been lighted up by our message, the world has become daily a worse place.' 'Disunity (amongst the princes and estates), usury and avarice, tyranny, unchastity, wantonness, are to be seen overwhelming us like the Flood, so that things will never be put right – not with ten councils and twenty *Reichstags*.'

Melanchthon was shattered by the 'immoderate exploitation of freedom in gratifying every desire'. He spoke of a new barbar-ism, in which complete and utter contempt for religion flourished. He had wept more tears over the calamity of the Reformation – so he said – than there was water in the Elbe.

If Butzer had complained in 1523 that there were almost no churches in Strasbourg, no respect for 'the Word', no longer any use of the sacraments, in 1538 his friend Capito was much more detailed and dreary: 'The Lord is now showing us how much damage we have done by our haste, by the thoughtless vehemence with which we have rejected the papacy. The mob, used to unres-traint, almost educated to it, have now become completely intractable. By throwing off papal authority it would seem that we have destroyed the power of the word, of the sacraments, and of the whole pastoral office. For the people shout: we understand the gospel well enough; we can read it for ourselves. What help do we need from you? Preach to those who will listen, and let them choose to accept what they will. We need tremendous patience in this mess in which we find ourselves.'

Does this not corroborate the impression and verdict of Willibald Pirkheimer, who turned away from Luther, because he saw no improvement but only a deterioration, because the 'former deceit' was not removed, but many even less tolerable were put in its place, in comparison with which the former was a mere joke? At the *Reichstags* the Catholic estates were able to reproach the Protestants with this decline. In Worms in 1545 they asked where public worship and the schools had gone, and what had happened to the endowments and alms for the poor, as they had known them twenty or thirty years ago. 'What the Protestants mean by preaching is mostly – as they themselves complain – decrying and scolding the pope and clergy, and sheer malice against all and sundry.' The pulpit has become a scolding box.

We do not forget all that was said about Luther's coarseness, and about the obstacle this put in the way of accurate exegesis of the Reformer. Certain manifestations of corruption provoked Luther to use exactly the same imprecise and immoderate superlatives as he did about the 'papists'. 'Usurers ought to be allowed to die like dogs, and the devil should gobble them up, body and soul; they should be broken on the wheel and bled to death; every miser should be chased out, cursed, beheaded.' Luther exaggerated; but does this allow us to deny the basis of fact behind his multitudinous, noisy complaints? Besides this, what do we make of the affirmations of other Reformers, who show the same aberration? The mass of complaints from Luther's side as from the Catholic side, prevents us from dismissing these things as isolated cases, uncharacteristic of the situation as a whole.

We must, rather, affirm the following. The Evangelicals adopted towards the corruption they saw within Protestantism the same sort of attitude as the Catholics adopted towards abuses within the Church of their time. People know about these various complaints, now and again they mention them, but on the Protestant side they are seldom given their full place in the historical picture. Some may wish to justify this weakness as a reaction to the exaggerated one-sidedness of Döllinger and Janssen; but surely now, all sensible people would agree that the time is past for all calculating balancing out methods, in the treatment of such important topics. For all of us as Christians and as citizens, the Reformation has become an event, fateful beyond comparison. It has become a destiny that we have still not been able to master. Such an event must be treated with the openest of minds, with a holy reverence for truth, and in deadly earnest. Döllinger's material does not lose its value simply because he does not give enough place to the positive elements in the Reformation.

We must, therefore, squarely face the fact, that a considerable decline in religion and morality came in the wake of the Reformation, that had been designed to restore the purity of Christian life, and we must incorporate this fact in our over-all assessment. This is the only way to work out a true balance.

Important conclusions are thus to be drawn from the development we have discovered in the sixteenth century. We have just recalled how Luther repeatedly sought to justify his renunciation of the Church and his attack upon it by the abuses he saw in the Church. At the end of his life he was compelled very largely to admit that his 'purified gospel' had not succeeded in accomplishing the desired improvement. What are we to make of this? Does it not imply a most damaging criticism of such a revolutionary attempt? For it is true, we may judge the Reformation only by those norms which Luther himself accepted as absolutely valid for time and eternity. These norms were purely religious and Christian, and they explicitly excluded any human autonomy. In fact, they demanded just the opposite.

And so we are brought back to the decisive question. Were Luther's basic theses correct and justified, and were they adequately realised, so that his apostasy from the Church was justified?

I do not propose meantime, for the purpose of this argument, to point out that according to Luther's ultimate concepts, everything was saved as long as the pure faith, as he formulated it, was held firm. Nor do I intend simply in passing, as it were, to refute Luther in a couple of sentences.

None the less, I consider it to be important, from a scientific and from a Christian standpoint, to consider, for example, in terms of our last question, that the purity of doctrine for which the

Reformers strove, stood or fell with the unity of doctrine. In this sense they did not achieve their goal.

Or again: the Reformation had as one of the great objectives in the fight, the abolition of the politicising of Christianity and the Church. This was not achieved either, neither in Luther's own time nor later. The state-Church system, in the sense of the aggregate prince-episcopate, became the great profiteer of the Reformation. In the end the paganism of the *Cuius regio, eius religio* came out on top.

Wider horizons are open to us today as we try to assess the Reformation historically. When, at the end of the sixteenth century, the Lutheran and Calvinist Reformation – to say nothing of Zwingli and the thousand fanatical splinter groups – had spent its energies, and had in great measure become stultified, the Church, whose plague and death Luther had wanted to be, was still there – renewed and producing new life. (No less a person than Harnack was deeply impressed by this fact.) Not only had the Church lived through the collapse of a whole world, and salvaged herself on the shore of a new world: she had cured herself of the poison of the Renaissance spirit, had weathered the storm of the Reformation, and had even shown herself capable of injecting undiminished life into the new European world, and into the foreign missions. Exemplary, heroic, creative, religious energies at work in Europe between 1550 and 1650, manifested a double century of saints in the Church – a sanctity of faith, prayer, charity and sacrifice. Whatever the value of these from the Evangelical angle, their Christian devotion very clearly made the kingdom of God a greater reality in the world around them; and it is obvious to all Christians that their imitation of Christ was much more intensive than the contemporary activity of Calvin. (In any case, the work of Calvin's organised militant Church emerged from a faith that roundly rejected definitive doctrines of Luther.) The moral poison of the spirit of the Renaissance at work in all classes of clergy, the threat to theology by the a-dogmatic and antidogmatic humanism, strongly advocated by representatives of the Church, the religious and, later, the ecclesio-political assault of the Reformation, were without doubt the most difficult and deadly crisis the Church had ever had to face. For many reasons, neither the threat from gnosticism, nor the threat from the corruptions of the tenth century, can be compared with it. No purely natural organism could have survived this combined attack from corruption within and assault from without, and then proceeded to revive and become filled with heroic life. If there is an historical proof on a grand scale of the supernatural power of the Church, then the sixteenth and seventeenth centuries provided it.

We do well to note, however, that this proof degenerates to the level of a popular apologetic short-cut and cheap rhetoric, if we do not admit the full seriousness of the terrible threat that there had been to the life of the Church. Only if we courageously admit this, may we speak of the supernatural triumph of the Church, which this revival represents. We have to see the decay of the Church in the spirit of the Renaissance and in politics, must see it as a deep wound in the Church of the Crucified; as Christians we must consider the monstrous fact that the leaders of this Church gambled away true religion for political stakes – perhaps not quite aware of what they were doing, but effectively doing it none the less; we must consider how the Reformation was a serious threat to the Church precisely because so much in the Reformation had a truly religious motive. Then and only then can we in some measure appreciate the fullness of the strength of the Church and bring that power effectively to light. It is easy for an intrinsically healthy organism, exposed to no attack from without, to keep alive. Resistance to a deeply rooted disease is a real test of the strength of an organism. Only if we know the length and steepness of the path that had to be trod, and the real size of the obstacles that had to be overcome, can we truly evaluate the strength that ended in triumph – rejuvenated and generating new life.

Let us look now at the other side of the coin – at the development of Luther's work in the centuries that followed. Impelled by his conscience, Luther had arisen to save revelation, to restore the pure word of God, to drive out the 'whore reason' from the realm of faith, to expunge all that was of man from the once and for all work and merits of Christ, and to make this completely accessible to men. What did he accomplish?

CONCLUSION 339

In these days when the world is moving so dangerously away from Christ, it would be a very poor Christian who rejoiced at the decline of any religious and Christian values. We leave unassailed everything in Luther and his work, in his own age or in ours, that honest research attributes to him in the way of prayer, sacrifice and various Christian activities. If we review all that Lutheranism has accomplished down the centuries; how it has brought the Christian message to millions of men, and given them power to face the trials of life and of death; how fruitful the witness to Christ the Lord in Protestant circles has been in faith and in love of one's neighbour; then we see much to praise. But at the moment this is not our theme.

The question cannot be avoided: seen as a whole, and in terms of the Reformation, did Luther's work lead to an edifying of the Christian people, and to an increase in faith? Or did the revolutionary attack against the old Church, in the name of conscience and the Word, simply lead logically to the exaltation of subjectivism (the human) in Christianity, and to the weakening of objectivity (the divine element in given revelation) – the objectivity of holiness in the *opus operatum* of the sacraments, and of the objectivity of truth in dogma? Did it not thus, in the course of its whole development, expose to dissolution, what is unique in Christianity as a religion of grace and redemption?

If we are permitted to treat of this vast and delicate theme in a few words, first to be mentioned would be the colossal diminution of specifically religious life, or religious activity in prayer within the new Church, and the diminution in the participation of the people in that prayer. This process has gone on until the present day in all Protestant Churches – including the Lutheran – with their approval. I do not primarily have in mind the general decline in religious life in modern times, which has affected Catholics as well. It was the Evangelical Churches themselves who gave up important supports, and made progressively fewer demands upon religious activity. The debasing of Luther's powerful theology of the cross to the level of a not very profound morality of humanist or Kantian stamp, is one of the most important aspects of this decline. Then there was the abandonment of frequent services on Sundays and feast-days, resulting in the churches being closed as a rule during the day. This phenomenon does represent a flagging of fervour, and its effect, which goes on quietly all the time, can never be fully measured. The ultimate cause of this phenomenon was the abolition of the mass, and this in itself provides a severe historical criticism of Luther's theological battle against this central point of Catholic piety. Abolition of aural confession ought also to be mentioned. Luther did not want to give it up. To him it was a precious possession. How many of his present-day followers know this and that in his catechism he directed the ordinary man in the use of private confession? Nor did Luther give up veneration of our Lady and of the saints, or of a sermon on their feast days. And yet in succeeding centuries their abandonment in the Protestant Churches – a serious impoverishment of devotional life – was carried out with such thoroughness, that it became an occasion for pride. It was regarded as the defeat of the Catholic or medieval residue, which Luther had not quite finished off.

In the Catholic Church, not the private moral or religious rectitude of the members but the correct and fruitful structure is the ultimately definitive thing. So it is with Protestantism. And so we now face this question: on the evidence of history must Protestant schism, Protestant subjectivism, Protestant narrowing down of the substance of revealed truth, definitively share in, and share the blame for, the unchristian life of modern culture? Does the religious impoverishment of modern Protestantism logically derive from the fundamental shape of Reformed doctrine?

Luther and Melanchthon and the Catholic opponents of the Reformation were agreed upon the dangerous starting-point from which the desired purification and enrichment of Christianity could be turned into the opposite: the new preaching of freedom. Rejection of a living teaching office made it impossible precisely to fix the content of revelation at any particular time, and make it binding upon all. An impressive proof of this fact was provided by the spontaneous splintering of Protestantism in Luther's time. In human speech, outside the sphere of quantity nothing is completely unequivocal. Hosius provided abundant proof of how this applies to the Bible (see above, p. 217 f.). Luther, the man of the absolutely binding word of God, the man of the Christian congregation, had in fact thrown man back upon himself, alone before the word of God. Every element of a concept of the Church in

Luther is powerless against this fundamental fact. This was the novelty he introduced, the decisive thing with which he filled men's minds, and which carried on its formative work down the centuries. Whatever of the Church Luther wanted to withhold from the caprice of the individual, was condemned from the start to remain in fundamental tension with his subjectivism and spiritualism. These were the foundations, and they were found to destroy objective fixity. In the end, logically, they were bound to lead each man to his own opinion. The individual had won. By the law of inner dialectic, the original ideas and deeds, once settled, determined that the development follow the course it did. It could not be otherwise. Intra-Protestant schism had to continue; and today we know, unfortunately, how far development had gone along this road.

We are happy to be able to say that in the recent Lutheran renaissance, and in sections of modern Protestant theology, a notable return can be seen to the objective elements in Luther's Christianity. What does that mean, however, for the picture as a whole? An astonishingly small percentage of the members of the Protestant Church stands upon the groundwork of doctrine which Luther, in a spirit of complete dogmatic intolerance, required as an indispensable precondition of entry into eternal life. Putting this in pointed language: Luther wanted to secure revelation; but the majority of Protestants ended in rationalism. He wanted to protect faith, to keep the 'Word' pure; but there emerged a spirit of self-destructive criticism. Luther wanted to be entirely the representative of old, primitive Christianity; but his work undoubtedly became an ecclesiastical revolution, in the wider sense, that it engendered something quite new.

The facts do not have to be proved: until the beginning of the twentieth century Protestantism became increasingly, alarmingly, unsure of what exactly Christianity is; the most arrogant biblical and dogmatic criticism, constantly revising its position, left very little behind as the sure content of the 'Word'; Protestants accepted, and still accept – although not all – that 'each takes out of the gospel, what is useful to him'; the selection Luther had made out of the total store of revelation, and the attractive one-sided simplification, which he could thank for much of the victory of his cause, turned in large measure into the opposite.

The sheer historical development through the centuries becomes a justification of the rejection of the Reformation by the Catholic Church. Today the Catholic Church may justly claim to have taken care of important concerns of the Reformers, better than they have done themselves. There is another parallel in the intra-Catholic reform, which we discussed in Volume II. Curialism in the bad sense, as it was before the Reformation, and during its critical years, simply did not continue. It is true that the *ancien régime* and its ecclesiastical way of life has continued since the Reformation, the intra-Catholic reform, and the Counter Reformation. But we cannot compare the Roman curia as it was under Pius X, Pius XI and Pius XII, with the Roman curia as we had to describe it in the fifteenth and sixteenth centuries.

In Luther's own day the separation of the spiritual from the secular resulted in very few departments of public life remaining within the sphere of faith. Luther had preferred to 'surrender most of the public spheres, intellectual life, politics, and the state, in particular, to the secular powers'. This meant that an extreme emphasis on the spiritual led to an expansion of the secular. In anything that affects man, who is a body-soul, no one-sided answer can permanently fit every aspect of a problem; and this weakness of one-sidedness was not removed by Luther's resolve to take real Christianity seriously – i.e. what he considered real Christianity to be. When his mighty religious energy was no longer there to act as a counterbalance, the reaction we have mentioned displayed its full force. The final result was the modern attitude of autonomy, acknowledging the liberal principle, that religion is a private matter. Without a doubt, that view of Christianity is diametrically opposed to the firm demands made by Luther.

On this point Luther's attitude was all the more dangerous because it all unwillingly brought assistance to the deadly enemy, humanist secularism (rationalist education and morality in place of the religion of the cross.) By this detour, this enemy, whom Luther had effectively beaten back in the interest of all Christians, once more came to power, and stayed there. Modern times are most certainly the product in part, of humanism. Humanism's break with medieval Christianity and the medieval Church system was, and is, much more radical than the break made by genuine Protestantism, of whatever colour, in so far as it did not directly link humanism with the Reformation movement – as Zwingli did. We have only to mention one of the chief characteristics of the moderns, as expressed in their affirmations to date, in order to establish this relationship: rationalism, moralism, relativism, ethical autonomy. In all of these things, it is humanism that has been the liberator of the subject (in contrast to its great ideal of a political community), and the destroyer of supernaturalism. Precisely in this liberation of the subject, the Reformation and humanism meet. The fact that, on the same issue, they come into deadly conflict (rational – irrational; rational – religious; power of the human will – grace) in no way cancels this definitive community.

The affirmation that Luther destroyed unity has a significance which extends far beyond the purely religious and ecclesiastical spheres. This verdict – serious above all others for the Christian – cannot be avoided by complaining that the old Church did not follow Luther. For it is plain, that it was out of his communion, following his basic views, that the fatal splintering of Protestantism itself emerged, so that today we find ourselves confronted by countless Protestant denominations, and observe within these various groups a lack of dogmatic cohesion. In so far as historical data can give evidence of essences, we may say, that schism is of the essence of what Luther created.

Unity – absolute unity is the essence of the Church. A doctrinal attitude which gives rise to a plurality of Churches, each with an essentially different doctrine, some denying redemption by the God-man, automatically arouses deep suspicion, and is in danger of refuting itself.

If this book has a purpose beyond the mere completion of a scientific investigation, it is this: to participate in the dialogue between the confessions, and also to create new possibilities for this dialogue.[3] Am I deceiving myself if I think, that a treatment

---

[3] This remark is not entirely unambiguous. It has led some critics into serious misinterpretation. It is not as though I have approached the study of the Reformation, guided by the desire to bring the confessions closer together. My research has neither been occasioned by such an intention, nor has it been accompanied and influenced by that intention during the progress of the work. My sole purpose in taking up a study of the Reformation was to find out the 'hard truth'. Without any secondary motive, the facts I have collected have

of Reformation history, such as I have carried out here, is the kind that will help create an atmosphere in which such dialogue can fruitfully take place? Today, influential Protestant circles have put behind them that attitude, which sees in the minimising of doctrinal propositions, a way to mutual understanding. In ecumenical negotiations amongst Protestants, the question of truth is plainly given priority over the question of unity. The same thing is a help in the dialogue between Protestants and Catholics. This represents a great and solid advance. It is a tactical advance, too, for this new attitude is calculated to exclude mistrust of conversations that might be conducted on dogmatically intolerant lines.

Unity can be achieved only through 'meeting in the centre'. Complete truth is the precondition, and the inflexibility of that truth possesses an absolute primacy.

The constant proclamation and stress of that principle by Rome is not an expression of 'Roman rigidity and hardness' – whatever personal inadequacies may be found in the curial representatives. It is the authentic expression of genuine, objectively true love, which can be realised only in perfect truth.

Even so – we must still remember and ponder what the Dominican, Congar, has written on this question:[4] 'At no time does the "conversion" of our separated brethren represent a diminution or even a destruction of what they already possess; it demands only the purification of what is negative, and the perfection of all positive values.'

It is not just a question of necessary, inflexible doctrine: it also has something to do with plumbing that doctrine right down to the depths. 'For no other foundation can any one lay than that which is laid, which is Jesus Christ' (1 Co 3:11).

---

led to the affirmations and verdicts which I have put forward in these volumes. These certainly do demand that one should take part in the ecumenical dialogue. In this sense such participation has become my deepest concern in publishing the book.

[4] Congar, *Chrétiens désunis* (Paris 1937).

POSTSCRIPT 1967

It is in the nature of history to be complex. As the years pass this complexity often resolves itself and we become better able than our forefathers to understand the meaning of what has been.

Today this is proved in a significant way by the phenomenon that has been described in this book.

There can be no doubt that by and large the world is becoming less Christian. Mankind today is not characterised by his strength of faith in God and in Jesus Christ, but by a secularisation of thought, which has reached a peak of development hitherto unknown and a corresponding autonomous this-worldly civilisation.

Even the Churches both Evangelical and Catholic are being hit by this ebbing away of the power of religion. The world has reached a crisis of faith such as it has never seen before. Millions today find it exceedingly difficult to believe, in the supernatural sense of the word.

In the Church which is named after Luther this development has gone so far that there are Evangelical bishops who seriously ask if the Reformation inheritance has not been all spent.

There is, however, another essential side to all of this: in the midst of the process that we describe as the disappearance of faith, in every Church we see a religious deepening such as the world has not experienced for a very long time.

The theme of this book directs our main interest to what is taking place today in the Reformed Churches. I say 'our main interest' because the phenomenon is closely linked with developments within the Catholic Church.

Of prime importance is the overthrow – associated with the name of Karl Barth and his commentary on Romans – of liberal Protestantism and the revival of Reformed Church thought. This has been an event of colossal importance. Thus nineteenth-century Protestantism, which had grown out of the Reformation, proved that it had not allowed the authentic Christian power of the preaching of faith in the crucified and risen Christ to be destroyed

by the Enlightenment of the eighteenth century and the material-
ism and criticism of the nineteenth century.

Obviously this victory over liberal Protestantism was not complete. There is a neo-Protestantism; and one of its leading expo-
nents, Walther von Loewenich, has confirmed the incipient subjectivism in Luther by making Luther – against his will, but quite
logically – the father of liberal Protestantism. At the same time,
however, he stressed in great depth the theology of the cross as the
core of Luther's faith.

In the theology of Rudolf Bultmann and his existentialist
pupils, however, this same return to a faithful acceptance of the
Biblical message has led at once to a threat to the objective re-
demptive events and to a universal and permanently valid objectively binding statement about them, never before so radically set
out.

The manifold results of large-scale historical and critical method
has completed the inner disintegration of Reformed preaching,
taking it further than the splintering of the nineteenth century, to
reach a condition that is closer to chaos than to creativity.

In this context there has been little that could be regarded as
fixed and binding. Through the logical over-development of certain elements in Luther the Reformation has come to be regarded
not so much as a preaching of a doctrine of faith as an intellectual
principle of the development overstressing the formal. In the process we are presented with astonishing portraits of Luther; and the
Luther of the decalogue, of the ancient creeds and of the sacraments largely loses his importance.

The most significant consequence of this historical theological
presentation is probably its destruction of the unity of the contents
of the Bible. At all events it sees this unity merely in a complete
reduction to an abstract point, in a mere way of looking, at things
(*vide* Ebeling).

More important than we realised is the fact that this style of
thinking has permeated Catholic theology and Catholic portrayals
of the Reformation. This has been in part an enrichment, in part a
threat to truth. It has enriched by giving depth and flexibility to
such basic concepts as tradition, sacrament, ministry, unity, infallibility. It has been a threat to the objectively existing, to the

static – which Luther himself took for granted as indispensable –
by an overstress on actual and dynamic elements.

While these many-sided developments have been in progress,
another phenomenon – perhaps even more characteristic of the
present critical world-situation and more pregnant of the future –
has been taking shape: ecumenism.

We have seen the rise of ecumenism in a double form. The
Churches of the Reformation are overcoming their separations and
oppositions and are drawing together. The most important result
of this is the formation of the World Council of Churches. No definition has been produced of the unity of the Church that is demanded by holy scripture, but it has been acknowledged that separation and opposition are contrary to the will of God and of Christ.
The Churches are drawing as closely together as possible, trusting
that the Holy Spirit will lead them along the right path.

The formation of the World Council of Churches is an event of
prime importance in the history of the Church. It represents a
magnanimous confirmation of the Christian power of the Reformation. Pope Pius XII pointed out to Catholics that this drawing
together of the Churches of the Reformation was the work of the
Holy Spirit.

(a) A major step forward was marked by the joining in of the
essentially sacramental and hierarchical Orthodox churches
in which the saints, including the virgin Mother of God, exercise
an essential function. (The Russians were last to join in 1961.)

(b) The most significant step forward resulted from a manifest
change in the attitude of the Roman Catholic Church under Pope
John XXIII and through the Second Vatican Council which he
called. Whereas hitherto the Roman Catholic Church had rigidly
refused to make contact with the World Council of Churches, John
XXIII formed a secretariat for Christian unity, having the status
of a Roman congregation.

This secretariat became responsible for enlisting Protestant and
Orthodox observers at Vatican II. The presence of these then
made the council ecumenical in a deeper sense than had previously
been the case. This council did not canonise Luther, nor did it revoke any anathemas; but it allowed many important Reformation
doctrines to come into their own. Most important of all: the word

M

'heretic' disappeared. In its place the Decree on Ecumenism speaks of 'separated brethren' in the 'Christian Churches and communities', who have preserved a Christian heritage and developed it, each in his own fashion, and in whom the Holy Spirit is redemptively at work.

Here in an important manner the Reformation has given fresh proof of its vocation; and that proof has been spelled out by no other than the Catholic Church.

The urge towards unity has now begun to reverse the trend towards schism.

CHRONOLOGICAL TABLE

Popes	Princes	Luther	Religion and Theology	World and Church Politics	Culture
1471–1484 Sixtus IV				1452 The first *Gravamina* of the German Nation (anti-Roman) 1461–1483 Louis XI of France: France's policy of conquest begins	1470 The *Germania* of Tacitus printed
			1475 Pilgrimage fever (Holy Blood of Wilsnack; Niklashausen; Children's Pilgrimage to Mont St Michel) 1476 Communistic, anticlerical preaching of repentance by Hans Böhm of Niklashausen. *Reformation of Emperor Sigismund* printed 1479–1552 Cochlaeus 1483–1542 Contarini 1486–1543 Dr John Eck		
		1483 10 Nov, born			
1484–1492 Innocent VIII	1486–1525 Elector Frederick of Saxony (the Wise)			1488 The Swabian League founded	
1492–1503 Alexander VI (Borgia)	1493–1519 Emperor Maximilian			1494 Charles VIII of France marches on Italy to annex Naples 1495 *RT* at Worms: reform of empire, perpetual Land Peace, Imperial High Court	1494 Sebastian Brant's *Ship of Fools*

1498 Dürer's *Apocalypse*

1499 Marsiglio Ficio, founder of the Platonic Academy in Florence, and teacher of Leo X, dies

1502 University of Wittenberg founded

1505 Erasmus publishes the *Adnotationes* of Laurentius Valla. James Wimpfeling's *Epitome* (first history of Germany)

1506 University of Frankfurt/O founded

1508 Celtis, the Archhumanist, dies

1509 Erasmus *In Praise of Folly*

1511–1514 Reuchlin controversy

1504 Naples falls to Spain (until 1713)

1512 Holy League in Italy against the French

1497–1560 Melanchthon (from 1518 at Wittenberg)

1507 Julius II issues the indulgence for reconstruction of St Peter's

1511 Reuchlin controversy

1512–1517 Lateran Council

1505 Enters monastery of Augustinian Eremites at Erfurt

1507 Ordination and first mass at Erfurt

1510–1511 Visits Rome

1512 Doctorate in theology at Wittenberg

1499–1535 Elector Joachim I of Brandenburg

1500–1539 Duke George of Saxony

1507–1548 Sigismund I of Poland

1509–1547 Henry VIII of England

1503–1513 Julius II (Rovere)

1509–1567 Landgrave Philip of Hesse

Popes	Princes	Luther	Religion and Theology	World and Church Politics	Culture
1513–1521 Leo X (Medici)	1514–1545 Albrecht of Brandenburg, archbishop and Elector of Mainz 1515–1547 Francis I of France	1513–1516 First lectures (on Psalms and Romans); reads Tauler			1514 'Poor Conrad in Wittenberg' Dürer's *Melancholia*
				1515 Milan falls to France	1515–1517 *Letters of Obscure Men*
					1516 Erasmus' Greek New Testament. More's *Utopia*
		1517 31 Oct, Indulgence theses		1517 War of plunder by duke of Gueldres in Holland. Creation of many cardinals by Leo X	1517 Donation of Constantine contested by von Hutten. Erasmus announces to Leo X the dawn of the Golden age
		1518 June: In Rome the process against Luther introduced. Oct–Nov: Luther before Cajetan in Augsburg; Luther appeals to the pope, then to the council		1518 *RT* at Augsburg: help against Turks refused	1517–1518 Veit Stoss, the Annunciation in St Laurence's, Nuremberg

Rulers / Popes	Luther	Church & Religion	Empire & Politics	Culture
1519–1556 Emperor Charles V	1519 July: Leipzig Disputation	1519 Leipzig Disputation	1519 Electoral campaign of Charles I (V) against Francis I	1519 Universities of Leipzig and Erfurt turn humanist
1520–1566 Suliman II, Sultan of Turkey	1520 June: bull threatening excommunication, *Exsurge Domine* Aug – Oct: The great pamphlets. 10 Dec: L. burns the bull threatening excommunication in Wittenberg	1521 In Worms L. refuses to recant. Edict of Worms. The mass abolished in Wittenberg, Communion under both kinds officially dispensed (Karlstadt); the Zwickau prophets	1521 *RT* at Worms: Imperial government. Supreme Court of Justice, Land Peace, *Gravamina*. Luther. Ferdinand receives Austrian Habsburg territories	1520 The *Book of the Shrine at Halle*
1522–1523 Adrian VI	1521 Bull of excommunication. *RT* at Worms. L. at the Wartburg (until 1 March, 1522; Translation of the New Testament). Edict of Worms	1521–1597 Peter Canisius	1521–1529 Charles V in Spain	1521 Eberlin von Günzburg's reform programme: the Fifteen Confederates
		1522 The German Augustinian congregation abolished. L.'s New Testament appears	1521 Alliance between emperor and pope against France	1522 Michael Ostendorfer – woodcut of the pilgrimage to the beautiful Madonna. Murner on the great fool Luther
			1521–1525 Charles V's first war with Francis I. Peace of Madrid 1526	
			1522 New regulation of life in Wittenberg by 'the common man'. Fraternal union of the west German knights	
			1522–1523 Sickingen's campaign against Trier. *RT* Nuremberg; the resolution	

Popes	Princes	Luther	Religion and Theology	World and Church Politics	Culture
1523–1534 Clement VII (Medici)	1525–1532 Elector John of Saxony	1524 Resumes lectures in Wittenberg 1525 Marries Catherine of Bora. *De servo arbitrio* (against Erasmus)	1523 Confession of guilt at Nuremberg by Adrian VI. Landgrave Philip of Hesse joins the Reformation 1524 Staupitz dies. Erasmus writes on free will	stresses the *Gravamina* and demands a council. Mandate of the imperial government: until a council – nothing but the true, pure, unadulterated gospel 1523 Alliance between Adrian VI and Charles V and Henry VIII and Ferdinand and Milan against France 1524 *RT* Nuremberg: Demand for a German National Council (which Charles forbids). Regensburg conference (Ferdinand, dukes of Bavaria, south German bishops) to execute Edict of Worms. Thomas Müntzer writes against Luther 1524–1525 Peasants' War 1525 Anti-Catholic unrest in Basel and Frankfurt. Alliance between Clement VII and Francis I against the emperor. Prussian Monastic property becomes a secular duchy as Polish fief. The cathedral chapters of the twelve suffragan sees of Mainz advise against Lutheranism	1523 Hutten dies. Hans Sachs, *The Wittenberg Nightingale* 1524 Expectation of prophesied Flood. Erasmus, *De libero arbitrio*

1526 RT at Speyer. Hesse now Evangelical	1526 Evangelical League – Saxony, Hesse, Brunswick and others 1526 Holy League of Cognac (France, the pope, Milan, Venice, Florence, England) against Charles V – RT at Speyer: each estate to live 'as it considers it must answer to God and his imperial majesty'. The Turks in Buda		
1527 Evangelical visitations begin in electoral Saxony	1527 The sack of Rome 1527–1529 Second war between Charles V and Francis I		1527 Machiavelli dies
1528 Bern Reformed. Outbreak of iconoclasm in Basel. Berthold Pirstinger writes first dogmatic treatise of the time	1528 The Pack forgery leads to first intra-German religious war through Philip of Hesse		1528 Wimpfeling, Peter Vischer, Dürer die. University of Marburg founded
1529 Marburg conversations between Luther and Zwingli	1529 RT Speyer: the Evangelicals protest. Basel forbids Catholic public worship. Suliman besieges Vienna. Lutheran assembly at Schmalkalden	1529 Larger and Shorter Catechisms	
1530 RT Augsburg	1530 Pope crowns Charles V in Bologna. RT Augsburg: Evangelical confessional documents	1530 At the Coburg (RT at Augsburg)	
	1531 Schmalkald League: Electoral Saxony, Hesse, Brunswick, Lüneberg, Brunswick-Grubenhagen, Lübeck, Magdeburg, etc.; Bavaria joins in. Church		1531 Tilman Riemenschneider dies

Popes	Princes	Luther	Religion and Theology	World and Church Politics	Culture
				of England breaks with Rome. Catholic victory over Zürich at Kappel. Zwingli dies	
	1532–1547 (1554) Elector John Frederick of Saxony		1532–1533 Negotiations about the council, between emperor and pope. The Schmalkald League, invited by the pope, demand a 'free' council in Germany. Erasmus writes on reunion	1532 *RT* Regensburg and religious Peace of Nuremberg. Turkish threat. Charles V grants religious toleration until the council. Imperial victory over Turks. Alliance between France, Bavaria, electoral Saxony and Hesse	
				1532–1540 Emperor again away from Germany	1533 Veit Stoss dies
				1532–1533 Pope and emperor negotiate in Bologna concerning the council	
				1534 Würtemberg falls again to Duke Ulrich, becomes Evangelical	
				1534–1535 Anabaptists in Münster	
1534–1549 Paul III (Farnese)	1535–1571 Elector Joachim II of Brandenburg		1535 Vergerio, as papal ambassador, tries to get a council. Paul III calls reforming cardinals, and calls councils for 1537 in Mantua	1535 Catholic Defence League: Charles V, Ferdinand, Bavaria, Palatinate-Neuburg, Brandenburg, etc. Francis I makes pact with Suliman	1535 Moore, Fisher, Ulrich Zazius die
				1535–1541 Charles V's wars in North Africa	
			1536 Wittenberg Concordat	1536 Denmark becomes Lutheran	1536 Erasmus dies

				1538 John Sturm founds the Protestant Gymnasium in Strasburg
		1537 Schmalkald League reject council (Luther's Schmalkald Articles). Reform proposals by the cardinals	1536–1538 Third war of Charles V with Francis I (ally of the Turks)	
			1537 Assembly at Schmalkalden rejects the council (Luther's Schmalkald Articles)	
			1537–1543 Charles V's war against William of Jülich-Cleves-Berg over Gueldres, which he annexes to Netherlands	
			1538 Holy League of Catholic princes (Charles V, Ferdinand, Paul III, Venice) against Turks. Catholic League in Nuremburg	
1539–1541 Duke Henry of Saxony (the pious)		1539 The council moved. Religious conversations attempted	1539 Duke George of Saxony dies. Saxony and electoral Brandenburg Evangelical. Frankfurt Truce between Charles and the Protestants	
1541–1553 Duke Maurice of Saxony – from 1548, Elector of Saxony	1541 *Wider Hans Worst* (Duke Henry of Brunswick)	1540 Religious conversation: Hagenau Worms-Regensburg (1541). Jesuits' order ratified by Paul III. Peter Faber, first Jesuit in Germany	1540 Bigamy of Philip of Hesse	
		1541 Karlstadt dies	1541 *RT* Regensburg. Charles V extends the truce with the Protestants. Turks conquer Buda	

357

Popes	Princes	Luther	Religion and Theology	World and Church Politics	Culture
			1542 Paul III calls council in Trent in 1543. Hermann von Wied introduces the Reformation in Cologne	1542 *RT* Speyer (aid against Turks). After expulsion of Duke Henry by the Schmalkald League, Brunswick becomes wholly Reformed. Palatinate-Neuburg and Regensburg Reformed. Hermann von Wied Reformer in Cologne	
				1542–1544 Fourth war of Francis I (and Suliman II) against Charles V	1543 Nicholas Copernicus dies
			1543 Eck dies. Canisius becomes a Jesuit	1543 *RT* Nuremberg (aid against Turks). Alliance between emperor and England	1544 University of Königsberg founded
			1544 Paul III protests against the religious concessions at Speyer, calls council to meet in Trent in 1545	1544 *RT* Speyer: Charles makes concession in religious matters and concerning secularisation to the Evangelicals who are prepared to join him against the Turks and against France, Peace of Crépy in Charles' favour (Francis renounces alliance with Protestants)	
			1544–1545 The Protestants reject the papal council. Cardinal Albrecht of Brandenburg dies	1544–1545 *RT* Worms. Truce between emperor and Suliman for eighteen months	
		1545 *Against the Papacy in Rome*. First collected edition of Latin			1545 Collected edition of Luther's Latin works

works, with auto-biographical reminiscence	1545–1547 (1549) The Council of Trent. Continued 1551–1552; 1562–1563	1546 Palatine Electorate becomes Evangelical (the last secular elector). *RT* Regensburg: the Schmalkald League do not attend. Alliance between pope and emperor. Alliance between emperor, Ferdinand, Bavaria; emperor and Maurice of Saxony. John Frederick of Saxony and Philip of Hesse outlawed
1546 Death	1546 Religious conversations Regensburg. Luther dies. Hermann von Wied deposed	1546–1547 Schmalkald War. Emperor victorious. Emperor concludes truce with Turks for five years
	1547 Cologne again Catholic	1547–1548 *RT* Augsburg: Imperial Interim (cup of the laity and marriage of clergy until the council)
1547–1553 Edward VI of England	1548 Interim and Reformation formula of the emperor. First Latin edition of the *Exercises* of St Ignatius of Loyola. Oratory of St Philip Neri	1548 Maurice of Saxony becomes an elector
1547–1559 Henry II of France	1549 Various provincial and diocesan synods. The Jesuits in Ingolstadt; Catholic university in Dillingen	
1548–1572 Sigismund II of Poland		

Popes	Princes	Luther	Religion and Theology	World and Church Politics	Culture
1550–1555 Julius III (Del Monte)				1550 Duke William IV of Bavaria dies. His chancellor, Leonard Eck dies. Imperial *RT* Augsburg 1551 Alliance between Henry II and German Protestants against the emperor at Lochau (1552 treaty of Chambord)	
			1552 Cochlaeus dies	1552 Maurice of Saxony abandons emperor. Henry II occupies Metz, Toul, Verdun. Revolt of princes against Charles V. Treaty of Passau: free ratification of religion until next *RT* 1552–1555 Plundering wars of Margrave Albrecht Alcibiades. Elector Maurice falls in battle 1553	1553 Luke Cranach dies 1554 University of Dillingen founded
	1553–1558 Mary Tudor of England (Catholic monarch)			1554 Emperor hands over German affairs to Ferdinand	
1555 Marcellinus I (Cervini) 1555–1559 Paul IV (Carafa)			1555 Catechism of Canisius	1555 *RT* Augsburg (without the pope): equal rights granted to followers of Augsburg Confession and to Catholics	1555 Sleidan, *De statu religionis*, the most important historical work of the times

1556–1598 Philip II of Spain	1556 Ignatius of Loyola dies	1556 Abdication of Charles V	1556 Flacius Illyricus, *Catalogus testium veritatis* (collection of all 'pre-Reformation' teachers)
		1557 Religious conversations at Worms: the last attempt initiated by the empire to achieve religious and Church unity	
		1558 Charles V dies. Ferdinand becomes Roman Emperor (no longer crowned by the pope)	

BIBLIOGRAPHY

Abbreviations

AKG   *Archiv für Kulturgeschichte*
BHR   *Bibliothèque d'Humanisme et Renaissance*
CC   *Corpus Catholicorum*
CT   *Concilium Tridentinum*
CTM   *Concordia Theological Monthly*
EEJ   *Erläuterungen und Ergänzungen in Janssen*
EKL   *Evangelisches Kirchenlexikon*
ELKZ   *Evangelisch–Lutherische Kirchenzeitung*
EvTH   *Evangelische Theologie*
HJG   *Historisches Jahrbuch der Görres-Gesellschaft*
GWU   *Geschichte in Wissenschaft und Unterricht*
DtPfrBl   *Deutsches Pfarrerblatt*
KD   *Kerygma und Dogma*
KZ   *Kirche in der Zeit*
MS   *Melanchthon Studien*
LQ   *Lutheran Quarterly*
LThK   *Lexikon für Theologie und Kirche*
LuthJb   *Lutherjahrbuch*
LuthMh   *Lutherische Monatshefte*
LuthRs   *Lutherische Rundschau*
MatDKfl   *Materialdienst des konfessionskundlichen Instituts Bensheim a.d.B.*
RGG   *Die Religion in Geschichte und Gegenwart*
RST   *Reformationsgeschichte Studien und Texte*
SVRG   *Schriften des Vereins für Reformationsgeschichte*
TL   *Theologische Literaturzeitung*
ThR   *Theologische Rundschau*
ZKG   *Zeitschrift für Kirchengeschichte Weltkirchenlexikon*

I. INTRODUCTION

This introduction to the literature of Reformation history is for the non-specialist and concentrates on ideas and religion, theology and Church, as well as suggesting some of the sources.

Archiv für Reformationsgeschichte together with *Verein für Reformationsgeschichte* W. Friedensburg, and since 1943, G. Ritter (eds). Leipzig, Vol 40, 1943; Tübingen, Vol 41, 1948, Parts 1 and 2; Gütersloh, Vol 42, 1951

Theologische Literaturzeitung Schürer, Harnack and H. G. Opitz (eds). Leipzig 1939

Bibliographisches Beiblatt der theologischen Literaturzeitung by various editors. Leipzig since 1922

Theologische Revue Diekamp and Struker (eds). Munster 1939 (with a good bibliography at the end of each volume)

Zeitschrift für Kirchengeschichte E. Seeberg and others (eds). Stuttgart 1939

Historisches Jahrbuch der Görres-Gesellschaft J. Spörl (ed). Cologne 1939

Luther-Jahrbuch J. Jordan (ed 1919–1941) Vols 1–23; F. Lau (ed 1957–1962) Vols 24–29

Bibliographie de la Réforme 1450–1648 Leiden 1958

BERGER A. E. 'Die Sturmtruppen der Reformation' *Deutsche Literatur* H. Kindermann (ed), 'Reformation Series', Vol 2. Leipzig 1931. (Also compare with Vols 3 and 4 of the same series)

BORNKAMM H. *Luther zwischen den Konfessionen. Vierhundert Jahre kath. Lutherforschung* Tübingen 1950, pp. 210–231

DAHLMANN–WAITZ *Quellenkunde der deutschen Geschichte* 9th edn. H. Haering (ed). Leipzig 1931. (He deals with the Reformation in Book 5, Section I, pp. 587–654)

HURTER H. *Nomenclator literarius theologiae catholicae* Vol 2, 3rd edn. Innsbruck 1906. (This deals with controversial Catholical theology and has not been surpassed)

GRIMM H. 'Luther Research since 1920' in *The Journal of Modern History* 32, 1960, pp. 105–118

LOEWENICH W. v. '10 Jahre Lutherforschung, 1938–1948' in *Theol. und Liturgie* L. Hennig (ed). Kassel 1952, pp. 121–170

—— 'Die Lutherforschung in Deutschland seit dem zweiten Weltkrieg' in *TL* 81, 1956, pp. 705–716

LÖFGREN D. 'Verschiedene Tendenzen in der neuren Lutherforschung' in *KD* 5, 1959, pp. 146–164

NYGREN A. 'Die Lutherforschung in Skandinavien' in *Gott ist am Werk* H. Brunotte and E. Ruppel (eds). Hamburg 1959, pp. 17–26

PETRY L. 'Die Reformatïon als Epoche der deutschen Universitätgeschichte. Eine Zwischenbilanz' in *Festgabe für Joseph Lortz* II, pp. 317–353

RUPP G. 'Lutherforschung in England, 1945–1956' in *TL* 81, 1956, pp. 753–756

SCHNABEL *Deutschalnds geschichtliche Quellen und Darstellungen* Vol I. Leipzig 1931

SCHOTTENLOHER K. *Flugblatt und Zeitung* (*Bibliothek für Antiquitäten-Sammler* Vol 21), Berlin 1922, pp. 21–224

—— *Bibliographie zur deutschen Geschichte im Zeitalter der Glaubensspaltung 1517–1585* Vol I–IV. Stuttgart 1956–1958. (Schottenloher deals with the literature up until 1937)

SUESS T. 'Lutherforschung in Frankreich' in *TL* 81, 1956, pp. 759–762

VAJTA V. (ed) *Lutherforschung heute*. (Reports of the first international Congress for Lutheran Studies at Aarhus, 1956), Berlin 1958

ZEEDEN E. W. 'Zeitalter der europäischen Glaubenskämpfe, Gegenreformation und katholische Reform. Ein Forschungsbericht' in *Saeculum* 7, 1956, pp. 321–368

Catholic Authors

AHLBRECHT A. 'Neuere katholische Versuche zur Würdigung der theologischen Anliegen Luthers' in *Una Sancta* 18Jg. (1963), pp. 174–183

BRANDENBURG A. 'Auf dem Wege zu einem ökumenischen Lutherverständnis. Anmerkungen zur Lutherdeutung nach den Prinzipien des Konzilsdekretes "De oecumenismo"' in *Reformata Reformanda* 1965, pp. 313–329

CONGAR Y. M.–J. 'Luther in katholischer Sicht' in *ELKZ* 17, 1951, pp. 261–264

HORST U. 'Wandlungen des Lutherbildes' in *Die neue Ordnung* 19, 1965, pp. 222–224

JEDIN H. 'Wandlungen des Lutherbildes in der katholischen Kirchengeschichtsschreibung' in *Wandlungen des Lutherbildes* 1966, pp. 77–101

LORTZ J. 'Zur Lutherforschung' in *HJ* 53, 1933, pp. 220–240

MANNS P. *Lutherforschung Heute. Krise und Aufbruch* Wiesbaden 1967

MERKLE S. 'Gutes an Luther und Übles an seinen Tadlern' in *Luther in ökumenischer Sicht* 1929, pp. 9–19

MERZ G. 'Der vorreformatorische Luther' in MERZ, *Um Glauben u. Leben nach Luthers Lehre* 1961, pp. 26–65

PESCH O. H. 'Abenteuer Lutherforschung. Wandlungen des Lutherbildes in katholischer Theologie' in *Die neue Ordnung* 6, 1966, pp. 417–430

—— 'Ein katholisches Anliegen an evangelische Darstellungen der Theologie Luthers' in *Catholica* 16, 1962, pp. 304–316

—— 'Zur Frage nach Luthers reformatorischer Wende. Ergebnisse u. Probleme der Diskussion um E. Bizer: Fides ex auditu' in *Catholica* 20, 1966, pp. 216–243; 264–280

—— 'Zwanzig Jahre katholische Lutherforschung' in *LuthRs* 16, 1966, pp. 392–406

PFANDL L. 'Das spanische Lutherbild des 16. Jahrhunderts. Studien und Vorarbeiten' in *HJG* 50, 1930, pp. 464–497

SARTORY T. 'Martin Luther in katholischer Sicht' in *Una Sancta* 16, 1961, pp. 38–54

Congress for Lutheran Studies 1) Aarhus 1956. 2) Münster 1960. Luther u. Melanchthon 1961. 3) Järvenpää 1966

Protestant Authors

ALBRECHT O. 'Kleine Beiträge zur Lutherforschung' in *ThStK* 2, 1915, pp. 239–263

BORNKAMM H. 'Beiträge zum katholischen Lutherbild' in *TL* 75, 1950, pp. 645–652

DILLENBERGER J. 'Literature in Luther Studies, 1950–1955' in *Church History* 25, 1956

—— 'Major Volumes and selected periodical literature in Luther Studies, 1956–1959' in *Church History* 30, 1961, pp. 61–87

FICKER J. 'Lutherorum acta' in *ThStK* N. F. 2, 1936

GEISSER H. 'Das Abenteuer der Lutherinterpretation als verbindendes Element zwischen den Konfessionen' in *MatDKonInst* 14Jg. 5, 1963, pp. 81–90

HERMANN R. 'Luthers geschichtliche und theologische Bedeutung als Gegenwartsproblem' (Wiedergabe e. Fest–Vorlesung bei d. Gedenkfeier d. 400. Todestages M. Luthers gehalten in d. Aula d. Universität Greifswald) in HERMANN R., *Gesammelte Studien z. Theologie Luthers u. d. Reformation* 1960, pp. 330–341

HERMELINK H. 'Die neuere Lutherforschung' in *ThR* 7, 1935, pp. 63–85; 131–156

KANTZENBACH F. W. 'Lutherforschung als kontroverstheologisches Problem' in *LuthRs* 16, 1966, pp. 335–352; *Wandlungen d. Lutherbildes* 1966, pp. 105–129

KOEBERLE A. 'Zweiter internationaler Kongress für Lutherforschung' in *ThLZ* 86, 1962, pp. 151 ff.

KOEHLER O. 'Eine Lutherkontroverse 1950–1953' in *HJG* 74, 1955, pp. 771–784

—— 'Der Wandel im Lutherbild des deutschen Katholizismus' in *LuthRs* 2, 1952

LAU F. 'Père Reinoud und Luther. Bemerkungen zu Reinhold Weijenborgs Lutherstudien' in *LuthJb* 1960, pp. 64–122

—— 'Lutherforschung' in *LuthMh* 5, 1966, pp. 512–519

LILJE H. 'Neue Kontroversen um Luther' in *LuthMh* 5, 1966, pp. 41–45

LOEFGREN D. 'Verschiedene Tendenzen in der neuren Lutherforschung' in *KD* 5, 1959, pp. 146–164

LOEWENICH W. v. 'Zehn Jahre Lutherforschung in Deutschland' in LOEWENICH, *Von Augustin zu Luther* 1959, pp. 307–378

—— 'Das Lutherbild der modernen Theologie in der evangelischen und in der katholischen Theologie' in *Informationsdienst d. konfessionskundl. Forschungsstelle d. Evang. Bundes* Vol 1, 1966, pp. 4–13

—— 'Evangelische und katholische Lutherdeutung der Gegenwart im Dialog' in *LuthJb* 1967, pp. 60–89

—— 'Wandlungen des evangelischen Lutherbildes im 19. u. 20. Jahrhundert' in *Wandlungen des Lutherbildes*, 1966, pp. 49–76

—— 'Lutherforschung in Deutschland' in *Lutherforschung heute*, 1958

—— 'Das Problem des "katholischen" Luther' in LOEWENICH, *Von Augustin zu Luther* 1959, pp. 238–249

—— 'Die Lutherforschung in Deutschalnd seit dem zweiten Weltkrieg' in *ThLZ* 81, 1956, pp. 705–716

—— 'Zehn Jahre Lutherforschung' in *Theologie u. Liturgie* 1952, pp. 119–170

—— 'Das Lutherbild in der gegenwärtigen Lutherforschung' in *Der evangelische Erzieher* 9, 1957, pp. 261–266

MEYER H. 'Der 3. Internationale Kongress für Lutherforschung' in *Kirche in der Zeit* 21, 1966, pp. 497–503

MUELLER H. M. 'Auf dem Wege zum wirklichen Luther' in *LuthMh* 6, 1967, pp. 365–371

PETERS A. 'Luther und die existentiale Interpretation' in *LuthMh* 4, 1965, pp. 466–473

ROST G. 'De libris. Aus der Arbeit der Lutherforschung' in *Luth. Rundbrief* 9, 1961, pp. 52–62

—— 'Zweiter internationaler Kongress für Lutherforschung' in *Luth. Rundblick* 8, 1960, p. 202 f.

STUPPERICH R. 'Lutherforschung und Reformationsgeschichte' in *AKG* 43, 1961, pp. 377–392

—— 'II. Internationaler Kongress für Lutherforschung in Münster, vom 8. bis 12. Aug. 1960' in *Luther* 31, 1960, pp. 139–141

WENDELBORN G. 'Luther in kirchengeschichtlicher Deutung' in *Evang. Pfarrblatt* 1963, pp. 131–133; pp. 149–152

WOLF E. 'Moderne Lutherdeutung'. Buchbesprechung von J. Lortz, 'Die Reformation in Deutschland' in *Verkündigung u. Forschung* 1940, pp. 88–104

—— 'Neuere Luther–Literatur und der Gang der Luther–Forschung' in *Christentum u. Wissenschaft* Vols 9–10, 1933

—— 'Martin Luther und die Prinzipien des Protestantismus in katholischer Sicht' in *ThLZ* 76, 1951, pp. 271–276

—— 'Was wollte Luther eigentlich?' in *Concilium* 2, 1966, pp. 236–240

II. SOURCES

The leading sources are (1) The Reichstag reports, (2) The writings of leading personalities, including their letters. As well as these there are an enormous number of reports, contemporary writings and Chronicles.

Die Reichstagsakten und die Chroniken der deutschen Städte published in 2 edns.

Die Bekenntnisschriften der evangelisch–lutherischen Kirche 3rd edn. Göttingen 1956

Deutsche Reichstagsakten Gotha 1893

Neue und vollständige Sammlung der Reichs–Abschiede 4 parts (to 1736). Frankfurt 1747

Der Augsburger Religionsfriede (1555) (Critical edn. K. Brandi) 2nd edn. Göttingen 1927

Flugschriften aus den ersten Jahren der Reformation O. Clemen (ed), Vols 1–4. Leipzig 1907–1910

'Flugschriften aus der Reformationszeit' in *Neudrucke deutscher Literaturwerke des 16 und 17 Jahrh* Vols 8–14. Halle 1889–1899

Kolde T. *Die Augusburger Konfession* 2nd edn. Gotha 1911

Legge T. 'Flug- und Streitschriften der Reformationszeit in Westfalen' (*RST* 58–59) Münster 1933

Müller–Kolde *Die symbolischen Bücher der evangelischlutherischen Kirche* 11th edn. Gütersloh 1912

III. GENERAL BACKGROUND

The most important work is still Ranke's, *Deutsche Geschichte im Zeitalter der Reformation*. The best new edition is by the German Academy, Vols 1–6. Munich 1925–1926

Handbuch der Kirchengeschichte 6 vols. Vol 4: *Reformation, kath. Reform und Gegenreformation* E. Iserloh, J. Glazik, H. Jedin (eds). 1967

The New Cambridge Modern History Vol I: *The Renaissance;* Vol II: *The Reformation 1520–1559.* G. R. Elton (ed). Cambridge 1959

Historia Mundi 10 vols. F. Valjavec (ed). Vol VI: *Hohes und spätes Mittelalter* 1958; Vol VII: *Übergang zur Moderne* 1957. Bern–Munich 1952–1961

Handbuch der deutschen Geschichte O. Brandt (ed). Vol I, 5: H. Heimpel, *Deutschland im späten Mittelalter;* Vol I, 6: M. Seidlmayer, *Weltbild und Kultur Deutschlands im Mittelalter;* Vol II: *Deutsche Geschichte vom Zeitalter der Reformation bis zum Tode Friedrichs d. Gr.* Constance 1956. (Also in this volume R. Stadelmann, E. Naujoks, *Das Zeitalter der Reformation* 2nd edn; J. Hashagen, *Die Gegenreformation*)

Deutsche Geschichte im Überblick. Ein Handbuch P. Rassow (ed), 2nd edn. Stuttgart 1962

Die Kirche in ihrer Geschichte. Ein Handbuch H. D. Schmidt, and E. Wolf (eds). Göttingen 1962

Bainton R. H. *The Age of the Reformation* Princeton 1958

—— *Studies in the Reformation* London 1964

Bezold Fr. v. *Geschichte der deutschen Reformation* [*Geschichte in Einzeldarstellungen* W. Oncken (ed)], Berlin 1890

Bihlmeyer K. and Tüchle H. *Kirchengeschichte* 16th edn. 3 vols. Paderborn 1958–1959

Bühler J. *Deutsche Geschichte* Vol 3: *Das Reformationszeitalter* Berlin 1938

Dickens A. G. *Reformation and Society in Sixteenth Century Europe* London 1966

Dilthey W. *Weltanschauung und Analyse des Menschen seit Renaissance und Reformation* 5th edn. Göttingen 1957

Fliche A. and Martin V. *Histoire de l'Énglise depuis les origines jusqu'à nos jours* Paris 1946. Vol 15: Aubenas–Ricard, *L'Église et Renaissance (1449–1517)* 1951; Vol 16: Moreau–Jourda–Jamelle, *La Crise religieuse du XVIe siècle* 1950; Vol 17: Christiani, *L'Église à l'époque du concile de Trente* 1948

GEBHARDT B. *Handbuch der deutschen Geschichte* H. Grundmann (ed), 8th edn. Vols I–IV. Stuttgart 1954. Vol II: *Von der Reformation bis zum Ende des Absolutismus* 1955 (Enlarged edn. 1956). Also in this volume W. P. FUCHS *Das Zeitalter der Reformation* E. W. ZEEDEN, *Das Zeitalter der Glaubenskämpfe*

GREEN V. H. H. *Luther and the Reformation. Landmarks in European History* London 1964

GRIMM H. J. *The Reformation Era, 1500–1650* New York 1961

HARTUNG F. *Deutsche Geschichte im Zeitalter der Reformation, der Gegenreformation und des 30 jähr. Krieges* Berlin 1951

HASSINGER E. 'Das Werden des neuzeitlichen Europa, 1300–1600' in *Geschichte der Neuzeit* G. Ritter (ed). Braunschweig 1959

HEER F. *Die dritte Kraft. Der europäische Humanismus zwischen den Fronten des konfessionellen Zeitalters* Frankfurt 1959

HOLBORN H. *The Age of the Reformation and of Absolutism* (Vol I of *A History of Modern Germany* 2 vols) London 1965

HUCH R. *Das Zeitalter der Glaubensspaltung* Berlin–Zürich 1937

IMBART DE LA TOUR *Les Origines de la Réforme* Vol 2: *L'église catholique. La crise et la renaissance* Paris 1909; Vol 3: *L'évangélisme* Paris 1914

JANSSEN J. *Geschichte des deutschen Volkes* Vols 1–8. Freiburg 189 off. (Many of the editions have been revised by L. v. Pastor)

JOACHIMSEN P. 'Das Zeitalter der Reformation' in *Propyläen–Weltgeschichte* Vol 5: *Das Zeitalter der religiösen Umwälzungen* Berlin 1930, pp. 1–216

—— *Die Reformation als Epoche der deutschen Geschichte* (1930) O. Schottenloher (ed), 2nd edn. Berlin 1951

KAULFUSS-DIESCH *Das Buch der Reformation, geschrieben von Mitlebenden* Leipzig 1917

MAURER–HERMELINK *Reformation und Gegenreformation* (*Handbuch der Kirchengeschichte* G. Krüger [ed], Vol 3) Tübingen 1931

MENTZ G. *Deutsche Geschichte im Zeitalter der Reformation, Gegenreformation und 30 jährigen Krieges* Tübingen 1913

—— *Propyläen–Weltgeschichte* Vol 7: *Von der Reformation zur Revolution* 1964

PEUKERT W.-E. *Die grosse Wende. Geistesgeschichte und Volkskunde* Hamburg 1948

RITTER G. *Die Neugestaltung Europas im 16 Jh* Berlin 1950

RÖSSLER H. *Europa im Zeitalter von Renaissance, Reformation und Gegenreformation, 1450–1650* Munich 1956

RÖSSLERU H. and FRANZ G. *Bibliographisches Wörtebuch zur deutschen Geschichte* Munich 1952

—— *Sachwörterbuch zur deutschen Geschichte* Munich 1958

SCHMIDT K. D. *Grundriss der Kirchengeschichte* Göttingen 1960

SCHÖFLER H. *Das Buch der Reformation, geschrieben von Mitlebenden* Leipzig 1917

STADELMANN R. 'Das Zeitalter der Reformation' in *Handbuch der deutschen Geschichte* Brandt, Meyer and Ullmann (eds), Vol 2. Berlin 1955, p. 1 ff.

WALTER J. v. *Die Geschichte des Christentums* Vol 2, I: *Die Reformation* Gütersloh 1935

WOLF G. 'Reformationszeit' in *Gebhardts Handbuch der deutschen Geschichte* (there is a completely new edition by R. HOLTZMANN. 7th edn. Stuttgart 1930, p. 556 ff.)

IV. PRE-REFORMATION PERIOD

In understanding Erasmus, the whole question of the relation of Humanism to sacrosanct dogma has to be re-examined. Only after this has been done can Charles V's attitude to the Church and the attitudes of the conciliators be understood; and the discussions of the forties and of the rôle of the great Humanists in Church history be given a clear background.

ALLEN P. S. *Erasmus. Collected Essays* Oxford 1934
——— *Opus Epistolarum Des. Erasmus Roterodami* Vols 1–12. Oxford 1906–1958

ANDREAS W. *Deutschland vor der Reformation* Stuttgart 1959. (The most comprehensive book on this topic, with a particularly fine study of Erasmus)

AUER A. *Die Vollkommene vor der Reformation. Nach dem Enchiridion Militis Christiani des Erasmus von Rotterdam* Düsseldorf 1954. (See also E. ISERLOH in *Trierer Theol. Z.* 64, 1955, p. 315 ff.)

BARON H. 'Religiöse Reformbewegungen des deutschen Humanismus' in *Hist. Zeitschrift* 132, 1925, p. 415 ff.

BELOW GG. v. *Die Ursachen der Reformation* Munich 1917

BERNHART J. *Die Symbolik im Menschwerdungsbild des Isenheimer Altars* Munich 1921

BEZOLD FR. v. 'Conrad Celtis, der deutsche Erzhumanist' in *Aus Mittelalter und Renaissance* Munich 1918, p. 82 ff.

BIER J. *Tilmann Riemenschneider. Ein Gedenkbuch* 4th edn. Augsburg 1936

BORGHI L. *Umanesimo e concezione religiosa* Florence 1935

BRAUN ALB. *Der Klerus des Bistums Konstanz im Ausgang des Mittelalters* Münster 1938

BÜHLER J. *Deutsche Geschichte* Vol 2: *Fürsten, Ritterschaft und Bürgertum von 1100 bis 1500* Berlin 1935

BURDACH K. *Reformation, Renaissance, Humanismus* 2nd edn. Berlin 1926

DEHIO GG. *Geschichte der deutschen Kunst* Vol 2, 4th edn. Berlin 1930; Vol 3, 2nd edn. 1931

DOLFEN C. *Die Stellung des Erasmus von Rotterdam zur scholastischen Methode* Münster 1936

DOLS J. M. E. *Bibliographie der moderne devotie* Nimwegen since 1936

Albrecht Dürers schriftlicher Nachlass E. Heidrich (ed). Berlin 1920. Dürer's judgment of the painting of the pilgrimage of the beautiful Maria in Regensburg (see Vol I, p. 72 – the ghost raised itself against Holy Scripture and was hanged by the bishop, but at the time it was not efficiently removed) offers a certain difficulty for my own interpretation of the religious and ecclesiastical position of Dürer (see Vol I, pp. 115–116) but is not a refutation.

EDER K. *Deutsche Geisteswende zwischen Mittelalter und Neuzeit.* (*Bücherei der Salzburger Hochschulwochen* Vol 8) Salzburg–Leipzig 1937

ERASMUS *Ausgewählte Werke* H. Holborn (ed). Munich 1933

——— *Vom freien Willen* German trans. O. Schuhmacher 2nd edn. Göttingen 1956

——— *Opera Omnia* J. le Clerc (ed). London 1962

——— *Erasmi Opuscula* a supplement to the *Opera Omnia.* Ed. with Introduction and Notes by W. K. Ferguson. The Hague 1933

FERGUSON W. K. *The Renaissance in Historical Thought* Cambridge, Mass. 1948

GEBHARDT B. *Die Gravamina der deutschen Nation gegen den römischen Hof* 2nd edn. Breslau 1895

GILL J. *The Council of Florence* Cambridge 1959

GODET P. 'Érasme' in *Dict. de théologie catholique* Vol 5, I. Paris 1924, p. 395 ff.

GORCE D. 'La patristique dans la réforme d'Érasme' in *Festgabe für Joseph Lortz* Vol I, pp. 233–276

HALLER J. *Die Ursachen der Reformation* Tübingen 1917

HARTUNG F. *Deutsche Verfassungsgeschichte vom 15 Jahrh. bis zur Gegenwart* 8th edn. Stuttgart 1964

HASHAGEN J. 'Die Devotio moderna in ihrer Einwirkung auf Humanismus, Reformation, Gegenreformation und spätere Richtungen' in *ZKG* 55, 1936, p. 523 ff.

——— *Staat und Kirche vor der Reformation* Essen 1931. (See also H. FINKE in *HJG* 51, 1931, p. 219 ff.)

HOFMANN G. *Papato, Consiliarismo, Patriarcato* Rome 1940

HUIZINGA J. *Erasmus* Trans. F. Homan. New York 1924

——— *Herbst des Mittelalters. Studien über Lebens- und Geistesformen des 14 und 15 Jahrh. in Frankreich und in den Niederlanden* Stuttgart 1953

ISERLOH E. *Gnade und Eucharistie in der philosophischen Theologie des Wilhelm von Ockham. Ihre Bedeutung für die Ursachen der Reformation* Vol 8. Wiesbaden 1956

JOACHIMSEN P. 'Vom Mittelalter zur Renaissance' in *Hist. Vierteljahrsschrift* 20 (Dresden 1922) p. 426 ff. (This puts forward an opposite point of view from K. BURDACH's *Reformation, Renaissance, Humanismus*)

JOHANN HUS *Opera Omnia* Prag: Acad. Scient. Bohem. Vol 7: *Sermones de tempore qui Collecta dicuntur* A. Schmidtova (ed). Prague 1959

KNAPP F. *Grünewald* 3rd edn. Bielefeld 1939

KÖHLER W. *Erasmus. Ein Lebensbild in Auszügen aus seinen Werken* Berlin 1917

—— *Erasmus Von Rotterdam, Briefe* Leipzig 1938

KUCKHOFF J. 'Thomas Morus und Desiderius Erasmus' in *Stimmen der Zeit* 66, 1935, p. 88 ff.

—— *Lob der Torheit* German trans. A Hartmann, with illustrations by Holbein. E. Major (ed). Basle 1929

LÖHR J. *Methodisch-kritische Beiträge zur Geschichte der Sittlichkeit des Klerus Besonders der Diözese Köln, am Ausgang des Mittelalters (RST 17)* Münster 1910

LORTZ J. *Zur Problematik der kirchlichen Missstände im Spätmittelalter. In memoriam Sebastian Merkle* Trier 1950

—— 'Erasmus – kirchengeschichtlich' in *Theologie und Philosophie* Düsseldorf 1950, pp. 271–326

LÜTZELER H. 'Vom Sinn der spätmittelalterlichen Schnitzaltäre' in *Hochland* 33 (1935–1936), p. 537 ff.

—— *Die christliche Kunst Deutschlands* Bonn 1935

—— *Die christliche Kunst des Abendlandes* 3rd edn. Bonn 1935

MONNERJAHN E. *Giovanni Pico della Mirandola* Wiesbaden 1960

THOMAS MORE *The correspondence of Sir Thomas More* L. F. Rogers (ed). Princeton 1947

—— *The Yale edition of the complete works* R. S. Sylvester (ed). New Haven 1963

OBERMAN H. A. *Forerunners of the Reformation* New York 1966

—— *The Harvest of Medieval Theology: Gabriel Biel and Late Nominalism* Havard University Press 1963

OELRICH K. H. *Der Späte Erasmus und die Reformation (RST 86)* Münster 1961

PAULUS N. *Geschichte des Ablasses am Ausgang des Mittelalters* Paderborn 1923

PFEIFFER R. *Humanitas Erasmiana* Leipzig and Berlin 1931. (See also the chapter on Erasmus in FUNCK–BRENTANO, *Luther*, p. 67 ff.)

PORKIN R. H. *The History of Scepticism from Erasmus to Descartes* Assen 1960

RITTER G. 'Romanische und revolutionäre Elemente in der deutschen Theologie am Vorabend der Reformation' in *Vierteljahrsschrift für Literatur und Geistesgesch* 5, p. 353

—— 'Die geistigen Ursachen der Reformation' in *Zeitwende* 7, 1931, ii, p. 1 ff.

—— *Die Heidelberger Universität* I, pp. 465–491 (Rudolf Agricola, Konrad Celtes, Jakob Wimpfeling)

RÜCKLIN–TEUSCHER G. *Religiöses Volksleben des ausgehenden Mittelalters in den Reichsstädten Halle und Heilbronn* (Hist. Studien 226). Berlin 1933

RUESS P. *Unsere Liebe Frau von Stuppach. Eine mystische Farbendichtung von*

Matthias Grünewald Bad Mergentheim 1934. (The author explains the artistic technique and especially the theological content of this wonderful work)

Schilling A. 'Beiträge zur Geschichte der Einführung der Reformation in Biberach. Zeitgenössische Aufzeichnungen des Weltpriesters Heinrich v. Pflummern' in *Freiburger Diözesan-Archiv* 9, 1875, p. 191 ff.

Schmitz W. *Der Einfluss der Religion auf das Leben beim ausgehenden Mittelalter* Freiburg 1894

Stein K. H. *Tilmann Riemenschneider im deutschen Bauernkrieg. Geschichte einer geistigen Haltung* Dresden 1936. (See also E. Kirschbaum in *Stimmen der Zeit,* July 1937)

Störmann A. *Die städtischen Gravamina gegen den Klerus (RST* 24–26) Münster 1916

Veit L. A. *Volksfrommes Brauchtum und Kirche im deutschen Mittelalter* Freiburg 1936

Vincke J. *Der Klerus des Bistums Osnabrück im späten Mittelalter. Vorreformationsgeschichte* Münster 1928

Vooght P. de *Hussiana* Louvain 1960

—— *L'hérésie de Jean Huss* Louvain 1960

Vorreformationsgeschichtliche Forschungen Vols 1–14 (Münster 1900–1938) H. Finke (ed); Vol 15, J. Lortz (ed)

Waetzold W. *Dürer und seine Zeit* 3rd edn. Wien 1936

Walser B. E. *Gesammelte Studien zur Geistesgeschichte der Renaissance* Basle 1932

Willburger A. 'Religiöse Versorgung Oberschwabens vor der Reformation' in *Hist. polit. Blätter* 152, 1918, Vols 3–5

Winter E. *Tausend Jahre Geisteskampf im Sudetenraum* Salzburg–Leipzig 1938

Zülch W. K. *Der historische Grünewald* Munich 1938

THOMAS MURNER and SEBASTIAN BRANT are accessible in various editions and translations. (Also published by *Reclam*). Critical editions: THOMAS MURNER 'Kleine Schriften' (*Prosaschriften gegen die Reformation* W. Pfeiffer–Belli [ed]). 3 vols Berlin 1927–1928. See Also Thomas Murner, *Deutsche Schriften* Vols 6–8)

V. MARTIN LUTHER

1. *Editions of Luther's Works*

Concordia Publishing House has undertaken to produce the most comprehensive and authoritative edition of Luther's writings available in English under the general editorship of Dr J. Pelikan and Dr H. T. Kehmann. When this edition is complete there will be 56 volumes, 20 devoted to Luther's writings on the Old Testament, 10 to his writings on the New Testament; the remaining 26 volumes contain other writings that are representative of his career: the historic debates, books and tracts setting forth his views, his personal conversation (Luther's Table Talk), letters, etc. The following list describes the contents of each volume. The ones in brackets have not yet been published.

Vols 1, 2, 3, 4, (5), (6), 7, 8	Luther's writings on Genesis
Vol 9	Lectures on Deuteronomy
Vols (10), (11), 12, 13, 14	Psalms
Vol (15)	Old Testament Commentaries
Vols (16), (17)	Isaiah
Vols (18), (19), (20)	The minor prophets
Vol 21	The Sermon on the Mount
Vol 22	John 1–4
Vol 23	John 6–8
Vol 24	John 14–16
Vol (25)	Romans
Vols 26, 27	Galatians
Vol (28)	Selected Pauline Epistles
Vol (29)	Commentary on Hebrews
Vol 30	Catholic Epistles
Vols 31, 32, (33), 34	Career of the Reformer
Vols 35, 36, 37, 38	The Word and the Sacrament
Vols 39, 40, 41	Church and Ministry
Vol (42), (43)	The Devotional Writings
Vols 44, 45, 46, (47)	The Christian in Society
Vols 48, (49), 50	Luther's Letters
Vols 51, (52)	Luther's Sermons
Vol 53	Liturgy and Hymns
Vol 54	Table Talk
Vol 55	Index
Vol 56	Bibliography

ALAND K. *Hilfsbuch zum Lutherstudium* Revised in collaboration with E. O. Reichert and G. Jordan, 2nd edn. Berlin 1958

BUCHWALD G. and KAWERAU G. *Luther–Kalendarium. Verzeichnis von Luthers Schriften (SVRG 147)* 2nd edn. Leipzig 1929

CLEMEN O. *Critical Edition of Luther's works* Vols 1–4. Bonn 1912–1913. (A further four volumes by various editors. Berlin 1930–1933)

FICKER J. *Anfänge reformatorischer Bibelauslegung* Vol I: *Luthers Vorlesung über den Römerbrief 1515–16* 4th edn. Leipzig 1930. (This is very important for knowledge of the young Luther and deals with his lecture on the *Epistle to the Romans*. (See also the German translation by E. ELLWEIN, *Martin Luther. Vorlesung über den Römerbrief 1515–16* 2 vols. Cologne 1960)

Luther Deutsch. Die Werke Martin Luthers in neuer Auswahl für die Gegenwart K. Aland (ed). Stuttgart 1957

Luthers Werke 7 vols and 5 supplementary vols. Munich 1913–1925. 2nd edn. 1934, C. Kaiser (ed). Vol 4: *Der Kampf gegen Schwarm– und Rottengeister* (including the Peasant's War); Vol 5: *Von der Obrigkeit in Familie, Volk und Staat* (single writings by Luther have also appeared in *Reclam*)

Münchener Luther–Ausgabe (The Latin writings are translated into German, the German writings are left unaltered linguistically – useful for the layman)

PINOMAA L. *Register der Bibelzitate in Luthers Schriften in den Jahren 1509–19* (Masch) 1951

—— *Register der Bibelzitate in Luthers Schriften in den Jahren 1520–21* (Masch) 1955

PLASS E. M. *What Luther says* Vols I–III. Concordia, St Louis 1959

RÜCKERT in *Lutherforschung heute*

SCHEEL O. *Dokumente zu Luthers Entwicklung* 2nd edn. Tübingen 1929

VOGELSANG E. in the final edition of the *Weimarer Ausgabe* (still the best for Luther's first lecture on the Psalms)

VOLZ *Die Religion in Geschichte und Gegenwart* 3rd edn. Vol IV, pp. 520–523. Tübingen 1960

2. General Background

BAINTON R. H. *Martin Luther* Mentor Books, New York

BOEHMER H. *Luther im Lichte der neueren Forschung* 5th edn. Leipzig 1918

—— *Martin Luther – Road to Reformation* Thomas & Hudson and Mentor Books 1957

CRISTIANI L. *Luther wie er wirklich war* Stuttgart 1957

DENIFLE H. *Luther und Luthertum* 2nd edn. Mainz 1904–1906

FAUSSEL H. D. *Martin Luther. Der Reformator im Kampf um Evangelium und Kirche* Stuttgart 1955

FEBVRE L. *Un destin. Martin Luther* Paris 1928

FUNCK–BRENTANO *Luther* 18th edn. Paris 1935

GRISAR H. *Luther* 3 vols. Freiburg 1911–1912 (Supplements to 2nd edn. 1924 and 1925)

—— *Martin Luthers Leben und sein Werk* 2nd edn. Freiburg 1927

HOLL K. *Gesammelte Aufsätze zur Kirchengeschichte* Vol I: *Luther* 4th and 5th edn. Tübingen 1927

KIEFL FR. X 'Martin Luthers religiöse Psyche' in *Kath. Weltanschauung und modernes Denken* (Regensburg 1922) p. 1 ff.

KÖHLER W. *Martin Luther und die deutsche Reformation* 2nd edn. Leipzig 1917

KÖSTLIN–KAWERAU *Martin Luther. Sein Leben und Seine Schriften* 2 vols. 2nd edn. Berlin 1905

LAU F. *Luther* Berlin 1959

MEISSINGER K. A. *Der katholische Luther* Munich 1952

MÖHLER J. A. *Symbolik oder Darstellung der dogmatischen Gegensätze der*

Katholiken und Protestanten nach ihren öffentlichen Bekenntnisschriften 7th edn. Regensburg 1909

RITTER G. *Luther, Gestalt und Takt* Munich 1959

SCHEEL O. *Martin Luther. Vom Katholizismus zur Reformation* Vol I, 3rd edn. Tübingen 1921; Vol 2, 3rd and 4th edn. 1930

SCHWIEBERT E. G. *Luther and His Times. The Reformation from a new perspective* Concordia, St Louis 1950

—— *The Protestant Reformation* L. W. Spitz (ed). Englewood Cliffs, N. J. 1966

THIEL R. *Luther* Vol I, 2nd edn. Leipzig 1936; Vol 2, 1935

THULIN O. *Martin Luther. Sein Leben in Bildern und Zeitdokumenten* Munich –Berlin 1958

The English Reformation

BROWN W. E. 'The Reformation in Scotland' in *European Civilisation* Vol 4, E. Eyre (ed)

CLEBSCH W. A. *England's Earliest Protestants, 1520–1535* (Yale Publications in Religion II) D. Horne (ed). Yale University Press 1964

THOMAS CRANMER *Cranmer's Selected Writings* (with introd. and bibliog. by C. S. Meyer) S.P.C.K., London 1961

HALLER W. *The Rise of Puritanism, Or: The Way to the New Jerusalem As Set Forth in Pulpit and Press from Thomas Cartwright to John Lilburne and John Milton, 1570–1643* Harper & Row 1957

MEYER C. S. *Elizabeth I and the Religious Settlement of 1559* Concordia, St Louis 1960

MILLER P. and JOHNSON T. H. *The Puritans* Harper & Row 1963

PEARCE E. G. 'Luther and the English Reformation' in *CTM XXXI*, 10 (October 1960) pp. 597–606

POWICKE SIR MAURICE *The Reformation in England* Oxford 1961

RENWICK A. M. *The Story of the Scottish Reformation* London 1960

TJERNAGEL N. S. *Henry VIII and the Lutherans: A Study in Anglo-Lutheran Relations from 1521 to 1547* Concordia, St Louis 1965

3. Luther's Theology

It is an alarming thought that after four hundred years, interpretation of the Reformation and of Luther's work is still so varied. It is vital that we arrive at an academically sound *opinio communis* on Luther. But it is not so easy to trace Luther's development; possibly it is too contradictory to analyse.

However, it is certain that the Catholic Luther is much more the central figure than most people have thought. Nevertheless the question, 'What is the Lutheran Reformation?' has still to be answered.

To attempt to answer it, a thorough investigation of Luther's way of thinking must be made. To some extent the existentialist approach has been helpful – made by BULTMANN and continued by EBELING.

ALTHAUS P. *Die Theologie Martin Luther* Gütersloh 1962

—— *Paulus und Luther über den Menschen* 3rd enlarged edn. Gütersloh 1958

ASENDORF U. *Eschatologie bei Luther* Göttingen 1967

AULÉN G. *Reformation and Catholicity* trans. E. H. Wahlstrom. Oliver & Boyd, Edinburgh 1962

BANDT H. *Luthers Lehre vom verborgenen Gott. Eine Untersuchung zu dem offenbarungsgeschichtlichen Ansatz seiner Theologie* Berlin 1958

BARGE H. *Luther und der Frühkapitalismus* (*SVRG* 168) Gütersloh 1951

BEINTKER H. *Die Überwindung der Anfechtung bei Luther* Berlin 1954

BEISSER F. *Claritas scripturae bei Martin Luther* Göttingen 1966

BIZER E. *Studien zur Geschichte des Abendmahlstreites im 16. Jahrhundert* Gütersloh 1940

—— *Fides ex auditu. Eine Untersuchung über die Entdeckung der Gerechtigkeit Gottes durch Martin Luther* 2nd enlarged edn. Neukirchen 1961

BORNKAMM H. *Luther als Schriftsteller* Heidelberg 1965

—— *Luthers geistige Welt* 4th edn. Gütersloh 1960

—— *Das Jahrhundert der Reformation* Göttingen 1961. (Including – 'Erasmus und Luther', 'Philipp Melanchthon', 'Humanismus und Reformation im Menschenbild Melanchthons', 'Martin Bucer, der dritte deutsche Reformator', 'Das Problem der Toleranz im 16. Jahrhundert')

BÖRSCH E. *Geber – Gabe – Aufgabe. Luthers Prophetie in den Entscheidungsjahren seiner Reformation 1520–25* Munich 1958

BRANDENBURG A. *Gericht und Evangelium. Zur Worttheologie in Luthers erster Psalmenvorlesung* Paderborn 1960

BRING R. *Gesetz und Evangelium und der dritte Brauch des Gesetzes in der luth. Theologie* Helsinki 1943

—— *Das Verhältnis von Glauben und Werken in der luth. Theologie* Munich 1955

BÜHLER P. TH. *Die Anfechtung bei Luther* Zürich 1942

GARRISON A. E. 'Luther and the Doctrine of the Holy Spirit' in *LQ XI* 2(May 1959) pp. 135—146

CHESTOV L. *Sola Fide. Luther et L'Église* (trans. from Russian by Sophie Seve) Paris 1957

EBELING G. *Luther. Einführung in sein Denken* Tübingen 1964

—— *Evangelische Evangelienauslegung. Eine Untersuchung zu Luthers Hermeneutik* Munich 1942 (Reprint: Darmstadt 1962)

—— *Wort und Glaube* (Collection) Tübingen 1960

EDEL G. *Das gemeinkatholische mittelalterliche Erbe beim jungen Luther* Marburg 1961

ELERT W. *Morphologie des Luthertums* 2 vols. Munich 1958

FORCK G. *Die Königsherrschaft Jesu Christi bei Luther* Berlin 1959

GENSICHEN H.–W. *Damnamus. Die Verwerfung von Irrlehre bei Luther und im Luthertum des 16. Jahrhunderts* Berlin 1959

GERDES H. *Luthers Streit mit den Schwärmern um das rechte Verständnis des Gesetzes Moses* Göttingen 1955

GERRISH B. A. *Grace and Reason. A study in the Theology of Luther* Oxford 1962

GERSTENKORN H. R. *Weltliches Regiment zwischen Gottesreich und Teufelsmacht. Die staatstheoretischen Auffassungen Martin Luthers und ihre politische Bedeutung* Bonn 1956

GRASS H. *Die Abendmahlslehre bei Luther und Calvin* 2nd edn. Gütersloh 1954

GROSCHE R. 'Gerecht und Sünder zugleich' in *Catholica* 4, 1935, p. 132 ff. (Now also in R. GROSCHE, *Pilgernde Kirche* Freiburg 1938, pp. 147–158)

GYLLENKROK A. *Rechtfertigung und Heiligung in der frühen ev. Theologie Luthers* Uppsala & Wiesbaden 1952

HACKER P. *Das Ich im Glauben bei Martin Luther* Graz 1966

HÄGGLUND B. *Theologie und Philosophie bei Luther und in der occamist. Tradition* Lund 1955

HARNACK T. *Luthers Theologie* new edn. Munich 1927

HECKEL J. *Lex charitatis. Eine jurist. Unters. über das Recht in der Theol. M. Luthers* Munich 1953

HEINTZE G. *Luthers Predigt von Gesetz und Evangelium* Munich 1958

HERMANN R. *Luthers These, Gerechte und Sünder zugleich* Gütersloh 1930

—— *Zu Luthers Lehre von Sünde Rechtfertigung* (*SgV* 200–201). Tübingen 1952

—— *Zum Streit um die Bedeutung des Gesetzes* Weimar 1958

—— *Von der Klarheit der Heiligen Schrift* Berlin 1959

—— *Gesammelte Studien zur Theologie Luthers und der Reformation* Göttingen 1960

HERMELINK H. 'Zu Luthers Gedanken über Idealgemeinden und weltliche Obrigkeit' in *ZKG* 29, 1908, p. 267 ff.

HIRSCH E. *Lutherstudien* I–II. Göttingen 1954

HOLL K. *Luther und das landeskirchliche Regiment* (above p. 374) p. 326 ff.

HOLSTEN W. *Christentum und nichtchristliche Religion nach der Auffassung Luthers* (*Missionsstudien* 13) Gütersloh 1932

ISERSLOH E. *Peter Manns* (Festgabe für Joseph Lortz, Vols I–II) Baden-Baden 1958. (Including – Vol I: E. KINDER, *Die Verborgenheit der Kirche nach Luther;* E. MONNERJAHN, *Zum Begriff der theologischen Unklarheit im Humanismus;* Vol II: W. SCHÜSSLER, *Deutschlutherischer Geist und Westeuropa*

IWAND H. J. *Um den rechten Glauben. Collected essays* ed. and introduced by K. G. Steck, Munich 1959. (Including – 'Die grundlegende Bedeutung der Lehre vom unfreien Willen für den Glauben. Eine Einführung in Luthers Schrift vom unfreien Willen', 'Die Freiheit des Christen und die Unfreiheit des Willens' (also *Festschr. R. Hermann* 1957, pp. 132–146)

—— *Glaubensgerechtigkeit nach Luthers Lehre* 2nd edn. Munich 1951

—— *Zur Entstehung von Luthers Kirchenbegriff* Neukirchen 1957, pp. 145–166

JOEST W. *Ontologie der Person bei Luther* Göttingen 1967

—— *Gesetz pnd Freiheit. Das Problem des Tertius usus legis bei Luther und neutestamentliche Parainese* 2nd edn. Göttingen 1956

KATTENBUSCH F. 'Pecca fortiter' in *Haering–Festschrift* (Tübingen 1918) p. 50 ff.

—— *Die Doppelschichtigkeit in Luthers Kirchenbegriff* Gotha 1928

KINDER E. 'Luthers Auffassung von der Ehe' in *Bekenntnis zur Kirche* Berlin 1950, pp. 325–334

KOEHLER W. *Zwingli und Luther* I–II. Gütersloh 1924–1953

KOHLSCHMIDT W. *Luther und die Mystik* Hamburg 1947

KRUMWIEDER *Glaube und Geschichte in der Theologie Luthers.* Göttingen 1953

LACKMANN M. 'Thesaurus sanctorum. Ein vergessener Beitrag Luthers zur Hagiologie' in *Festgabe J. Lortz* I, pp. 135–171

—— 'Luthers Beitrag zur Lehre vom Schatz der Verdienste der Heiligen' in M. LACKMANN, *Verehrung der Heiligen. Versuch einer lutherischen Lehre von den Heiligen* Stuttgart 1958

LAUK K. 'Luthers Kritik aller Religionen' in *Pastoraltheologie* 33 (Göttingen 1937) p. 219 ff.

LINK W. *Das Ringen Luthers um die Freiheit der Theologie von der Philosophie* 2nd edn. Munich 1955

LOEWENICH W. v. *Von Augustin zu Luther* Witten 1959. (Including – 'Macht und Ohnmacht in der Kirche'; 'Gregor VII'; 'Luthers Bedeutung für die Geschichte der menschl. Freiheit'; 'Die Frömmigkeit Martin Luthers'; 'Luther und das Schicksal des Abendlandes'; 'Reformation oder Revolution?'; 'Die Reformation: Verhängnis oder Segen für die deutsche Geschichte?')

—— *Luther als Ausleger der Synoptiker* Munich 1954

—— *Luthers Theologia crucis* 4th edn. Munich 1954

—— 'Das Problem des "katholischen Luther" ' in *Dank an Althaus* W. Künneth and W. Joest (eds). Gütersloh 1958, pp. 141–150

—— *Pharaos Verstockung. Zu Luthers Lehre von der Prädestination* Munich 1951, pp. 196–213

LÖFGREN D. *Die Theologie der Schöpfung bei Luther* Göttingen 1960

LOHSE B. *Ratio und Fides. Eine Untersuchung über die Ratio in der Theologie Luthers* Göttingen 1958

LORTZ J. 'Martin Luther. Grundzüge seiner geistigen Struktur' in *Reformata Reformanda* 1965, I, pp. 214–246

—— 'Zu W. v. Loewenichs Buch "Der moderne Katholizismus" ' in *Theologische Revue* 53, 1957, pp. 193–196

—— 'Luthers Römer briefvorlesung. Grundanliegen' in *Trierer Theologische Zeitschrift* 71, 1962, pp. 129–153, 216–247

—— 'Zum Kirchendenken des jungen Luther' in *Wahrheit und Verkündigung* 1967, Vol 2, pp. 947–986

LOVY R.–J. *Martin Luther* Paris 1964

MANNS P. *Die 'theologia crucis' als Grundanliegen Fénelons* Düsseldorf 1961

MAURER W. *Von der Freiheit eines Christenmenschen* Göttingen 1949

—— 'Die Einheit der Theologie Luthers' in *TL* 75, 1950, pp. 245–252

MAYER F. E. 'The "Una Sancta" in Luther's Theology' in *Christendom XIII* 3 (summer 1947) pp. 315–327. (Reprinted in *CTM XVIII* 2 (November 1947) pp. 801–815)

MEINHOLD P. *Römer 13. Obrigkeit, Widerstand, Revolution, Krieg* Stuttgart 1960

MEYER C. S. (ed) *Essays on Luther's Theology* Concordia, St Louis 1967

MEYER H.–B. *Luther und die Messe* Paderborn 1965

MIEGGE G. *Lutero giovane* Milan 1964

MUELLER G. 'Neuere Literatur zur Theologie des jungen Luther' in *KD II* 4, pp. 325–357

NAGEL N. 'The Incarnation and the Lord's Supper in Luther' in *CTM XXIV* 9 (September 1953) pp. 625–652

OESCH W. M. 'Luther on Faith' in *CTM XXVII* 3 (March 1956) pp. 184–196

OYER J. S. *Lutheran Reformers against Anabaptists* The Hague 1964

PELIKAN J. *Obedient Rebels. Catholic substance and Protestant principle in Luther's Reformation* SCM Press, London 1964

—— *From Luther to Kirkegaard. A study in the History of Theology* Concordia, St Louis 1963

—— *Luther the Expositor. Introduction to the Reformer's Exegetical writings* (Companion volume to the American edition of Luther's Works) Concordia, St Louis 1959

PFÜRTNER S. *Luther and Aquinas. A Conversation* London 1964

PINOMAA L. *Sieg des Glaubens. Grundlinien der Theologie Luthers* Göttingen 1964

—— *Der existentielle Charakter der Theologie Luthers* Helsinki 1940

—— *Die Heiligen in Luthers Frühtheologie* Lund 1959

PLASS E. *This is Luther. A Character study* Concordia, St Louis 1948

POHLMANN H. *Hat Luther Paulus entdeckt? Eine Frage zur theologischen Besinnung* Berlin 1959

PRENTER R. *Spiritus Creator. Studien zu Luthers Theologie* 2nd edn. Munich 1954

PREUSS H. D. *Maria bei Luther* Gütersloh 1954

RADE M. 'Der Sprung in Luthers Kirchenbegriff und die Entstehung der Landeskirche' in *Zeitschr. f. Theologie u. Kirche* Tübingen 245,

REIMANN H. W. 'Luther on Creation: A Study in Theocentric Theology' *CTM XXIV* 1 (January 1953) pp. 26–40

REU J. M. 'Luther and the Scriptures' *The Springfielder XXIV* 2 (August 1960) pp. 3–11. (The whole issue is devoted to a reprint of REU's, *Luther and the Scriptures* Columbus, Ohio; The Wartburg Press 1944

RIETSCHEL E. *Das Problem der unsichtbaren Kirche bei Luther* (*SRVG* 154) Leipzig 1933

RUPP E. G. *The Righteousness of God* London 1953

RUTH E. *Sakrament nach Luther* Berlin 1952

SASSE H. *This is my Body. Luther's Contention for the Real Presence in the Sacrament of the Altar* Minneapolis 1959

—— *Kirchenregiment und weltliche Obrigkeit nach Luthers Lehre* Munich 1935

SCHEMPP P. *Gesammelte Aufsätze* E. Bizer (ed). Munich 1960. (Including – 'Die christliche Freiheit nach Luther'; 'Ist Luthers Stellung zum Staat heute revisionsbedürftig?'; 'Der Mensch Luther als theologisches Problem')

SCHWARTZ R. *Fides, spes und caritas beim jungen Luther unter bes. Berücksichtigung der mittelalterlichen Tradition* Berlin 1962

SEEBERG E. *Luthers Theologie in ihren Grundzügen* 2nd edn. Stuttgart 1950

SEILS M. *Der Gedanke vom Zusammenwirken Gottes und der Mesnschen in Luthers Theologie* Gütersloh 1962

SIRRALA A. *Gottes Gebot bei Martin Luther* Helsinki 1956

SPITZ L. W. 'The Universal Priesthood of Believers with Luther's Comments' in *CTM XXII* 1 (January 1952) pp. 1–15

STANGE C. *Die ältesten enthischen Disputationen Luthers* Leipzig 1932. (The author argues that, in his fight against the Church, Luther's main point was ethical)

—— *Der johanneische Typus der Heilslehre Luthers im Verhältnis zur paulin. Rechtfertigungslehre* Gütersloh 1949

—— *Die Anfänge der Theologie Luthers* Berlin 1957

STECK K. G. *Lehre und Kirche bei Luther* Munich 1963

STOCKMANN R. E. *Der königliche Weg* Mainz 1965

STORCK H. *Das allgemeine Priestertum bei Luther* Munich 1953

SUBURG R. F. 'The Significance of Luther's Hermeneutics for the Protestant Reformation' *CTM XXIV* 4 (April 1953) pp. 241–261

SWIHART A. K. *Luther and the Lutheran Church, 1483–1960* London 1961

TIMME H. *Christi Bedeutung für den Glauben* Gütersloh 1933

TÖRNVALL G. *Geistliches und weltliches Regiment bei Luther* 2nd edn. Munich 1947

VAJTA V. *Die Theologie des Gottesdienstes bei Luther* Göttingen 1952

VOGELSANG H. *Der angefochtene Christus bei Luther* Berlin–Leipzig 1932

WALTER J. v. *Die Theologie Luthers* Gütersloh 1940

WATSON P. *Let God be God. An Interpretation of the Theology of Martin Luther* Epworth Press, London 1947

WERNLE P. *Der evangelische Glaube* Vol 1: *Luther;* Vol 2: *Zwingli;* Vol 3: *Calvin* Tübingen 1918–1919

WINGREN G. *Luthers Lehre vom Beruf* Munich 1952

WÖLFEL E. *Luther und die Skepsis. Eine Studie zur Köhelet–Exegese Luthers* Munich 1958

ZAHRNT H. *Luther deutet Geschichte* Munich 1952

4. Various

ALAND K. 'Luthers Thesenanschlag, Tatsache oder Legende?' in *DPfBl* 1962, pp. 241–244

—— 'Der Thesenanschlag fand – und zwar am 31 Oktober 1517 statt.' in *GWU* 16, 1965, pp. 695–699

ALGERMISSEN K. 'An welchem Tag schlug Luther seine Thesen an?' in *Catholica* II, 1958, pp. 75–79

BARTH F. 'Materialien zu Entstehung und Bedeutung der Ablässe' in *MatDKfl* 18, 1967, pp. 47–54

BORNKAMM H. 'Thesen und Thesenanschlag Luthers' in *Geist und Geschichte der Reformation* 1966, pp. 179–218

—— *Luther im Spiegel der dt. Geistesgeschichte* Heidelberg 1955

BRUNNER P. 'Reform – Reformation, Einst – Heute. Elemente eines ökumenischen Dialoges im 450. Gedächtnisjahr von Luthers Ablassthesen' in *KD* 13, 1967, pp. 159–183

CAMPENHAUSEN H. FRHR. V. *Tradition und Leben. Aufsätze und Vorträge* Tübingen 1960. (Including – 'Die Bilderfrage in der Reformation'; 'Reformatorisches Selbstbewusstsein und reformator. Geshichtsbewusstsein bei Luther 1517–1522'; 'Gottesgericht und Menschengerechtigkeit bei Luther')

CLEMEN O. *Luther und die Volksfrömmigkeit seiner Zeit* Dresden–Leipzig 1938

DÖRRIES H. *Luther und Deutschland* pp. 83–102

ERIKSON E. H. *Young Man Luther. A Study in Psychoanalysis and History* New York 1958

GRISAR H. *Der Deutsche Luther im Weltkrieg und der Gegenwart* Augsburg 1924

GROSSMANN E. 'Beiträge zur psychologischen Analyse der Reformatoren und Calvin' in *Monatsschrift für Psychiatrie und Neurologie* 132, 1956, pp. 274–290. Basel–New York 1958

HERMANN F. 'Luthers Tractatus de Indulgentiis' in *ZKG* 28, 1907, pp. 370–373

HERTE A. *Das kath. Lutherbild im Bann der Luther-kommentare des Cochläus* 3 vols. Münster 1943

HOESS I. 'Diskussion über "Luthers Thesenanschlag" ' in *GeschWiss-Unt* 16, 1965, pp. 695–699

HUMBERT C. *Erasme et Luther. Leur polémique sur le libre arbitre* Paris 1909

IMBART DE LA TOUR 'Pourquoi Luther n'a-t-il créé qu'un christianisme allemand?' in *Revue de métaphysique et de morale* 1918, p. 579 ff.

ISERLOH E. 'Luther–Kritik oder Luther–Polemik? Zu einer neuen Deutung der Entwicklung Luthers zum Reformator' in *Festgabe für Joseph Lortz* I, pp. 15–42

—— *Luthers Thesenanschlag. Tatsache oder Legende?* Wiesbaden 1962

—— 'Der Thesenanschlag fand nicht statt' in *GeschWissUnt* 16, 1965, pp. 675–682

KAWERAU P. 'Das Datum von Luthers Thesenanschlag' in *DPfBl* 58, 1958

KROKER E. *Katharina von Bora, Martin Luthers Frau. Ein Lebens– und Charakterbild* 5th edn. Berlin 1959

LAU F. 'Père Reinoud und Luther. Bemerkungen zu Reinhold Weijenborgs Lutherstudien' in *Bekenntnis zur Kirche* Berlin 1960
—— 'Die gegenwärtige Diskussion um Luthers Thesenanschlag. Sachstandsbericht und Versuch e. Weiterführung durch Neuinterpretation von Dokumenten' in *LuthJb* 1967, p. 11
—— 'Zweifel um den 31. Oktober 1517?' in *Luth. Monatsch.* I, 1962, pp. 459–463
LEUBE H. *Deutschlandbild und Lutherauffassung in Frankreich* Stuttgart–Berlin 1941
LILE H. *Luthers Geschichtsanschauung* Berlin 1922. (See also E. SEEBERG in *ZKG* 52, 1933, p. 432 ff; F. KATTENBUSCH in *Christl. Welt* 47, 1933, p. 977 ff.)
LOHSE B. 'Der Stand der Debatte über Luthers Thesenanschlag' in *Luther* 34, 1963, pp. 132–136
LUTHER B. *Legenden und Luther* Leipzig 1933
MANTEY K.–G. 'Traditionstag der Reformation' in *Luther* 37, 1966, pp. 34–36
MEINHOLD P. *Luthers Sprachphilosophie* Berlin 1958
MÜLLER–BARDORFF J. *Geschichte und Kreuz bei Luther* Weimar 1938
MÜLLER H. *Erfahrung und Glaube bei Luther* Leipzig 1929
RAEDER S. *Das Hebräische bei Luther untersucht bis zum Ende der ersten Psalmenvorlesung* Tübingen 1961
REITER P. J. *Martin Luthers Umwelt, Charakter und Psychose sowie die Bedeutung dieser Faktoren für seine Entwicklung und Lehre* Vols 1–2. Copenhagen 1937–1941
SCHILLEBEECK E. 'Der Sinn der katholischen Ablasspraxis' in *LuthRs* 17, 1967, pp. 328–353
SCHUSTER H. *Der Prophet der Deutschen* Frankfurt 1936. (See also J. FICKER in *TL* 1936, p. 290)
SERTORIUS L. 'Luther der Deutsche' in *Catholica* 4, 1935, p. 61 ff.
STEITZ H. 'Martin Luthers Ablassthesen von 1517' in *GeschWissUnt* 16, 1965, pp. 661–674
—— 'Luther 95 Thesen. Stationen eines Gelehrtenstreites' in *Jahrbuch d. hess. kirchengeschichtl. Vereinigung* 14, 1963, pp. 179–191
STEPHAN H. *Luther in den Wandlungen seiner Kirche* 2nd edn. Berlin 1951
STEUBING H. 'Hat Luther die 95 Thesen wirklich angeschlagen?' in *KZ* 20, 1965, pp. 447–452
TAPPOLET W. *Das Marienlob der Reformatoren. Martin Luther, Johannes Calvin, Huldreych Zwingli, Heinrich Bullinger* Tübingen 1962
VOGELSANG E. 'Das Deutsche in Luthers Christentum' in *Lutherjahrbuch* 16, 1934, pp. 83–102
VOLZ H. *Erzbischof Albrecht von Mainz und Martin Luther 95 Thesen* 1962, pp. 3–44
—— *Martin Luthers Thesenanschlag und dessen Vorgeschichte* Weimar 1959
—— 'Die Urfassung von Luthers 95 Thesen' in *ZKG* 78, 1967, pp. 67–93

WEIJENBORG P. R. O.F.M. 'Neuentdeckte Dokumente im Zusammen-
hang mit Luthers Romreise' in *Antonianum* 33, 1957, pp. 147–202
—— 'Luther et les cinquante et un Augustins d'Erfurt d'après une
lettre d'indulgences inédite du 18 avril, 1508' in *Revue d'histoire
ecclésiastiques* 55, 1960, pp. 819–875
—— 'Miraculum a Martino Luthero confictum explicante eius refor-
mationem?' in *Antonianum* 31, 1956, pp. 247–300
WERLE H. *Allegorie und Erlebnis bei Luther* Basle 1960

VI. POLITICAL FORCES

BORNKAMM H. 'Moritz von Sachsen' in *Zeitschr. f. deutsche Geisteswissen-
schaft* 5, 1938, p. 398 ff.
BRANDT K. *Kaiser Karl V. Werden und Schicksal einer Persönlichkeit und eines
Weltreiches* Munich 1959
—— *Karl V* Trans. C. V. Wedgewood, 2 vols. London 1939
HACKETT F. *Francis the First* London 1934
KIRN P. *Friederich der Weise und die Kirche. Seine Kirchenpolitik vor und nach
Luthers Hervortreten im Jahre 1517* Leipzig 1926
LEMONNIER H. in ERNEST LAVISSE, *Histoire de France* Vol 5, I (Paris) p.
187 ff.
MOREL–FATION A. *Historiographie de Charles–Quint* text and French trans-
lation. Paris 1913
RASSOW P. *Die Kaiser–Idee Karls V* (Hist. Studien 217) Berlin 1932
—— and F. SCHALK (ed) *Karl V Der Kaiser und seine Zeit* (Kölner Col-
loquium 1958) Cologne 1960
TRISCH W. *Karl V. Mährisch–Ostrau* 1935. (Strongly journalistic, but
with some valuable remarks about sources and literature)

VII. THE COURSE OF THE REFORMATION

BARGE H. *Der deutsche Bauernkrieg in zeitgenössischen Quellenzeugnissen*
(Voigtländers Quellenbücher 71)
BECK–MALLECZEWEN F. *Bockelson. Geschichte eines Massenwahns* Berlin
1937
BÖHMER H. *Urkunden zur Geschichte des Bauernkrieges und der Wieder-
täufer* (LIETZMANN, *Kleine Texte* 50–51) Berlin 1911
BRANDT O. H. *Der grosse Bauernkrieg. Zeitgenössische Berichte und Akten-
stücke* Berlin 1926
BRIEGER T. *Aleander und Luther, 1521. Die vollständigen Aleanderdepeschen
vom Wormser Reichstag, 1521* Gotha 1884. (These have been trans-
lated by P. Kalkoff [*SVRG* 17] 2nd edn. Halle 1897. For Alean-
der's appreciation of the situation in Germany see also I. DOL-
LINGER, *Beiträge* 3, p. 268 ff. Wien 1882)
BUCHNER M. 'Volks– und Stammescharakter und Konfession' in *Gelbe
Hefte* 14, pp. 25 ff., 57 ff. Munich 1937

N

COLLINET R. *La réformation en Belgique au XVIᵉ siècle* Brussels 1958

DONALDSON G. *The Scottish Reformation (1517–1573)* Cambridge 1960

FEBVRE L. *Au coeur religieux du XVIᵉ siècle* Paris 1957

FRANZ G. *Der deutsche Bauernkrieg* Berlin 1926

—— *Der deutsche Bauernkrieg* Vol 1, Munich 1934; Vol 2 (reports), 1935. (For opposition to Franz's thesis that the peasants were not in such a bad plight before the war, see BÜHLER, *Deutsche Geschichte* p. 493. Cf. FRANZ in *Vergangenheit und Gegenwart* 24, 1934, p. 32 ff.)

HOFFMANN H. *Reformation und Gewissensfreiheit* Giessen 1932

HUGHES P. *The Reformation in England* 3 vols. London 1950–1954

ISERLOH E. *Luthers Thesenanschlag, Tatsache oder Legende?* Wiesbaden 1962

JANNASCH W. *Reformationsgeschichte Lübecks vom Petersablass bis zum Augsburger Reichstag, 1515–1530* Lübeck 1958

JOERGENSEN K. E. J. *Ökumen. Bestrebungen unter den poln. Protestanten bis 1645* 1942

KALKOFF P. *Der Wormser Reichstag von 1521* Munich 1922

—— *Entscheidungsjahre der Reformation* Munich 1917

KERSSENBROIK H. V. *Anabaptistici furoris . . . historica narratio* H. Detmer (ed). Münster 1899–1900

KISCH G. *Zasius und Reuchlin. Eine rechtsgeschichtlich-vergleichende Studie zum Toleranzproblem in 16. Jahrhundert* Constance–Stuttgart 1961

LECLER J. S.J. *Toleration and the Reformation* Vol I and II, London 1960

LEHNERT H. *Kirchengut und Reformation* Erlangen 1935

LÖFFLER KI. *Die Wiedertäufer zu Münster 1534–35* (Reports, Sayings and Acts) Jena 1923

LORTZ J. 'Germanicum und Gegenreformation' in *Korrespondenzblatt für die Alumnen des Collegium Germanicum* (Rome Pont. Università Gregoriana 1952) pp. 139–151

MEISSNER P. *England im Zeitalter von Renaissance, Humanismus und Reformation* Heidelberg 1952

MOELLER B. *Reichsstadt und Reformation (SVRG* 180) Gütersloh 1962

MOURS S. *Le protestantisme en France au XVIᵉ siècle* Paris 1959

THOMAS MÜNTZER *Sein Leben und seine Schriften* O. H. Brandt (ed). Jena 1932

NAUJOKS E. *Obrigkeitsgedanke, Zunftverfassung und Reformation* Stuttgart 1958

PARKER T. M. *The English Reformation to 1558* London 1950

PAULUS N. *Protestantimus und Toleranz im 16. Jahrh* Freiburg 1911

REITSMAU J. and LINDEROOM F. J. *Geschiedenis van de Hervorming en de Hervormde Kerk der Nederlanden*'s-Gravenhage 1949

RICAN R. *Das Reich Gottes in den Böhmischen Ländern. Geschichte des tschechischen Protestantismus* German trans. B. Popelar. Stuttgart 1957

RITTER G. *Die Weltwirkung der Reformation* 2nd edn. Munich 1959

RÜSTOW A. 'Lutherana Tragoedia artis' in *Schweizer Monatshefte* 39. 1959. pp. 891—906

SCHLOSSER J. *Die Lehre vom Widerstandsrecht der Untertanen gegen die legitime Fürstengewalt bei den Katholiken des 16. Jahrh* Diss 1914

SCHÖFFLER H. *Wirkungen der Reformation* 2nd edn. Frankfurt 1960

SCHORNBAUM K. *Quellen zur Geschichte der Wiedertäufer* Vol 1 : *Herzogtum Württemberg* G. Bossert (ed), Leipzig 1930; Vol 2 : *Markgrafschaft Brandenburg* Schornbaum (ed), 1930–1934

SCHWAIGER G. *Die Reformation in den nordischen Ländern* Munich 1962

SMIRIN M. M. *Die Volksreformation des Thomas Münzer und der grosse Bauernkrieg* German trans H. Nichtweiss. 2nd edn. Berlin 1956

STEITZ H. *Geschichte der Evangelischen Kirche in Hessen und Nassau* Vol I : *Reformatorische Bewegungen, Reformationen, Nachreformationen* Marburg 1961

STOLZE W. *Bauernkrieg und Reformation* (*SVRG* 141) Leipzig 1926

TETLEBEN V. *Protokoll des Augsburger Reichstages 1530* (*Acta conventus imperialis Augustensis anno 1530*) Ed. and introd. H. Grundmann. Göttingen 1958

THIEME H. *Die Ehescheidung Heinrichs VIII. und die europäischen Universitäten* Karlsruhe 1957

ULRICH P. *Studien zur Geschichte des Nationalbewusstseins im Zeitalter des Humanismus und der Reformation* (Hist. Studien 298) Berlin 1936

WALTER L. G. *Thomas Münzer (1489–1525) et les luttes sociales à l'époque de la réforme* Paris 1927

ZEEDEN E. W. *Martin Luther und die Reformation im Urteil des dt. Luthertums* (*bis zum Beginn der Goethezeit*) 2 vols. Freiburg 1950–1952

VIII. OTHER PROTESTANT REFORMERS

ANRICH G. *Martin Bucer* Strasbourg 1914

BAINTON R. H. *Hunted Heretic: The Life and Death of Michael Servetus, 1511–1553* The Beacon Press 1964

BARGE H. *Andreas Bodenstein v. Karlstadt* 2 vols. Leipzig 1905

BIZER E. *Theologie der Verheissung. Studien zur theologischen Entwicklung des jungen Melanchthon, 1519–1524* Neukirchen–Vluyn 1964

—— 'Zur Methode der Melanchthonforschung' in *EvTh* 24, 1964, pp. 1–24

BLASS F. 'Melanchthon als Humanist und Pädagoge' in *NKZ* 8, 1897, pp. 165–194

BORNKAMM H. *Martin Bucers Bedeutung für die europ. Reformationgeschichte* (*SVRG* 169) Gütersloh 1952

BRUNNER P. *Nikolaus von Amsdorf als Bischof von Naumburg. Eine Untersuchung zur Gestalt des evan. Bischofsamtes in der Reformationszeit* (*SVRG* 179) Gütersloh 1961

MARTIN BUCER *Opera Omnia* Series I: *Deutsche Schriften* R. Stupperich (ed), Vol 1 : *Frühschriften 1520 bis 1524* Gütersloh

1960. Series 2: *Opera Latina*, Vol 15: *De regno Christi 1550* F. Wendel (ed). Paris–Gütersloh 1955

BUGENHAGEN J. *Beiträge zu seinem 400. Todestag* Dr. W. Rautenberg (ed). Berlin 1958

BUTTLER G. 'Das Melanchthonbild der neueren Forschung' in *MPTh* 49, 1960, pp. 129–137

JOHN CALVIN *Calvin: Institutes of the Christian Religion* trans F. L. Battles; J. T. McNeill (ed) *The Library of Christian Classics* Vols XX and XXI, London 1961

—— *Institutes of the Christian Religion* trans H. Beveridge; Introd. by John Murray. 2 vols. W. B. Eerdmans Publishing Co. 1962

—— *On the Christian Faith: Selections from the Institutes, Commentaries, and Tracts* ed. with Introd. by J. T. McNeill, New York 1957

—— and *JACOPO SADOLETO A Reformation Debate: Sadoleto's Letter to the Genevans and Calvin's Reply, with an Appendix on the Justification Controversy* ed. with Introd. by J. C. Olin. New York 1966

Calvinism and the Political Order: Essays Prepared for the Woodrow Wilson Lectureship of The National Presbyterian Center, Washington, D.C. G. L. Hunt and J. T. McNeill (eds). Westminster Press, Philadelphia 1965

COURVOISIER J. *Zwingli, A Reformed Theologian* Epworth Press, London 1964

CUNZ D. *Ulrich Zwingli* Aarau 1937

DOWEY E. A. *The Knowledge of God in Calvin's Theology* Columbia University Press, New York 1952

ELLINGER G. *Philipp Melanchthon* Berlin 1902

ENGELLAND H. *Melanchthon, Glauben und Handeln* Munich 1931

FARNER O. *Das Zwinglibild Luthers* Tübingen 1931

—— *Zwingli the Reformer: His Life and Work* trans. D. G. Sear, Lutterworth Press, London 1952

FINSLER G. *Zwingli–Bibliographie. Verzeichnis der gedruckten Schriften von und über Ulrich Zwingli* Nieuwkoop 1962

FRAENKEL P. 'Fünfzehn Jahre Melanchthonforschung' in *BHR* 22, 1960, pp. 582–624; 23, 1961, pp. 593–602; 24, 1962, pp. 443–478; 26, 1964, pp. 191–241

—— 'Melanchthon Jubilaria II' in *BHR* 16, 1964, pp. 191–241

—— *Revelation und Tradition (Studia Theologica)* Lund 1958

—— *Testimonia Patrum. The Function of the Patristic Argument in the Theology of Philip Melanchthon* (Travaux d'Humanisme et Renaissance Vol XLVI), Geneva 1961

GARSIDE C. *Zwingli and the Arts* (Yale Historical Publications, Miscellany 82) Yale University Press, New Haven 1966

GEYER H.-G. *Von der Geburt des wahren Menschen. Probleme aus den Anfängen der Theologie Melanchthon.* Neukirchen 1965

GREEN L. C. 'Die exegetischen Vorlesungen des jungen Melanchthon und ihre Chronologie' in *KD* 3, 1957, pp. 140–149

GRESCHAT M. *Melanchthon neben Luther* Witten 1965
—— 'Melanchthoniana Nova. Literaturbericht' in *BHR* 29, 1967, pp. 189–219
GUMMERUS J. *Michael Agricola, Der Reformator Finnlands* Helsinki 1941
HAENDLER K. 'Ecclesia consociata verbo Dei. Zur Struktur der Kirche bei Melanchthon' in *KD* 8, 1962, pp. 173–201
—— 'Melanchthons Kirchenverständnis im Licht seiner Auslegungsgeschichte' in *NZSThR* 8, 1966, pp. 122–151
HEINSIUS M. *Das Bekenntnis der Frau Argula von Grumbach* Munich 1935
HELD P. *Ulrich v. Hutten. Seine religiösgeistige Auseinandersetzung mit Katholizismus, Humanismus und Reformation* Leipzig 1928
HOPPE T. 'Die Ansätze der späteren theologischen Entwicklung Melanchthons in den Loci 1521' in *ZSTh* 6, 1928, pp. 101–125
HÖSS I *Georg Spalatin, 1484–1545. Ein Leben in der Zeit des Humanismus und der Reformation* Weimar 1956
ULRICH VON HUTTEN *Opera Omnia* Böcking (ed). 7 vols. Leipzig 1859–1870
JONES R. M. *Spiritual Reformers in the 16th and 17th Centuries* The Beacon Press 1959
KALKOFF P. *Ulrich von Hutten. Ein kritische Geschichte seiner Lebenszeit und der Entscheidungsjahre der Reformation (1517–1523)* Leipzig 1920
—— *Huttens Vagantenzeit und Untergang. Der geschichtliche Ulrich von Hutten* Weimar 1925
ANDREAS BODENSTEIN VON KARLSTADT *Karlstadts Schriften aus den Jahren 1523–25* selected and edited by E. Hertzsch, Vols 1–2. (Reprints of German literary works of the 16th–17th centuries, 325) Halle 1956–1957
KARPE G. 'Melanchthon in Jena und die Melanchthon-überlieferung der Universitätsbibliothek' in *In Disciplina Domini. Thüringer Kirchl. Studien* I, 1963, pp. 45–54
KLAUS B. *Veit Dietrich. Leben und Werk* Nürnberg 1958
KÖHLER W. *Die Geisteswelt Ulrich Zwinglis. Christentum und Antike* Gotha 1920
KOOIMAN W. J. 'Literatuur over Melanchthon' in *Tweemaandelijks bulletin d. theol. readiocolleges* 4, 1962, pp. 19–22
LITTELL F. H. *The Origins of Sectarian Protestantism* New York 1964
LOCHER G. W. 'Die Wandlung des Zwingli–Bildes in der neueren Forschung' in *Zwingliana* II, 1963, pp. 560–585
LOHSE B. 'Melanchthon als Theologe' in *Luther* 31, 1960, pp. 14–23
MANSCHRECK C. *Melanchthon. The Quiet Reformer* Nashville 1958
MAURER W. 'Melanchthons Anteil am Streit zwischen Luther und Erasmus' in MAURER *MS* 1964, pp. 137–162
—— 'Der Einfluss Augustins auf Melanchthons theologische Entwicklung' in MAURER *MS* 1964, pp. 67–102

—— 'Geschichte und Tradition bei Melanchthon' in *Geschichtswirklichkeit u. Glaubensbewährung* 1967, pp. 167–191

—— *Melanchthon–Studien* Gütersloh 1964

—— 'Zur Komposition der Loci Melanchthons von 1521. Ein Beitrag zur Frage Melanchthon und Luther' in *LuthJb*, 1958, pp. 146–180

—— 'Der Laie in der Reformationszeit' in *Zeitwende* 33, 1962, pp. 21–29

—— 'Lex spiritualis bei Melanchthon bis 1521' in Maurer *MS* 1964, pp. 103–136

—— 'Melanchthons Loci communes von 1521 als wissenschaftliche Programmschrift' in *LuthJb* 1960, pp. 1–50

—— 'Melanchthon als Humanist' in Maurer *MS* 1964, pp. 20–38

—— 'Melanchthon als Laienchrist' in Maurer *MS* 1964, pp. 9–19

—— 'Melanchthon und die Naturwissenschaft seiner Zeit' in Maurer *MS* 1964, pp. 39–66

—— 'Melanchthon als Verfasser der Augustana' in *LuthRs* 10, 1960, pp. 164–179

—— 'Studien über Melanchthons Anteil an der Entstehung der Confessio Augustana' in *ARG* 51 1961, pp. 158–222

McNeill J. T. *The History and Character of Calvinism* Oxford 1954

Meinhold P. *Philipp Melanchthon. Der Lehrer der Kirche* Berlin 1960

PHILIPP MELANCHTHON *Forschungsbeiträge zur 400. Wiederkehr seines Todestages, dargeboten in Wittenberg 1960* W. Ellinger (ed). Göttingen–Berlin 1961

Mennonite Encyclopedia A Comprehensive Reference Work on the Anabaptist–Mennonite Movement. H. S. Bender, C. H. Smith and others (eds). 4 vols. Mennonite Publishing House 1955–1959

Moeller B. *Johannes Zwick und die Reformation in Konstanz* (*QFRG XXVIII*) Gütersloh 1961

Müller G. *Franz Lambert von Avignon und die Reformation in Hessen* Marburg 1958

Näf W. *Vadian und seine Stadt St. Gallen* 2 vols. St Gallen 1954–1957

Niesel W. *Calvin–Bibliographie 1901–1959* Munich 1961

Plitt–Kolde *Die loci communes Philipp Melanchthon in ihrer Urgestalt* Leipzig 1900

Pollet J. V. o.p. *Martin Bucer, Études sur la correspondance*, I Paris 1958

Rendenbach K. J. *Die Fehde Franz von Sickingens gegen Trier* (Hist. Studien 224) Berlin 1933. (See also O. Clemen in *ZKG* 52 (Stuttgart 1933), p. 440 ff. Also J. v. Staupitz, *Luthers Vater und Schüler* Berlin 1928)

Rogge J. *Zwingli und Erasmus* Stuttgart 1962

—— 'Melanchthon im Kreise der Humanisten' in *Theologia viatorum* 7, 1959–1960, pp. 130–143

SCHAFER R. 'Melanchthons Hermeneutik im Römerbrief–Kommentar von 1532' in *ZThK* 60, 1963, pp. 216–235
—— 'Zur Prädestinationslehre beim jungen Melanchthon' in *ZThK* 63, 1966, pp. 352–378
—— *Christologie und Sittlichkeit in Melanchthon frühen Loci* Tübingen 1961
SCHEIBLE H. 'Melanchthons Brief an Carlowitz' in *ARG* 57, 1966, pp. 102–130
SCHIRMER A. *Das Paulusverständnis Melanchthons 1518–1522* Wiesbaden 1967
SCHMIDT–CLAUSING F. *Huldrych Zwingli* Berlin 1965
SICK H. *Melanchthon als Ausleger des Alten Testaments* Tübingen 1959
SMITH H. M. *Henry VIII and the Reformation* London 1964
SPERL A. 'Eine bisher unbeachtete Vorlesung Melanchthons über den Römerbrief im Herbst 1521' in *ZKG* 59, 1958, pp. 115–120
—— *Melanchthon zwischen Humanismus und Reformation* Munich 1959
SPITZ L. W. *The Religious Renaissance of the German Humanists* Havard Univeristy Press 1963
STRAUSS D. FR. *Ulrich von Hutten* O. Clemen (ed). Leipzig 1927
STUPPERICH R. 'Melanchthon – der Mensch und sein Werk' in *Luther* 31, 1960, pp. 1–13
—— 'Melanchthon und die Täufer' in *KD* 3, 1957, p. 150 ff.
—— 'Das Melanchthonverständnis der letzten 100 Jahre' in *ELKZ* 1952, pp. 253–255
—— 'Melanchthons Weg zu einer theologisch–philosophischen Gesamtanschauung' in *LuthRs* 1960–1961, pp. 150–163
—— 'Das Melanchthon – Gedenkjahr 1960 und sein wissenschaftlicher Ertrag' in *TL* 87, April 1962, pp. 241–254
—— *Der unbekannte Melanchthon. Wirken und Denken des Praeceptor Germaniae in neuer Sicht* Stuttgart 1961
SZAMATÒLSKI S. *Ulrichs von Hutten deutsche Schriften* Strasbourg 1891
VAJTA V. (ed) *Luther und Melanchthon* Göttingen 1961
WALSER F. *Die politische Entwicklung Ulrich von Hutten* Munich 1928. (This presents an opposite point of view from Kalkoff)
WENDEL F. *Calvin: The Origins and Development of His Religious Thought* trans. P. Mairet. Collins, London 1963
WILLIAMS G. H. *The Radical Reformation* Westminster Press, Philadelphia 1962
WOLF E. *Staupitz und Luther* Leipzig 1927

IX CATHOLIC FORCES

SCHEUBER J. *Kirche und Reformation. Aufblühendes katholisches Leben im 16. und 17. Jahrh* 6th edn. Bonn 1928
1. Material concerning the popes of the Reformation era is available in all the volumes of L. v. PASTOR's *Geschichte der Päpste seit dem Ausgang des Mittelalters* Freiburg 1906 ff. Vol 4, 1 for Leo X; Vol 4, 2 for Adrian VI

and Clement VII; Vol 5 for Paul III; Vol 6 for Julius III. Ranke's, *Päpste* Vol I does not have the incomparable archivistic basis of Pastor's book. For Adrian VI see also E. Hock's, *Der letzte deutsche Papst, Adrian VI* Freiburg 1939; for Paul III–W. Friedensburg, *Kaiser Karl V und Papst Paul III (SVRG* 153) Leipzig 1932; W. H. Edwards, *Paul der Dritte oder die geistliche Gegenreformation* Leipzig 1933. (See also Jedin in *HJG* 54, 1934, p. 259 ff.)

2. Sources

Acta reformationis catholicae Germaniae concernentia saeculi 16. Die Reform-verhandlungen des dt. Episkopats v. 1520 bis 1570 G. Pfeilschrifter (ed). Regensburg 1959, Vol 1: *1520–1532* 1959; Vol 2: *1532–1542* 1960

Corpus Catholicorum. Werke katholischer Schriftsteller im Zeitalter der Galubens-spaltung 28 vols to date. Münster 1961

Franziskanische Studien Münster–Werl i. W. 1914

Greven J. *Die Kölner Kartause und die Anfänge der katholischen Reform in Deutschland* Münster 1935

Jedin H. *Die Erforschung der kirchlichen Reformationsgeschichte seit 1876* Münster 1931

Katholisches Leben und Kämpfen im Zeitalter der Glaubensspaltung. Vereins-schr. d. Gesellschaft z. Herausgabe des Corpus Catholicorum 20 vols to date. Münster 1962

Reformationsgeschichtliche Studien und Texte H. Jedin (ed). 38 vols to date. Münster 1962

Römische Quartalschrift für christliche Altertumskunde und Kirchengeschichte Freiburg 1891

3. Background

Iserloh E. *Der Kampf um die Messe in den ersten Jahren der Auseinanderset-zung mit Luther* Münster 1952

4. Individual Personalities

Albert P. P. *Konrad Koch Wimpina von Buchen* Buchen 1931

Brandt A. *Johann Ecks Predigttätigkeit (RST* 27–28) Münster 1914

Douglas R. M. *Jacopo Sadolets, 1477–1547, Humanist und Reformer* Cambridge 1959

Feifel E. *Grundzüge einer Theologie des Gottesdienstes. Motive und Konzeption der Glaubensverkündigung Michael Heldings (1506–1561) als Ausdruck einer katholischen 'Reform'* Freiburg 1960

—— *Der Mainzer Weihbischof Michael Helding (1506–1561) zwischen Reformation und katholischer Reform* Wiesbaden 1962

Greving J. *Johann Ecks Pfarrbuch für U. L. Frau in Ingolstadt (RST* 4–5) Münster 1908

Groetken A. *Dietrich v. Kolde von Münster (Deutsche Priestergestalten)* Kevelaer 1935

GULIK W. v. *Johannes Gropper* (*EEJ* 5, 1–2) Freiburg 1901

HERTE A. *Die Lutherkommentare des Johannes Cochläus* (*RST* 33) Münster 1935

HÖFLER C. *Der hochberühmten Charitas Pirkheimer, Äbtissin von St. Clara zu Nürnberg, Denkwürdigkeiten* Bamberg 1852

ISERLOH E. *Die Eucharistie in der Darstellung des Johannes Eck. Ein Beitrag zur vortridentinischen Kontroverstheologie über das Messopfer* (*RST* 73–74) Münster 1950

JEDIN H. *Der Abschluss des Trienter Konzils 1562–3* Münster 1963

—— *Des Joh. Cochläus Streitschrift De libero arbitrio hominis* (*1525*) Breslau 1927

KAWERAU W. *Murner und die deutsche Reformation* (*SVRG* 32) Halle 1891

—— *Hieronymus Esmer* (*SVRG* 61) Halle 1898

KURTEN E. *Franz Lambert von Avignon und Nikolaus Herborn in ihrer Stellung zum Ordensgedanken und zum Franziskanertum in besonderen* (*RST* 72) Münster 1950

LIEBENAU T. v. *Der Franziskaner Dr Th. Murner* (*EEJ* 9, 4–5) Freiburg 1913

LORTZ J. *Kardinal Stanislaus Hosius* Braunsberg 1931

MANDONNET P. *Jean Tetzel et sa prédication des indulgences* Paris 1901

NEGWER J. *Konrad Wimpina* Berslau 1909

NEUHOFER T. *Gabriel v. Eyb, Fürstbischof von Eichstätt 1455–1535* Eichstätt 1934

NEWALD R. 'Wandlungen des Murnerbildes' in *Festschrift für Franz Schultz* Frankfurt 1938

—— *Thomas Murner und seine Dichtungen* Regensburg 1915

PAULUS N. *Die deutschen Dominikaner im Kampfe gegen Luther, 1518–1563* (*EEJ* 4, 1–2) Freiburg 1903

—— *Kaspar Schatzgeyer, ein Vorkämpfer der katholischen Kirche gegeng Luther in Süddeutschland* (*Strassburger theol. Studien* 3, I) Freiburg 1897

—— *Johann Tetzel als Ablassprediger* Mainz 1899

—— *Der Augustinermönch Joh. Hoffmeister* Freiburg 1891

POSTINA A. *Der Karmelit Eberhard Billick* (*EEJ* 2, 2–3) Freiburg 1901

RICHTER G. *Die Schriften Georg Witzels ... nebst einigen Reformationsgutachten und Briefen Witzels* Fulda 1913

RIED K. *Moritz v. Hutten, Fürstbischof von Eichstätt* (*1539–1557*) *und die Glaubensspaltung* (*RST* 43–44) Münster 1925

SCHARTZ W. E. *Zehn Gutachten über die Lage der katholischen Kirche in Deutschland 1570–76* Paderborn 1891

SCHENK W. *Reginald Pole, Cardinal of England* London 1950

SCHUHMANN G. *Thomas Murner und seine Dichtungen* Regensburg 1915

SPAHN M. *Johannes Cochläus* Berlin 1898

TRUSSEN W. *Um die Reform und Einheit der Kirche* Münster 1957

WIEDEMANN T. *Dr. Joh. Eck* Regensburg 1865. (For essential additions see also J. METZLER in *CC* Vol 2, 1921; Vol 16, 1930)

5. Jesuits

BRAUNSBERGER O. *B. Petri Canisii S.J. Epistulae et Acta* Freiburg 1896–1923

—— *Petrus Canisius. Ein Lebensbild* 2nd edn. Freiburg 1921

BÖHMER H. *Die Jesuiten* 4th edn. Leipzig 1921

CRISTIANI L. *Le bienh. Canisius* (Les Saints) Paris 1925

DUHR B. *Geschichte der Jesuiten in den Ländern deutscher Zunge* Vol I. Freiburg 1907

FRIEDENSBURG W. *Die ersten Jesuiten in Deutschland* Halle 1905

GENOUD J. *Le bienh. Pierre Canisius* Freiburg 1915

GUILLERMOU A. *Ignatius von Loyola in Selbstzeugnissen und Bilddokumenten* Reinbeck b. Hamburg 1962

HUONDER A. *Ignatius von Loyola* Cologne 1932

IGNATIUS OF LOYOLA *Der Bericht des Pilgers* trans. B. Schneider. Freiburg 1956

—— *Das geistliche Tagebuch* A. Hass, P. Knauer (eds). Freiburg 1961

—— *Exercitia spiritualia* Regensburg 1911

JOLY H. *St. Ignace de Loyola* (Les Saints) 11th edn. Paris 1925

LETURIA P. s.j. *El Gentilhombre Iñigo López de Loyola* 2nd edn. Barcelona 1949

—— *Estudios Ignatianos* 2 vols. Rome 1957

METZLER J. *Der heilige Petrus Canisius und die Neuerer seiner Zeit* Münster 1927

—— *Die Bekenntnisse des sel. Petrus Canisius und sein Testament* German trans. from the Latin, 2nd edn. M.–Gladbach 1921

RAHNER H. *Ignatius von Loyola als Mensch und Theologe* Freiburg 1964

—— *St Ignatius of Loyola: Letters to Women* 1960

—— and MATT L. *Ignatius von Loyola* Würzburg 1955

SCHÄFER W. *Petrus Canisius. Kampf eines Jesuiten um die Reform der katholischen Kirche in Deutschland* Göttingen 1931. (See also *Allgem. Lit.-Ztg.* 3, 4 (1933) p. 2209 ff.

SCHURHAMMER G. *Franz Xaver, sein Leben und seine Zeit* Vol I: *Europa 1506–1541* Freiburg 1955

WOLTER H. s.j. 'Gestalt und Werk der Reformatoren im Urteil des hl. Ignatius von Loyola' in *Festgabe Joseph Lortz* I, pp. 43–67

6. The Council of Trent

BIZER E. 'Die Wittenberger Theologen und das Konzil 1537' in *ARG* 47, 1956, pp. 77–101

Concilium Tridentinum published by the Görres–Gesellschaft, 13 vols, 1901–1961 (In 4 parts *Diaries, Minutes, Letters* and *Tracts*)

CONSTANT G. *Concession à l'Allemagne de la communion sous les deux espèces, I,* Paris 1923

Decreta septem priorum sessionum Concilii Tridentini sub Paul III Facsimile edition of Massarell's autograph of the first seven sessions. Introd. H. Kuttner.

EBNETER A. *Luther und das Konzil* Zürich 1962

JEDIN H. *Krisis und Wendepunkt des Trienter Konzils (1562–63)* Würzburg 1941

—— *The Council of Trent* Vols I and II. Nelson 1957 and 1961 respectively

—— 'Überblick über die Jubiläumsliteratur vor und nach 1945' in G. SCHREIBER's collection, *Das Weltkonzil von Trient, I*, pp. 11–31 Freiburg 1950

—— *Geschichte des Konzils von Trient* 2 vols. Freiburg 1950–1957. Vol I in 2nd edn. 1951. (See also J. LORTZ, 'Um das Konzil von Trient. Zu Jedin Gesch. des Konzils von Trient' in *Theol. Revue* Münster 47, 1951, pp. 157–170; 55, 1959, pp. 151–160; 193–204)

—— *Kleine Konziliengeschichte* (Herder–Bücherei 51) Freiburg 1959

—— 'Tridentinum und Protestantismus' in *Catholica* 3, 1934, p. 137 ff.

LORTZ J. *Um die Zielsetzung des Konzils von Trient* Mainz 1960

MERKLE S. 'Die weltgeschichtliche Bedeutung des Konzils von Trient' in *Görres-Gesellschaft*, 3 vols, Cologne 1936

TIERNEY B. *Foundations of the Conciliar Theory* Cambridge 1955

WOLF G. *Deutsche Geschichtsblätter* 18, 1917; 19, 1918

X. THE QUESTION OF UNION

ASMUSSEN H. *Das Christentum eine Einheit. Biblisch–Reformatorisch – Ökumenisch* Wiesbaden 1958

—— and SATORY T. *Gespräch zwischen den Konfessionen* Frankfurt a. M. 1959

—— and BRANDENBURG A. *Wege zur Einheit. Zur Praxis interkonfessioneller Zusammenarbeit* Osnabrück 1960

BIOT F. *Evangelische Ordensgemeinschaften* French trans. H. Schüssler, Mainz 1962

BOSS G. *Die Erbschuld der Glaubensspaltung* Klotz 1927

BOUYER L. *Wort, Kirche, Sakrament in evangelischer und katholischer Sicht* French trans. W. Neubert. Mainz 1962

CONGAR Y. *Vraie et fausse Réforme dans l'Église* Paris 1950

—— *Chrétiens désunis. Principes d'un 'oecuménisme' catholique* Paris 1937. (See also L. LAMBINET, 'Kontroverstheologische Perspektiven' in *Catholica* 7, 1938, p. 150 ff; P. SIMON in *Hochland* 35, 1937–1938, p. 429 ff.)

DILSCHNEIDER O. A. *Gabe und Aufgabe der Reformation* Wiesbaden 1954

HESSEN J. *Luther in katholischer Sicht* 2nd edn. Bonn 1948

KARRER O. 'Eucharistie im Gespräch der Konfessionen' in *Una Sancta* 15 (Meitingen 1960) p. 250 ff.

—— and CULLMANN O. (ed) *Einheit in Christus* Vols 1–3, Zürich 1960–1966

LACKMANN M. *Credo Ecclesiam catholicam. Evangelisches Bekenntnis gegen den Protestantismus* Graz 1960

LAROS M. 'Kardinal Newmans ökumenische Sendung' in *Festgabe Joseph Lortz* I, pp. 469–479
—— *Schöpferischer Friede der Konfessionen* Recklinghausen 1950
LORTZ J. *Thesen zur Handreichung bei ökumenischen Gesprächen* 3rd edn. Meitingen 1945
—— *Die Reformation als religiöses Anliegen heute* Trier 1948
—— *Von den Ursachen der christlichen Spaltung und der rechten Art davon zu sprechen* Recklinghausen 1960
—— *Die Einheit der Christenheit* Trier 1959
—— (ed) *Europa und das Christentum* 3 vols by W. v. Loewenich, F. Stepun and J. Lortz. Wiesbaden 1959
MARGULL H. J. (ed) *Die ökemenischen Konzile der Christenheit* Stuttgart 1961
MARTIN A. v. *Luther in ökumenischer Sicht* Stuttgart 1929
MEINHOLD P. *Konzile der Kirche in evangelischer Sicht* Stuttgart 1961
—— *Ökumenische Kirchenkunde* Stuttgart 1962
—— and ISERLOH E. *Abendmahl und Opfer* Stuttgart 1960
PINSK J. *Schritte zur Mitte* Recklinghausen 1950
POL W. H. VAN DE *Der Weltprotestantismus* German trans. M. de Weijer. Essen 1960
—— *Das reformatorische Christentum in phänomenologischer Betrachtung* Dutch trans. O. Karrer. Cologne–Einsiedeln 1956
—— *Probleme und Chancen der Ökumene* Munich 1962
—— *Das Zuegnis der Reformation* Essen 1963
PRIBILLA M. *Um die Wiedervereinigung im Glauben* Freiburg 1926
—— *Um kirchliche Einheit. Stockholm–Lausanne–Rome* Freiburg 1929
RADEMACHER A. *Die innere Einheit des Glaubens* Bonn 1937
—— *Die Wiedervereinigung der christlichen Kirchen* Bonn 1937
—— *Der religiöse Sinn unserer Zeit und der ökumenische Gedanke* Bonn 1939
ROESSLE M. and CULLMANN O. (ed) *Begegnung der Christen. Studien evangelischer und katholischer Theologen* Stuttgart–Frankfurt 1959
SARTORY T. *The Ecumenical Movement and the Church* trans. H. Graef. Oxford 1963
—— *Mut zur Katholizität* Salzburg 1962
—— *Die Eucharistie im Verständnis der Konfessionen* Recklinghausen 1961
SASSE H. and others *Vom Sakrament des Altars* Leipzig 1941
SCHLINK E. *Der kommende Christus und die kirchlichen Traditionen* Göttingen 1962
SCHÜTTE H. *Um die Wiedervereinigung im Glauben* Essen 1959
SKYDSGAARD K. E. (ed) *Konzil und Evangelium. Lutherische Stimmen zum kommenden römisch–katholischen Konzil* Göttingen 1962
STÄHLIN W. *Allein. Recht und Gefahr einer polemischen Formel* Stuttgart 1950
WEBER H. C. and WOLF E. *Begegnung* Munich 1941
WEIGEL G. s.j. *The Ecumenical Movement* London 1958

INDEX

I = Volume One   **II** = Volume Two

Voes, H., formerly o.f.m., Protestant martyr **I** 401

Wackinger, G. **II** 210
Waldburg, Gebhard Truchsess v. **II** 134
Waldburg, George Truchsess v. **I** 368
Waldburg, Otto Truchsess v. **II** 134, 147, 154
Waldeck, F., bishop **II** 90, 268, 271
Waldensians **I** 15, 80
Wann, P., Catholic preacher **I** 111
Wanner, J., cathedral preacher **I** 382
Warham, W., archbishop **I** 97
Wasa, G. **II** 91
Wealth, of the Church **I** 93
see annates, benefices, fiscalism
Weather and nature **I** 116
Weigand, F., peasant leader **I** 368
Weller, J., friend of Luther **I** 332
Welser **I** 47
Wendelin, O., o.p. **I** 382
Work-righteousness **I** 126, 220, 438; **II** 200
World, decline and renewal of **I** 56
Wycliffe **I** 15, 82; **II** 23
Wider Hans Worst **I** 227, 460, 468, 479
Wied, H., archbishop **I** 392; **II** 245, 263, 267
Wild, J., o.f.m. **I** 244, 246
William, duke of Bavaria **I** 278; **II** 117, 171, 236, 294
William of Brunswick **II** 321
William of Hesse **II** 311
Wilsnack **I** 115, 122
Wimpfeling, J. **I** 59, 61, 103, 107, 149, 221, 383, 466
Wimpina, C., Catholic theologian **II** 59, 117, 126, 142, 190, 197
Windesheim congregation **I** 104
Witch-hunting **I** 114, 116, 127

Wittenberg **I** 203, 227, 410, 427, 473
university of **I** 240; **II** 110
Anabaptists and troubles **I** 343, 348
concordat (1536) **II** 77
Wittenberg Nightingale **I** 384
Witzel, G. **I** 335, 442; **II** 131, 180, 195, 225, 239, 243, 247
Wolf, G. **I** 259
Wolffenbüttel **I** 391
see Brunswick-W.
Wolfgang, Count Palatine **II** 282
Wolrab, N., Catholic printer **I** 421
Wolsey, T., cardinal **I** 26, 308
Woodcuts **I** 275
see pamphlets
Word of God **I** 402
see scripture principle
Worms **I** 155, 246, 291, 303, 309
Reichstag (1495) **I** 41; (1521) **I** 57; **II** 4
edict of **I** 320, 384, 390; **II** 11, 14, 33, 47
Wullenweder, J. **II** 91
Würtemberg **I** 301, 308, 391
Würzburg **I** 120, 132

Ximenes, F., archbishop, cardinal, regent **I** 154; **II** 4

Yuste, monastery **II** 335

Zabern, battle of (1525) **I** 369
Zapolya, **I** 36; **II** 13, 50, 74
Zasius, U., humanist and jurist **I** 59, 71, 335
Zevenberghe, van, imperial counsellor **I** 301
Zürich **I** 382, 466; **II** 34
Zwickau **I** 348, 354, 418
Zwingli **I** 154, 254, 260, 269, 336, 338, 348, 352; **II** 22, 34, 47, 51, 180, 343
ratio fidei **II** 60